MW00576060

THOU WHO ART

THOU WHO ART

The Concept of the Personality of God

John A. T. Robinson

continuum
NEW YORK • LONDON

Continuum
The Tower Building
11 York Road
London SE1 7NX

15 East 26th Street
New York
NY 10010

www.continuumbooks.com

Text © The Estate of John A.T. Robinson, 2006

Introduction © Rowan Williams 2006

All rights reserved. No part of this publication may be reproduced or transmitted in any form or by any means, electronic or mechanical, including photocopying, recording, or any information storage or retrieval system, without prior permission from the publishers.

First published 2006

British Library Cataloguing-in-Publication Data
A catalogue record for this book is available from the British Library.

ISBN 0–8264–8897–8

Typset by RefineCatch Limited, Bungay, Suffolk
Printed and bound in Great Britain by
MPG Books Ltd, Bodmin, Cornwall

CONTENTS

PREFACE

This essay is offered as a study in biblical philosophy. It is an attempt to rethink the most fundamental theme of Christian metaphysics – that of the personality of God – in terms of the 'Hebraic' categories of word and will, of speech and action, with which the biblical writers constantly work. Only by allowing the dynamic categories of the Bible itself to determine its expression can there emerge a theology adequate to the experience of the 'living', personal God of the Hebraeo-Christian tradition. But the Bible is not itself philosophy, and every essay, however limited, in systematic theology requires to be guided by some set of ideas or principles with the aid of which the truths apprehended by prophet and apostle may be ordered and integrated in the light of experience as a whole. The traditional theology of the Church, which found its culmination and epitome in the *Summa Theologica* of St Thomas Aquinas, has always relied on Greek thought for the intellectual formulation of its insights. But the categories of this philosophical tradition are not such as can do justice to the 'living' God of the biblical revelation. They are static and impersonal, and quite inadequate to that creative, dynamic centre of loving will and energy of which the Scriptures speak. Is there, then, an alternative philosophy which can enable us to formulate a doctrine of God in categories drawn from specifically personal existence and more fitted, therefore, to describe the grace and challenge of that peculiar encounter of two wills in love which the Bible sees as the norm of the divine-human relationship? It will be submitted that such a philosophy has now been made available in the writings of Dr Martin Buber and others, who, in their analysis of the 'I–Thou' relationship, have given us precisely those categories we require. Much will be drawn in the course of what follows from the work of Buber, Emil Brunner and a large number of other writers on the same theme, as also from such similarly 'existential' theologians as Søren Kierkegaard and Karl Barth. But the systematic elaboration and application of these ideas in connection with the philosophical concept of the personality of God and his relation to the world is a need which we feel has hitherto hardly been met. It is in some little way to supply such a want that this essay is offered.

Apart from acknowledgments to published works which occur in references and notes, I am beholden to very many who in discussion and comment have frequently helped me in ways of which both they and I were largely unaware at the time. If there is one point at which I am convinced of the validity of Buber's emphasis, it is in his insistence that the truth is to be found, not in the thoughts of a solitary individual, but always and essentially in the meeting between the 'I' and the 'Thou'. In particular, however, I should like to express my indebtedness to conversations with Dr Hans Ehrenberg and the Revd F. B. Welbourn in relation to matter in Chapters 3 and 6 respectively. Above all, I must thank Professor H. H. Farmer, without whose encouragement and unfailingly helpful comments this would have been a very different work. The extent to which I have, consciously and unconsciously, absorbed and availed myself of his thought I am by now quite incapable of assessing, and I hope that both he and the reader will pardon any unacknowledged plagiarisms.

INTRODUCTION

It is astonishing to think that this massive and magisterial work was composed in barely three years, in the midst of many other pressing concerns. John Robinson graduated in Theology at Cambridge in 1942, having already begun his training for pastoral ministry in 1941. In 1943, he was accepted as a doctoral student, supervised by the veteran Free Church philosopher of religion, H. H. Farmer. The doctorate was awarded in 1946, a year after his ordination as deacon. Doctoral theses vary a good deal in both length and quality, but by any standards this was an outstanding piece of work, twice the length of what would now be normal, and constituting a very ambitious programme for rethinking several fundamental themes in doctrine and philosophical theology. The late Donald MacKinnon, a demanding critic, regarded it as a very serious essay in reconstruction, as did those who supervised and examined it.

How well has it worn? It begins with a premise very much of its time and place – that there is a deep antipathy between the 'static' thought forms of the Greek world and the dynamic and relational concepts of the Hebrew and Christian Scriptures. This is typical of the Biblical Theology movement of the mid-century, and it is a model that finds few if any defenders now. In the course of the work, Robinson has almost no good words to say of the patristic or mediaeval scholastic tradition: Aquinas is discussed as an unqualified adherent of 'Greek' ideas, committed to a basically impersonal view of God, and, in a clear foretaste of the later Robinson, the Christology of Chalcedon and its later refinements is regarded as both intellectually and devotionally sterile. The title of the thesis, as Robinson's biographer notes, was a deliberate counter to Eric Mascall's Thomist essay, *He Who Is* (published in 1943). The Aquinas who can be read as precisely the philosopher of being as active relation – an Aquinas already discernible in Mascall's early work and, less directly, in Austin Farrer's *Finite and Infinite* of 1943 – was still obscured for Robinson by a selective textbook scholasticism insensitive to Aquinas as a theologian.

The immediate influences are a variety of 'personalist' thinkers of the early twentieth century, Martin Buber in particular, and a number of lesser-known European writers, including Unamuno – but also Kierkegaard, John Macmurray, Emil Brunner and a few British theologians like John Oman and Oliver Quick. It is therefore a fairly eclectic work from the philosophical point of view, though it clearly belongs to the same world as the work of Farmer, Oman and F. R. Tennant, reflective, complex but untechnical, absorbed by the problem of how to speak adequately of the mysteries of freedom and personality. It is a long way from the concerns of most professional philosophers of the period; but it is quite remarkable in the quantity of European, especially German, material with which it shows familiarity.

The central governing idea is that there is not and cannot be an 'I' existing prior to relationship with an other who addresses and is addressed. A philosophy of human nature which begins from the abstract self is bound to be inadequate; but equally a theology which thinks in terms of a God 'in himself' as an object of thought will completely miss the heart of biblical revelation, which depicts a God known only in relationship, as personal will engaging finite selves. In contrast to the 'Greek' emphasis on seeing, contemplation of the Good, an aesthetic of wisdom and virtue, the Biblical world is one of hearing – a point that reminds the reader of Barth and his disciples, though Barth's presence is not easily to be discerned in these pages.

On this basis, various traditional formulations of doctrine are reassessed – Christological and Trinitarian, but also concepts of creation and omnipotence. Robinson's discussion is always impassioned and often visionary; at times it is also diffuse and none too clear. When he turns to issues like the relation of divine nature to divine will, the 'necessity' or otherwise to God of the act of creation, the nature of omnipotence or of eternity, the reader may feel that the account of other positions is a little Aunt-Sallyish and that the resolutions proposed by Robinson do not really take us much further. Just as with *Honest to God*, you wonder if he has done justice to what he wants to dismiss. It is interesting too to see that he is cautious about any Trinitarian theology that makes God's life a model for intersubjectivity. In his later writing, a certain reserve about Trinitarian speculation is often evident, and he had limited sympathy with the dramatic Trinitarian pluralism of a Moltmann, for example. The discussions of the topic here are of special note in elucidating some aspects of the mature Robinson.

All that being said, some of his writing here is as profound and moving as anything he ever did. The whole account of what human selfhood actually is remains compelling. The reflections on the cross as the expression of the very nature of God's power, the passages on universal salvation and eternal punishment – these must be among the most engaged pages in any doctoral thesis ever. They are spiritual reading of the highest quality. And the overall intent of the work is clear on every page; stripped of some of its polemical angularity, it is a passionate vindication of the true and living God, who mysteriously and unpredictably addresses and invites creation into his love. Read the extracts from Robinson's journals during the years in which he was composing the thesis printed in Eric James's wonderful biography, and you can hear the same level of passion. Nor is it any accident that these were also the years of his engagement to Ruth Grace, which unlocked emotional depths previously unsounded for him.

As I have suggested, this is really a pretty comprehensive essay on major doctrinal themes. Had it been published at the time, it would certainly have attracted critical discussion, not least from some of those, like Mascall, whom Robinson so sharply challenges, and its insistent, even repetitious, rhetoric would have caused problems for some readers; but it would have established John Robinson publicly as a precociously mature commentator on the whole landscape of fundamental theology. The later popularizing work would have had to be read against this background, and a good many superficial criticisms might have been silenced. It is a very great gift to have this work at last publicly available. I suspect that it will provoke and illuminate in just the way that the rest of the Robinson corpus does; but also that it will stimulate the loving and grateful admiration that is always appropriate when we realize what it is like to a person speaking who is genuinely in love with God.

Part One

Chapter One

THE CONCEPT OF THE PERSONALITY OF GOD

It would obviously be convenient if a study in the personality of God could begin with a definition of the concept to be considered. This, however, cannot be offered. For personality, human or divine, is one of the most elusive of all things to contain within the bounds of a definition. He would be rash who would seek to produce in advance an account of the term which would do full justice to all the richness of content, expressible and inexpressible, with which each, out of the store of experience, could fill the empty concept. Its full connotation can be set forth only after examination of its many and various denotations. In this it differs from objects of mathematical knowledge. When the subject under discussion is a triangle, the mind moves straight to a definition. For the adult at least, its nature is not demonstrated ostensibly by pointing to triangular patches of various shapes and sizes. The definition comes at the beginning. But in the case of personality it is possible to proceed only tentatively and empirically. One can say, 'that is a characteristic of a person', or 'if you excluded this your definition would be too narrow', or 'you could hardly include this in the category of person'. A definition, if it is to be reached at all, can only come at the end. And what is true of human personality holds with even greater force of the divine.

But in the case of personality it is not merely that the concept is one whose complexity makes adequate definition extremely difficult. It will also be maintained in the course of what follows that what the term connotes is in fact strictly indefinable. If it were patient of being totally comprehended within the bounds of a definition it would *ipso facto* cease to be personality. But demonstration of this point must await further examination of its essential nature.

When all this has been said, however, it still remains true that some indication is required which will explain and justify the use of the terms 'personality', 'personal', 'impersonal' and so on, with which we shall be working. Certain basic assumptions have to be made, if only for later modification. There are, of course, numerous aspects of personal life on which it would be possible to fix and to say that without them there could not be personality. Thus, in the first place, there are the various characteristics by which men have sought to distinguish humanity from the beasts. Man is a rational animal, a tool-making animal, a laughing animal. Again, such notions as those of individuality, self-consciousness, purposiveness, freedom, the capacity for moral and spiritual values have always been prominent in discussions of the marks of personality. While not in any way wishing to deny the necessity of introducing any or all of these qualities, we shall maintain that over and above them there is a further element whose presence is a minimum condition for any satisfactory definition, and without which all other qualities could not together form that kind of existence which we know as personal.

This is not just one more quality which could be appended to the others. It is rather the way in which a person who possesses all these characteristics relates himself as a totality to the existence of other persons over against whom he is set. It is not being maintained here that this is *the* factor in terms of which personality must be defined, that it is its essence. Such a thing, if it were true, would need to be defended and justified by careful argument: it could not form part of one's presuppositions or assumptions. We only claim that it can be said that any account which ignores it is necessarily describing something less than personality as we know it. Reference to popular usage, we hope, will reveal that this is not an arbitrary statement, and thereby justify our right to take it as a point of departure.

To a large extent, the purpose of all that follows is to make explicit the nature of the peculiarly personal relationship which characterizes human existence. Nothing therefore will be said at this stage except to point to it in a way which will indicate exactly to what reference is being made.

When we say of a man or of an organized group of men that they are 'impersonal' in their dealings with us, we do not mean that they do not possess rationality, self-consciousness, purposiveness, or even that they are not pursuing high moral or spiritual ideals. They may have all these characteristics, and their relationship to us may yet continue to be impersonal. We mean, rather, that the individual or group in question does not reveal that personal interest in us which is shown in a caring concern for us as individuals, for no other reason than that we are persons. For most of us, our relations with the chimney sweep or the dentist or the Department of Inland Revenue are of such a kind. They are personal in the sense that the transaction involved between us could not be conducted by animals or by anything less than persons. They are, however, in a much more important sense impersonal. We are interested in the other and he in us, not for what we are as whole personalities, but simply for those parts of us or those activities by reason of which we happen to come into contact. I meet him as a possessor of a chimney that is full of soot: he meets me as one who is skilled in removing that soot. Apart from that we might never have met, and the chances are that my contact with him will be limited strictly to the transaction of sweeping. Such relationships could be called 'functional': I am interested in the other simply as the performer of a certain function in life, for what he does rather than for what he is.

There are, of course, many degrees in such a relationship. At the one end of the scale there is what virtually amounts to an 'instrumental' relation. (At this stage there is no need to differentiate clearly between the 'functional' and 'instrumental' relations; cf. Ch. 6 below. Here we are only concerned to mark off the 'personal' from all kinds of 'impersonal' encounter.) A firm takes an interest in a man as a 'hand', in the same way as it shows concern for the smooth running of its machines. When a man is regarded *solely* for what he does, then he is treated not as a person but as a thing, that is of no significance for what it is apart from what it does. This is what Kant referred to when he said it was immoral to treat a person merely as a means and not also as an end in himself, of value simply for what he is. At the other end of the scale, there are those human contacts where a much greater part of the life of each party is involved in that of the other. Between two scientists engaged on a common piece of research or between members of a cultural or religious society, the community of interest is far more extensive. In the last case the necessity for lifting relationships above a functional level altogether is explicitly asserted, if not in practice achieved. He would hardly be regarded as a good churchman who was interested in his fellow communicants solely as partakers of the same Sunday worship.

However much they may merge into each other, there is a clearly recognizable distinction between the instrumental and functional relationships on the one hand and the fully personal relationship on the other. In the latter case there is a respect for the other as an individual of supreme value in himself, quite apart from his character or function in life. In a true communion of love, which is the most authentic expression of the fully personal relationship, the other is not regarded and valued for something he does or for 'something there is about him' – neither because he is the bearer of certain values or skilled in some trade, nor because he is handsome or rich or happens to be a neighbour or relation. He is loved simply and solely for the fact that he is a human being.

Now the use of the word 'personal' to describe a certain type of relation between human beings and the denial of it to other relations is very significant. For it implies the recognition, whether conscious or unconscious, that a certain norm of relationship is bound up with the idea of personality. There is one particular kind of dealing – which, as we have described it in its purity, is the relationship of love – that is 'proper' to personality. It forms part of its norm, in the sense that to act otherwise is to act 'impersonally', to betray a lack of something which is essential to one's definition as a person. But are we then to conclude that a man who does not continuously exhibit this personal relationship, who does not love, is *ipso facto* not a person, and has no claim to be treated as such? That would certainly not be a conclusion easy to harmonize with the deliverances of our experience and conscience.

At this point there is involved a paradox which is a source of constant complication to the treatment of personality – the paradox that man is a being divided against himself, affirming, at the same time as he denies, the norm of his existence. Popular usage testifies to the recognition that anything less than love is to some degree 'improper' to personality: man recognizes the exalted nature of his norm and its relevance for judging his actions. And yet nowhere is it possible to see this norm embodied – it is certainly not derived as an inference from the 'normal' behaviour of human beings. The 'personal' relationship continually remains unrealized in its purity: it can never completely rid itself of a 'functional' taint. Natural human love always seems to be dependent on something *in* the 'other' for its evocation and maintenance. It attaches itself to him because of a particular thing there is about him, for example, the fact that he is in some way attractive or is connected to the subject by natural ties. Love simply for the man, as a man, and for all men as men, however unlovable they may be, remains an 'impossible possibility' (Reinhold Niebuhr). And yet the 'personal' is constantly recognized and affirmed by man as the norm of relationship in which his life is to be lived – though in such a way that failure to fulfil it does not abrogate the title and claims of personality.

The situation may perhaps be stated thus. In the application of the word 'impersonal' to anything less than the love-relation, it is recognized that personality involves the 'responsibility' to treat the 'other' 'personally', that is, to love him. The failure to fulfil this responsibility, or even to admit its existence, however, does not mean to say that a man is not a person, or that he thereby relinquishes all the claims and duties such existence involves. It just means that he is a bad person. He is still to be judged by the standards required of persons and accorded the treatment due to persons. It is not the fulfilment of the responsibility, nor even the recognition of it, which makes a man a person, but simply the fact of that responsibility itself. The content of this responsibility is defined in terms of the love-relationship. A person is one who at any rate *ought* to exist in this relationship. It is not accidental to his personhood: it forms part of the definition of his norm. So much we may learn simply from examination of popular usage, which embodies the presuppositions which we use in thinking about personality.

Now if this norm of relationship is involved in the idea of personality, we should expect that if there were a being in whose case the norm was ex hypothesi fulfilled, then to call him personal would be to say, not merely that he had a *responsibility* to act 'personally' (i.e., lovingly) but that he actually *did* so act. In other words, we should expect that what people mean if they talked of a personal God would be that he was a God who *had* such a relation with his creatures. The assertion that he was impersonal would *mean* that he was not the sort of God whose very existence was existence-in-love.

Now this is in fact exactly what we find. We find that, no more than in the case of human personality, is it sufficient to speak of the presence of personal qualities in God in order to assert personal existence of him. There are numerous systems of thought in which different personal properties are appropriated to the Supreme Being, which yet leave no room for belief in a personal God. Even those philosophies which are professedly impersonal often speak of their god in terms which are strictly applicable only to persons. Edwyn Bevan points out that Vedantic Hinduism ascribes to its supreme reality *anada* or joy, while the Stoics predicated of their divine Fire qualities of reason and infallible wisdom (*Symbolism and Belief*, 1938, 26).[1] Mr H. G. Wells appears to regard all world-movement as a Purpose, though not the purpose of any individual person. Again, though Aristotle could speak of God as a Being separate from the world in a sense that these other purely pantheistic systems cannot, yet the mere fact that he is the eternal Thinker engaged upon a timeless act of self-contemplation hardly justifies the ascription of personality. Similarly, though the great Mathematician of Sir James Jeans doubtless possesses powers of calculation predicable only of persons, this does not of itself make him what people have in mind when they speak of belief in a personal God.

Their concern is rather with a Being with whom they can enter into personal relations and whom they believe to be personally interested in them. He must be one for whom each individual is an object of care and love; for whom every man is precious, simply as a man, and not because he is a necessary element in the attainment of history's goal, or because he may have decisively influenced its course, or even because he has shown himself righteous or otherwise deserving of divine favour. It is the presence of such a relationship by which a genuinely personalistic view of God is to be recognized. All impersonal Theologies[2] are to be distinguished by their assertion of some other relation of God to man. Either they deny the existence of one altogether (Aristotle); or it is merely an instrumental relation (e.g. the Potter and the pot of Omar Khayyam); or this may merge, as in Mohammadenism, into a functional relationship. All religions of 'works' conceive of a relationship of this kind: the individual is precious to God not simply for what he is but for what he does. Again, other systems cannot believe that the Almighty really concerns himself over the petty fortunes of individual men and women; rather does he exercise a general providence by which he orders all things for the best, in terms, not of the individual's hopes and fears, but of the universal laws and values which govern his existence as a human being. All deism conceives a 'functional' relation between God and man, in that it regards God as concerned with men, not as whole individuals of flesh and bone, unique and irreplaceable, but simply in virtue of that element in them which they share in common with humanity as a whole. There are many varieties of sub-personal Theologies of this kind. But there is no need to say more at this point, since much of what follows will be concerned precisely with their shortcomings. All we wish to make clear here is exactly what is and is not intended by speaking of a Theology as 'impersonal'. We do not mean that its author does not ascribe to God many or even all the individual qualities by which persons are distinguished from other forms of being. Against Christian writers at any rate there can be no ground for an accusation of impersonality in this sense. What we do mean is that in such systems there is insufficient allowance made for that peculiarly individuating love between God and man which characterizes his dealings as 'personal' and not merely as 'instrumental' or 'functional'.

Such, at any rate, is the place from which it is proposed to begin this investigation of the divine Personality. And we repeat we have good confidence that it is no arbitrary or artificial starting point. For we think that all who have an interest in the existence of a personal God would agree that the capacity for such a 'personal' way of relating himself to men was essential to what they understood by the doctrine. In fact, to many it will doubtless appear that this is but another way of stating the idea of God as 'Father' as he is conceived by the Christian religion. What distinguishes the God of the Judaeo-Christian tradition is not primarily the particular personal attributes predicated of him, most of which can be paralleled in other religious or philosophical systems. It is just this continuous 'personal' relation in which it teaches that he stands to the world. The personality of God in this sense would be regarded as central to, if indeed not actually distinctive of, the peculiarly Christian Theology.

With this judgment we should concur; and it is indeed precisely such an idea of God as wholly and utterly personal which it will be our concern to expound as the only genuinely biblical doctrine. Nevertheless, at this point we encounter a fact which is not only the occasion of considerable surprise to those who meet it for the first time, but which is also highly illuminating for the deeper understanding of the idea of divine personality. Professor C. C. J. Webb states the matter thus:

> It is so often taken for granted nowadays that the Personality of God is a principal tenet of Christianity that it is not without surprise that we find this expression not only entirely absent from the historical creeds and confessions of the Christian Church, but even, until quite modern times, in the estimation of all but the minority of Christians who rejected the doctrine of the Trinity, regarded as unorthodox. Nevertheless, it is beyond question that historically it was in connection with the doctrine of the Trinity that the words 'person' and 'personality' came to be used of the Divine Being; and that God was first described as 'a person' by certain theologians of the sixteenth century not so much by way of positively asserting an important truth of theology as by way of denying that He was rightly said to be *three persons*. (*God and Personality*, 1918, 61–2)

It was in the Trinitarian controversies of the eighteenth century that the idea of God as a 'person' in the modern sense of the term began to undergo the process of its prolonged and difficult parturition. There can be little doubt that it is to Unitarian heterodoxy that the credit must be given for first insisting on the concept of the divine personality. The orthodox dogma of the three Persons was quoted in opposition without any clear understanding that the word 'person' in its new meaning and the translation of the old *persona* were far from identical. There was little realization at first that the ascription of personality to God might in any way be compatible with the belief in three divine Hypostases. The former was denied in the supposed interests of Trinitarian Theology. But the illogical implications of such a denial were seized upon by the other side.

> When, therefore, you maintain that God, taken absolutely, cannot be said to be a Person, you introduce nothing but confusion: For God is always described by the sacred writers, as a Person . . . When you speak of God being an intelligent Agent, and at the same time deny Him to be a Person, you talk in a language not possible to be understood. (*The Trinitarian Controversy Reviewed: or a Defence of the Appeal to the Common Sense of all Christian People*, 6. By the Author of the Appeal. Quoted, L. Hodgson, *The Doctrine of the Trinity*, 1943, 221–2)

That was written in 1760. But it was not until the eighteenth century was passing into the nineteenth that the phrase lost its Unitarian colour and was employed by orthodox theologians and philosophers to express the idea for which it now stands. Schleiermacher's *Speeches on Religion* (1799), Paley's *Natural Theology* (1802) and Kant's *Opus Posthumum* (Kant d. 1804) are mentioned by Professor Webb as among the earliest works in which the modern usage makes its appearance.

But even when we find the term personality thus applied in Christian philosophy to the conception of God, there is as yet little indication that the writers are referring to anything beyond the predication of certain personal qualities to the Godhead. What our eighteenth-century pamphleteer had in mind was clearly the idea of God as 'an intelligent Agent'. The peculiar relationship which makes such an agent 'impersonal' or 'personal' in the sense defined above does not enter into consideration. According to their terms, even the God of the deists would have been described as 'personal': in fact it was for the most part a deistic faith which they themselves were concerned to advocate.

It would require much greater research into the writings of the period than we have been able to give to discover the first use of the term 'personal' of God in a sense which includes or points to something over and above the predication of isolable personal attributes. It would not be surprising to find that such a use first occurs as late as the works of Kierkegaard. There is a passage in this author's literary autobiography which is worth citing in this connection. It occurs in the note *Concerning the Dedication to 'that Individual'*, which he appended to *The Point of View*, 119–20. He is putting forward the thesis that 'the communicator of the truth can only be a single individual. And again the communication of it can only be addressed to the individual; for the truth consists precisely in the conception of life which is expressed by the individual'. What this conception is will be discussed at greater length below (Ch. 3). Suffice it here to say that to be 'an individual' is for Kierkegaard the norm of human existence. It is the task of each to become what it essentially is, 'an individual before God'. There is involved in this concept the thought of a 'personal' relationship of faith and responsibility in which every man is ultimately alone in the presence of God and eternally answerable for his own soul. The call to each is to be 'in' the truth, which is God as revealed in Christ. He can only do this in so far as he is an 'individual', relating himself to God in this personal way. 'The crowd', which is the aggregate of human beings not so personally related, is for this reason essentially 'untruth'. It does not see that truth is something which each has to appropriate subjectively for himself by a decisive personal committal to him who is the Truth. It believes it can bring men to it simply by the direct dissemination of objective information. It is for this reason, not because it lacks any specific personal qualities, but because it dispenses with the personal relationship, that Kierkegaard can describe it as 'impersonal'. And because it is thus impersonal it excludes God; 'for the *personal* God cannot be a middle term in an *impersonal* relationship' (italics his).

It is clear that the sense in which personality is here being applied to God is genuinely identical with that which we decided above to regard as normative. It is not the fact of his possession of certain relational attributes, but his existence in a certain relationship, that is the decisive thing. God is *personal* as the subject of that relationship to which humanly there corresponds 'the individual'. This is a great advance over the somewhat barren deistic rationalism of earlier writers. But the passage in question was not written till 1847, and Kierkegaard never himself worked out the philosophical implications of the idea of divine personality. We have no right to regret that Kierkegaard was no 'systematizer', but, had he been such, the development of this concept might not have been subject to the retardation which continued to affect it.

It will doubtless be said that the above discussion pays too much attention to the actual appearance of the words 'personal' and 'personality' with reference to God. The matter of terminology, after all, is of minor significance. What is really important is the idea which the word expresses; and the notion of Divine personality had been present long prior to the nineteenth century. Although it may not be accurate to say that 'God is always described by the sacred writers as a Person', yet it is nevertheless clear that the biblical awareness of God is throughout conceived as intensely personal. The experience of the prophets and apostles, and the nature of the Divine existence to which it testifies, was always that which the modern term 'personal' exists to describe. And the same has been true of the experience of Christians ever since. In consequence, it is hard to believe that the introduction of the actual word 'personality' into philosophical theology could represent anything more than the somewhat belated discovery of a convenient shorthand expression for what was already firmly established doctrine.

But this is by no means clearly the case. And it brings us up against another remarkable fact in the history of the idea of Divine personality, of great significance for its true understanding. Between the intensely personal Christian experience of God and its elaboration in a correspondingly personalistic theology and philosophy there exists a strange gap, at first sight inexplicable. And it is a gap which, *mutatis mutandis*, is observable in other religions than that of Christendom. The late appearance of the term 'the personality of God' is in fact far from accidental. It is symptomatic of something much deeper. The truth of this may be indicated in two ways. First, philosophically, it can be shown that the full implications of the idea were not felt until considerably after the term first became current. It is historically not true that the idea had been present the whole time and that it was left to the nineteenth century merely to add the name. And, secondly, from the more strictly theological point of view, there is a good deal of evidence for a considerable lag, which shows itself in a curious incompatibility between the original personal experience and the impersonal doctrines of God formulated to give it conceptual expression.

First, then, there is the evidence of philosophy. Can it be shown that there existed prior to, or even contemporaneously with, the adoption of the description of God as 'personal' an independent understanding of the significance of the attribution to him of such a form of existence? Some test is required to discover whether the implications, if not the name, of personality in God were already familiar. Various leading questions might be put. We could ask, for instance, whether certain attributes were conceived as present or not. But this would not take us very far. For (as we have seen) none of these attributes in itself could give any guarantee that God is conceived as personal in the sense which we have taken as determinative. Only if the *relationship*, in the sense in which the Divine Being exists, is itself fully 'personal' may we be sure that the doctrine of God under discussion can also be so judged. The personal attributes are not irrelevant: and if our condition is satisfied then they also will certainly not be absent. But in themselves they are not decisive.

It is, then, the relationship which a writer regards as obtaining between God and the world which should most surely indicate whether his conception of the Deity is fully personal. Now the personal quality of this relation might be judged from any of several points of view. The second section of this work will largely be devoted to indicating some of these. We shall seek to show that there are particular conceptions of the relation, say, between the infinite and the finite, or eternity and time, which are alone compatible with a thorough-going personalism. The views of a given writer could be submitted to any of these criteria for test. But there is a simpler and surer method which can here be applied. This concerns not the quality of the relationship but the necessity for it.

The possibility of describing certain relations between human beings as 'impersonal' implies the recognition of a norm of relationship as bound up with the definition of personality. Even where this norm is not fulfilled, the existence of a 'responsibility' to do so implies a structure of relationship in which it can be fulfilled. The idea of living 'in relation' is therefore integral to the idea of personality. An environment of other persons is presupposed. In the case of a personal God this and more is implied: he must not only have an 'other' over against him, but he must exist towards it in the love-relationship. But this idea of God's 'other' is obviously attended with great difficulties. If he, too, can only exist 'in relation', does he not then require the existence of someone else for the possibility of his own? And if so, is he not rendered as dependent on creation as it is on him? What of his infinity and self-subsistence if he only exists as a person through being bounded by another?

With the various solutions offered for this problem, which is usually regarded as the most formidable objection to the ascription of personality to God, we are not here concerned. They will present themselves for attention at different points later on. There have been three main lines along which it has been tackled. The first is to deny that in the case of an infinite personality the necessity for an 'other' would in fact be involved. This is in sum the answer by Rudolf Hermann Lotze. Another course adopted by Christian philosophers has been to seek God's 'other' within his own being, by making use of the doctrine of the Trinity in this connection. The third way of approach is to accept the implication that God must have an 'other' and to place this outside himself, and yet to deny that the consequences are in fact destructive of a doctrine of divine transcendence.

Here, however, all we are concerned to note is the consciousness of the existence of the problem, not the attempts at its solution. For at this point the mere awareness of a problem at all is the surest indication that the decisive step has been taken towards a truly personal conception of the Godhead. For it is only a genuinely personalistic theism for which such a difficulty can exist. Personality is the sole form of divine being which may not be conceived as existing completely *in se* (in itself) and *per se* (through itself). It is only love which, by its very nature, is incapable of life in and for itself. Neither Aristotle nor even St Thomas had any difficulty in thinking of God as a sole self-subsistent Absolute: the necessity for living in a particular kind of relationship formed no part of his definition. They were not troubled by the thought of his existing alone from everlasting to everlasting. On the contrary, they treated this possibility as the axiomatic presupposition of any doctrine of creation, and would have been considerably disturbed by any other suggestion.

But it is certainly not merely the Aristotelian-Thomistic school for whom the idea of the sole self-subsistence of the Deity presented no difficulty. It is a remarkable fact that it is apparently impossible to light on any definite evidence for consciousness of such a problem before the latter part of the nineteenth century. By this is not meant that there was no realization of the structure of the love-relationship, wherein the possibility of love implies that there be one who is loved. Clearly the Augustinian formula for the Trinity in which the three Persons are '*amans, amatus, et amor*' ('loving, loved, and love') reveals such an analysis. Again, there is a remarkable passage quoted by R. C. Moberly in his *Atonement and Personality*, 1901, 164–5, recording the views about God held by the Valentinians:

ἐπεὶ δὲ ἦν γόνιμος ἔδοξεν αὐτῷ ποτε τὸ κάλλιστον καὶ τελεώτατον, ὃ εἶχεν ἐν αὐτῷ, γεννῆσαι καὶ προαγαγεῖν. φιλέρημος γὰρ οὐκ ἦν, ἀγάπη γαρ, φησὶν, ἦν ὅλος, ἡ δὲ ἀγάπη οὐκ ἔστιν ἀγάπη ἐὰν μη ᾖ τὸ ἀγαπώμενον.

['When, however, he became productive, it seemed to him expedient at one time to generate and lead forth the most beautiful and perfect (of those germs of existence) which he possessed within himself, for (the Father) was not fond of solitariness. For, says he, he was all love, but love is not love except there may be some object of affection.'] (Hippolytus, *Refut. omn. Haer.*, vi, 24). But such statements were not propounded as answers to the philosophical problem of how God could exist without an 'other'. Such a problem was just not formulated, and any suggestions of the existence of love-relationships within the Trinity were made from quite different motives – largely in order to satisfy what were regarded as the requirements of biblical and, in particular, Johannine, terminology.[3] The first author whom, without having gone into the subject in detail, we have discovered to have been consciously concerned with the philosophical question is the Swedish historian E. G. Geijer (1783–1847), whose work is referred to in J. Cullberg's *Das Du und die Wirklichkeit*, 26–30, and of whom we shall have more to say later (Ch. 3). In his *Über falsche und wahre Aufklärung hinsichtlich der Religion* (*Sämtliche Werke*, I, 214ff.), which was published in 1842, Geijer set out a theory of personality in which he insisted upon the impossibility of the existence of a person except in relation to other persons. Elsewhere he applies this principle to God, making the bold statement that 'even the Divine personality is unthinkable in isolation; God can only be conceived as a person if He has from all eternity made His counterpart as free as Himself' (*Sämtliche Werke*, X, 215). But Geijer stands quite outside the line of philosophical development, and his influence on other writers may be discounted.

It is not till after the work of Lotze (*Microcosmos* (vol. III, pub. 1864, ET, II, 678–87; cf. *Outlines of a Philosophy of Religion*, 70) that the difficulty in question became a regular theme for theistic apologetic, and even he only grasped the problem very imperfectly. As he saw it, it consisted merely in the fact that self-consciousness (for him the distinctive characteristic of personality) is impossible unless the ego is seen to be differentiated from something which is not the self. He never raises the real problem, which is not that of the not-self but of the 'Thou', the problem of how a person can exist except in relation to other *persons*.

An adequate historical survey would require a far greater expansion of what has just been said, but it would hardly be relevant here. It will be recalled that the question of God's 'other' – of the necessity of his being 'in relation' if he is to be a person – was introduced simply as a test of how far a view of divine personality could be regarded as already assumed before the name was explicitly applied. Is it true that the emergence of the phrase 'the personality of God' is just an unaccountably retarded description of an idea already well established and understood? The evidence of this, the *philosophical* test, is certainly to say that it is not. On the contrary, it is not until half a century *after* the appearance of the term that implications were drawn which revealed that its significance was beginning to be appreciated. And even then the process of realization was rather halting.[4]

This late and uncertain emergence of the philosophical understanding of the personality of God is paralleled by a similar phenomenon in the more strictly theological field. Although the religious awareness of a personal God had been present from the very beginning of the Christian Church, and indeed, in large degree, in the Old Israel before it, it is probably true to say that a correspondingly personalistic Theology which can do full justice to its insights has not yet been developed, or at least is only in the process of development. A similar lag could be traced in the relation between the religion and theology of other traditions (e.g., those of ancient Greece), but they do not furnish such clear examples of the point at issue. In the case of non-Christian religions one has always to take into consideration the fact that the original experience is often far from fully 'personal'. And, although we should maintain that the lag in question still existed, one cause for an impersonalistic Theology in such instances will always be a corresponding deficiency in the religion. But in the case of Christianity there is no doubt that a fully personal relationship between God and man has been asserted from the beginning. The Gospels and Epistles are a final witness to this fact of experience. When, therefore, we meet within this tradition a series of Theologies which are frankly impersonal in the relationship they conceive between God and man an explanation of the discrepancy is required.

The substantiation of the charge of impersonality must wait till the next chapter, when the process of thought which may account for the discrepancy we have mentioned will be investigated. Here a few broad, and in themselves somewhat sweeping, statements will be made to illustrate the kind of situation we shall have to consider.

From the beginning the Christian Church found that if it were to give systematic intellectual formulation to the new truths which the gospel had brought to light, and thereby commend its religion to 'its cultured despisers', there was only one direction in which it could look. To the philosophy of Greece there was no serious alternative. That the Church turned to it is in no way remarkable. What is worthy of comment is the avidity with which, on the whole, the Fathers embraced it. One might have expected a certain uneasiness or hesitation about attempts to express the Christian experience in the terms of philosophical systems which were so obviously unable to do justice to its fundamental ascription of full personality to the Godhead. But there seems to have been no compunction in the minds of the Alexandrian scholars when they set out to demonstrate that Plato found his fulfilment in Christ and that the current speculations of the Neoplatonists merely needed to be crowned by the incarnation of the Logos in Jesus in order to be transformed into a genuinely Christian philosophy. They did not appear to reflect that they were trying to combine the fullest revelation of the personal love of God with a system of thought which allowed no place either for personality or love. The whole Hellenic philosophical tradition made impossible any love on the part of God: there could only be human *Eros*, never anything like divine *Agape*. It is true that Neoplatonism differed from Aristotelianism in denying a completely static conception of the First Cause. There was a continuous flow out of and into the Godhead, and – in the words of a prayer which can only be called Christian by a generous extension – it was the privilege of the philosopher to be able to 'feel and know that all things are returning to perfection through Him from whom they took their origin'. But this effluence and reabsorption were pictured in entirely impersonalistic imagery and differed *toto caelo* from the relationship between God and man set out in the biblical scheme of creation and redemption.

If one moves on a thousand years the same eager appropriation of an impersonalistic philosophy as a vehicle for the expression of the Christian doctrine of God meets one in the system of St Thomas Aquinas. It is not merely that the Aristotelian categories were regarded as the best available in a somewhat unpropitious philosophical environment. They were welcomed with a readiness which saw in them the most admirably suited modes of expression for Christian truth which human reason had ever evolved. They were capable of providing a basis for what could confidently be claimed by a later age as a final philosophical presentation of the Faith – a *philosophia perennis* which need never be superseded. In exactly what respects the

Thomistic system is necessarily impersonal in its doctrine of God will appear later. Indeed its very merits as the clearest and most coherent of such Theologies will cause us to give it much attention in various connections.

Here we may simply note the inadequate conception of the requirements of a truly personalistic Theology which is revealed in the whole Thomistic method of synthesizing Aristotle and the Bible. The impersonalism of the Aristotelian Absolute is corrected by the introduction of attributes and functions predicable only of persons. For the *κινεῖ ὡς ἐρώμενον* of the Greek there is substituted a doctrine of creation by the divine *ἀγάπη* (love). Qualities of will and purpose, of omnipotence and omniscience, are added as the necessary presuppositions of the biblical revelation. Above all, ground is safeguarded in natural theology for the possibility of a historical self-disclosure and incarnation on the part of God which was wholly out of the question for Aristotle. But, as we saw before, the mere addition of personal qualities and functions is not sufficient to establish a properly personalistic doctrine of God. What requires to be asserted is a genuinely 'personal' relation between God and each of his creatures. This, we shall maintain, Thomism cannot provide. To justify this statement is the work of another place. But the reason, in sum, is the retention – in a form not in principle affected by the introduction of personal attributes – of the Aristotelian analysis of Pure Being and Substance from which the element of personal relatedness is necessarily excluded.

It is not denied that the Thomistic system – any more than the efforts of the earlier Christian Platonists and of numerous later theologians – was thoroughly Christian in its intention and inspiration. Indeed the real problem is not so much how such incompatibilities between experience and theology arose and persisted (though this certainly requires explanation), but why they were not, and in many quarters are not, recognized as incompatibilities. An inadequate conception of what is involved in the idea of the personality of God seems as rife in the ranks of the theologians as we found it among the philosophers. And yet the concept is hardly strange to the mind of the ordinary believer. It is one which conveys a fairly definite impression and which most people are astonished to hear has ever been in dispute in Christian theology. But a brief examination of the history of the idea has revealed a situation which is more complicated than at first appears. We have touched on the story of its emergence because we believe it to reflect something which is of considerable importance for the understanding of its true nature. Whether this is so or not, we should not be satisfied until some attempt has been made to account for the strange phenomena which the course of this chapter has uncovered.

Chapter Two

THE 'CLASSICAL' THEORY OF PERSONALITY

The discovery of the late appearance of the idea of the personality of God is always at first a source of some surprise to the unknowing. But its realization leads on to another discovery, namely, that that whole notion of personality in general is a modern development. It is often difficult for a classical scholar to realize that the culture he admires is the product of a civilization to which the concept of personality, or at least any term which gives evidence for it, was entirely unknown. Neither the Greeks nor the Romans in classical times had any word to express what the modern world means by personality. Sufficient testimony for this is to be seen merely in the fact that when the Christian Church was seeking a terminology in which to express the threefold distinctions within its personal God, there was nothing available which was in the least degree distinctively personal in its connotation or associations. Terms had to be borrowed from quite different contexts, pressed into a new service, and largely redefined.

Now it is fairly clear that, in a situation in which the concept of personality in general was either completely unformulated or merely embryonic in its development, the application of the idea to God, even though the experience of him as personal was already present, was bound to be retarded. To a large extent, therefore, the phenomena we noted in the last chapter can be explained by this fact. But this in itself does not carry us very far. It only drives the question further back. We still want to know why the idea of human personality was so late in emerging, and also why even so there is a considerable gap between the elaboration of the concept in general and its application to God only in the nineteenth century. And, moreover, ought we to be satisfied with the hidden assumption that the idea of divine personality must necessarily wait upon the development of that of the human? Might it not be claimed, as many have claimed, that it is in fact from seeing God that we derive any notion we have of what human personality truly is? If man is made in the image of God, may it not be that it is by looking at him that we should expect to discover what man is? Or is the situation rather the reverse? Whatever may be true of the *ordo essendi* (order of being) are we perhaps forced for the purposes of knowing to proceed analogically from the human to the divine, and, to some extent, make God in our own image? Is Brunner right in saying, 'Show me what kind of a god you have, and I will tell you what kind of a humanity you possess' (*Man in Revolt*, 1937, ET 1939, 34), or could the statement with equal or greater truth be reversed?

It is questions like this that drive us deeper into the essential meaning of the concept with which we are dealing. They do not admit of an easy or an *a-priori* answer. It is not possible to say in advance whether it is human or divine personality which is the prior in the process of development. We can only look to the actual course of that development and try to pick out its significant features. From them we may be able to draw conclusions, not only for this immediate question which is not in itself of decisive importance, but also for the inner meaning of the concept of personality to which the course of its emergence may be an index.

The most convenient place for starting will be that at which we were left at the end of the last chapter. We noticed the willingness, and even avidity, of many Christian theologians to embrace, for the purpose of giving philosophical expression to their beliefs, systems of thought which are clearly incapable of doing justice to the fundamental personalism of their experience of God. Now this fact clearly betrays a failure to realize the philosophical implications of the idea of personality in general. In particular, it is not seen that, if it is to be faithful to experience, a concept of personality must necessarily include within it some reference to the peculiarly personal relationship. Because of the backward state of the philosophy of personality the implications were not grasped and impersonal doctrines of God admitted. We have here an example of the influence of philosophical development, or rather the lack of it, on theology.

But if we go on to ask what it is that has chiefly affected the philosophical development, we find it is theology, or rather theologians. At all the significant stages of the emergence of the idea of personality it is the *religious* interest that has been decisive. In the first place it is an undeniable fact that the crucial point in the history of the word *persona* occurred when it became connected with the Trinitarian controversy (Ch. 20 below). It was through its baptism into Christianity that it was later able to express a wholly new idea in the world both of the schools and of the marketplace. Before Christ there was little or no conception of what we now understand by personality. And it was Christianity that made possible the classical definition of Boethius – '*persona est naturae rationabilis individua substantia*' ['a person is an individual substance of a rational nature'] – which has largely dominated subsequent thinking on the subject.

Moreover, it is possible to show that throughout the history of the development of the idea of personality it is thinkers brought up in the Christian tradition that have made the most important contributions. Two illustrations may suffice. The first is that of Kant. Although Kant cannot properly be called Christian, it is undeniable that he was a religiously minded man and the influence of his Christian upbringing on his thought is very marked. It led him, for instance, to advocate a profound and thorough-going theory of sin, despite the fact that it was really incompatible with the rest of his ethical writings and the humanistic presuppositions on which they were based. But even in his ethics proper the influence of Christianity is wide and deep. In fact, in several places he is at pains to show that his own moral teaching is really none other than that of the gospel in philosophical guise (e.g., T. K. Abbott, *Kant's Theory of Ethics* (6th edn), 15). And nowhere in his ethics does he so obviously incorporate essentially Christian principles than in the stress he lays on personality as the ground of all values and the end of all moral action. Kant's central affirmation that, whether in oneself or in another, personality must always be treated as an end and never merely as a means, strikes us as so self-evident that we forget its novelty. Yet stress on the moral implications of personality and its rights marked a real departure from the traditional view of the self, dominated as it was by the epistemological or psychological bias given it by Descartes – itself the product of Christian influences at work in the Renaissance and Reformation. Kant's teaching clearly issues from, and (despite his own denial) is really only tenable on, the assumption of the Christian doctrine that all men are equal as children of God and derive their value from the fact that they are infinitely precious in his eyes.

The second and more notable example of the influence of religious, and especially Christian, thinkers on the philosophical development of personality may be taken from the present [twentieth] century. There will be much occasion later to discuss one of the most original and positive movements in recent and contemporary philosophy – the reopening of the question of personality and personal relationships by the school of writers under the influence of Dr Martin Buber. The point which is relevant here is that all the writers concerned are theologians and, with very few exceptions, Christian theologians. Ebner, Heim, Gogarten, Grisebach and Brunner in the German-speaking lands; Cullberg in Sweden, and Professors J. Baillie and H. H. Farmer in this country have all come to this question of philosophy from a religious background and with religious convictions. Moreover, our survey of the previous history of the movement in the next chapter will bear out the same point even more strikingly. It will introduce us to a series of names possessing very little continuity and having very little in common beyond a unifying religious, and for the most part Christian, interest and concern.

From this it would not be unreasonable to conclude that there was a fairly close connection between religious conviction and the development of the philosophical idea of personality. In fact, it seems that awareness of the divine personality rather than experience of human personal relationships is the decisive factor in bringing to birth the conceptual idea of personality. The contention that this latter depends on a mature consciousness of personality in God is supported by the consideration that it did not in fact emerge until after the full revelation of the divine personality had been made in Christ and appropriated in the experience of the Church. It must remain an interesting speculation whether, if Judaism had not been so isolated from the cultural centres of the Graeco-Roman world, it could have effected at least a partial development of the philosophical idea of personality. But whereas it is ultimately from experience of God that the idea of personality seems to be derived, there is another equally important fact to be considered. This is that, although it is religiously and theologically minded thinkers who have been most prominent in forwarding the development of the concept, it is to the idea of *human* personality that in the first place they have applied what their experience taught them. In other words, it was not the case that the implications were worked out with reference to God's personality of which they had had experience, and then applied to human personality and personal relationships; rather, the conception of the human formed the ground and analogy for that of the divine. Thus, in his published works, Kant was concerned exclusively with human personality, and was only just beginning to think in terms of the divine in the papers which make up his *Opus Posthumum*. Again, it is only on the basis of a careful previous analysis of finite personal relationships that the contemporary theologians of whom we spoke go on to discuss the relationship with God, the eternal personal.

But perhaps it is in the contribution of Boethius that this somewhat paradoxical combination of interests is most succinctly expressed. It will be maintained later (Ch. 20) that within the theological debates of the early Christian centuries the most significant step in the evolution of the word 'personal' was its application to Christology. It was this more than anything else that assured its later development into the concept of personality as we now know it. And in this we have once again a very clear case of *theological* interest expressing itself in the elaboration of the idea of *human* personality.

The fact that Boethius' famous definition of *persona* as 'rationabilis naturae individua substantia' (the individual subsistence of a rational nature) appears in a *Christological* context (*Contra Eutychen et Nestorium*, III) well summarizes the tendency we have noticed, that the development of personality is advanced by fixing attention neither on the divine nor on the human in isolation, but by an interaction between the two. The interest behind the development of *persona* was in the first place strictly Theological. But it did not lead at once to a concept of the divine personality: the establishment of the formula 'una substantia et tres personae' (one substance and three persons) had little or nothing to do with what we discuss under the heading of the personality of God. Yet, through its application to the human personality of God in Christ, a definition of personality was evolved which eventually had its effect in personalizing the Theological conception of the Godhead. The slowness of this last process can be attributed to, first, the misplaced fear that to call God a person involved a denial of his triune nature; secondly, the enormously strong grip of the Hellenic tradition of Christian theology and philosophy which had to be broken; and, thirdly, the intrinsic inadequacy of the actual theory of personality which was in fact evolved.

As a result of this brief investigation, a dialectic of development can be observed which enables us to give some answer to the question concerning the connection between the ideas of divine and human personality.

Every concept is distilled from experience, and the concept of personality is no exception. But there does seem to be evidence to show that the experience which gives rise to it is not – as might be expected – that of human personal relationships, but of the relationship to God, especially as this is known in its fully personal form in Christianity. It is religious writers who have had the most to contribute to the modern understanding of personality. The personality of God is therefore prior, not only in the *ordo essendi* [order of being], but also in a real sense in the *ordo cognoscendi* [order of knowing]. For apart from the relationship to God as personal there would appear to have been evolved little knowledge or appreciation of the meaning of human personality.

But, secondly, what we first come to know, in the sense of being able to formulate a rational concept of it, is not the divine personality. The development of the concept has indeed been forwarded by religious authors, but by religious authors whose main attention has been given to the personality, not of God, but of man. Although it is the experience of the divine which enables the perception of the human, it is only the elaboration of the philosophical significance of the human which leads to an appreciation of such a significance in the divine. The religious awareness of

God as personal is ultimately, of course, the source of the doctrine of the divine personality. But there is not a direct relationship between them. For between the first stage and the last there needs to come an elaboration of a concept of personality as it has reference to human selves and their relationships.

This brief historical survey, then, has yielded evidence of two movements of thought which wisdom would bid one observe in seeking the truth about the personality of God. In the first place, one would be prudent to remember that the concept of divine personality which one reaches will to a large extent be the reflection of the general theory of personality from which one starts. It is important therefore to be sure to begin with as correct an analysis as one can of the human personal situation. And, secondly, the most valuable insight into this situation is likely to be drawn from those whose gaze has been fixed, not on human persons, but on the divine. For it is out of religious experience of God as personal – which means, in effect, the experience of him within the Hebraeo-Christian tradition – that the most fruitful philosophy of personality appears to spring. As a result of combining these two principles, one could argue, if one had not already accepted the fact, that the true concept of the personality of God was that of the biblical revelation. For it is that which alone corresponds with, or can be yielded by, the biblical doctrine of man, in its turn the only analysis of the human situation adequate to the personal awareness of God from which one started. The fact that it is Christians who have alone for the most part achieved anything in the elaboration of the most essential concept of human personality provides some appreciable pragmatic attestation to the truth of the experience from which they have derived it and of the Theology to which it impels them.

This examination of the history of the idea of personality has therefore helped to formulate the programme which we should be wise to follow in seeking the truth of the divine personality. But equally, it is relevant for tracing and explaining the errors in conceptions of it which are less than adequate. For there are many doctrines of God formulated by Christian theologians which lack a conception of his personality capable of doing anything like justice to the utterly personalistic nature of Christian experience. This discrepancy is recognized and lamented in such a book as Dr W. R. Matthews's *God in Christian Thought and Experience* (1939 2nd edn) which is typical of a good deal of modern theological discontent. In different ways, William Temple and Nicolas Berdyaev have voiced their dissatisfaction with the Hellenic ontology of 'substance' which has dominated traditional Western theology. But no real alternative has been offered which provides categories more favourable to the expression of a truly biblical personalism.

The method of procedure worked out above, however, does indicate some line along which to diagnose, if not to heal, this theological malaise. What our conclusions would lead us to undertake is, first of all, a closer scrutiny of the particular concept or concepts of *human* personality and personal relationships which have influenced, and in large measure determined, the inadequate notions of the divine Person. If these are in error, then it is at this level that we should seek a remedy for the Theological situation.

As a matter of fact, if we may anticipate, the various underlying concepts of human personality will reveal themselves upon examination to be but variants upon a single theory which has dominated Western philosophy for nearly 1,500 years. There have been many differences of expression and emphasis, but fundamentally the same presuppositions have been accepted. Historically this view of personality was born out of the classical Hellenic tradition. For this reason, and for lack of a better name, we shall call it the 'classical' theory. But its influence has permeated every school of philosophical thought, and it may be found to lie behind much recent theology which is not professedly Hellenic in its inspiration.

It is therefore proposed to make an examination of a representative modern philosophical theologian whom we should regard as failing to provide a fully personal conception of God, and try to uncover the conception of human personality which underlies and influences his Theology. For this purpose the thought of Dr F. R. Tennant offers many advantages. In the first place, the choice will show that the 'impersonalism' we have indicated is not peculiar to those, such as the Thomists, who are consciously and deliberately working with the categories of a Hellenic metaphysic. And, secondly, such are the merits of Dr Tennant's exposition, that the connection between his doctrine of the divine Person and his analysis of human personality is made abundantly clear. There are few theologians who are so careful to state their philosophical assumptions about the nature of the self and its relationships as the author of *Philosophical Theology* (1928 and 1930). In the first volume of that book there is as good an introduction as can be found to the 'classical' theory of personality to which we have referred.

At this point it may be well to remind the reader of the sense in which we are using the words 'personal' and 'impersonal'. For it will perhaps seem strange to quote in this connection an author who is definitely concerned to state that a personalistic interpretation of the universe is the only one which satisfies an empirically grounded theology (*Philosophical Theology*, II, 165–8). But when we apply the word 'impersonal' to his doctrine of God there is no thought of denying or overlooking anything he says there. We mean rather that his philosophy does not provide for that peculiar form of relationship between God and man which we agreed to be distinctive of a fully personal conception of the divine existence. To call God personal implies in him the capacity for, and exercise of, a love which is wholly individuating in its dealing with people. It is the belief that he has relationships with his children in which each is irreplaceably precious, being created for an inalienable contribution to the total glory. The personal is the realm of Kierkegaard's 'individual', where every man has his own 'charge to keep' and 'soul to save' and 'calling to fulfil' (C. Wesley, *A Collection of Hymns for the Use of the People called Methodists*, 318). It thus will be in God's ability to impart to different persons the different insights they require into his nature and will and to give wholly individual guidance and succour in the unrepeatable situations of each man's circumstances – in other words in the sphere of particular revelation and special providence – that his personality will express itself most unmistakably. 'The idea of providence is that God is concerned about the individual and for what is most individual in him' (Kierkegaard, *Journals*). This is not to deny that the regularities of natural laws are not equally essential factors in the personal dealing of God with his creatures. But they are not the peculiar distinctive signs of a personal relationship. To all outward appearances such regularities might equally well be the marks of a purely mechanical structure of the universe. What distinguishes personality is the capacity to deal with each case on its merits – to act in terms of the nature of the *object* in accordance with the demands of its changing situation, as Professor John Macmurray puts it (*Reason and Emotion*, 1935, 19–21). It is the exceptional acts called forth by the particular nature or circumstances of the object in question that are most 'revealing' or expressive of the quality of a man's personality. 'It tells us something about a man's character if we know that he rises from bed every day at the same hour; it tells us much more about him if we know that he even once rose a great deal earlier to do some act of kindness' (W. Temple, *Nature, Man and God*, 1934, 305).

It is, then, by his personal dealing with individuals that the personality of the God of the various theologians is primarily to be judged. The impersonality of pagan Greek thought on this subject is never more clearly revealed than when it is put to this test. The only type of theology which allowed a place for special revelations and providence was the Olympian. And here the interventions of the gods in human life were so haphazard and indiscriminate as to be completely destructive of moral personality if systematized into a philosophical doctrine of providence. What took the place of providence for the Greek was an impersonal Fate, whether this was conceived, as in Aeschylus, as a rigid chain of ethical cause and effect, or, as in Euripides, as an amoral τύχη [act of God, fate]. In the Theologies of the philosophers even this was abandoned: where there was no philosophy of history, there could be no views about its providential guidance.

The Christian theologian, however, is committed to a doctrine of history, and with it to an assertion or denial of special providence. From this point of view, we propose to examine the claim of Dr Tennant to present a genuinely personalistic view of the nature of God and his dealings with men. This is also a good starting point on the ground that his chapter (II, 7) on the problem of evil (which, as he treats it, is really the same as the problem of special providence) is usually regarded as a particularly valuable contribution. Tennant sees very clearly that the sort of indiscriminate interference in the affairs of men which the Olympian religion and many Christians have supposed of God is destructive alike of science and morality. Unless a certain independence and dependability can be ascribed to the natural order no personal life is thinkable. This order, he maintains, is still under God's control, in the sense that it is subject to his laws, but God is such, and the possibility of science and morality demands, that he does not interfere with their working to suit the desires or prayers of individuals; and this is to the individual's ultimate advantage. We cannot, then, look for evidence of God's direct action in the kingdom of nature, which is determined by its own laws. But this by no means excludes its possibility in the kingdom of ends. It is here that his guiding influence and revelation is visible – in the working of men's minds and wills. The moralist is not primarily interested in whether a man suffers, but in whether he is capable of using his suffering for the production of good, and good of a kind perhaps impossible without it. It is in this that God can be seen at work, guiding, inspiring and upholding. What is 'overruled for good' is not events but the attitude to those events, which in its turn influences the future course of history. Our bodies may be under the indirect control of God, but it is only for our souls that he has direct concern. It is for deliverance from doing rather than from suffering evil that we are told to ask. Prayer must always take the form 'We ask not that Thou wilt keep us safe, but that Thou wilt keep us loyal'.

The foregoing statement is not expressly set out in *Philosophical Theology*, which, in fact, has very little positive to say on the question of special providence. But Dr Tennant would agree that *some* sort of individual care and guidance on the part of God must be asserted by theism if it is not to become entirely deistic. And it is such a view as is outlined above to which his treatment of the problem of evil commits him and to which he would in fact subscribe.

First of all, the large amount of truth which such a view contains must be freely admitted. It is manifestly impossible to see behind each instance of suffering a special providential purpose. Order in the physical world is an absolute precondition of prediction and purpose, of character and culture, and in fact of all specifically human activities. A constancy in God's ways is required both for the development of human personality and not less for saving the divine personality from revealing itself as irresponsible wilfulness or irrational caprice. Self-direction according to a consistent purpose is implied in the very idea of personality.

But the constancy is the constancy of a will and not of a machine. A person will act in a certain way on a certain occasion because his overruling purpose demands it, and not because he always has so acted and always must. He will be continually adjusting his actions to the circumstances, not in the sense, subjectively, of trimming his sails to the wind, but of always acting in terms of the nature of the object, treating each case individually on its merits. A wise and loving father will know what is best for each of his children on every occasion, and it will not always be the same. This constancy of will will not mean that he acts in an absolutely uniform fashion for ninety-nine times out of a hundred and then the hundredth time makes an exception in favour of some deserving case. That is the kind of view of miracle to which Tennant rightly objects. What it does mean is that there is no mechanically rigid consistency at all. For if such a constancy is postulated, then, in order to find a place for special providence, one has to introduce the idea of exceptions, which destroys the constancy. Rather, God's hand is tied by no self-made uniformities, but only by the singleness of his overruling purpose to win all to free and perfect communion with himself. Because he is what he is and we are what we are, the conditions of the achievement of this truly personal relationship will be similar for all; and that will result in uniformities in events on which we can, and must, rely. Let no attempt be made to minimize their significance. But to make these uniformities a rigid basis on which to exclude what *eo facto* become 'exceptions' is to reveal an impersonalistic view of the dealings of God with men.

Tennant's approach to the problem of evil and providence, in fact, does regard men as things and not as persons. All have to be treated in exactly the same way, despite the fact that each man's problem is in some degree peculiar to himself. The conditions for the attainment of moral personality are fixed in advance, and the process set going. The fact that this will inevitably involve many 'hard cases' cannot be helped – to go on steadily is the only hope for all and thus for any. To pull the communication cord because of individual instances of distress would mean to dislocate the whole railway system, whose smooth running along can enable any of us to reach our destination. But to imagine God so ordering the world is to imagine him as less than personal. No person, save perhaps a madman, ever acts with a constancy *of that kind*.

It is for this reason that Tennant's answer does not, and cannot, really penetrate to the heart of the problem of evil. He attempts to find in an 'impersonal' world-order, even though it be one which exists ultimately solely for the promotion of moral personality, a solution for an intensely personal problem. For while he bids fair to justify the ways of God to man as far as the *existence* of evil is concerned, its distribution is left entirely unexplained. And it is in the latter that the real tragedy lies. Natural disasters only become a problem, an evil, because they affect persons. And, except for the philosopher in the security of his study, the real poignancy of the problem is connected, not with the fact that evil affects persons in general, but with how it affects individuals in particular. For every one person whose faith in God is destroyed by the general existence of evil, or even by the occurrence of a world war, there are very many more who lose it through being confronted by the arbitrary distribution of its effects. It is the lack of equality and meaningful proportion in suffering that desolates. For how many in the last few years has the inexplicable arbitrariness of the Scripture prophecy come only too vividly true: 'Then shall two men be in the field; one is taken, and one is left: two women shall be grinding at the mill; one is taken, and one is left' (Matt. 24:40–1). The question why this man and not that is more haunting than why anyone at all. In Mr Thornton Wilder's book (*The Bridge of San Luis Rey*, 1927) the fact that demanded explanation and justification was not that five apparently innocent people were killed by the collapse of the bridge of San Luis Rey, but that it should have been these particular five and no others. A personal problem demands an explanation in terms of personal relationships, and that means in terms of particulars and individuals: to be given general assurances that all is for the best in the end is no explanation at all.

Another point arising from the view of providence under consideration will be seen to be important for what follows. This concerns the dichotomy between body and soul to which any view is committed that seeks to combine a place for a personal religion with a theory of an invariable mechanical causation in the physical order. If God's direct influence cannot be traced in material events, then it must be sought, if at all, only in our attitude to them. This dichotomy is wholly untenable. A state of mind is just as much an event as a change in the weather, a fact which is assumed when it is admitted, as it must be, that ideas influence the course of material happenings. Such a theory is impossible to reconcile with the clear experience of the close connection between mind and body, making character-formation inexplicable and encouraging a naively indeterministic view of freedom.

This dichotomy also has its effects in the sphere of values, and therefore on personality itself, the ground of values. It destroys the integrity of the personal ideal by setting up one essential part of it in opposition to another. For in attempting to satisfy the requirements of morality the theory in question unwarrantably ignores or minimizes other values, notably those of beauty and happiness. If my physical circumstances are determined by laws working themselves out independently of God's direct will, then my happiness or misery is purely a matter of coincidence, and is significant only in providing material for moral choices. And if life is merely a vale of soul-making then the beauty or pleasantness of its scenery should not interest us except as our moral reaction is affected by it. But this is not how we think about beauty and happiness. Both are good in themselves, even though neither can be held to be so without qualification.

Unless providence is concerned with material events it is concerned with nothing. The conviction expressed in the saying that even the hairs of our head are numbered is central to the doctrine. It is noticeable that the religion which more than all others seeks to dispense with this doctrine is that which not only conceives God as fundamentally impersonal but which writes off the material world as *maya* and as subject to that *karma* which is but another name for the rigid system of cause and effect postulated by the view we have been discussing. Any theology which assigns any significance to happiness or bodily welfare cannot possibly accept a theory of providence which denies God's direct control over and interest in material events. For one who subscribes to the religion of the Incarnation to embrace it is simply a contradiction.

Dr Tennant's observation that all true theism must be tinged with deism is unexceptionable if all that it means is that a proper place must be found for the divine transcendence. But in fact, a 'deistic tinge' is admirably fitted to summarize the error which pervades his own doctrine of God and inevitably renders it an impersonalistic Theology. For it is just what deism denies that is lacking in Tennant's exposition, that is, a continuous individuating personal relationship of love on the part of God, which lays its inescapable demands upon the whole man, body and soul, at every moment of his existence, at the same time as it upholds, guides and provides for him in the uniqueness of his historical situation. It is the love of the divine Shepherd, who knows his own sheep and calls them all by name, and who for every individual is prepared to give himself totally. Man is created by this love, born into the context of it, and called to find his freedom and fulfilment in its service. He cannot escape its relevance to any part of his life, whether material or spiritual, whether social or incommunicably private. Neither God nor man can be understood out of that relationship: the fact that they are so related constitutes part of the definition of their being. Tennant indeed grants that God in relation to the world is the only God of whom we may ever legitimately speak. But this relation is not properly personal. It is just a correlation – a mere statement that one cannot be spoken of in isolation from the other, in the same way as one term in a pair of correlatives, such as subject and object, cannot be treated as existing *per se* (by itself). Such a relation need be no more than a logical or epistemological connection.

If we were right in the relation we established above between the inadequacies of an impersonalistic Theology and the conception of human personality which underlies it, we should be led to expect that Tennant's analysis of the nature of the self would also reveal a similar abstraction from that peculiarly individual relationship which we agreed to be an indispensable condition of personal existence. And this is, in fact, exactly what we find. It happens, moreover, to be the most telling characteristic of what we have described as the 'classical' view of personality. Starting, then, from the point to which Tennant's Theology has drawn attention, we may try to set out in general terms the essential features of this theory.

The introduction of the concept of personality into the philosophical world had its origin, as we saw, in the attempt to give intellectual formulation to the new depth of personal relationship to God opened up by the Christian revelation. The terms, however, which were used in this connection were not of the Church's own choosing. They were terms taken over from other contexts, and contexts not in themselves specifically personal. For this reason they committed their theological employers to no one theory of personality. Nevertheless, the fact that these particular terms were chosen, and, through their Latin forms, continued to serve their purpose for centuries, is extremely significant.

Professor Webb has pointed out the connection between the terms in which the Trinitarian formulae were expressed and Boethius' famous definition of personality that served to mark the close of one era and determine the development of the next. The idea of 'individual subsistence' was taken out of the connotation of ὑπόστασις, that of 'rational nature' from the associations of *persona* (*God and Personality*, 50–1). Through this definition, the influence of the terms has been extended to all subsequent philosophy. St Thomas took his start from it, adopting it without alteration as an account of human personality. Ockham's *suppositum intellectuale*, i.e. – a distinct individual existence, differs only in still greater concentration. Webb refers to very similar expressions among philosophical theologians of the sixteenth and early seventeenth centuries (*op. cit.*, 55, n. 29). From the period of the *Aufklärung* we have the same thing again in Wolff's definition of a person as '*ein Ding das Sich bewusst ist*' (something conscious of itself) (*Vernünftige Gedanken von Gott, der Welt, und der Seele*, 570. Webb, *op. cit.*, 58). J. R. Illingworth, writing in 1894, can still say: 'The fundamental characteristic of personality is self-consciousness, the quality in a subject of becoming an object to itself, or, in Locke's language, "considering itself as itself" and saying "I am I" ' (*Personality Human and Divine*, 28). And, lastly, we find this in a passage from a writer of the twentieth century:

> By 'person' we mean an existent of such a kind as can form a real unity, despite the multiplicity of its parts, having its own nature and value, and as such, in spite of the diversity of function among its parts, can achieve an independent individuality which is both unified and purposive. (W. Stern, *Die menschliche Persönlichkeit*, 4–5)

The last phrase ('eine einheitliche zielstrebige Selbsttätigkeit') [a unitary purposive activity of the self] is almost a translation of Boethius' '*naturae rationabilis individua substantia*'.

This classical idea of personality survived the 'Copernican revolutions' of both Descartes and Kant. In fact, these thinkers only served to establish it more firmly than ever. Descartes put additional meaning into both 'rational nature' and 'individual substance'. By his '*cogito ergo sum*' (I think therefore I am) he made self-consciousness and thought the only sure basis of existence, an emphasis which is clearly reflected in the preoccupation of the later rationalists with *Selbstbewusstsein* (self-consciousness) as the essential characteristic of personality. Again, by isolating the subject of knowledge as the one entity concerning whose existence certainty was possible, he gave a solipsistic bias to epistemology. The *individua substantia* of personality was no longer just one existent among many, but the one true existent from which knowledge of all others was derived.

What Descartes did in the sphere of the theoretical reason Kant did in that of the practical. He too is insistent on the *natura rationabilis*: 'Moral personality is nothing but the freedom of a rational being under moral laws' (Abbott, *Kant's Theory of Ethics*, 279). It is only because a person is for him essentially rational that he is free and must always be respected as an end in himself. And, secondly, in Kant there appears for the first time a serious attempt to give complete centrality in philosophical ethics to the sanctity of the individual conscience. In this he was indeed but giving expression to his heritage as a German Protestant derived from Luther and the Reformation. But he was also translating into moral terms the older characterization of a person as an 'individual substance'. The rights of a person as a rational being are individual rights – his person is not to be used merely as a means to the welfare of the group. So, too, are his duties – he is responsible before God for his own inner life alone. He has duties, of course, in regard to other persons – that is part of the definition of personality according to Kant; for it is involved in the universality of reason. But with regard to others his aim can never be more than to promote their happiness. No man can ever make another more moral: that is something each must achieve for himself or not at all. For Kant morality *is autonomy*. The Kingdom of Ends is the ethical version of Leibniz's Pre-established Harmony. No monad can penetrate or affect another – the harmony is established by each perfecting itself by reflecting within it the perfect order of the whole. The difference is that in the case of Kant this harmony with the universal reason is to be achieved through moral freedom. It can, therefore, only be the final stage: it cannot be established in advance and set going like a clock.

The essence of this 'classical' view of personality is its definition of a person in terms of a self-conscious substance, a noumenal self, a pure ego. As Dr Tennant remarks (*Philosophical Theology*, I, 124–5) with reference to Professor Webb, the various presentations of this view have represented but glosses on the different parts of Boethius' definition – according to whether the words *rationabilis naturae* or *individua substantia* have been selected for emphasis. It does not seem to Tennant himself that there is any alternative to continuing such a line of thought, apart from lapsing into a behaviourist psychology. His own statement that anything less than 'self-consciousness plus anything that may be superadded through the mediation of social life' (*Philosophical Theology*, I, 126) is too narrow as a definition of personality, clearly reflecting his acceptance of the traditional view. It assumes that self-consciousness is something which a person possesses as an individual – the rational nature in virtue of which he is equipped to go out into the world of persons and things, cognizing them, using them, and entering into moral and functional relationships with them. Personality is modified and enriched by social life, but it remains something which can be defined in terms of itself, and it exists – if not chronologically at least metaphysically – as the *prius* of all that may be added through contact with others. The starting point is the consciousness of the 'I'. Within this idealistic framework the individual's presentational world is built up. By 'idealistic' nothing is here implied about the metaphysical status of what is perceived; nothing, that is, about realism, idealism or phenomenalism as theories of knowledge. Rather the reference is to the assumption that the knower starts from a private world of his own self-consciousness, from which world he later concludes to the existence of other centres of consciousness. In other words, a theoretical solipsism is postulated as the necessary epistemological basis of all subsequent development. Tennant is not an idealist in the usual sense of the term; he holds that one must believe in some kind of 'thing in itself' existing independently of the subject. At the same time, he is essentially idealistic in his centring of all on the self. His starting point is the Cartesian '*cogito ergo sum*'. From this he proceeds to establish the reality of the material world, of other selves and of God. But none of these even when established can ever be thought of out of my own 'consciousness-space' (to use a phrase of Karl Heim's) – they remain parts of my presentational field, 'constructs' of my own thought processes. I can have no 'certainty' of their independent existence, to however great a degree their 'probability' may be attested by practical verification.

What is to be said to this theory of the self and of personality? Comments and criticisms will reveal themselves as we proceed. Here we may just draw out the connection before asserted between this view and the corresponding inadequacies we noted in the impersonal Theologies which presuppose it.

First and foremost, there is the same omission of reference to the peculiarly personal relationship, on account of which we felt obliged to deem Tennant's view of God impersonal, despite the ascription of personal qualities to him. According to this view of the self, a person is defined in terms of his own being without reference to his relations to others. The distinguishing qualities of personality, included under the comprehensive *rationalis*, are grounded in a self-contained 'individual substance' from which the idea of any necessary relations is excluded. The 'classical' theory defines man not merely as a rational being, but as an *autonomous* rational being (Brunner, *Man in Revolt*, 109). According to this view, a person would still be a person, even though he had with his fellows either purely impersonal relations or none at all. The formula always runs 'the self, plus . . .'. The central core of personality is self-constitutive: it is because it partakes of reason rather than relation that it is what it is. And on this account the peculiarly personal relationship of love is excluded from consideration as in any way essential. According to the 'classical' theory, our relation to our fellow men is based on the idea that the Other is also the bearer of the same Reason as I am myself; thus between him and me there exists a relation of identity in view of the essential, to which there corresponds, subjectively, respect but not love. (Brunner, *Man in Revolt*, 326–7)

This one essential element, therefore, in the last resort, makes the one independent of the other. He can always 'tell himself' what the other could tell him. He has no need of the other . . . To be dependent upon others and connected with others seems to be something accidental or transient. (ibid., 437)

The connection of this view with an impersonalistic Theology is evident. Neither in the case of God nor man is reference to the peculiarly personal relationship of love contained in the definition of personality.[5] If one works with the 'classical' theory there is no reason why one should consider the God of Tennant's Theology impersonal; all the relevant qualities are there, and he is explicitly claimed as personal. And yet we have had occasion to doubt whether the absence of such a continuous, individuating love-relation between divine and human of which we have spoken does not destroy the very essence of what experience requires of a truly personalistic Theology.

Out of the omission of this relationship from the definition of personality two consequences inevitably follow, both of which are clearly reflected in Tennant's Theology. The first is the lack of provision on the part of rationalistic individualism (that is to say, the definition of personality in terms of the '*rationabilis naturae individua substantia*') for any genuine individuality. This will be discussed at greater length in Ch. 7 below. Here it is enough to point out that, according to this view, the essence of personality is regarded as something universal. All men are equal, in the sense that all partake of the one reason. This is the one thing that really matters. The Kantian 'Kingdom of Ends' is achieved by regarding men purely in the light of this one essential, by 'abstracting from all individual differences'.

Individual differences are accidental and contingent: they are but a negative limitation and restriction of reason. The peculiar uniqueness of each personality, which makes it impossible to treat him exactly like any other and impossible to exchange him for any other, is of no essential importance. This finds reflection in the case of the divine personality in the deistic tinge that infects such Theologies as those of Tennant. Because the individual has no unique, peculiar and inalienable value there is nothing that would require him to be treated in a wholly individual manner. There is no need of any idea of special providence. God shows his goodness by treating men as rational moral beings, and as such all men are the same. The contingencies of life's course are morally a matter of indifference. They are just the conditions and raw materials for the moral life, and it is therefore essential that they should be governed by constant and reliable laws, however arbitrary their impact upon the individual.

This abstract individualism which destroys individuality is the direct consequence of divorcing the person from that unique and unrepeatable relation to others in which alone we have claimed that the norm of his personality is fulfilled. For it is only this relation, the relation of love, that gives significance and value to the particular and to the individual. It is not merely that we can only love a person as an individual. This is clear enough; though Tennant would seem to depict a God who loves everyone in general and no one in particular, whereas Kant strove to introduce an idea of 'practical love', which never succeeds in differentiating itself from 'respect', simply because it is directed only to what is universal in man. It is also true that only because a man is an object of love is he fully an individual. I am loved for what I am because of the uniqueness of my particular nature; I am respected for what I am despite it. It is love which gives significance and value to that element in a man which makes it impossible to exchange him for anyone else. Love not only appreciates individuality, it bestows it. A man loves a woman simply because she is that particular woman and no one else. It would be a sheer insult to him to suggest that another would do equally well. But remove the bond of love – take the woman out of that peculiar relationship – and the significance of her being that particular one is gone. The less intense the love the less individuality counts. Abstract the individual from the personal relationship altogether – which is just what rationalism does – and one is as good as another.

Secondly, indissolubly connected with the abstraction of the 'classical' theory from the peculiarly personal relationship and its failure to find a place for individuality is its inability to assign a proper significance to the body. For the body is the vehicle through which individuality comes to expression. Rationalism can speak of 'pure spirit' as the ideal essence of man as a god simply because individuality is for it of no account. It is fundamental to a Christian personalism to insist on the resurrection of the body. The body, whatever form it may take, is the medium of all communication of personality, of all relation. Abstract a man's soul from his body and you have at once removed him from the possibility of that relationship in which alone he can be an individual and a person.

The connection between the body and the personal relation will receive further attention at a later stage (Ch. 7). It is only relevant at this point to recall the previous association in our discussion of Tennant's Theology of an absence of individual or special providence with the underestimation of the significance of the body and the divine direction of material events caused by an exclusive concentration on the moral goal. If it is the 'soul' alone that matters, then it is explicable that God should take but an indirect and impersonal interest in the collocation of material factors which compose the vale of this 'making'. And it is the 'classical' theory of personality which gives the basis for such a view. For compared with the rational element in man, which makes him a man, the body is but a temporary shack of little value. If, however, it is the relation in which a man stands to others which makes him personal, then the body becomes an essential condition of such existence.

Chapter Three

A NEW BEGINNING

The 'classical' theory of personality, which has dominated Western philosophical thought to such a remarkable degree for so many centuries, was thrust upon our attention, it will be recalled, by the inability of much theology to provide a doctrine of God capable of doing justice to the essentially personalistic nature of Christian experience. History seemed to suggest that the reason for such a deficiency might be found in the influence of a notion of *human* personality which showed similar inadequacies. This connection has been substantiated by consideration of a recent (at the time of writing) defence of a theistic position open to just such charges of impersonalism as we had in mind. The absence of the peculiarly 'personal' relationship in Dr Tennant's otherwise personalistic Theology corresponds exactly to the criticism we have noted of the 'classical' theory of personality. This theory gives due place to the various qualities which distinguish personal from other forms of existence – notably those of rationality and self-consciousness. But it pays no attention to the factor which we agreed to be a minimum requirement for any definition of personality – namely, the responsibility to exist in the peculiarly 'personal', as opposed to the merely 'functional' or 'instrumental', relationship with other persons. This is a fact of experience for which a theory of personality has got to find room if it is not to stand self-condemned. For not all the ways in which persons relate themselves to each other are equally personal. Some are definitely impersonal: they constitute an abuse or violation of personality. That is to say, it is recognized that there is a kind of relationship which is 'proper' to existence as a person. Such a relation cannot, therefore, be treated merely as one way in which a being with personal attributes may choose to act towards his environment. Rather must it be considered as the *only* way of existing which is not in some degree a betrayal of the norm of his being.

It is the absence of any such element from the 'classical' definition of personality that constitutes its basic failure. And, since it does not include it from the beginning, it is unable to introduce it afterwards. Starting from a theoretical solipsism, it can never hope to reach a position in which the fact of relatedness is part of the essence of personality. The most it can assert is that a relationship with other persons is possible on such a basis and is in fact achieved.[6] Actually it is not hard to demonstrate that this assertion involves an impossible epistemology. The argument is that knowledge of other selves arises as an analogical inference from the combination of the consciousness of one's own self and the apprehension of objects (in particular the observation of other bodies). It can be shown, however, that both these two forms of knowledge presuppose what they are used to prove, namely, the awareness of other selves, and that, even if they did not, they could never in themselves unite to produce it. But we do not intend to expand these statements here, partly because the case has already been set forth at length by others,[7] and we would only be repeating what has been said much better elsewhere. But also, and more importantly, it is because, even if the analogical theory of the knowledge of other selves that goes with the 'classical' theory of personality[8] could establish a genuine '*cogito ergo es*' (I think therefore you are), relationship to others could never be shown to be more than of the *bene esse* (well-being) of personality. It would constitute the means of expansion and enrichment of self-consciousness. But self-consciousness itself, which is regarded as the *esse* of personality, would always be epistemologically prior to it and independent of it. The autarchical ideal, which grounds man's personality in his own rational nature, destroys the necessity of relationship. 'If I possess the essential in myself, I have no need of the other' (Brunner, *Man in Revolt*, 557). Nor, moreover, could any one class of relationship to other selves, such as the 'personal' relationship, be regarded as normative. Unless it forms part of the definition from the beginning, it is purely arbitrary to say that out of several ways, this particular one of relating oneself to others is *the* personal way, and that its absence justifies the application of the epithet 'impersonal' to a man's dealings.

It is against the background of the failure of the 'classical' approach to the understanding of personality that the work of a school of writers, of whom the most well known is Dr Martin Buber, acquires its significance. For what it has achieved is nothing less than the reversal of the traditional starting point of all Western philosophy, especially as it has been formulated since the days of Descartes. This traditional point of departure has been the idea of 'individual substance'. Descartes only revealed his acceptance of its presupposition when he declared that of the many 'individual substances' one only, the self, could provide the philosopher with something behind which it was impossible to go. For, among the attributes of the 'rational nature' by which an earlier generation had distinguished personal substances from others, there was one, self-consciousness, which was unique. It was the one primary 'clear and distinct idea' from which all the rest of experience was derived and by which it could be validated. The '*cogito ergo sum*' was but the logical conclusion of the search for the ideal starting point of a really individual substance, which does not presuppose or depend on anything else, but which can be defined and established with reference to itself alone. It is the Ego as the embodiment of the autarchical ideal, whether epistemologically considered or, as in the case of Kant, ethically also, which modern philosophy has taken as the 'knot in the thread' with which it does all its sewing.

This is the position that Buber reverses when he states from the very beginning: 'There is no "I" taken in itself' – no '*Ich an Sich*' (*Ich und Du*, 10; all translations, except where otherwise indicated, will be taken from the English version *I and Thou* by R. Gregor Smith, 1937, to which for convenience references will be made). Rather, the *Grundworte*, which stand for the primary things in our experience, represent not individual substances but relationships. These he divides into two types, the relation of 'I' to 'Thou' and of 'I' to 'It'. The difference between them will be discussed in detail later. Here it is sufficient to say that, in our dealings with others, the 'I–Thou' relation corresponds to what we have been calling the distinctively 'personal' relationship, while the 'I–It' represents roughly what we have included under the 'functional' and 'instrumental'.

Buber is saying that the different relationships into which a man enters are not additional to the essence of personality but constitutive of it. The primary fact from which we have to start (and he is prepared to demonstrate its epistemological primacy) is not the 'Ego' but the 'Ego-in-relationship'. 'There is not "I" taken in itself, but only the "I" of the primary word "I–Thou" and the "I" of the primary word "I–It" ' (*I and Thou*, 4). For him the real is the relational. His study of the meaning of personality – and, for that matter, of reality – takes the form of an analysis of the personal relationship. Thereby a genuinely new start is made. The 'classical' approach, by not taking this relationship into its definition from the beginning, never succeeded in finding a place for it. In consequence, it produced a theory of personality which, both in the case of the human and the divine, is inadequate to the experience it seeks to represent. For by its starting point it rendered itself incapable of giving room to a fact about persons which on any count must be regarded as distinctive of them. Although the peculiarly personal relationship is difficult to describe in words, it is something which is easily recognized by all. It is its absence which makes the various traditional accounts of personality so depressingly abstract and uninspiring.

So much warmth and reality is lost by the time we arrive at a definition such as that of Boethius that it seems at the end hardly worth achieving – so little does it tell us of what it would be like to meet a person. The same is true even when the expression is couched in the comparatively modern terms, say, of Illingworth's *Personality, Human and Divine* (1894), or even of Temple's *Nature of Personality* (1911).

Buber's work, in contrast, makes an intense appeal to those who read it, even though they may have little philosophical training and may find his mode of expression at times extremely perplexing. Their reaction is that here at any rate is to be found something real and living, something which they have actually experienced and known for themselves. There is presented in his pages such 'a man of flesh and bone' as Miguel de Unamuno cried for as an alternative to the generalized abstractions of humanity with which philosophy so frequently deals (*The Tragic Sense of Life in Men and in Peoples* (ET 1926), Ch. I). The speed and avidity with which the idea of the 'Thou' relationship is being taken up and applied in connections far removed from the sphere of academic philosophy is an indication that men are finding in it something which they can really make their own, which they can constantly verify in their own living, and which can lead to a really creative understanding of their personal and social situations. Buber inevitably strikes one as writing of something which one has known all the time. To some this may appear to indicate that he has little new to offer. But to most people it is a revelation and an inspiration to see for the first time the true significance of what they had always taken for granted. Ideas are liberated which lead them to ever-fresh discoveries about themselves and the world of relationships in which they are set. And in particular, for the religious man, a new insight is gained into the organic connection between his personal experience of God and the whole nexus of finite 'Thou' relationships by which this is mediated to him. At last a conception of the personality of God is offered which seems genuinely to correspond with the reality which religion has always known.

This, in Hume's phrase, may appear to 'savour more of panegyric than philosophy', but it is relevant to the theme of this chapter. For, before going on to a more detailed account of Buber's contribution to the understanding of personality, we should try to see it against the background of the problem as a whole and to estimate it in connection with the need to be satisfied and the attempts of other philosophers to meet it. On the first two of these points something has now been said. The third may perhaps be met by a rapid survey of the genesis in the history of philosophy of the kind of ideas with which Buber has familiarized us. It is therefore proposed to spend the remaining pages of this chapter in exploring what, even at the lowest estimation, is a remarkably interesting by-way in the history of ideas.

The significance of the 'Thou' relationship had in different ways and degrees made itself felt long before the second decade of the twentieth century when Buber's *I and Thou* appeared. The contribution of this author has largely been to recognize its central importance, and, by advancing it to the position occupied by the Cartesian '*cogito ergo sum*', to expound it as the clue, not only to the nature of personality, but also to the interpretation of the whole of truth and reality. What is so tantalizing in the various glimpses won at different times by different thinkers is often just that they have not applied radically enough the insights they have gained. In consequence, what they saw was usually lost and forgotten, only to be discovered again quite independently by later generations.

Of the ancients probably only Socrates had any conception of the significance of personal meeting. His famous remark that 'the men who dwell in the city are my teachers, not the trees or the country' (*Phaedrus*, 230, d) impressed itself on the whole form of Plato's work. The dialogue is not merely a literary artifice: it is a necessary expression of the underlying conviction that the road to knowledge is the *via dialectica* (the way of question and answer). The truth is not something spun from the brain of the philosopher in his study, but hammered out in the discussion of the marketplace.[9]

But the significance of this insight was qualified and limited in two respects. In the first place, what was really involved in the Socratic method was not necessarily the confrontation of different persons but the meeting of rival 'arguments' or 'theories'. It is true that these always tend to be embodied in separate collocutors, and it was doubtless real conversations and discussions which provided the source of much of Socrates' philosophy. But such a reciprocal relationship is not essenial: the debate might equally well be carried on 'within the heart of a single enquirer, as his "soul" questions itself and answers its own questions' (Taylor, *Socrates*, 157). And, if we are honest with ourselves, we have often to admit the impression that some Platonic dialogues could fare quite well if Socrates were the sole interlocutor and himself provided the easy expressions of assent or the Aunt Sallies to be demolished.

And secondly, while Socrates and Plato may have grasped the importance for method that truth has to emerge from the debate of the marketplace, they show no signs of having recognized its significance for metaphysics. Personal contacts might be the method of arriving at the truth; but there was no suggestion that the truth was to be found *in* them, and in a real sense, consisted *of* them. Reality, on the contrary, was something entirely removed from the life of the market. The good by open confession was to be reached by a process of abstraction from actual personal relationships (cf. the recipe for arriving at the notion of absolute beauty given by Socrates by Diotima in the *Symposium*, 211). Platonic Realism (in this respect recently revived in an interesting way as the basis of an avowedly atheistic philosophy by Nicolai von Hartmann) is probably the most impersonal of all metaphysical systems. For his 'Ideas' neither exist in the minds of human persons (as the Nominalists asserted), nor are they embodied in a divine Person. They just 'subsist', *a se* and *per se* (from and of themselves), with a relevance to personal living, it is true, but with no basis in it.[10]

The Socratic conception of the connection between truth and personal relationships has been discussed in a fascinating way by Kierkegaard in his *Philosophical Fragments*. The theme of the book is the difference between the relation in which Socrates believes himself to stand to the truth and that of Christ. The position of the former, as he himself described it, was that of the midwife. His was the 'maieutic' art of bringing to birth a knowledge which was already present within the subject (cf. especially *Meno*, 81, a – 85, e, and *Phaedo*, 72, e ff.). A man, on account of the natural immortality of his soul and its affinity for the things of the spirit, was already 'in the truth' and the truth in him. The function of human contacts and of the 'teacher' was to elicit this knowledge, by putting him in mind of what the lure of physical existence had caused him to forget.

But the work of Christ, says Kierkegaard, is much more than to act as the 'occasion' of the birth of a truth already within a man. For Christ denies that men are in the truth. He asserts rather that they are very far from being so. For *he* is the truth. It is something outside them, which they must enter into, by coming to 'abide' in him. The process required is not calling to mind but changing the mind, i.e. repentance. He does not stand in relation to them as the 'teacher' of a Truth which has no connection with personal relationships and to which the historical mode of its communication is accidental. For the Truth is a Person: 'I am the Truth', says Christ. To be in the truth is to relate oneself personally to him. The truth consists in the personal relationship which is its communication.

Kierkegaard here puts his finger on the inadequacy of the conception of truth held by the one ancient for whom he had an almost unbounded admiration. The 'Thou' relationship may be necessary for its understanding and impartation, but it has no essential connection with the nature of the reality which it reveals. In exactly the same way Hegel regarded the truth of Christianity as essentially a set of ideas, to which their historical communication through a Person stood in no more than a purely contingent relation. In both cases we are very far from a doctrine of a personal God, although we may feel that Socrates the pagan would be the more likely to lead us to it.

The significance of the 'I–Thou' relationship, which flashed uncertainly across the mind of Socrates, seems to have been increasingly lost as Plato advanced in age. The later Dialogues lose their realistic touch; they take on the character of an art form rather than a real conversation necessitated by the conviction that philosophy *is* dialogue. In Aristotle there is no trace remaining. Truth resides in the thoughts of the Eternal Thinker, who is wholly confined to his own mental processes. This idealistic bias, this location of the real within the consciousness of the 'I', whether divine or human, was unbroken until the nineteenth century. Jacobi's '*ohne Du kein Ich*' ('no thou – no I') foreshadows the modern connection. Yet on Jacobi's lips the phrase had none of its later significance. By *Du* he had in mind merely the external world of objects, and he was not referring specifically to other persons. The words occur in an attack on the rejection of the '*Ding an sich*' (thing in itself) by post-Kantian idealism: they do not indicate a disruption of the whole idealistic framework.

Nor should too much significance be attached to some sentences quoted by Buber (*Zweisprache*, 1932, 72) from Wilhelm von Humboldt's *Abhandlung über den Dualis* (1827): 'Man longs, even purely for the purpose of his own thinking, for a "Thou" corresponding to the "I"; concepts only disclose themselves with definiteness and certainty through being reflected back from some other and different thinking centre.' The process of ideation, von Humboldt says, presupposes an objectivity which is only established by the communication of two minds through the medium of speech.

But the 'Thou' which is here posited as a precondition of thought is little more than simply that. There is no idea of the relation as of significance in itself, no interest in the 'other' as a man, apart from as a thinker. We have here, as Buber says, simply an ideal, inner 'Thou' of thought, not a whole embodied personality, an 'other' in all its otherness. But von Humboldt's words are significant in pointing beyond themselves to the position that true thinking, and indeed all 'real living', implies such a relation to a real concrete 'Thou'.

It is at this point that we meet what must be one of the most remarkable phenomena in the history of philosophy. In the midst of a period in which the Hegelian tradition dominated the intellectual world and which produced both before and after it no trace of a consciousness of the problem of the 'Thou', there appeared in the course of six years from 1842 to 1848 works by three men in three different languages and completely uninfluenced by each other, wherein not only does the 'I–Thou' terminology appear but also there is revealed a remarkably deep understanding of the deficiencies of the idealistic position and of the corrective it required. United in their opposition to Hegel and all his works, they were similar in little else.

The first was the Swedish historian and poet Erik Gustaf Geijer (1783–1847), Professor of History at Upsala University. From this somewhat unlikely source John Cullberg, in the sole historico-critical survey of the 'Thou' philosophy which has yet appeared (*Das Du und die Wirklichkeit*, Upsala, 1933), draws much that is prophetic, though in no way determinative of later movements. We need not concern ourselves here with Geijer's radical criticism of the monism of Hegel and Schelling, nor with his refusal to base knowledge of other selves on a self-consciousness which presupposes it – however interesting these may be in view of later developments. Rather, let us turn to the theory of personality which he formulated towards the end of his life in the course of a work published in 1842, *Über falsche und wahre Aufklärung hinsichtlich der Religion* (*Sämtliche Werke*, I, 214ff.). The real antithesis of philosophy, he maintains, is not between spirit and nature, or subject and object, or any other hypostatizations of the abstractions of thought processes, but between subject and subject. The real opposite of the 'I' is another 'I' or a 'Thou'. This realization is fundamental for the understanding of personality. An isolated person is an impossibility. There is 'no personality except in and through another. No thou – no I' (I, 226; quoted by Cullberg, *Das Du und die Wirklichkeit*, 26). Experience of other persons is the sole basis of consciousness.

Geijer anticipates much, but he had no influence on philosophical development. Even in Sweden, says Cullberg, his thought was only 'a parenthetical episode'. The other personalistic philosophers, such as Kristoffer Jacob Boström (1797–1866), returned to the traditional philosophy of the 'I' and viewed God as the Infinite Spirit after the manner of Hegel.

This absence of any determining influence on the immediate course of development in the understanding of personality is typical of each of the three writers with whom we are concerned. But in the case of the next, Ludwig Andreas Feuerbach (1804–72),[11] whose small book *Grundsätze der Philosophie der Zukunft* was published within a year of that of Geijer's mentioned above, the insights were obscured more by the rest of his own writings than by those of posterity. For a genuine understanding of the significance of personal relations, both for epistemology and ontology, was spoiled by an inadequate sensualistic conception of the love which is their basis. Both Geijer and Feuerbach were in their own ways religious men (cf. H. Ehrenberg, *Disputation*, I, 167: '*Feuerbachs Atheismus beruht überhaupt auf eine durchaus religiösen, ja christlichen Denkentdeckung*' [Feuerbach's atheism rests on a discovery of religious, indeed Christian, thought]). But there was a difference between their Theologies which is reflected in their differing conceptions of human love. For Geijer, who was a Christian, the norm of the personal relation was an *agape* derived from the transcendent relation of the *agape* of God to man, which was the ultimate fact of the universe. But for Feuerbach there was no such transcendent relation. Reacting strongly from an ecclesiastical upbringing and from what he regarded as the blasphemy of the Hegelian Theology, he aimed at 'the transformation and resolution of theology into anthropology' (*Philosophie der Zukunft*, 1843, 1). In the encounter in love of one man of flesh and bone with another, he felt that he had found a reality far more ultimate than the bloodless categories which idealism graced with the name of God. This was for him what was represented by God, '*Mensch mit Mensch – die Einheit von Ich und Du – ist Gott*' [The human being with the human being – the unity of I and Thou – is God] (ibid., 62). As against the Hegelian philosophy of identity he insisted that this unity rested 'only on the reality of the *difference* between I and Thou' (59). Yet, though the two confronted each other in a real otherness, neither might be thought of in isolation. For, like Geijer, he saw that, except in relationship to an 'other', personality was impossible. 'The real "I" is only the "I" that stands over against another "I"; but for the "I" of the idealists there exists no object at all and no "Thou".' And he goes on, even more strongly: 'First and last and from the very ground of my being, I am essentially a being relating myself to another being outside myself; out of this relation I am nothing' (*Sämtliche Werke*, X, 214; quoted, Ehrenberg, *Disputation*, I, 165–6). This relation too is for him the key to the problem of truth. No more than he can admit the '*L'être c'est moi*' of the Hegelian Absolute, can he tolerate the '*La verité c'est moi*' of the idealist philosopher (*Philosophie der Zukunft*, 61). 'The true dialectic is no monologue between I and Thou' (ibid., 62). 'The personal relationship (*Gemeinschaft*) of one human being with another is the first principle and criterion of truth and universality (*Allgemeinheit*)' (41). Or, even more succinctly, '*Wo keine Liebe, ist auch keine Wahrheit*' [where there is no love there is no truth] (35).

Yet, for all this, one cannot but feel that in this insistence on the ultimacy of the personal relationship ('*nichts sein und nichts lieben ist identisch*' [not being and not loving are identical], 35), Feuerbach never really reaches a conception of love in which the circle of egocentricity is broken. His remains an *Eros* which is centred on the 'I', and in which the 'Thou' still appears as a point on the circumference of its self-satisfaction. Just as for von Humboldt a 'Thou' of thought was necessary for the thinking subject, so Feuerbach's infinitely richer and more concrete 'Thou' is presented as the necessary complement of the sense-experiencing man of flesh and bone. There is here no absolute valuation placed upon the 'other' in his own right, in obedience to whose imperious claim the lover can alone reach self-fulfilment. Until the 'Thou' is accorded more than a relative justification, the absolute 'I' of idealism remains on the throne. The inadequacies of Feuerbach's position will become manifest by a comparison with the conception of love to be set forth half a century later by Soloviev. It will also be clear that they are such as are directly due to the lack of that from which Feuerbach for all his religious spirit turned away; namely, a conception of a 'Thou' wholly and transcendentally 'other', which disrupts the simple identification of theology with anthropology. Only as the embodiment of the absolute love of God can the human 'Thou' meet the self with that unconditional gift-in-demand which is capable of lifting it out of its 'I'-centred existence and establishing a true reciprocity of personal communion.

It is just this awareness of an unconditioned, transcendentally 'other' Person which was absent from Feuerbach's thought that formed that knot in the thread – as he himself called it – with which Søren Kierkegaard (1813–55), the last of the three strange contemporaries we have to consider, did all his thinking and – which was for him the same thing – all his existing. For it was this ('the God-relationship') which was constitutive of his central idea, the concept of 'the individual' (*det Enkelte*, 'my category', as he used to style it). It is worth examining this idea, because it has led to some misunderstanding of the significance of this Danish writer for the movement we are considering. Cullberg dismisses Kierkegaard in a footnote by saying that his otherwise relevant attack on 'the system' of the idealists led him to a concentration on the 'individual', which meant that the problem of the 'Thou' did not arise. The assumption is that the two, 'the individual' and the 'I–Thou' relation, are mutually exclusive, and the term Kierkegaard uses has led others to think the same.

Buber himself, in *Die Frage an den Einzelnen* (1936, ET 'The Question of the Single One', in *Between Man and Man*, tr. Ronald Gregor Smith, 1947. Ed. note.), accuses Kierkegaard of encouraging a view of the God-relation which involves an abstraction from the finite 'Thou' relationships of human contacts. Rather, he says, 'it is God's will that we should come to Him through the Reginas [the name of Kierkegaard's prospective betrothed, thus

= marriage, the world. Ed. note.] He has made, and not by a renunciation of them' (ibid., 34). It must be confessed that there is much that lends colour to such an accusation. Such is his concentration upon the necessity for each to become 'an individual before God' that Kierkegaard has practically nothing to say about the corporate nature of Christianity. His doctrine of the Church is really 'an aggregation of millions of individuals each of whom severally has his own God-relationship' (*Training in Christianity*, 1850, 92). As far as this world is concerned ' "fellowship" is a lower category than "the single individual" ' (ibid., 218). 'The congregation' only properly belongs to eternity. In the Church militant each man has to battle as a single individual, and it is as an individual that he will be judged.

It is, however, important to see the reasons for this one-sided concentration. It was certainly not that Kierkegaard believed in the *via negativa* of the mystic, namely, that God can only be reached by an abstraction from all finite relationships. Of this there is no evidence. It was rather that he saw the decision involved in the Christian life to be so utterly individual, and the responsibility so completely inalienable, that, in the face of the Christendom of his day, he could but affirm and reaffirm the appeal to consider its absolute centrality and seriousness. He constantly pictured God as the great Examiner, demanding from each an individual answer, which he could only give if he kept his eye sternly on his own paper without gazing round to see what progress others were making (*Training in Christianity*, 220).

It is this continuous sense of the 'seriousness' of existence, of the ultimate responsibility of each man before the throne of heaven, that gives Kierkegaard his importance in the history of the 'Thou' relationship. For 'the individual' is always 'in relationship'. Even though he may think to cut himself off from everyone and deny all claims, he can never escape from the context of his relation to God. 'Let him now forget everything, but think passionately upon one fact, that he is not altogether alone in the dark room, but that God is present and says to him: "Art thou a Christian?" ' (quoted, W. Lowrie, *Kierkegaard*, 1938, 526). And no more can he seek to avert that question by immersing himself in the multitudinous claims of the world: 'As a single individual he is alone, alone in the whole world, alone before God' (Kierkegaard, *The Point of View*, 137; cf. *Purify Your Hearts*, 152). The concept of 'the individual' is simply the correlative of the idea of a 'living', speaking, active God: 'To God as the decisive factor corresponds the individual' (*The Point of View*, 136). Everyone, in the norm of his being, is such 'an individual' (ibid., 121). He is essentially what he is because of his relationship to God, and to 'become a man' is precisely 'to become an individual before God' (ibid., 154).

But though in the concept of 'the individual' Kierkegaard expresses the essence of the truth of the 'I–Thou' relation, there is another connection in which he goes yet further and employs the actual terminology. It occurs in a passage on preaching (*Training in Christianity*, 228–30; cf. *Purify Your Hearts*, 147–8) which anticipates in a remarkable way the introductory argument of Professor Farmer's *Servant of the Word* (1941). In preaching, he says, one cannot, as contemporary custom would suggest, merely deliver oneself of 'reflections' upon some topic or other.

> Christian truth cannot properly be the object of 'reflection'. 'For Christian truth, if I may say so, has itself eyes to see with, yea is all eye; but it would be very disquieting, rather quite impossible, to look at a painting or a piece of cloth, if when I was about to look I discovered that the painting or the cloth was looking at me – and precisely such is the case with Christian truth, it is that which is looking at me to see whether I do what it says I should do . . . It has itself, if I may say so, ears to hear with, yea, it is as it were all ears, it listens attentively while the speaker talks; one cannot talk about it as about an absentee or as a thing present only objectively, for since it is from God and God is in it, it is present in a very special sense while one is speaking about it, and not as an object, rather it is the speaker that is the object of its regard, in speaking he has conjured up a spirit which examines him. (*op. cit.*, 228–9)

When we come to Buber's description of the 'reciprocity' of the 'I–Thou' relation, we shall see how exactly this account of it fits. It is because when one is in the proper sense 'in the truth' that one is always in a relation of this kind, that preaching is a thing of the utmost seriousness and responsibility. For God is always in the congregation.

> So venturesome a thing is it to be the 'I' which preaches, to be the speaker, an 'I' who by preaching and in the act of preaching puts himself absolutely under obligation, lays his life bare so that if it were possible one might look directly into his soul – to be such an 'I', that were a venturesome thing. Therefore little by little the parson found out how to draw his eye back into himself, indicating thereby that nobody had any business to look at him. In fact it was not (so he thought) about himself he was speaking, it was about the thing at issue; and this was admired as an extraordinary advance in wisdom that the speaker ceased to be an 'I' and became, if possible, a thing. Anyhow, in this way it became far easier to be a parson – the speaker no longer preached, he employed these moments to introduce some reflections . . . So it is that the 'I', who was the speaker, dropped out; the speaker is not an 'I', he is the thing at issue, the reflection. And as the 'I' fell out, so also the 'Thou' was done away with, thou the hearer, the fact that thou who sittest there art the person to whom the discourse is addressed.

The personal relationship is the reciprocity between 'I' and 'Thou': when one goes the other goes too; and the relationship becomes purely impersonal, though it is still between the same human beings. For it is the relationship established rather than anything in the beings themselves, which constitutes their form of existence personal. This is the authentic note of the new view.

The next figure whose significance for the movement should be noted is the Russian Christian philosopher, Vladimir Soloviev (1853–1900. For an introduction to his thought, see N. Zernov, *Three Russian Prophets*, 1944). In 1892 he published a small book called *The Meaning of Love* (ET, 1945, by Jane Marshall), which, particularly through the writings of Berdyaev, has exercised a considerable influence. Though he never actually employs the terms 'I' and 'Thou', his conception of the significance of love reveals a very similar understanding of the structure of the personal relationship. He challenges the adequacy of the notion of 'individual substance' as the norm of existence. 'That which lies at the basis of our world is Being in a state of disintegration, Being dismembered into parts and moments which exclude one another' (ET, 72–3). 'If the root of false existence consists in impenetrability, *i.e.*, in the mutual exclusion of creatures by each other, then true existence is to live in another, as in oneself, to find in another the positive and unconditional completion of one's own being' (77). Human egoism, rightly fastening upon man's own unconditional significance as an individual, wrongly refuses this same significance to others: 'He relegates others to the circumference of his own being and leaves them only an external and relative value' (23). By thus seeking to establish his individuality in isolation, he in fact destroys it: for he only exists as a person in relation to others. 'Asserting himself apart from all that is other, a man by his very act divests his own authentic being of meaning, deprives himself of the true content of existence, and reduces his individuality to an empty form' (24). The only salvation from this self-centredness is that 'the living force of egoism' should 'encounter another living force opposed to it' (21), 'a life equally concrete and determinate, permeating the whole of our nature, and taking possession of everything in it' (25). The love which, par excellence, Soloviev regards as capable of effecting this liberation from the castle of egocentricity is the love between a man and a woman. But he views it in a very different way from Feuerbach, for whom, in such a relation, the other person remained essentially a point on the circumference of the experiencing 'I'. Soloviev insists that the 'Thou' be 'effectually other' (26), with a self-subsistence and absolute significance completely independent of the subject. Indeed it is this fact that gives love its whole 'meaning and worth', which consists precisely in this, that

> it effectually constrains us, in all our nature, to acknowledge for *another* [italics his] the unconditional central significance, of which, in virtue of our egoism, we are conscious only in our own selves. Love is of importance; not only as one of our feelings, but as the transfer of all our interest in life from ourselves to another, as the shifting of the very centre of our personal life. (30)

But at this point an objection arises which leads Soloviev to a crucial transition, the same transition to which all writers of this school who understand the significance of the 'Thou' find themselves forced.

> The radical meaning of love, as has already been shown, consists in the acknowledgment for another creature of unconditional significance. But this creature in its empirical being, as the subject of actual sensuous reception, is not possessed of unconditional significance: it is imperfect in its simplicity and transient as to its existence. (59)

In itself the 'other' can exercise no absolute claim upon us capable of drawing us out of the prison-house of our egoism. It is only 'by faith', by 'the affirmation of this object as it exists in God' (59), that we are justified in according it eternal significance; only, that is to say, as in this 'other' we meet the divine Other, which 'receives its concrete embodiment in the relation to a single person of the other sex, who represents in itself this complementary "all" in one' (76). But this very act of faith presupposes (and herein lies its power for salvation) a radical revaluation of a man's own existence as having its centre not in himself but in the divine 'Thou'.

> I can only acknowledge the unconditional significance of a given person, or believe in him (without which true love is impossible), by affirming him in God, and therefore by belief in God Himself, and in myself, as possessing in God the centre and root of my own existence. (59)

It is in my relation to God, not in my own 'individual substance', that the essence of my personality resides. Thus, once again, we find in Soloviev the phenomenon noted before – a genuine recognition of the truth of the 'Thou', yet arising apparently completely independently and equally without direct influence on the course of succeeding thought.

With the name of Hermann Cohen, head of the Neo-Kantian school of philosophy at Marburg, we come for the first time to a thinker who exercised a direct influence on the circle out of which Buber's *I and Thou* was to emerge. It was not until 1919 that his book *Die Religion der Vernunft aus den Quellen des Judentums* was published posthumously at Leipzig, though his personal influence had been at work many years previously. In the context of Old Testament study he sought to work out on its ethical side the conviction that a man's existence is given only in and through his relation to a 'Thou'. The headings of three successive chapters in the book mentioned will give some indication of the sequence of his thinking: Ch. VIII 'The Discovery of Man as Man-in-community (*Mitmensch*)'; Ch. IX 'The Problem of Religious Love'; Ch. X 'The Individual as "I" '.

In the years immediately preceding 1914 a number of friends, including Martin Buber, Franz Rosenzweig, Eugene Rosenstock and Hans Ehrenberg,[12] were beginning to feel their way towards a break with the idealistic tradition which had dominated German philosophy since the days of Kant and Hegel. The incidence of the Great War, which brought about the final crash of the whole liberal idealistic structure of thought and values, hastened this process. By the spring of 1916 Buber had begun on the process of thought which led to his *Ich und Du*. It was first written down, he tells us, in the autumn of 1919 and attained its final form in the spring of 1922. Publication followed a year later. At the same time Ehrenberg brought out the first of three *Disputationen über Fichte, Schelling und Hegel*, which contained an elaboration of Feuerbach's conception of the 'I–Thou' relation in opposition to what he called the 'Es–Ich' of Fichte's idealism.

Meanwhile in 1921 Rosenzweig had published his great book *Der Stern der Erlösung*. This was begun while he was in the army in Macedonia in 1918 and completed the following year. It took shape out of a remarkable series of letters between him and the Christian Rosenstock on the relations between Judaism and the Church. In the course of the book he propounds a doctrine of creation as the address of the Divine 'I' to the human 'Thou', the Lover to the beloved. God's creative love is not a timeless attribute, 'no quality but an event' (209), an ever-fresh Word (*reinste Gegenwart*) meeting each man in the peculiarities of his personal situation, calling him by his own name, as in the Garden of Eden he called, 'Adam, where art thou?' It is this individual address by name which makes man a man and distinguishes him from the rest of creation. 'He ceases to be a substantive, a thing, and he no longer displays the fundamental characteristic of things, to be a thing among things' (237). As man he is an 'individual' because, as for Kierkegaard, he stands in a peculiar relation to God. 'With the calling of the proper name, the Word of revelation enters upon a real conversation (*Wechselrede*); with the proper name a breach is made in the rigid wall of thing-hood' (237). To the 'Thou art mine' of the divine Lover man answers 'I am Thine' (233). And this 'conversation of love', though grievously marred by sin, 'is there to the end' (235–6): it is the basis of all commerce between the Creator and his creation.

The last name, without reference to whom it would be impossible to close this chapter, is that of a writer who stood quite outside this circle and worked completely independently of them. Ferdinand Ebner, an Austrian elementary school teacher, anticipated the appearance of *I and Thou* by two years, by publishing at Innsbruck in 1921 a book entitled *Das Wort und die geistigen Realitäten*. Actually both authors had begun writing several years beforehand (Ebner in the winter 1918/19, Buber, as we saw, in the autumn of 1919), and the many close parallels between them are all the more remarkable because of the absence of any direct connection or mutual influence. It is impossible to do justice to Ebner's work in the course of a few paragraphs. It is in many ways a great book, and for proper treatment would demand a chapter to itself. How great may be judged by the fact that Karl Heim has seen fit to accord to Ebner's achievement in administering the first decisive rebuff to the whole idealistic position the honoured description of '*eine kopernikanische Tat*' ['a Copernican act'] (Cullberg, *Das Du und die Wirklichkeit*, 38).

Ebner's work affords ample evidence that the new approach was the outcome of a real wrestling with concrete personal experience. The same hard facts which in theology evoked the onslaught on liberalism of Barth's *Römerbrief* (1918, 1921 2nd edn, ET tr. E. C. Hoskyns 1933) provoked Ebner to declare, with many similar emphases, the total bankruptcy of the idealistic philosophical tradition. 'The dream of the poet and the philosopher . . . is now finally dreamt out of Europe', he writes (*Das Wort*, 243): only the two Christians Kierkegaard and Dostoevsky foresaw the present disruptions. There is a strongly anti-intellectualist bias throughout. Theology as an objective science is falsehood (144–5), and a Christian culture of *Weltanschauung* a contradiction in terms. All culture is relative and nationally conditioned (232–3). The only hope for Christianity and the world is to renounce the idealistic dreaming of the mystic and the metaphysician and return to the one reality of the individual believer's relation to God. Ebner was essentially a man of one idea, and herein lay both his strength and weakness. The effect of the War, without which the book might never have been written, shows itself only too clearly in the lack of coherence and stability in form and style. It is composed of a series of fragments, which, from different angles and with much repetition, drive home the one central theme.

The basis of the whole is that the solitary 'I' (the *Icheinsamkeit*) from which the traditional idealistic philosophy started is but an abstraction (15). Concrete personal being is 'always the existence of the "I" in relation to the "Thou" ' (36) – a 'Thou' who is really 'other' and not merely an ideal

'Thou' of thought or fiction. Man is not first an 'I' in isolation who later acquires socialization: rather, the relation to the 'Thou' is the presupposition of his capacity for socialization (32). It is the 'I' and the 'Thou' in their mutually constitutive relation which alone are the 'spiritual realities' of the title. The existence of the 'I' is only given in relation to the 'Thou' (16), but this means, in the last resort, only in relation to God (22). For in every real 'Thou' relation it is God who confronts us in and through the 'other': 'In the ultimate depths of our spiritual life God is the true "Thou" of the true "I" in man' (17). Man's being presupposes that of God (26): atheism in denying God denies man (29–32). 'Without God the "I" sinks into the abyss of nothingness, since he exists only in relation to Him as his "Thou" ' (152).

The personal relation is characterized on its subjective side as love, and objectively, as the outward condition of its possibility, by speech (51). 'Personality is unthinkable except in relation to the word' (18): 'the "Thou" is the "addressability" (*Ansprechbarkeit*) in others' (18). Ebner attaches great significance to the fact of speech, not merely as a sign of rationality, but as making possible the relation in which all human existence, consciousness and rationality is rooted (34). 'The problem of speech is not a philosophical nor a psychological nor indeed a scientific problem of any kind, but a pneumatological one' (52). 'In the word lies the key of the spiritual life' (52). The distinctive thing about human existence is that 'man "has" the word' (24). Only with Christianity, he claims, could there come a proper understanding of religion as '*das Ihmgegebensein-des-Wortes*' ['his being given the word'] and therefore a proper understanding of man (57). St John was the first to see the inner connection of man's spiritual life with the word, whose divine source he recognized, and saw embodied in the life of Jesus (52–3). The Word of God is the ultimate ground of human existence: 'That God created man means nothing else than that He spoke to him. In creating him He said to him "I am, and through me thou art" ' (26). All true human living, all prayer, is nothing but the response of faith to this Word: 'Thou art and through thee I am' (37). When referred to God, the second person (the 'Thou') is in fact the first person, and the human 'I' possesses but a responsive existence. 'The existence of the "Thou" (God) does not presuppose that of the "I", but rather *vice versa*, the "I" the "Thou" ' (37). This he expresses elsewhere by saying that, whereas the form of the 'In the relationship to the Thou, the "I" comes into being'. '*Im Verhältnis zum Du, wird das Ich*' (177).

Though Ebner does not call it the 'I–It' relation, he says much that is similar to Buber on the attitude to existence which is characterized by

Dulosigkeit [Thoulessness], when the 'Thou' is 'far off'. The 'I' in its *Icheinsamkeit*, the centre of its own little world which takes no account of other centres (132–3), is confined within the 'Chinese Wall' of its own egoism, which only the love of God as it meets us in others, and pre-eminently in Jesus Christ, can break down (116–17). The whole system of idealist ethics is just a structure erected for the purpose of 'raising to the level of an ethical demand respect for the "Chinese Wall" of the "I" in man, respect for his "*Icheinsamkeit*" ["solitude of the 'I' "] and "*Duverschlossenheit*" ["being closed to the 'Thou' "]' (114). But as long as man remains in this self-isolation he cannot be 'in' the truth, which is something which only exists between the 'I' and the 'Thou', in speech (78). All so-called 'objective' knowledge of the type pursued by mathematics and the sciences (including theology) is based on the abstraction of the 'I' from the pure 'subjectivity' of the 'Thou' relation, in Kierkegaard's sense of the term (130). 'Absolute objectification would be . . . the death of the spirit' (94). Such thinking works with categories of 'substance', which are diametrically opposed to those of true personal existence (140–1). When theology uses these terms, as for instance when it seems an 'objective' demonstrable knowledge of God, it 'robs Him of His personality' and profiteth nothing. 'Existence as a person' and 'existence as substance' are 'two utterly incompatible things' (144–5). It is the characteristic of such objective thinking to make its statements in the third person. But the truth lies in the meeting between the first and the second persons – the 'I am' and the 'Thou art'. To say that the 'I' *is* is already to have destroyed it and emptied it of meaning. The realm of the 'is' and the 'are' is that where law is valid and determinism reigns. Only in the 'Thou' relation is there true personal freedom (96). And this cannot be analysed away by psychology or speculated away by metaphysics; for both of these can only deal with being in the third person, where, ex hypothesi, the real 'I' cannot be (109). ' "Is" always indicates some kind of impersonal being; not only when it is used in relation to something intrinsically impersonal – animals, plants, things – but also in relation to a person, be it a man or God' (167–8). Speaking *about* God, though unavoidable, never brings us to his reality (171). 'God in the third person' is a mere fantasy, a product and a counter of human thought (192).

It would be possible to quote many other passages from Ebner which reveal a similarity to Buber's work that makes it almost incredible that the two should have been working in complete independence. But we must now leave him and pass on to an examination of the latter's *I and Thou*, making but the single observation that the high degree of independence which has all along characterized the sporadic insights into the truth of the 'Thou' does appear to indicate, as indeed does the acceptation which it is now receiving, that it is something which lies very close to the experience of every individual; though – and this our historical survey has also surely abundantly established – it is an element in experience whose recognition is very nearly related to a *religious* awareness of the personal God of the Hebraic-Christian tradition.

Chapter Four

THE 'I–THOU' RELATION

'Primary words do not signify things, but they intimate relations' (*I and Thou*, 3). This is the basis of all that Buber has to say. The fundamental data of all experience are relational events – the 'I' bound up with the world, and the world given only in relation to the 'I'. 'There is no "I" taken in itself' (ibid., 4). Yet within this comprehensive relatedness there are two distinguishable kinds of attitude which man adopts towards his environment. He may relate himself to it personally or impersonally, by addressing it as a 'Thou' or treating it as an 'It'. He cannot help but act towards it in one of these ways. He himself only exists as a being in one of these relations. For the 'I' is not a reality in itself, which enters into certain relationships but which could go on existing, without essential alteration whether it did so or not. That was the 'classical' view, and the cause of its inability to give any significance to the personal relationship. There is no 'I' except an 'I' in relation. 'The existence of the "I" and the speaking of the "I" are one and the same thing' (ibid., 4). So Buber puts it. For since the relationship a man takes up, the attitude he adopts, depends on him, it can be described as the way he addresses himself to the world. He can say 'Thou' or 'It'. But what he says is nothing external to himself; he cannot say it, as a man may utter words, and remain unaltered. For Buber says himself: 'Primary words are spoken from the being' (3): 'When a primary word is spoken the speaker enters the word and takes his stand in it' (4). He *is* what he says: he *is* the relationship he adopts; for out of that relationship the 'I' has no existence. Relationship is constitutive of a man's essence; and the 'I' of the one relationship is different from that of the other. A man cannot say 'Thou' or 'It' without being the 'I' of one or the other relationship. The person who lives his life in an 'It' world will not be the same as he would have been if he had related himself to his environment as 'Thou'.

In exactly the same way as there is no 'I' in isolation, so there is no 'Thou' or 'It' in itself. 'Thou' and 'It' are constituted simply and solely by the fact that the person or thing in question is in this particular relation to an 'I'. It is important to insist on this rather strongly, for it is a source of much misrepresentation of Buber's position. It is commonly supposed that the difference between the two relations lies in the fact that one describes a man's relationship to persons and the other to things. It would be admitted indeed that a man may treat persons as things and act towards a 'Thou' as though it were an 'It'. But the two relations would be regarded as representing the attitudes 'proper' to the two different natures of that which confronts him. That is to say, on this interpretation, the relationships are differentiated by the object by which the 'I' is opposed: the 'Thou' relation represents the attitude required when that which faces the 'I' is possessed of personal characteristics and qualities, the 'It' when these are absent.

But this interpretation really destroys all that Buber is trying to establish. It involves a reversion to the idea that it is possible to define an 'I' or a 'Thou' or an 'It' in terms of itself and its own qualities. Rather a 'Thou' is constituted by the fact that, whatever it is (be it a person or a thing), it is *related in a certain way to an 'I'*, and an 'It' by the fact that it is related in another way. The object of the relationship is entirely irrelevant. It is not that which constitutes the distinction. The difference lies strictly in the *relatio* and not in the *relata*. An 'I–It' relationship may be had with persons as well as things. Not so obvious, but equally true, is that 'I–Thou' relationships are possible with things just as much as with persons. This does not mean to say that 'I–Thou' relations with persons and things may not qualitatively differ from one another. But the kind of *relata* will not affect the genus of the *relatio* (i.e., alter it from an 'I–Thou' to an 'I–It' relationship, or vice versa), even though it will affect the quality of the relation within either genus.

Unless this point is perfectly clear there will be considerable confusion later. According to Buber there are two distinct attitudes we may adopt to the world. We may see it as a 'Thou' or we may see it as an 'It'. In actual fact everyone is continually doing both. These are two ways of knowing, or, what comes to the same thing, two ways of existing. Now within the world to which I am related in these two ways, there is the fundamental distinction of persons and things. If we like, we may use the terms 'Thou' and 'It' to denote this distinction; and this is in fact how they have most frequently been used by those who have adopted Buber's terminology.[13] But this is not, and could not be, Buber's own usage. Not only does it reverse the essential step he has taken in rejecting this 'classical' assumption, but in other respects also (which will become evident as we proceed) it would impoverish the value of his contribution.

The merit of Buber lies not merely in the fact that he sees there is or should be a difference in the way we relate ourselves to persons and things (which is obvious in experience, even if it has been ignored in philosophy), but in the fact that he sees this difference as but one expression of a much more fundamental divide in our whole attitude and relation to the universe. It is not until it is recognized that the 'proper' way of knowing, that is, of existing towards, persons is but a part of a way of relating ourselves to the whole realm of nature, persons and values (a relation, if we may anticipate, which is fundamentally a recognition of 'responsibility', an 'obedience') – it is not until then that a true understanding is possible either of the personality of man or of God. This means that it will be an essential preliminary to examine the 'I–Thou' relationship as Buber analyses it in all its forms and not merely in that case when the 'Thou' is another person. That is not to say that for the purposes of the characterization of this general relationship it will not be necessary to concentrate on that expression of it in which its distinctive quality of mutual 'responsibility' is most explicit, that is, where the primary word can actually be spoken and answered in human conversation.

But before we can proceed further it is necessary to be more precise over the meaning of the word 'relation', or 'relationship', which has hitherto been used in two senses without discrimination. In the first sense of the term all being is relational. There is no reality outside the fundamental knowledge complex 'I–Thou–It'. It is impossible to have a subject without at the same time having something given together with it which is not subject; impossible to conceive an 'It' or a 'Thou' which is not related to an 'I', and vice versa. This is only to state that the primary fact of experience is not, as Descartes said, 'I think', but 'I, a social being, think something'. This sense of the word 'relation' Buber distinguishes from his later usage, in a way which is unfortunately not brought out in the English translation, by employing the term *Verhältnis*. This stands for an entirely passive and colourless connection, and might be used of a geometrical ratio or proportion. The *relata* (e.g., subject and object) are correlative in the sense that you cannot have the one without the other. This is the word employed in the sentence 'primary words do not signify things, but they intimate relations' (*I and Thou*, 3); which is just another way of saying 'the primary words are not isolated words, but combined words' (*Wortpaar*, a pair of correlatives).

But in this relatedness of the 'I' to the world generally there are, as we have seen, two different 'attitudes' to be distinguished. 'I perceive something' (or 'someone', since 'He' and 'She' can replace 'It' without altering the primary word 'I–It'). 'I am sensible of something, I imagine something. I will something. I feel something. I think something . . . This and the like establish the word of "It" ' (4). To this approach to the world Buber gives the name of 'experience' (*Erfahrung*), and the things or persons so related to the subject he names as the 'objects' of experience. But the life of man is not made up of all this and the like alone. For besides knowing a person as an object, it is also possible to be confronted by him as another subject – to enter into an active relationship with him, to face him and be faced by him in personal contact. This active commerce or rapport he distinguishes from mere correlation (*Verhältnis*) as *Beziehung*. This word is used only with reference to the 'I–Thou' relation, never to the 'I–It'. The difference between them is well stated in another connection by Dr Ehrenberg: 'Between subject and object stands only a hyphen, but between "I" and "Thou" sounds the living word' (*Disputation*, I, 184). (This distinction of usage is one of the points where Buber differs from Ebner, who uses *Verhältnis*, *Beziehung*, and even 'Relation', interchangeably.)

This has led us to the point at which it is possible to analyse the nature of the two relationships in greater detail. We shall deal with the 'It' relation first. Actually, as later investigation will show, the world of 'It' is posterior to that of the 'Thou' in the development of consciousness, both for the individual and the race. But there are good reasons for reversing the order for the purposes of exposition.

In the first place, there is the factor of familiarity. Life as we know it is such that most people spend most of their time in the world of 'It'. That is the world in which they feel 'at home'. In comparison with its solid benefits and securities,

> the moments of the 'Thou' appear as strange lyric and dramatic episodes, seductive and magical, but tearing us away to dangerous extremes, loosening the well-tried context, leaving more questions than satisfaction behind them, shattering security – in short, uncanny moments we can well dispense with. (*I and Thou*, 34)

To many, the idea of a 'Thou' relationship to things and values is incomprehensible or fantastic. And even in their relations with other people there are none for whom really 'personal' encounters represent more than a fraction of the thousands of 'functional' contacts which go to make up the daily round. In a depersonalized society a pure 'Thou' relationship, in Buber's imagery, comes to appear like a flash of lightning across the night sky – momentary, strange and sometimes even frightening.

But there is a yet more fundamental reason for the difficulty involved in expounding the contents of this 'I–Thou' relation. For by its very nature it cannot be explained, analysed or reduced to the concepts of thought, without at once ceasing to be itself and becoming part of the world of 'It'. The 'Thou' can only be known for what it is at the moment of meeting, in the crucible of decision, and not in the cool of the laboratory or the philosopher's study. The fundamental distinction between the two worlds is stated by Buber as that between *Gegenwart* and *Gegenstand* (12). Now *Gegenwart* means both 'presence' and 'the present time', and both significations are included. We can only know the world of 'Thou' when we are in the *presence* of a 'Thou', and that is only *at the present moment*. The time of the 'I–Thou' relationship is always the creative 'now'. Then reality is in the melting-pot, in the process of being formed at the point where the 'I' meets with its 'Thou'. The moment of the world of 'It', in contrast, is always the part. The *Gegenstand* is what stands over against the subject in a static, objectified form. It is a 'product' (a past participle passive) rather than a 'producing'. In another context, with characteristic poetic imagery, Buber refers to the 'Thou' as 'the eternal butterfly'. It is here one moment, gone the next, defeating the power of the eye to plot its swift, irregular track. Pin it down for examination on the epistemologist's board, and it at once becomes a thing that has been, an object, an 'It'. The only hope of arriving at even an inadequate description of the world of 'Thou' is by the *via negationis* [way of negation]; by starting from the realm of 'It' and seeing what it is not.

Here, then, is a description by Buber of man's experience of the world of 'It'.

> He perceives what exists round about him – simply things, and beings as things; and what happens round about him – simply events, and actions as events; things consisting of qualities, events of moments; things entered in the graph of place, events in that of time; things and events bounded by other things and events, measured by them, comparable with them: he perceives an ordered and detached world. It is to some extent a reliable world, having density and duration. Its organisation can be surveyed and brought out again and again; gone over with closed eyes, and verified with open eyes. It is always there, next to your skin, if you look on it that way, cowering in your soul, if you prefer it so. It is your object, remains it as long as you wish, and remains a total stranger, within you and without. You perceive it, take it to yourself as the 'truth', and it lets itself be taken; but it does not give itself to you. Only concerning it may you make yourself 'understood' with others; it is ready, though attached to everyone in a different way, to be an object common to you all. But you cannot meet others in it. You cannot hold on to life without it; its reliability sustains you; but should you die in it, your grave would be in nothingness (*I and Thou*, 31–2). The man who experiences (*der Erfahrende*) has no part in the world. For it is 'in him' and not between him and the world that the experience arises. The world has no part in the experience. It permits

itself to be experienced, but has no concern in the matter. For it does nothing to the experience, and the experience does nothing to it. (5)

Perhaps the essential difference between the world of experience and the world of 'Thou' may best be introduced by using an illustration. The reader will recall the dramatic moment in Gilbert's opera *Ruddigore*, when the ancestral masters of the house of Ruddigore, being roused to life, come down from the frames in which they have been so securely fixed on the walls of the manorial hall, and confront their unfortunate descendant. Up to that moment these gentlemen had formed part of the realm of 'It', a *Stück Welt*, a section of the continuum, spatial and temporal, which formed the object of Sir Roger Murgatroyd's awareness. The pictures were set in the context of the room, in the same way as the furniture or any other 'thing'. They could be manipulated, shifted or ignored at will, in which treatment they would play an entirely passive role. But now the situation is entirely different. Professor Farmer has written some words of a similar situation, that of Pygmalion confronted by the statue as it begins to speak, which well describe the 'Copernican revolution' which takes place.

The point is not that one would be exceedingly startled that a dead object should suddenly become alive; rather it is that, whether startled or not, there is in the awareness of having now in the room a personal being in addition to oneself a profound reorientation of the whole mind. There is, as it were, a shift in the foundation, a change of key, with the result that the whole pattern of awareness becomes different. The statue's addressing of itself to *you* in speech is like the sudden moving of the lever of a kaleidoscope; the bits of glass fall into such an entirely new pattern that it is difficult to believe that they have not themselves been transformed into entirely different things. (Farmer, *The World and God*, 14. Cf. Heim, *God Transcendent*, 99)

The new situation brought about by the coming to life of the pictures or the statue may be summed up in the idea of reciprocity (cf. the illustration of Kierkegaard's given above, p. 48). Whereas before, in Buber's words, the experience was *in* the subject, and not between him and the world, which just permitted itself to be experienced but had no concern in the matter; now what stands over against the subject confronts him in its own right, it affects him as well as being affected by him. A mutual relationship is set up.

When 'Thou' is spoken the speaker has no 'thing' for his object. For where there is a thing there is another thing. Every 'It' is bounded by others; 'It' only exists through being bounded by others. But when 'Thou' is spoken, there is no thing. 'Thou' has no bounds. (Buber, *I and Thou*, 4)

This requires a little explication. As has been seen, every 'It' forms part of an ordered world. It is the world that science studies – where everything can be referred to everything else in terms of cause and effect and plotted on the space–time graph. Something exists as an 'It' only in so far as it is marked off by certain limits from something else. Like the pictures on the wall every 'It' has its frame, its certain size, shape, colour, which enables it to remain part of the field of awareness, and yet remain a distinct, isolable part. What happens when a thing ceases to be an 'It' and becomes a 'Thou' is just that it leaves its frame. 'In the face of the directness of the relation everything indirect becomes irrelevant' (12). 'I have been seized by the power of exclusiveness' (7). Everything else has fallen into the background. Measure and comparison have disappeared: at the moment of meeting the 'Thou' alone matters. Confronted by a 'Thou', I can only respond by recognizing its total claim upon my attention, by addressing myself wholly to it. If I try to make it my object, to experience and use it, the kaleidoscope is shifted, the bits of glass fall back into their original position, and the 'Thou' is once more an 'It', a thing among things, a man among men. Buber sums this up as follows.

> The 'Thou' appears, to be sure, in space, but in the exclusive situation of what is over against it, where everything else can only be the background out of which it emerges, not its boundary and measured limit. It appears, too, in time, but in that of the event which is fulfilled in itself: it is not lived as a part of a continuous and organised sequence, but it is lived in a 'duration' whose purely intensive dimension is definable only in terms of itself (i.e., it is apprehended as a meaningful whole like a musical phrase, not just as one of a succession of moments occupying a certain amount of 'clock time'). It appears, lastly, simultaneously acting and being acted upon – not, however, linked to a chain of causes, but, in its relation of mutual action with the 'I', as the beginning and end of the event. This is part of the basic truth of the human world, that only 'It' can be arranged in order. Only when things, from being our 'Thou', become our 'It', can they be co-ordinated. The 'Thou' knows no system of co-ordination. (30–1)

The impression may have been left by the illustration used that the transition from the world of 'It' to that of 'Thou' is effected by *things* 'coming alive', that is, becoming *persons*. But it was made clear earlier that the difference does not consist in this. The 'Thou' relationship, though most explicit in the meeting between two persons, is not confined to this. Buber holds that the relation may arise in any of the three spheres in which a man lives his life – in his contact with nature, with man and with the world of values ('*mit den geistigen Wesenheiten*') (6).

Concerning the second – relationships with human beings – enough has perhaps been said for the present. But before passing on we may just look at a passage from Eberhard Grisebach, which, while it deals with characteristics of the awareness of 'Thou' in general, is written in the terms of the encounter of personalities. It will serve to make clear the connection between the two meanings of the word *Gegenwart* – 'presence' and 'the present' – which is not just an etymological conceit but an insight of the greatest importance both for philosophy and theology. Grisebach is describing the 'now' of moral decision and its relation to the temporal and spatial continuity of the world of 'It', which is apprehended as something fixed and past.

> The span of time which demands our investigation lies at the point where that succession which is apprehended as a continuous process is interrupted; where the man whose knowledge is concerned with what is past is forced to come to a halt, through being met by something future (*Zukunft*), which he is unable to include within the present. This that meets him (*Zu-kunft*) is no longer an abstraction, but that something which comes to him from without – the other person, the knowledge of whose presence is inescapable. Thus the narrow bounds of the present (*Gegenwart*) are constituted by two persons mutually in each other's presence (*Gegen-wartende*). A problem therefore confronts us. For all temporal measurements are inadequate to describe this glancing moment (*Augenblick*). Within the narrow bounds of the present this is a real momentary glance (*Augen-blick*) between persons who meet each other and themselves constitute the boundaries of this span of time.
>
> The same is consequently also true of spatial limits. The ethical sphere of becoming is enclosed within two boundaries. On this spot the man whose knowledge is related to the past finds himself brought to a check, with all his designs and intentions. This point can no longer be conceived as anywhere and everywhere, but is given to us, quite definitely, at that spot where, here and now, we just have to interrupt our course, since we encounter one who comes to meet us from without. In each particular case the spatial delimitation signifies the urgency of the situation, which we can neither escape nor evade. It is here, at this spot, that the personal relation between one human being and another must be worked out. Our concern is therefore not with the judgment of a spatial situation but with the explication of an ethical situation, within which the knower is narrowly confined. It is because at this spot it is a claim that limits us, and a claim which we cannot avoid, that all spatial measurements are no longer relevant. Moreover, no spatial law has any further significance where the proximity of another human being to us is just given in an entirely contingent manner. This contingent spot cannot be shifted at will. It is a particular spot, with a uniqueness, an unrepeatability, that

> upsets all calculation and precludes every attempt to alter it. The space which the present occupies is not therefore the unlimited space of nature, but the narrow bounds within which two human beings limit each other in claim and counter-claim. That interval is, to be sure, so constricted, that the free spirit may well shrink back for fear of being stifled. However, it remains the task of a critical ethic to investigate precisely this narrow space of the present and to point out its reality. Here all spatial measurements are useless. He who possesses an unlimited power of measurement finds himself here, to his surprise, severely limited. (Grisebach, *Gegenwart*, 148–9)

It is this limitation, not by other things in space and time, but by an exclusive and inescapable claim which is the authentic mark of the 'Thou'. This demand reaches us at its highest in the meeting of person with person. But there is the same note in all forms of this relationship. Even in our relations with the natural order this reciprocity is in evidence. 'My "Thou" affects me', says Buber, 'as I affect it'. A man may be changed by living with a dog or by the contemplation of a landscape. In the 'I–It' relationship there is not this mutuality; the 'It' is just an object of experience or manipulation – all the activity is on one side. But to meet a 'Thou' a man must be prepared to listen to its claims, to be obedient to what it has to teach him. What is required, in Grisebach's phrase, is an open ear, not an open mouth (*Gegenwart*, 577). But is this meaningful in reference to our attitude to the subhuman order? Let Buber answer, in his own poetic way.

> I CONSIDER A TREE.
>
> I can look on it as a picture: stiff column in a shock of light, or splash of green shot with the delicate blue and silver of the background.
>
> I can perceive it as movement: flowing veins on clinging, pressing pith, suck of the roots, breathing of the leaves, ceaseless commerce with earth and air – and the obscure growth itself.
>
> I can classify it in a species and study it as a type in its structure and mode of life.
>
> I can subdue its actual presence and form so sternly that I recognise it only as an expression of law – of the laws in accordance with which a constant opposition of forces is continually adjusted, or of those in accordance with which the component substances mingle and separate.
>
> I can dissipate it and perpetuate it in number, in pure numerical relation.
>
> In all this the tree remains my object, occupies space and time, and has its nature and constitution.
>
> It can, however, also come about, if I have both will and grace, that in considering the tree I become bound up in relation to it. The tree is now no longer 'It'. I have been seized by the power of exclusiveness.
>
> To effect this it is not necessary for me to give up any of the ways in which

> I consider the tree. There is nothing from which I would have to turn my eyes away in order to see, and no knowledge that I would have to forget. Rather is everything, picture and movement, species and type, law and number, indivisibly united in this event.
>
> Everything belonging to the tree is in this: its form and structure, its colours and chemical composition, its intercourse with the elements and with the stars, are all present in a single whole.
>
> The tree is no impression, no play of my imagination, no value depending on my mood; but it is bodied over against me and has to do with me, as I with it – only in a different way.
>
> Let no attempt be made to sap the strength from the meaning of the relation: relation is reciprocity [*Gegenseitigkeit* – more is implied than merely 'relation is mutual', which the ET has]. (*I and Thou*, 7–8)

This is not to say that what is given and taken will be the same on both sides. Even between two persons this will vary according to the personality of each. In the case of the tree there is no suggestion that it has consciousness or a soul: it will not affect me *in the same way* as I affect it. Nor is it necessarily implied that the action and reaction is equal and opposite in any strict mechanical proportion. The wind bloweth where it listeth: so is every relation that is born of the spirit.

We may now look briefly at the third sphere in which the 'I–Thou' relationship may be realized – the supersensible or 'intelligible' world, the realm of value and validity. The difference here between the 'I–Thou' and the 'I–It' relation may perhaps be illustrated by the difference between the word 'idea' in the Platonic and modern meanings of the term. In the latter sense it is a concept, whose abstraction from the concrete world of the particular is governed by interest. A man of culture makes such abstractions as will assist in the understanding and ordering of the external world. General concepts are indispensable for any thought, or communication of thoughts, of any complexity whatever. The history of science is the history of the formulation, and ever-more adequate elaboration, of general concepts and hypotheses which will facilitate the classification of phenomena in such a way that, by the method of analysis and redistribution of substances, new phenomena may be discovered and explained. An idea in the modern sense of the word is twice removed from reality. It is an abstraction from the world of 'It', which in its turn is but a precipitate of the world of 'Thou'.

Or we can change the metaphor. We may imagine the real world of relation (*Beziehung*) as a compass, in which the needle of the 'I' is in a perpetual state of gentle oscillation as it swings freely in response to the 'Thou' which attracts it from without. We press down the lever, and the needle is arrested and held in a state of fixation. This gives us the world of 'It'. It is necessary to press the lever before we can *use* the compass; only then can accurate deductions be made concerning our position or direction. Before the machinery of thought and ideas which gives the compass its practical value can be brought into play the data on which it is to work must have already been 'fixed'.

When we turn to the Platonic 'Ideas' we find something quite different. They are not abstractions twice removed from reality. They are reality itself, of which the empirical world of 'appearances' in varying degree 'partakes'. In contact with this eternal, unseen world lies man's only true knowledge and his only true good. The organ of knowledge, of salvation, is the pure and disinterested love of the true, the good and the beautiful – that is φιλοσοφία (philosophy). In philosophizing alone is the norm of man's nature attained. This is at once the source and goal of 'all real living' (Buber, *I and Thou*, 11). Now Buber would not agree that the intelligible world of 'Ideas' or values was the only, or even the chief, point of contact of the 'I' with its 'Thou'. But he would acknowledge in Plato's thought a very important insight into the nature of real life. For it is essential to the Platonic view that the intelligible world is not an arena in which man may exercise the products of his own conceptual thinking, but a world existing in its own right over against him, with a relevance for his life and claim on the obedience of his whole personality. It is a world with which the human spirit is called to enter into a relation of communion: it is to be reverenced and respected, and not to be regarded either as the product of man's mental processes or as material for his manipulation.

This action, like all actions in which the 'I' takes its stand in relation to a 'Thou', is also a suffering. 'Action is suffering and suffering action' – that is the leitmotif of T. S. Eliot's *Murder in the Cathedral*. So Buber: 'Relation means being chosen and choosing, suffering and action in one' (*I and Thou*, 11). If 'all real life is meeting', then half the secret of living is obedience, keeping an 'open ear' (both in Latin and Greek the word for 'to obey' is derived from that meaning 'to listen'). That means willing recognition of, and co-operation with, the true being of that which confronts one.

This quality of the 'Thou' relation is to be found in all the forms of its manifestation, not least in the sphere of art, which is also the most obviously creative of human activities. There is a double obedience required of the artist. There is the sacrifice which is necessitated by the 'exclusiveness' that characterizes what meets him as a 'Thou'. In this case it is the uncompromising demand of form for mastery, to the rigorous exclusion of all the possibilities with which the mind may entertain itself prior to the act of creation.

Secondly, there is the spending of the whole being, the complete self-giving which is demanded of the true artist.

> The primary word can only be spoken with the whole being. He who gives himself to it may withhold nothing of himself. The work does not suffer me . . . to turn aside and relax in the world of 'It'; but it commands. If I do not serve it aright it is broken, or it breaks me. (Buber, *I and Thou*, 10)

The result of this act of creative obedience is the bodying forth of the form. But it is just at this point that the tragedy of life, which is well exemplified in artistic creation, is revealed. For 'the work produced is a thing among things, able to be experienced and described as a sum of qualities' (10). In other words, the very fulfilment of the meeting of the 'I' with its 'Thou' results in what is potentially just one more 'It'. Such relation may be 'the cradle of real life' (9), but what profit is it if the child is still-born? The relationship of the 'Thou' to the world of 'It', and the possibility of the latter's salvation from meaninglessness, is the theme of the second section of Buber's book. Here we are merely concerned to establish the inevitability of this decline of the 'Thou', which is of great importance for the discussion of the personality of God and of the possibility of a ' "Thou" that by its nature cannot become "It" ' (75). Buber thus describes this falling away:

> This is the exalted melancholy of our fate, that every 'Thou' in our world must become an 'It'. It does not matter how exclusively present the 'Thou' was in direct relation. As soon as the relation has been worked out or has become permeated with a means, the 'Thou' becomes an object among objects – perhaps the chief, but still one of them, fixed in its size and limits. In the work of art realisation in one sense means loss of reality in another. Genuine contemplation is over in a short time; now the life in nature, that first unlocked itself to me in the mystery of mutual action, can again be described, taken to pieces, and classified – the meeting point of manifold systems of laws. And love itself cannot persist in direct relation, it endures, but in interchange of actual and potential being. The human being who was even now single and unconditioned, not something lying to hand, only present, not able to be experienced, only able to be fulfilled, has now become again a 'He' or a 'She', a sum of qualities, a given quantity of a certain shape. Now I may take out from him again the colour of his hair or of his speech or of his goodness. But so long as I can do this he is no more my 'Thou' and cannot yet be my 'Thou' again. (16–17)

The question arises, can an 'It' ever become a 'Thou' again? Can the portrait, the static product of the moment of relation, ever come down from its frame and rise up before an 'I' in present meeting? To this Buber returns the answer 'yes', and he devotes a good deal of space to a discussion of the means, both false and true, whereby depersonalized modern society may be revivified and brought back to that living personal relationship of man with man wherein alone contact with reality is maintained. But it is not to our point here to pursue this further. Moreover, the question of the redemption of the world of 'It' can only properly be understood in the light of its origin and its genetic relation to that state of being to which it is to be restored.

Now the genesis of the two primary words is also of considerable importance for the right understanding of personality. We encountered above the vitiating influence which false epistemological presuppositions could exercise on the notions of personality and personal relationships. So it is significant to note the alternative hypothesis which Buber puts forward to the theoretical solipsism which involved the 'classical' view in such shortcomings.

'In the beginning is relation' (27). This, as always, is the starting point. But at first this relation is not the full conscious 'I–Thou' relationship which it later becomes. The antenatal life of the child is for Buber symbolic of the undivided union which characterizes man's primal relation with mother earth. This natural connection with the cosmos, which is manifested for all men during the hours of sleep, is gradually transformed into a spiritual connection – that is, *relation* (*Beziehung*). This transformation the child must achieve for itself, reaching out with timid glances and movements to meet what is over against it. 'Little, disjointed, meaningless sounds go out persistently into the void. But one day, unforeseen, they will have become conversation – does it matter that it is perhaps with the simmering kettle? It is conversation' (27). What Buber calls 'the *a priori* of relation, the inborn "Thou" ' (27) is gradually explicated, passing through a state in which the 'Thou' is addressed as such, yet still in a form of address which precedes words. Though the child cannot name it, his teddy bear or the patch of red on the carpet may possess that 'power of exclusiveness' for him such as to evoke a wondering stare undistractedly focused upon it.

The 'I' of self-consciousness from which Descartes started is not yet developed. It only emerges as a single element at an advanced stage of the evolution of the primal relational situation. As Tennyson says of the advancing child, 'his isolation grows defined'.[14] 'I' and 'Thou' develop as two poles of one relationship. '*Ich werde am Du*' (*Ich und Du*, 18; ET, 11) – 'I come into being as over against the Thou', as Professor J. Baillie translates (*Our Knowledge of God*, 1939, 208). The self-conscious 'I' is formed by a process of abstraction from this single 'I–Thou' complex. As the various 'Thous' lose their exclusiveness, retire and remain isolated in the memory, the consciousness of the permanent partner in the relationship becomes stronger. Though still held in the nexus of relation and given only in and through it, there comes a time when the 'I' bursts its bounds and confronts itself for a moment, separated as though it were a 'Thou'. It is only at this advanced stage of abstraction that the Cartesian situation arises. It is not from this that we reach the knowledge of other selves – a sort of '*cogito ergo es*' [I think therefore you are]. It is exactly the reverse. In Gogarten's phrase, '*Ich bin durch dich*' – 'Through thee I am' (*Glaube und Wirklichkeit*, 57).

At this stage two movements are possible. On the one hand, one may enter into the full 'I–Thou' relationship with a consciousness of doing so which was hitherto impossible. But, alternatively, the 'I' is able now for the first time, lifted out of the web of the primary relation in which it was given, to set itself up as an experiencing and using subject. The objects of its experience and manipulation are the fleeting 'Thous' of relation, at the time just forgotten, but now ready to be recalled to form part of a new relational event. The 'I–It' relationship systematizes the chance deposits of the other primary word, plotting their position on the graph of determined being by means of the co-ordinates of space and time.

It is important to avoid misunderstanding in stating that the 'I–It' relationship is subsequent upon that with the 'Thou'. It might be said that here is a vicious circle. I can only know another 'Thou' through my senses, through material signs or bodily movements, despite the fact that these alone will not give consciousness of another self. Yet it is only through knowing the other person as a 'Thou' that I can subsequently know the material world of things. But this circle is only apparent. It arises from a lapse into the identification of the 'Thou' with persons and the 'It' with things. There is no suggestion in Buber (though possibly Grisebach and Berdyaev and certainly Heim are not so free from criticism) that the meeting of persons with persons constitutes the creative present and that the 'deposit' of this continuous process is the world of things. The 'It' is not an 'object' in the sense of being a 'thing', but in the sense of being 'objectified' in relation to an 'I'. Persons also, and our relations to them, can become – and according to Buber (cf. *I and Thou*, 37–8) increasingly have become – objectified and depersonalized. The 'It' is something I have made an 'It' by my relation to it (it only exists, like the 'Thou' in that relation), and so, in theory at least, can be unmade or redeemed to 'Thou-hood'. 'Thou-ness' and 'It-ness' are not qualities belonging to different sets of precepts, one of which I know before the other. They characterize the relation I have with the world around me as it is presented in its totality. When I am confronted by another person, my 'Thou' is his complete personality, body and soul. The whole is presented as a 'Thou' and the whole can subsequently become an 'It'. What I perceive is not a self and then its body, or, as on the analogical theory, a body and then the self which animates it. I know a person, in Farmer's words,

> as self active in and through its unity with a body, as body acting in and through its unity with a self, neither being prior to the other, but both being given together. When a man who is angry with me glares at me with clenched fist, his personal attitude, as a conscious being, to myself is not inferred from the physical manifestations, but is apprehended as being dynamically contained in, and continuous with, them; he presents himself as a single personal totality containing, as it were, the two mutually involved and quite inseparable dimension of mind and body. (*The World and God*, 17; cf. Berdyaev, *Solitude and Society*, 109, 166)

The stress on the indivisibility of body and soul is important in view of the tendency which was noted above for the 'classical' theory of personality to divorce them. It is, moreover, a merit of the theory of personality we shall be expounding that it can go further than this and demonstrate to some degree the necessity of the purely physical for peculiarly personal existence. Starting from the 'I–Thou' relation, it can show that its very possibility implies the existence of some form of bodily media. But it is not possible to draw conclusions for a new theory of personality in this or any other respect purely on the basis of an analysis of the 'Thou' relations so far undertaken. For Buber and the others are insistent that neither man's nature nor indeed the full truth even of these finite relationships can be understood without taking into account the most fundamental relation of all – that between man and the eternal personal 'Thou' of God.

Chapter Five

THE DIVINE 'THOU'

The fundamental error of the idealistic rationalistic view of personality is its abstractness. Because man is taken out of the relational situation in which he finds himself over against his world the account of his nature is distorted. The new anthropology insists that personality can only be discussed in terms of personal relationships. Man is confronted with an 'other', which is presented both as something 'given' – a real limit to his own Ego, through and over against which alone self-consciousness is developed – and also as a 'claim', something demanding realization. Consequently the 'Thou' to which I must relate myself, in the terms of German theology, confronts me both as a *Gabe* and as an *Aufgabe*, a gift and a task. The 'I' stands in a relation of 'responsibility' to the 'Thou', and the 'response' it must make is the acceptance of this double 'word', the fact and the demand. (The etymological connection is brought out in the German: *Wort*, *Antwort*, *Verantwortung*). This response is thus both suffering and action. It is suffering because it involves humility, to listen, to learn, to wait upon the nature of the other; it means not treating this other as an 'It' to be experienced and used in a one-sided relationship. It is action, because the 'word' of the other is a demand upon me to do something, a claim which I can only ignore by escaping into the world of 'It'.

The 'other' may meet me as a 'Thou' in any form – there need not necessarily be present another human will. The 'I' is brought to development by, and confronted with the claim of, the 'Thou' of its material and 'intelligible' environment in the same way as by the 'Thou' of other selves. Knowledge of the self, of other selves, of the material order, and of the world of values is given simultaneously. No one element can be understood except in the light of this total context. That is why it has been necessary to view the 'I–Thou' relationship in all its manifestations in order to grasp its significance for personality. Real knowledge is afforded and its true being achieved only when the 'I' stands in its 'proper' relationship to this complex as a whole. This relation – the meeting of the 'other' in all its forms as a

'Thou' – may be described as one of 'responsibility', a recognition that one's own true freedom and existence as a person lies in willing acknowledgment of, and co-operation with, the true nature of what stands over against oneself. The quality of this relationship, from the side of the subject, is obedience, yet an obedience which is also the highest form of creativity – a paradox seen as clearly in the case of the artist as it is experienced in our dealings with our friends. (The substance of this paragraph will receive expansion below, Ch. 6.)

But this is not the whole picture. For the complex of relationships in which I am placed is not exhaustively analysed in terms of the above three forms in which the 'Thou' confronts me – the world of nature, of persons and of values. A characteristic which is shared by all these forms of its presentation is that the 'Thou' is not finally inescapable. As Buber puts it, it is always possible to 'relax in the world of "It" ' (*I and Thou*, 10). The sense of dependence which I feel in regard to these various 'Thous' for the existence of my own personality is not absolute. If I wish, I can repudiate my responsibility towards them and treat them, not as persons or things in obedient relation to whom I can alone find my true existence, but as objects at my disposal for enjoyment or exploitation. Again, with regard to the 'claim' which is presented along with the 'givenness' of the fact – I can, if I will, ignore it. To recognize a person's 'Thou-hood' is to respect him as an end in himself. But this demand for reverence is not such as makes it impossible for me when convenient to use him as a mere means. Indeed it is 'the exalted melancholy of our fate' that every 'Thou' must become an 'It'. The moment of 'meeting' cannot be held.

But, over and above all these finite 'Thous', there is also the experience of meeting with and being confronted by a 'Thou' from whom no escape is possible.

> Whither shall I go from Thy spirit? or whither shall I flee from thy presence? If I ascend up into heaven, thou art there: if I make my bed in hell, behold, thou art there. If I take the wings of the morning, and dwell in the uttermost parts of the sea; even there shall thy hand lead me, and thy right hand shall hold me. If I say, Surely the darkness shall cover me; even the night shall be light about me. Yea, the darkness hideth not from thee; but the night shineth as the day: the darkness and the light are both alike to thee. (Psalm 139:7–12)

Here is a 'Thou' from whom it is not possible to relax in the world of 'It'. We cannot get outside our relation to it, and in it alone do we live and move and have our being. The fact, the *Gabe*, is inescapable: dependence on the 'other' is here absolute. This is the doctrine of creation. 'Thine eyes did see my substance, yet being imperfect; and in thy book all my members were written, which in continuance were fashioned, when as yet there was none of them' (Psalm 139:16). Here alone is it possible to say without qualification: 'Through Thee I am.'

Equally inescapable is the 'claim' of this 'Thou' – the *Aufgabe*. 'O Lord, thou hast searched me, and known me . . . Thou hast beset me behind and before and laid thine hand upon me' (Psalm 139:1, 5). The penetrating demands of omniscient holiness, which require complete purity in the inward parts, cannot be lifted at will. There is no avoiding the claim for absolute obedience, for final surrender – even, if necessary, of life itself. There is a note of unconditionality, an experience of being confronted from without by a will before which all must yield – even though it be at the same time conceived as a will in which alone is our peace.

This dual awareness of every 'Thou', culminating in the knowledge of God both as 'final succour' (since what is 'given' is not confined to one act of creation, but embraces the whole working of the divine 'Thou', through whom human personality is preserved, developed and consummated) and as 'absolute demand', has been worked out by Professor Farmer in his book *The World and God* (19–26). He sees a double movement in all personal relationships, and especially in that relation between will and will which we know as trust. There is, first, the awareness of a certain polarity or tension. The frontier of my neighbour's personality is to be respected, and only to be crossed on his invitation.

> The other's will stands as a limit to ours. Physical objects also limit our purposes, but the limitation is of an entirely different kind, as our response to it clearly shows. The resistance of physical objects can only be overcome, if it is overcome at all, by direct and manipulative control. The resistance of a will can never be overcome save by what we call agreement or reconciliation. For in the degree that it is otherwise overcome it ceases to be a personal will any longer, and so, *qua* will, cannot be said to be overcome at all. (*The World and God*, 21–2)

Mere manipulation of another is an 'abuse of personality' and one who submits to it is regarded as having no personality, being just a 'rubber stamp'. To force someone's will by appealing to his instincts or fears is to show that we do not and cannot trust him. It is just in what Farmer calls 'purpose – or value-resistance' that personality is most a reality.

But if we are to give ourselves to what is thus entirely inaccessible to our control a second element is required. 'We are ready to commit ourselves to it in so far as we are able to believe that both his will and ours, though not subject to one another, are subject to the same standards of *unconditional* worth or value' (ibid., 20). We can trust another if we know he shares our standards and will abide by them, come what may. Indeed it is only this community of ultimate loyalties (this 'value–co-operation') that makes possible the kind of tension referred to above.

> The other man's peculiar power to resist and frustrate me – so very different from the inert resistance of things or the blind resistance of animals – lies in his power to understand what I am doing and to adjust himself accordingly; but that implies also his power to co-operate and help. (22)

In the light of this double quality of human person relationships, Farmer sets our experience of God as, at the same time, 'a consuming fire' and 'our refuge and strength'. These two experiences are inseparable from one another.

> The divine will resists and sets a limit to our personal desires and preferences of a peculiarly absolute kind; none the less it can be trustfully obeyed for it is in the same world of values with ourselves, or rather it is the ultimate foundation of it. In its very resistance, therefore, it is in a unique and ultimate way, co-operative. (25)

The close connection between the awareness that man cannot be defined in terms of himself but only in relation to God, with whom his life – from its inception to its consummation – is hid, and the awareness of his responsibility in face of God's absolute claims, is well brought out in consecutive verses from the book of Jeremiah. 'O Lord I know that the way of man is not in himself: it is not in man that walketh to direct his steps. O Lord correct me, but with judgment; not in thine anger, lest thou bring me to nothing' (10:23–4). Man's essential being lies in his responsibility to God. He has to make answer both for what he is and for what he ought to be – to say 'yes' both to the divine *Gabe* and to the divine *Aufgabe*. This division is not indeed an ultimate one – it is due to man, to man's sin. But the fact remains that this polarity is visible in every 'I–Thou' relationship in which the 'I' is a sinful human being divided against himself (a '*Mensch im Widerspruch*', to use the title of Brunner's book). Yet even for us *in via* the unity is more important than the duality. For 'I come into being through the "Thou"' only by being faced with the claims of the 'Thou'.

Professor Farmer, as we have seen, builds the awareness of God as a 'Thou' on the experience of an analogous relationship between human persons. But he makes no attempt to find adumbrations of this awareness in other forms of knowledge, besides that of other selves. This is because he limits the 'I–Thou' relation exclusively to the meeting of person with person. Our knowledge of things is therefore knowledge of the world of 'It', and can thus supply no analogy for our awareness of One who is eternally 'Thou'. Buber denies the 'Thou' relationship not in terms of the kind of object encountered but in terms of the quality of the relationship established, and consequently he is able to broaden the epistemological foundation of his theism. For him every contact of an 'I' with a finite 'Thou' points beyond itself to [an] encounter with an infinite 'Thou', and in whatever sphere it occurs there is a similarity of structure.

> The external lines of relation meet in the eternal 'Thou'. Every particular 'Thou' is a glimpse through to the eternal 'Thou'; by means of every particular 'Thou' the primary word addresses the eternal 'Thou'. Through this mediation of the 'Thou' of all beings fulfilment and non-fulfilment of relations come to them: the inborn 'Thou' is realised in each relation and consummated in none. It is consummated only in the direct relation with the 'Thou' that by its nature cannot become an 'It'. (*I and Thou*, 75)

By a 'direct' relation with the eternal 'Thou' Buber does not mean that a relationship to God can be established which takes no account of the media of finite 'Thous'. He is insistent that it is only in and through our meeting with other persons and things that the unconditioned 'Thou' of the divine is encountered. He will have nothing to do with the *via remotionis* of the mystic.

> God is not an object among objects, and cannot therefore be reached through a renunciation of objects. God indeed is not just everything, but he is equally certainly not Being minus everything. He is not to be found through withdrawal and not to be loved through abstraction. (M. Buber, *Die Frage an den Einzelnen*, 1936, 44)

This is not to deny a place for renunciation. Any particular 'Thou' may become a *σκάνδαλον* (offence, stumbling block), barring rather than mediating the divine approach. But this is only a possibility precisely because every particular 'Thou' is potentially a *Durchblick* to the eternal. It is in them, and not by turning our eyes away from them, that the divine presence may be found if it is to be found at all.

Through every real meeting with our environment something of that finality and unconditionality may be mediated, something of the 'ultimacy and intimacy' (to use a phrase of Webb's) of the Eternal Person shines through. 'Form's silent asking, man's living speech, the mute proclamation of the creature, are all gates leading into the presence of the

Word' (Buber, *I and Thou*, 102). But while we must insist on this broad basis for the knowledge of the divine 'Thou', we must not lose sight of the fact that the central gateway will always be the meeting of man with man, in which the full mutuality of relation is consummated, in the give and take of speech. This is the truest image and medium of the God-relationship. Here is the central point through which passes what from different sides we call religious experience and revelation. It is primarily, then, in that full reciprocity of personal relationship which we know as love that we must expect the nature of God chiefly to be discovered and revealed.

But before it is possible to go on to say anything about the divine nature, it must be reiterated that to this philosophy it is fundamental that nothing can be known of God except what is revealed in and through meeting with him. God outside a relational context is not God but something else. And this does not mean merely that God cannot be discussed except in connection (*Verhältnis*) with the world. This is obviously true, and Dr Tennant's insistence on it is salutary. But something very much more is asserted. It means that God can only exist in real relation (*Beziehung*) – that is, he can only be a 'Thou'. This implies, negatively, two things.

It involves a denial that it is possible to talk of God as the 'Eternal I', as in the writings of the Absolute Idealists. Such a '*Gott an sich*' is a pure abstraction. Kierkegaard's scathing criticisms of Hegel were being paralleled, as we have seen, by those of his lesser-known contemporary Geijer who, on the basis of his principle 'No Thou – no I', maintained that the '*Alles und Eines*' [all and one] of Hegel and Schelling was in reality simply '*Alles und Nichts*' [all and nothing]. He condemned what Ebner later described as *Icheinsamkeit* [the solitude of the I] as rigorously in the case of God as of man. For Feuerbach, too, the 'L'être c'est moi' of the Hegelian Absolute was completely destructive of what he regarded as the truth about personal existence (*Philosophie der Zukunft*, 61). The nature of this peculiarly personal form of existence in God will be the subject of a later chapter (Ch. 9). Here we may simply state that, as Cullberg has said of Gogarten, the new philosophy 'arrived at the recognition that the question of God for ontology has to be worked out, not in terms of the Divine "I", but of the Divine "Thou" ' (*Das Du und die Wirklichkeit*, 89).

The second implicate of the statement that God can never be anything but a 'Thou' is that he cannot be known or experienced as an 'It'. His personality can never be conceived, as the traditional view conceives it, in terms of a substance in possession of personal attributes. For by its nature the eternal 'Thou'

> cannot be understood as a sum of qualities raised to a transcendental level; . . . for it cannot be experienced, or thought; for we miss Him, Him who is, if we say 'I believe that He is' – 'He' is also a metaphor, but 'Thou' is not. (Buber, *I and Thou*, 112)

It is impossible to say that he exists or does not exist in the sense that we say it of objects of experience – 'existence in the third person', as Ebner called it, cannot be his. That would make him a part of his world or an inference from it. We cannot reach God by arguing from the world – that only gives us one more 'It'. This does not mean to say that there is no place for what is called natural theology. But it does mean that if this 'natural' theology is set up in antithesis to 'revelation', as it usually is, then it cannot give knowledge of God. A God who is the last stage of an argument will never be more than a hypothesis, of service, possibly, in explaining and co-ordinating experience, whether for theory or practice, but never qualitatively different from the world of 'It' which he is used to interpret.[15]

The truth of natural theology lies in this assertion that God's presence may be mediated in and through every part of creation; that is to say, he may be 'met' in everything. All 'I–Thou' relations, of whatever kind, lead to him. 'Earth's crammed with heaven, And every common bush afire with God' (E. B. Browning). In the words of Goethe, which Buber takes as the text of his work, it is possible to discover 'in allen Elementen Gottes Gegenwart' ['God's presence in all elements']. But it is important to see that the sense in which Buber adopts these words is very different from that in which they were originally written. Largely on the strength of this quotation Cullberg accuses Buber of himself falling into those pantheistic notions which he vigorously attacks on the ground that they destroy the whole basis of a genuine 'I–Thou' reciprocity. But this is to miss Buber's meaning. For him, God's 'presence' in every element does not mean that God is objectively everywhere, but that he can become present to an 'I' in personal encounter through the medium of any part of creation. Anything may become the 'Locus' of revelation. That does not imply that everything is in some sense impregnated with divinity in its own right. It means that anything at any time may spring into relation as a 'Thou'; and through this, as through every 'Thou', the divine 'Thou' shines for those who have the eyes to see.

This 'pansacramentalism', as he himself elsewhere calls it, is derived by Buber from his Chassidic background. In order to make clear its difference from pantheism, we may perhaps analyse more closely the structure of this God-relation, which in all its forms is essentially a personal relation, the meeting of personal will with personal will, in '*Gabe und Aufgabe*'. Like all such contacts, it must allow for the possibility of 'value-resistance' if 'value–co-operation' is to be achieved. This is only another way of saying that the relation must be what Kierkegaard called 'indirect', if it is not to override personality.

In this connection Professor Farmer has stressed the importance of symbols for the communication of person with person. In man the isolation of the individual and the definition of the frontier which divides one psychical existence from another has reached a high degree of development. In many lower creatures 'there are no frontiers to their mental life, no, so to say, immigration barriers on the frontier turning back undesirables'. 'Their psychical being flows in and out of one another like a stream of water flowing in and around porous pots' (*The World and God*, 71). This isolation of mind from mind on the human level is overcome by a method of communication which does not override the individual's integrity. Here lies the supreme significance for personality of symbolism, and especially the highly complex form of it manifested in speech and language. It is no accident that the personal 'I–Thou' relationship should have been worked out in the terminology of the speech-situation. The type of every such relation was seen by its first expounders to be conversation (*Gespräch*), and it was at once formulated in terms of *Wort* and *Antwort* [word and answer], *Rede* and *Gegenrede* [discourse and counter-discourse], *Spruch* and *Widerspruch* [saying and contradiction]. Speech is of prime significance for personality *not* merely because it is an accomplishment of a peculiarly high degree of rationality, but because only through the symbolism of which it is the most perfect form could personal life have become possible. It alone secures the other person against that direct exercise of manipulative power which constitutes an abuse of personality by denying the need for the element of 'value-resistance'.

> In the highest personal relationship the other does what I desire, not because my will has been imposed on his, but because we are in the same world of values, because my insights have become his insights, my meanings his meanings . . . When I speak to a friend, I cannot thrust my meaning directly into his mind, however much I may be disposed to think that it would be to his advantage if I could. I can only come so far as the frontier and signal my meaning, and the latter can only become his after he has interpreted the signals and taken up their significance into his own personal awareness. He may, however, reject their meaning, but the fact that it was first symbolised is precisely what gives him the opportunity to accept or reject it, to hold it, so to say, at arm's length and consider it. (Farmer, *The World and God*, 70–2)

It is just where this opportunity is not given, as when an attempt is made to influence the mind of another by suggestion or propaganda, that human relations become depersonalized.

This principle is also valid in interpreting the relation between God and man. Where the necessity for this indirect method of converse is denied, personality disappears. There must be an independent world standing over against both God and man to provide the medium or symbol through which alone there is rendered possible a communication compatible with respect for personal integrity. This does not imply that the created order has no significance for itself, apart from being a means for the preservation and perfecting of personality. But this is a function it performs which must not be belittled. Pantheistic denials of an independent world invariably depersonalize God and his relations with men. This point may be put in different language. If we did not always meet God – the eternal 'Thou' – under the form of 'Thous' which may also become 'Its', our freedom and personality would be destroyed. If we had no chance to reject the 'gift' and the 'demand' of the divine 'Thou' by treating the vehicle of potential revelation, whether it be a human being or a thing, as a mere 'It'; if we could not blind ourselves to its 'transparent' or revelatory quality by regarding it simply as an object for our use or enjoyment – then our response would be forced and valueless. As it is essential for human personal relationships that the 'word' of communication can also be regarded as a mere 'It' among 'Its', so it is only because 'a man that looks on glass, on it may stay his eye' that he can 'if he pleaseth, through it pass, and then the heaven espy' (G. Herbert, 'The Elixir').[16]

Recognition of this necessity for God to work through symbols is absolutely essential to the understanding of his personality. If there is to be a gracious personal relationship between God and man, in which the individuality and freedom of the latter is not overwhelmed, then God must withdraw himself from direct gaze. He must verily be a God that hideth himself. As Farmer has put it, 'Jesus said: "It is expedient for you that I go away"; God said from the beginning: "It is expedient for you that I keep away" ' (Farmer, *The World and God*, 73).

This is not to deny God's immanence or omnipresence. But it is possible to see him '*in allen Elementen*' only because it is possible to see him in none. Kierkegaard expresses this in his own delightful way.

> If God . . . had taken on the figure of a very rare and tremendously large green bird, with a red beak, sitting in a tree on the mound, and perhaps even whistling in an unheard of manner – then the society man would have been able to get his eyes open . . . All paganism consists in this, that God is related to men directly, as the obviously extraordinary to the astonished observer.

> But the spiritual relationship to God in the truth, that is, inwardness, is conditioned by a prior inruption of inwardness, which corresponds to the divine elusiveness that God has absolutely nothing obvious about Him, that God is so far from being obvious that He is invisible. It cannot immediately occur to anyone that He exists, although His invisibility is again His omnipresence. An omnipresent person is one that is everywhere to be seen, like a policeman, for example: how deceptive then, that an omnipresent being should be recognisable precisely by being invisible, only and alone recognisable by this trait, since His visibility would annul His omnipresence . . . The spiritual relationship to God in truth, when God refuses to deceive, requires precisely that there should be nothing remarkable about the figure, so that the society man would have to say: 'There is nothing whatever to see' . . . It would help very little if one persuaded millions of men to accept the truth, if precisely by the method of their acceptance they were transferred into error. (*Concluding Unscientific Postscript*, 219–21)

This way of communicating the truth is necessitated by the kind of truth to be communicated, namely, a personal presence requiring a personal response. In a different context John Oman wrote that revelation 'approves itself, as it reconciles and not as it informs' (*Grace and Personality*, 1917, 1925 3rd edn, 147), that is, as it initiates, or reinitiates, a personal relationship. Unlike a set of facts, it cannot be instilled directly. It can only be presented indirectly, as a possibility for the other to appropriate existentially, to make it his own by living it. 'A communication in the form of a possibility compels the recipient to face the problem of existing in it . . . In the form of a possibility it becomes a requirement' (Kierkegaard, *Concluding Unscientific Postscript*, 320). The 'Thou' is always so presented. But because the possibility, to be capable of realization, has also to be capable of being repudiated, the 'Thou' must always admit of being turned into an 'It'. This raises two problems. First, what right have we then to speak of a ' "Thou" that by its nature cannot become an "It" '? And, secondly, if we admit this to be legitimate, how are we to conceive the connection between this eternal 'Thou' and the finite 'Thous' through which it must mediate itself if it is not to override the freedom of the human personality?

To speak of God as omnipresent is to speak of one who is always and everywhere a 'Thou'. This is the only valid meaning of the word for a personalistic theism. If God is immanent in any 'objective' sense – as a spiritual substance which permeates creation in the way that pantheism asserts – then there is no real difference between him and the world. He is simply '*ein Stück Welt*', a part of the objective continuum, just one more factor to be reckoned among many 'Its'. This theory not only gives us an impersonal deity, but, as we saw, makes any personal relations impossible by denying the existence of an independent sphere to serve as a medium through which will may meet will. To think of God as personal means to think of him as being personally related to oneself, that is, to think of him as one's 'Thou'. But to know him as one's 'Thou' is to know him as the writer of Psalm 139 did – as a 'Thou' from whom neither time nor space nor desire for an undisturbed life make it possible to escape. There is no 'where' and no 'when' in which God is not already there, confronting the soul in mercy and judgment. Such omnipresence is clearly not open to logical demonstration. There can be no *proof* that God is everywhere – or even that he is anywhere. If his presence could be so verified it would not be the presence of a person. It can be known, not by the impartial investigator of an interesting phenomenon, but only by one who in seeking is prepared to discover himself under its judgment and who is open to the call for decision and commitment which its finding brings. The omnipresence of God is not the objective presentation of a ubiquitous *Gegenstand* [object], but continuous 'confrontation' by the *Gegenwart* [presence] of a 'Thou' which demands all as it gives everything.

Against this fact of the eternal 'Thou' we have to set the equally incontestable experience of the turning of this 'Thou' into an 'It'. The history of religion abounds in examples of mankind's continual attempts to make God into a thing – an object of possession or use, of creed or cultus. And the same, of course, is ever true of the individual. This denial of the 'Thou' is exactly what is meant by sin. In St Paul's words, it is to know God and to glorify him not as God (Rom. 1:21): to perceive him as a 'Thou' and yet to change that 'Thou' into an 'It' (1:23, 25). How then are we to reconcile the idea of a 'Thou' that by its nature cannot become an 'It' with the necessity that this 'Thou' must, if human freedom is to be preserved, be manifested in and through 'Thous' that may, and in actual fact do, continually become 'Its'?

The answer lies in what was said before about the nature of man. Man must always be defined in terms not of himself alone as an individual substance, in the categories of self-consciousness or self-determination, but in terms of his relationship to others and the world, as a being-in-responsibility. (This will be expanded as a theory of personality in Ch. 7.) And the fulfilling of this responsibility, life in a true 'I–Thou' relation to his environment, expresses itself in its highest form as love between human beings. Brunner limits the 'Thou' to other selves, but what he says can be applied, *mutatis mutandis*, to all such relations.

> Man [he asserts] cannot be man 'by himself'; he can only be man in community. For love can only operate in community, and only in this operation of love is man human. The human 'Thou' is not an accident of human existence, something which gives to his present human existence a new content and richness; but it is that which conditions his human existence. Only if he is loving can he be truly man. This means the discovery of a new idea of humanity, which does not find the distinctively human element, the core of humanity, in the creative or perceptive reason, but in community, as the fulfilment of responsibility. 'Love is the fulfilling of the law' – not merely of the moral law, but of the law of the law of life. (Brunner, *Man in Revolt*, 106)

> Being-for-love is not one attribute of human existence among others, but it is human existence itself. Man is man to the exact extent in which he lives in love. The degree of his alienation from love is the degree of his inhumanity. (ibid., 74)

But, Brunner goes on, 'only as an answer to the divine love is human love the fulfilment of responsibility and the realisation of humanity' (74). Man is man only in the 'I–Thou' relationship; but that means, first and foremost, in his relationship to the eternal 'Thou', which is the ground of all other relation. His is not merely 'existence in responsibility' but 'existence in the Word of God'. Man lives literally by every word that proceedeth out of the mouth of God. 'The essential being of man as man . . . is identical with his relation to God.' 'The humanity of man rests in nothing else than the divine Word addressed to him' (ibid., 157, 160).[17] In everything he has to give an answer to the word of creation – and he is that answer. He alone of all creatures knows that he is a responsible being: he is 'called' into existence. His life depends on a spiritual relation to his Maker – he must answer that call. He is not merely a product but a receiver of the divine word. He is therefore a 'being-in-decision'; he stands over against God and must respond.

> But this responsibility – and here the biblical understanding of man finally parts company with the Idealistic understanding of man – is not first of all a task but a gift; it is not first of all a demand but life; not law but grace. The word which – requiring an answer – calls man, is not a 'Thou shalt' but a 'Thou mayest be'. The primal word is not an imperative, but it is the indicative of the divine love: 'Thou art Mine'. (ibid., 98; cf. *The Divine Imperative*, 1942, 116)

This self-communication is not forced on man: man must receive it by accepting the gift of life.

> He must 'repeat' the original divine word – he must not make a word of his own, but of his own accord he must give it back saying: 'Yes, I am thine.' Man is destined to answer God in believing, responsive love, to accept in grateful dependence his destiny to which God has called him, as his life. (Brunner, *Man in Revolt*, 98)

The word of God, in which alone man exists, is a word of love which is presented as a gift which we have to appropriate through obedience – the *Gabe* and the *Aufgabe* are one and indivisible. According to the divine ordinance, to love is to live, and the 'answer' man must make is the answer he longs to make: responsibility is just responsiveness. Yet responsibility is for our minds inevitably bound up, not, primarily, with love, but with law – with the moral law. To act responsibly is enjoined as a matter of duty. But it is important so to frame our definition of responsibility that this more familiar sense of the term does not become the norm. Only as a perversion of a situation in which we desire to make a spontaneous response under the constraint of love can we hope to understand the state of affairs in which we experience an obligation to act responsibly under the pressure of law. It is important to recognize the continuity between the two states.

> Although, through sin, we cease to express our responsibility, we do not cease to be responsible. We do not even cease to be aware of responsibility. Responsibility still remains the characteristic formula for the nature of man, for fallen man as well as for man in his origin. But responsibility is now no longer the formula of his reality, but only the formula of his obligation. It is true that man does not love God and his neighbour, but himself; yet he ought to love God and his neighbour. The divine law of nature has become a law of obligation. (Brunner, *Man in Revolt*, 156)

What is of significance here is not the gulf between man's ideal and actual situation, but the continuity. The form of the responsibility remains, even if its content has been changed from love to law. Yet the change is never complete. The law by which we must measure our responsibility is the law of love, and it is obeyed as law only because it is seen for something higher. Commenting on the words 'Thou shalt love the Lord thy God with all thy heart, and with all thy soul, and with all thy mind. This is the first commandment. And the second is like unto it, Thou shalt love thy neighbour as thyself', Professor Reinhold Niebuhr has said:

> Such a commandment can be understood as stating an ultimate condition of complete harmony between the soul and God, its neighbour and itself in a situation in which this harmony is not a reality. If it were a reality the 'thou

> shalt' would be meaningless. If there were not some possibility of sensing the ultimate perfection in a state of sin the 'thou shalt' would be irrelevant. (*The Nature and Destiny of Man*, 1941, I, 303–4)

We are now in a position to answer the question whether we have any right to speak of an eternal 'Thou' which cannot become an 'It', for this is intimately bound up with the idea of responsibility. God has made us for himself; that is, he has created us to give a free and loving response to the love wherewith he so loves the world. Responsibility is therefore of the essence of our humanity. 'In virtue of the divine creation we are irrevocably bound to this form of existence: we must either love or hate, we cannot leave this dimension of love-hate' (Brunner, *Man in Revolt*, 136). We may deny our responsibility to God, ignore or flout his claims, and think to rest undisturbed in the security of the world of 'It'. But the love of the eternal 'Thou' confronts us and will not let us go. The 'Hound of Heaven', seek to escape where we will, still dogs us 'with unhurrying chase, And unperturbed pace, Deliberate speed, majestic instancy' (Francis Thompson). To speak of an eternal 'Thou' is not to say that any human beings live their lives in the consciousness of a loving presence continuously about them. But it does mean that this ideal is of perpetual relevance to the life of all, whether saint or sinner, and that man's attempt to turn the divine 'Thou' into an 'It' can never wholly succeed. Man's responsibility which he denies as love returns upon him as wrath. All efforts to find repose in a merely 'neuter God' who makes no claims are doomed to failure. There remains a 'Thou', as the psalmist knew, who never ceases to confront the sinner, pursuing, accusing, chastening, entreating, if haply he may at length turn to seek after him and find him (cf. Baillie, *Our Knowledge of God*, 3–16).

The second question we posed arose out of the fact that this eternal 'Thou' is always presented to man in a broken and refracted form, in and through many finite 'Thous'. These continually rise up before us out of the world of 'It', demanding exclusive attention and then as quickly sinking back once more into the ordered continuum of the spatio-temporal process. These flashes, as transitory as they are immortal, reveal the meaning of things (cf. Berdyaev, *Solitude and Society*, 72, 160–2, where personality is called an 'axiological' category, as illuminative and creative of 'meaning'). They are 'the moments of silent depth in which you look on the world order fully present' (Buber, *I and Thou*, 31). 'The living relation with the Centre' (ibid., 49) which they afford alone enables the power of personality to be preserved and to conquer in a depersonalized age. These glimpses are vouchsafed to any wherever they have the eyes to see them, whether in the everlasting hills or in the unrepeatability of historical event, in the contemplation of the artist and the mystic or in the cup of cold water given in love.

Such is the divine omnipresence. God is never absent; and yet his presence is such as never to compel our presence. Though God is ever looking, man may shut his eyes, and does. The divine revelation is necessarily received successively and partially. It is broken and refracted by the fact that the 'Thous' that mediate it are continuously sinking back to become 'Its' as men turn from them. Though his desire is that we should live in the continuous sun of his presence, he will not force us to this. He prefers, as it were, to meet us in the flickering snatches of light reflected from the shimmering poplars, than to compel us to endure the inescapable glare of a treeless desert. The omnipresence of God wills to be revealed as apparent absence, since sin will have it so: otherwise it would not be the omnipresence of love, but a power for whom the response of freedom was irrelevant.

And it is just this divine permission which leaves man without consciousness of his presence that is the occasion of the further sin of setting up the 'It'-God of creed and cultus. Man in his contradiction both wills to escape God and yet cannot bear to be without God. He turns away from the consuming fire of the divine presence, and yet seeks to perpetuate his God-relationship as a permanent possession. He makes to himself a God who can be contained within the propositions of a creed or is available through book or sacrament under the control of an institution. Thus God is always there when wanted – and not when he is not. He can be summoned as required, held at arms' length, confirmed and proved. Instead of the continual pilgrimage back to the centre, back to the place of meeting, involving ever afresh that patient awaiting for the breath of the Spirit and the moving of the waters, man seeks to 'fix' the encounter by getting it under his control, as an object for his comfort and enjoyment, to be dispensed to the faithful through assured ecclesiastical channels (cf. Buber, *I and Thou*, 113–14; Brunner, *The Divine-Human Encounter*, 15–17). But, just because God *is* eternally 'Thou', he is ever greater than the God man builds to ward off the real presence. He ever breaks into the system of defences constructed for the comfortable enjoyment of the 'It'. The man who says in his heart 'there is no God', or, what is for the Bible the same thing, that he does not interfere masterfully in the world organized without reference to him, is always ultimately revealed as a 'fool'.

But does this Word of the eternal break in only in judgment, in the 'Thou fool' to him who thinks to order his life within the predictable reliabilities of the 'It'? Is the divine revelation always such as simply to work wrath, by disclosing to man his inability to respond to it with his whole being and thereby establishing his sin? Christianity answers No. For in Christ, it claims, there is presented to man not simply another finite 'Thou' which, just because it is not identical and coextensive with the boundless 'Thou' of the divine, is one more among the many transitory and partial revelations of that presence. Rather, there meets him one in whom 'dwells all the fullness of the Godhead bodily' (Col. 2:9), the incarnation of the infinite Word itself. The possibility of aversion and judgment is still present. The form of his revelation is indeed such that the 'indirectness' of his communication and the liability of 'offence' is at its height. Only in 'faith', which presupposes the chance of rejection, is it possible to see God and live. But to those who have it is given the ability to encounter in Jesus, and in Jesus alone, the divine 'Thou' in its unconditioned fullness. Though there is no part of the universe in which God has left himself without witness, it is here alone that the eternal 'Thou' is to be met *in a saving manner*. In our other encounters this is not so, and that not merely because of the transitoriness of the revelation of the 'Thou' to which sin condemns us. For that, to some extent, can be remedied, if, as Buber says, we have both grace and the will to do it, by an ever-repeated return in humility to the centre. But all our 'Thou' relations, when they come, are partial and incomplete. Thus, we find it impossible ever to achieve purely 'personal' relations with other people. Our dealings always have a mixed and ambiguous character: even in our highest relationships the 'other' remains to some extent an object of experience or feeling, use or satisfaction. Our giving of ourselves, our venturing out from the 'I', our handing over of ourselves in obedience for the disposal of another, is never complete and unhesitating. To the end, our lives remain centred upon the 'I' and careful for it, rather than about the 'Thou'. And as long as this is so the revelation of the 'Thou', with its summons to the unconditional surrender of love, will necessarily present itself as judgment and as law. And this in itself is never saving.

It is only encounter with the Unconditioned which can evoke the unconditional response required. No finite 'Thou' can dispose of the love necessary to break down the resistance of the ego.

> That total self-giving, that complete renunciation of one's own security, that utter dependence . . . is only possible face to face with one whose being and acts are such that face to face with him one *can* afford to renounce his own security. Man stays concealed in his secure hiding place, secreted behind the walls of his 'I'-castle; and nothing can really entice him out until one meets him who overcomes all the mistrust and anxiety about his very existence, which drives him into his self-security and there imprisons him. Man remains imprisoned within himself until the one meets him who can free him, who

> can break down his system of defences, so that he can surrender himself, and in this surrender of self receive what he needs to enable him to abandon his securities; that is to say, until that one comes who gives man the life for which he was created. Only unconditional love, which brings man to self-fulfilment, and therewith gives him his true selfhood and eternal life, can call out in him complete, unconditional trust. (Brunner, *The Divine-Human Encounter*, 51)

That unconditional love Christianity declares to be presented in Jesus Christ, in the only form in which love can confront us *in concreto*. For whereas, on the one hand, no human being can exercise the love necessary, yet, on the other hand, as Gogarten says, 'There is . . . only one single possible way of being loved; that is, that another human being should love us.' As men, we can have direct experience only of finite 'Thous'. But they in themselves, though mediating the Infinite, can never effect that reorientation of our being which the 'Thou' always demands: they can never therefore be realized in their purity. Only in Christ, where the finite 'Thou' who meets us is identical and coextensive with the Infinite in the power of his love, can we be drawn wholly out of ourselves to achieve that perfect relation to God, which is salvation and eternal life.

Chapter Six

THE DOUBLE 'RESPONSIBILITY' OF PERSONAL EXISTENCE

In the two previous chapters we have sought to give some account of the structure of the 'Thou' and 'It' relationships to his finite and infinite environment, which, according to Buber and others, make up the nature of a man's existence. In the next chapter we shall be drawing these insights together with a view to formulating a theory of personality which will both serve as an alternative to the 'classical' view and also provide a basis upon which to rest a concept of the divine personality more congruent with the 'personal' nature of Christian religious experience. But, before we can pass on to that, it is necessary to analyse a little more closely and critically the nature of the peculiarly 'personal' relationship from which we started in Chapter 1, to set it in the light of Buber's discussion of 'I' and 'Thou', and to mark it off more carefully from the other relations upon which persons may enter. For what we called the 'personal' relation is not simply identical with the 'I–Thou' relationship which Buber describes, if only because the latter is extended to cover encounters in which the 'other' is not a personal will.

This difference affords an obvious point from which to start our analysis. It will be recalled that we noted a similar difference in the two usages of the 'I–Thou' terminology adopted by its various exponents. There are some who distinguish the two relations according to the differing nature of their objects. For them the 'Thou' is the 'proper' relationship to persons, and is confined to such encounters. This norm may indeed be violated by treating persons as if they were things, by applying to them in fact the 'It' relation, which is that 'proper' to the non-personal. But the norm of the two relationships is governed by the nature – personal or otherwise – of that which confronts the subject. But, secondly, there are others, of whom Buber is the most consistent, who define 'Thou' and 'It' without reference to the nature of the object. For them these are constituted solely by the relation they bear to the 'I', and apart from that relation they represent nothing. Anything may be a 'Thou'; and again anything, and the same things, may at any time become 'Its'. The two relations are defined, not in terms of the nature of the object, but of the attitude of the subject. In the 'Thou' relation the 'I' is fully himself and takes his stand over against the 'other' with his whole being, the total personality being committed. The 'It' relation, in contrast, can never be more than a partial expression of what, as a person, he is. In it he never gives himself entirely in love, trust and obedience. 'The primary word "I–It" can never be spoken with the whole being' (*I and Thou*, 3). We may sum up this usage in contrast to the former by saying that the 'Thou' is the 'proper' relationship to everything, whereas the 'It' is the improper relation to everything, 'proper' being used, as before, with reference to the norm of what existence as a person implies and demands. Our present purpose will be served if we consider for a little the problem posed by the juxtaposition of these two usages. What is the connection between them? Clearly they are different. Yet are they so different that they have nothing of importance in common? Both draw attention to facts of experience which all recognize, or at least can be led to recognize, as valid and true. Both, therefore, have an independent value. But is there nothing more? And if they are really simply concerned with two different sets of facts and problems, how is it that the one passes so easily into the other, and that the very presence of such a difference of terminology is for the most part unrecognized by those who employ the terms?

In trying to discover what, if any, is the connection between them, it would seem wise to start with the common ground they share. Both are agreed that the 'Thou' relation is the 'proper' relationship of persons with persons. And this is not only the common ground between the two usages; it is also clearly the starting point of each. From an analysis of this, the 'speech situation', both begin. What they go on to say is by way of application, in extension or contrast, of what this analysis reveals, to other relationships. This is quite clearly the case even in Buber, for whom the 'Thou' relation is much more general in its denotation. On the basis of an understanding of reciprocal *personal* relationships, and only on this basis, he extends the application of the 'Thou' to a man's whole relational environment. The personal determines its norm, and to a large extent governs its description.

But we shall have to ask – and this on the face of it is the chief difference between the two usages – why is it necessary to extend it at all? It is not immediately evident what is the appropriateness of applying to things and 'values' a term which, in its origin and connotation, is so distinctively personal as the concept of the 'Thou'. Why is such a term required to describe relations with that part of our environment which is, ex hypothesi, non-personal? This is a question which probably arises in the minds even of those who recognize and appreciate what Buber is trying to describe when he speaks of 'Thou' relationships with nature or beauty. Yes, they would say, this is a genuine experience, and a man would be the poorer who could claim no knowledge of it. But why the description in terms of the 'Thou'? Does not this give the impression that the earth is being peopled with a multitude of spirits after the fashion of primitive animism?

This supposition Buber explicitly denies (*I and Thou*, 8, 27): he never means to assert any form of panpsychism (*Allbeseelung*). The use of the term 'Thou' does not necessarily imply the full mutuality of word and response, which is to be found in the personal relationship alone. There is no suggestion that the 'other' must possess a soul or consciousness. No, what necessitates the application of the word 'Thou' is nothing in the 'other' itself. It is because Buber sees every 'Thou' in this world, whether it possesses consciousness or not, as a point of meeting, or potential point of meeting, with the eternal personal 'Thou' of God (ibid., 6). Every 'Thou' relationship is for him potentially a personal relationship, because it may mediate an encounter with a Will. In what a man receives from a 'Thou' relationship with a thing or some ideal or value (and it is essential to the idea of this relationship that he must receive as well as order and dispose: some sort of reciprocity is necessary), he may recognize the 'summons and the sending' of the divine revelation. Buber would not say that it was necessary that this recognition should take place: in most cases it does not. Nor would he say that a man cannot genuinely relate himself to the non-personal any more than to the personal, in his environment, unless he views it as the medium of the Infinite Personal. The true artist must be capable of such a relation; yet most artists are not religious. The scientist who pursues his investigations conscious of the imperious claim of the truth upon his efforts need not be aware of meeting therein any personal demand. And even the moralist, whose material is the distinctively personal, can have a burning sense of the imperative of the moral law without necessarily hearing in and through it the voice of the holy God. Kant, who was a religious man, saw no reason for basing the moral law in anything but itself, reserving its identification with the divine will as a permissible extra for the pious.

Nevertheless, Buber would claim that such a reading of the demands of the 'Thou' in all its forms as points of meeting with the personal God was the truth about their nature. It is not our purpose to substantiate such a claim by logical demonstration, even if that were possible. We are only concerned to establish that it is the underlying presence of this insight which in fact explains and justifies Buber's usage of the 'I–Thou' terminology. Without this there would be no ground, let alone necessity, for extending the very personal word 'Thou' to relationships with non-personal objects and for seeing their claims as essentially continuous with that exercise by a fellow human being.

It is this awareness that in all 'real living', in every 'Thou' relationship with whatever part of our environment, we are or may be in contact with the personal God that gives to the 'Thou' its peculiar quality, in contradistinction to the 'It' where this meeting is denied. This awareness may be described as the constant memory, that, whatever we do, we do all in God's presence, since he is there to meet and be met if we so will. And he is there not as spectator but as judge. In every decision we are answerable or responsible to God. And it is this sense of *responsibility* which characterizes the 'Thou' relation in all its forms, distinguishing it once and for all from the 'It'. It is this fundamental difference of attitude to the whole of life – which, at bottom, is that between the religious and the irreligious, though it may not be recognized as such – that constitutes for Buber the fundamental divide. This is what he characterizes by the words 'Thou' and 'It'. The former describes the 'proper' relationship of a person to the world, the latter the 'improper'. And 'proper' has now defined itself in terms of 'responsibility'.

If this is the fundamental truth which Buber's terminology is seeking to express, what of the other usage? For it, too, corresponds to a real fact of experience. We all recognize that there is a difference in the way in which we ought to treat persons and things, even though we may often obscure it in action. From one point of view there is a single 'proper' way in which we ought to relate ourselves to everything. But within this identity there are also real and genuine differences. For there is a 'proper' way in which to relate ourselves to persons, which is *not* the same as the 'proper' attitude to things. It is this truth which the other terminology is intent to uphold.

Can we state this difference more exactly and apply to it the same kind of analysis which we undertook in the case of Buber's distinction? We believe that it is possible, and that by means of this process we shall not only uncover the real ground of the distinction, but also reveal the connection which exists between the two sets of facts to which the two terminologies testify.

In what follows reference will be made to a similar analysis undertaken by Professor John Macmurray, which appears in his book *Interpreting the Universe* (1933, 1936 2nd edn), and also, later, in his *Reason and Emotion* (1935). The first thing which strikes the reader is that Macmurray's division is threefold and not twofold. We believe that he is correct in this, and that the 'Thou–It' dualism which the other writers take over from a terminology formulated for a different purpose obscures a necessary distinction. We shall therefore be adopting and working with his three categories.

The three categories are the three ways in which man's 'rationality' expresses itself in the world in which he is set. Rationality, for Macmurray the distinctive mark of personality, is the capacity for acting in terms of the nature of the object with which one is dealing. Other things behave in terms of their own nature. One has only to find out how a thing is constituted to understand why it responds to a stimulus in a certain way: the reaction is automatic, and can be calculated from the nature of the subject. There is here no freedom and, as long as the seat of freedom is sought in an analysis of their inner constitution, none will be found in the case of human beings either. Freedom lies in the possibilities of choosing one's reaction to a given stimulus. The difference between this and automatic response is well illustrated in the example Macmurray gives of 'objectivity' in action.

> A little boy starts to run across a busy street. His mother sees him from the pavement and sees that he is in imminent danger of running in front of a motor car. Her natural impulse is to call out to him in terror. If she did so she would reacting subjectively in terms of her own natural constitution, responding to a stimulus from the environment. But she does not. She recognises that to shout to the boy would only increase his danger by distracting his attention, so she suppresses her impulse. Her behaviour is rational, because it is determined not by her subjective impulse but by her recognition of the nature of the situation outside her. She acts in terms of the nature of the object. (*Reason and Emotion*, 20–1)

It is this capacity for objectivity which Macmurray sees as the essence of the personal. Since the rational approach depends on the nature of that which confronts one, it will naturally differ from case to case. Here the threefold division, of which we spoke, comes in. For it is possible to classify the different rational or 'proper' personal responses under three main heads, according to whether the 'other' is inorganic, organic or personal in its constitution.

In the case of the first, the inorganic, the nature of the object is the sum of its causes. It can be understood and dealt with on the hypothesis that it is a complex of mechanical causation. To alter its nature one has merely to alter the determining conditions or the arrangement of the substances which go to make it up (e.g., water becomes ice by lowering the surrounding temperature or hydrogen by the elimination of its oxygen content). To act in terms of the nature of the object is here to act in terms of the nature of the causal laws which determine it. The object has no existence or significance in itself apart from these laws: it is simply the aim of its determinations and no more. There is no 'proper' form of existence for the combination of hydrogen and oxygen in itself: what it is depends entirely on the proportions in which they come together and on the surrounding temperature. As long, therefore, as one studies and observes these laws, there is nothing more to take into account, and in terms of which one should act. There is no independent nature of water which one violates by turning it into ice or steam. One has merely made use of the causal laws which constitute what it is, but which under other conditions would equally well combine to form something else. To act in terms of the nature of an inorganic object is simply to observe the laws which condition it. The use or manipulation of these laws to create some other object is a perfectly rational and 'proper' procedure, and forms the basis of all progress in a science such as chemistry. This relation, the 'proper' relation of persons to things of this nature, may be called the *instrumental*.

When we come to the class of organic substances, however, we find that the principles which held for the interpretation of the inorganic are not adequate. A living being is incapable of being explained merely as the sum of its causes. It can only be properly understood, as Aristotle insisted, teleologically, in terms of the end or function which it is striving to fulfil. It is true that it is possible to examine organisms *as if* they were merely complexes of mechanical causation. In fact, as Kant pointed out in his *Critique of Judgment*, science is bound to proceed on this assumption. For science is that activity of the human reason which studies everything – inorganic, organic and personal – in so far as it can be treated as a complex of mechanical causation. This is just what the scientific method means, and within its limits it is perfectly legitimate. But not much is required to see that it has its limits, and to understand that life, let alone personality, cannot be completely comprehended on the presuppositions with which it is bound to start. Biological science, by its very nature, 'cannot be an attempt to define the nature of life but only an effort to represent and understand the mechanism through which life works' (Macmurray, *Interpreting the Universe*, 117).

If we turn from theory to practice we quickly observe that the same thing is true. In the same way as one can study organisms as if they were no more than the sum of certain laws, so, within limits, it is possible to treat them as such. It is possible, by manipulating its environmental conditions, to stunt or to force a plant. Above all, by mutilating it or by denying it water or oxygen, it is possible to kill it altogether. This is the practical concomitant which haunts the application of the scientific method to the field of organisms. Biology is ineluctably committed to studying much of its life dead.

But this purely instrumental relation is not the 'proper' way of treating an organism. It is very far from acting in accordance with the nature of the object. In fact, the logical conclusion of such treatment is to destroy its nature altogether. To act thus is always, as it were, to go against the grain. It is unnatural because it takes no account of the function which it exists to perform. The plant or animal is significant in itself over and above the conditions which determine it, and this is derived from, and must be defined in terms of, its particular end. In the case of the inorganic there was no nature or self to be violated by a redistribution of the atoms which composed it. But in a living organism this is not so. As Gerard Manley Hopkins expressed it in his 'Binsey Poplars', 'ten or twelve, only ten or twelve strokes' will '*unselve*' the growing tree, and 'but a prick will make no eye at all'. The whole pain and poignancy of his lines

> Oh if we but knew what we do
> When we delve or hew –
> Hack and rack the growing green!

depend on recognizing a real violation here, comparable to the destruction of a man's manhood. Such treatment is in a true sense 'improper', because it ignores or flouts the nature of the object, which in the case of an organism is the end or function it exists to perform. The 'proper' relation is one that takes this into account and co-operates with this purpose. This relation we may therefore call the *functional*.

Yet the purpose here is not conscious (it is what Kant described by the paradox of '*Zweckmässigkeit ohne Zweck*' [purposefulness without purpose]) and the function is not self-justifying. Each organism has its own end, but this is not an end in itself. It is possible to relate oneself to organisms in the 'proper' functional relationship and yet to co-operate with them for ends more inclusive than those which they fulfil. A person can take up such functional relationships into his own designs in exactly the same way as he can manipulate inorganic matter to serve his own ends. And just as he can apply the 'instrumental' relationship to organisms, so he can apply the 'functional' to persons. It is possible, and easy, to relate oneself to other people by co-operating with them in the function they are performing, but co-operating with them only so far as they are performing it, and only so far also as that function can help to forward the purpose one has in mind. This is to treat persons as organisms pursuing an end (for all one is concerned they might just as well be pursuing it unconsciously) and showing an interest in them only from this point of view. This is, indeed, less 'improper' than the use of the 'instrumental' relationship to persons, which just means manipulating them by effecting a change in the forces which determine them mechanically. The most blatant example of this 'instrumental' relation is physical compulsion or duress; but there are other techniques – such as suggestion by advertisement or propaganda or economic dictatorship by control of the means of production – which are no less potent for being less direct.[18] But, though the 'functional' relationship at least does not treat men as chattels, it cannot yet claim to be action in terms of the nature of the object if it prefers to consider them as intelligent animals.

For a person is characterized not merely by an immanent unconscious purposiveness but by the capacity for deliberate design. And intelligent purpose, with which one can sympathize, is the only final explanation, beyond which one cannot ask 'why'? It constitutes the ultimate self-justifying category. With it we reach what is genuinely an end in itself, needing to be referred to nothing beyond itself. The 'proper' relation of persons will show recognition of this capacity in their nature of being their own justification. To treat them as means to some other end, as the 'functional' relation does, even while respecting their own end, is to deny this and to act towards them 'improperly'.

This may be expressed in another way by saying that a person must be regarded as a being who is equally capable as the subject of constituting himself an 'I' in a 'Thou' or 'It' relation to everything else, the subject included. In the 'proper' *personal* relationship I relate myself to the 'other' simply as another being possessed of this relation. Acting in terms of the nature of the object is here acting in terms of a nature exactly similar to my own. And in so far as I am acting simply in terms of what he is, and not in terms of what he does or can be made to do, he is absolutely my equal. I may consider myself in every way superior, and deem therefore that his purpose should be subordinated to mine. But this superiority, if it exists, is entirely irrelevant. In the functional relationship human differences and inequalities are very important: it is only in so far as a person is good at something or has certain qualities or performs a certain function that I am interested in him. But in the 'personal' relation, while these differences and inequalities remain and enrich its quality they have no effect on the fundamental equality. As a person, as a being capable of relating himself rationally or objectively to the world, or, in another terminology, as a being capable of 'Thou' relationships, all men are equal and one is as good as another. Men are unequal in what they can do, but equal in what they are. In the personal relationship I relate myself to the *nature* of the other, which is not, as in the case of organisms, to be defined in terms of his function. In human beings, a man's function is only part of him. As a person I am not interested merely in 'something there is about him' or something he can do, but in the whole man, just for what he is. And this 'total' nature of the relationship has its counterpart on the side of the subject. In all the other relationships of life, I give myself to the 'other' only in so far as I am interested in getting something done. In the 'personal' relationship, I commit my whole self with no ulterior motive. Such a relationship is simply another way of expressing what it means to be a person. It is therefore an end in itself and completely self-justifying.

In this survey of the different kinds of relationships which it is 'proper' for a person to establish with different parts of his environment, we have seen that rationality (which for Macmurray is the essence of personality) is 'objectivity'. To act 'properly' as a person is always to act in terms of the nature of the object. But this is only another way of saying that we should act towards everything *responsibly* – giving to each the response that its nature requires. Impropriety is irresponsibility.

Through this word we are led back again to the first usage of the 'I–Thou' terminology, in which we also found the essence of the 'Thou' relation to be 'responsibility'. But in the two cases the emphasis is significantly different. For Buber the primary reference of the word, and the reference which necessitates the employment of the personal term 'Thou', is the responsibility for all things to God, which goes with the recognition of them as his gifts to us and as opportunities for encountering his presence. In the second usage, wherein the distinction between 'Thou' and 'It' corresponds with Macmurray's division (except that 'It' has to cover both the 'instrumental' and 'functional' relations), the emphasis is rather on acting responsibly towards the nature of that which is over against one. There is no necessary reference to any ulterior claim to be met.

The truth seems to be (and here it is possible really to see a synthesis of the two usages) that the 'I–Thou' relationship in fact involves *both* these responsibilities, immediate and ultimate. This Buber sees. The ultimate responsibility is there, very obviously, and, as we have seen, this determines his use of the term 'Thou' of all 'proper' relations. But the immediate responsibility is there too, and is that from which he starts. Moreover, he does not regard it as essential for the possibility of a 'Thou' relation that there should be any further (religious) awareness though, unlike Kant with the moral law, he does not believe it can be fully understood without it. It is true that Buber is not concerned to examine in very great detail the differences in this 'proper' 'Thou' relation constituted by the nature of the objects over against which one stands. But he does divide it into three types – relations with the world of nature (which is meant to include both inorganic and organic, though his examples are mainly taken from the latter), the world of persons and the noetic world of 'intelligible forms' or values. And he definitely notes that in each case the quality of the 'Thou' relation will not be identical – there is an obvious gulf between the complete reciprocity of the personal relation and that of the other two.

In this matter of determining more precisely that nature of the immediate responsibility, an analysis which works with the categories Macmurray adopts can be useful in supplementing Buber. But while Buber allows room for the double nature of the responsibility involved in the 'Thou' relation, Macmurray does not and cannot. The fact that he gives the name 'rationality' to what Buber describes as the attitude which always says 'Thou' is in itself significant of this defect. He has no room for the idea of an ultimate responsibility just because there is no being over and above the complex of immediate relations to whom one has to make an answer. There is no independent divine 'Thou' transcending the nature and claims of the personal, with claims of its own capable of demanding the renunciation even, say, of the human love which mediates it.[19]

Macmurray's analysis in this matter, however, does not do justice to the accent of unconditionality always attached to the peculiarly religious awareness. For in our finite relations, even in those with other persons, there meets us no *absolute* demand, no *final* refuge. To no other human being have I the right to accord an unconditional obedience, and no other human being can provide a fulfilment and assurance of which not even death can deprive me. We cannot, it is true, know this demand and assurance apart from the human relationships in which they meet us. The Infinite works through the language of the finite: it has no special tongue of its own. But while the letters are human, the accent which is placed upon them is divine. It cannot be explained in terms of the letters themselves. It is explicable only if another whole dimension is taken into the reckoning – the dimension of the supernatural, of the sense of the holy and the judgment of the sacred.

It is this that Buber introduces. And once it has been introduced it becomes the all-important one. The difference between the 'proper' and the 'improper' relation to *this* aspect of reality is infinitely more important than any distinctions within the field of finite human relationships. That is why Buber is right in employing the 'Thou–It' distinction with reference to the fulfilment and non-fulfilment of this responsibility, rather than to the differences in the 'proper' finite relationship occasioned by the different nature of the objects confronting one. Indeed, for this latter distinction, the 'Thou–It' terminology is not really very suitable. As we have seen, what is required is not a twofold but a threefold division (or even a fourfold if Buber's '*Beziehung mit den geistigen Wesenheiten*' [relationship with spiritual beings] is to be reckoned as an independent category of 'Thou' relations over and above Macmurray's other three).

Our conclusion is that the two usages of the 'I–Thou' terminology with which we began are concerned with different, but complementary, 'responsibilities' involved in the relation they are seeking to describe. Each of these we have seen to represent real facts of experience and to be indispensable for a full understanding of the relation. We cannot end, however, without giving a little consideration to the question of the connection between these two responsibilities. For that connection is clearly close. It would seem unlikely that the ultimate responsibility to God could be discharged through action which flouts the more immediate responsibility of acting in terms of the true nature of what confronts one. But if the former automatically involves the latter, are they really two at all? Could they not, in the end, be reduced to one? And if they could, would not Ockham's razor demand that they should?

We noted above that, though Buber may use the category of the 'Thou' to cover a man's relations with any aspect of his existence, his starting point, in terms of which his definitions are framed, is the relationship of person with person. It is here too that we must start if we are to formulate any clear guiding principle which will also help us in the other instances.

The problem in the case of the personal relationship is that which is raised, in a Christian context, by the mutual relation of the two great commandments, love of God and love of neighbour. It is obvious that, though many succeed in loving their neighbours without any knowledge or love of God, it is impossible sincerely to love God without loving one's neighbour too (1 Jn 4:20), or even to love God apart from this and other finite relationships. The two commandments cannot be treated simply as existing independently side by side: fulfilment of the commandment to love God implies that of the other. Yet must they remain two at all? Granted that it is impossible to reduce both to the second, as Macmurray tries to do, should we not meet with more success if we assimilated the second to the first? May we not say that, when we love men, we are not doing anything other than loving God, but are in reality 'loving God in man' (Ebner)? Is not our fellow man just a *Durchgangspunkt* [passageway] through whom the love of God is revealed to us, and by loving whom we are enabled to give our response?

To this we must again return a negative answer. For that would not be to treat a person as the end in himself which he essentially is. It would not be fulfilling our immediate responsibility to respect him for what by his nature he is. To know someone as a 'Thou' is to respect his *Selbstständigkeit* [independence]. I can never treat him as a mere means to an end – even if that end is the knowledge and service of God. I owe an answer to my neighbour as well as to God, and one answer will not do for both. I cannot serve God but through my neighbour, nor love my neighbour truly except in so far as I see him in God. Yet the polarity remains. The human 'Thou' has a status in its own right over against me and demands my love, just because he is a 'Thou' for God and is loved by him.

Moreover, to wish to resolve this tension and to reduce the two terms – the divine and human 'Thou' – to one would be as destructive of the personality of God as it is of man's. For it would undermine the whole basis of the 'I–Thou' relationship as the foundation of the universe. To attempt to minimize the *Selbstständigkeit* of man over against God is to make impossible that tension of will with will which is the only safeguard against the invasions of a pantheistic mysticism. Unless the relation between God and man is such that God can and must say: 'Son of man, stand upon thy feet and I will speak with thee' (Ezek. 2:1); unless, that is, life is a real dialogue, then the dialectical, ethical relationship of communion will be swallowed up in a monistic doctrine of absorption (cf. Buber, *I and Thou*, 83–95).

At this point we may seek to illustrate from the three different spheres of human activity which we described before the abiding duality of responsibility involved in the single 'Thou' relationship. The principle throughout is that which Buber states when, in the context of the 'personal' relation, he defines 'love' as 'responsibility of an "I" for a "Thou" ' (*I and Thou*, 15). For there is here included the double reference of which we spoke. In the first place, the very word 'responsibility' implies that in such a relation I am answerable *to* someone. And this, as in all my doings, is the divine 'Thou'. But it is possible to be responsible to someone for something (e.g., for carrying out an undertaking) without being involved in a further responsibility to the thing itself. This might be called responsibility for an 'It'. But in 'responsibility for a "Thou" ' there is something else as well. A probation officer, for instance, is answerable to the court which committed to him his charge, but he is also answerable to the charge himself. The fact that he can only fulfil the one by fulfilling the other too does not mean that he has only a single responsibility.

The meaning of such 'responsibility for a "Thou" ' in the realm of 'personal' relations can be observed in the claim which others exercise upon oneself. The demand which God lays upon my life is always mediated through the claims of finite persons. Yet, so far from meeting these claims only as a means to an end, the call is to satisfy them absolutely. The matter of the claim is concerned with the human: in its form it assumes the unconditionality of the divine. The sphere in which the eternal must be realized is the historical 'now', the *Gegenwart* of the meeting of men with men. Human history is never in itself self-explanatory: the contact of 'I' with 'Thou', which is what constitutes it, always points beyond itself to a 'Thou' transcending and giving meaning to the whole. Yet it is the 'now' and 'here' which are the time and place of decision and salvation; and as such they acquire a significance which makes it impossible to think of them as mere means to some future state. The religious man who regards this world purely as a vale of soul-making will always minimize the claim of others to be served simply for their own sakes.

In the organic field, responsibility for a 'Thou' does not involve treating the 'other' as an end in itself. For it is not the nature of the object to be such, and it would be 'improper' so to treat it. Religions, such as Hinduism, which regard responsibility to God as implying the treating of some animal as sacred, apply to that animal categories which are proper only of personality. But equally 'improper' is the application to organisms of the instrumental relation. Exploitation of the earth's resources, by irresponsible cropping or deforestation, involves for the religious man a double betrayal. It is an offence against the nature of that with which one is dealing, which is being manipulated for ends that pay no regard to the function it exists to perform. And, secondly, such action disregards the true significance of these processes as means of grace, and the inescapable responsibility to God to which their use commits one.

It is important to recognize the real difference between exploitation and the 'proper' use of natural processes. The latter does not consist simply in leaving them as we find them. That would be to condemn all forms of agriculture as sinful, and to accord to natural functions a status as ends in themselves which they do not enjoy. It is possible and proper to use these functions for personal ends. If we believe that they have been set in the world for the sake of persons, or at least partly for that reason, then they will be being used most properly when they are serving such ends, and not when they are left to run wild in a pure 'state of nature'. A garden may be nearer God's ideal for the organic world than a wilderness, and ears which yield some thirty, some sixty, some a hundred, more truly 'natural' than wild oats. In this connection we may quote a footnote of Professor Hodgson's.

> If this argument be sound [he writes], then the old saying that nature is conquered by being obeyed is a half-truth. It is true if it be taken to mean simply that we must understand the workings of nature in order to control them. But it is a dangerous error if it be held to mean also that our aim in seeking to understand these workings should be to conform our ways to them rather than to enlist them in the service of our own purposes. (*The Doctrine of the Trinity*, 1943, 75)

The criterion will always be the double standard of responsibility for the 'Thou' and to the 'Thou'. Use of organic processes for other ends is justified only if it involves a genuine co-operation with the natural function, that is, if this is taken up into a more inclusive whole, and not merely destroyed or ignored – in an act of mechanical manipulation. And, secondly, the purpose for which they are used must be such as can be undertaken consciously in the presence of God and laid before him in prayer. For man is ultimately answerable to God for the use of everything he finds in nature. And if this last responsibility is taken seriously, the former will certainly not go by default.

Finally, there is the realm in which the 'instrumental' relation is the 'proper' one. There is a certain tendency among those who use the 'I–Thou' terminology to suggest that there is something wrong about *using* anything: for that would be to treat it as an 'It', and we have been told that we must relate ourselves to everything as 'Thou'. But this is to indulge in a dangerous sentimentality. To act responsibly in terms of the nature of the 'other' is to treat it as one's 'Thou'. And if the nature of the 'other' is such that the 'instrumental' is the 'proper' relation to it, then to use it is not to treat it as an 'It'. It is precisely to adopt some other attitude which is improper. Of course, in such use one must observe the nature of the laws which determine it. Magic, which tries to bypass the necessity to act in terms of the nature of the object, because either the nature is unknown or the process laborious, is 'improper'. But then, it is also useless – for the simple reason that it will not work. In the case of persons and organisms it is still possible, and often easier, to treat them in a way proper to a lower form of existence. But in the case of inorganic substances that temptation is absent: for there is only way only of subjecting them to one's will, and that is to obey the laws of their nature.

But there is, at the same time, the danger of according them a relative or a final justification as ends, which they do not possess. And it is this which constitutes the main consideration when the question of the ulterior responsibility comes to be faced. For the material is given by God to be used, not to be treated as possessing a value other than instrumental. Money and goods are held from God and a man must render an account of his stewardship. They must not be hoarded or prized or worshipped for themselves: the 'proper' relation to them is the instrumental. It was the perversion of this relationship that was the sin of the Chaldean: 'He sacrificeth unto his net, and burneth incense unto his drag; because by them his portion is fat, and his meat plenteous' (Hab. 1:16). And, secondly, the use to which such things are put must be continuously reviewed as though in the presence of the divine auditor. And what this ulterior responsibility directs will also involve the true relationship which the more immediate one requires. But though they coincide, and though one meets the subject only in and through the other, yet neither here nor anywhere else are they identical. Such is the dialectical nature of the responsibility which constitutes the 'Thou' relationship in all its forms.

We have hitherto been proceeding on the assumption that the act a man feels he ought to do after conscientious regard to his ultimate responsibility will in fact always coincide with the 'proper' act as the nature of his immediate object defines it. And it would obviously be satisfactory if we could say that this supposition must always be true. But such a pattern of responsibility is actually disturbed by several judgments of experience, which it would be dishonest to exclude from account. For we do in fact apply to objects both higher and lower categories than their nature would 'properly' demand, without thereby feeling that we are acting improperly in the sight of God. Some rather important modifications, therefore, need to be made in what has been said. They have been reserved till now so as not to confuse a clear exposition of the underlying principle.

In the first place, there are cases in which both inorganic and organic objects seem to require of us an attitude which, purely by the criterion of their own nature, they could not rightfully demand. By their association with persons they acquire a value which lifts them out of the class to which they properly belong and gives them a certain claim to be treated as ends in themselves. This does not mean that they become good in themselves without qualification – a description which, as Kant saw, must be reserved for the good will alone. But they do become in a real sense good in themselves, and not merely as a means to something else.

Things in this class are those which, over and above the status attaching to them for what they are in themselves, acquire an additional significance as the locus of some value, or as possessed of some association, sacred, historical or 'sentimental'. This extra association causes a disturbance of normal value judgments. There are cases where we should regard it as perfectly 'proper' to destroy an organic function in order to preserve an inanimate object. Most of us would be prepared to shoot a tiger rather than allow it to rip up a canvas of Raphael. Indeed the value of works of art may constitute a serious challenge when compared even with that of human lives. The debate occasioned by the balancing of the destruction of the monastery at Cassino against the risk of increased Allied casualties revealed a real division even in Christian circles. The questions raised for ethics by such a class of problems are ones for which no fixed criteria of judgment appear to exist.

The second class of cases are those in which a lower relationship is adopted than that which is 'proper' to the object, and yet where it is difficult to see that an ultimate 'impropriety' is involved. There are two relationships included here, which require to be treated rather differently.

The first is the application of the 'instrumental' relation to the organic. It would indeed be satisfactory if it were possible to achieve all the personal purposes which we deem ultimately 'proper' in a way involving a relation to organic objects which was always one of *co-operation* with their natural function. But such an exact correspondence of 'proprieties', in the world as we know it, is quite unattainable. The very effort to keep alive involves the frustration of organic functions in the destruction of vegetable and, usually, animal life too. The Binsey poplars so dear to Hopkins's heart may have been required as timber for the most necessary purposes; and at any rate the felling of *some* trees is quite indispensable for the needs of civilization. Again, such is the competition of nature that the survival of crops or flowers which we wish to perpetuate cannot be achieved except through the elimination of other growth. To this 'impropriety' we appear to be committed by the fact that men, in so far as they are biologically conditioned, cannot escape from the laws of natural selection. We cannot say that it is sinful, though the justification of it is far from evident. Here we seem to be touching the edge of the dark mystery surrounding the whole problem of animal suffering and the maintenance of organic life solely by the destruction of other organic life.

Finally, there is the question of the application of the 'functional' relationship to other persons. This we saw before must in itself be strictly 'improper': it is only the 'personal' relation which in this case can do justice to the nature of the object. And yet in fact most of us spend most of our lives in functional relationships with others, without being conscious of sinning thereby. There are, of course, degrees in such relations, according to the area of intersection between two lives which different functions involve. Clearly, the connection established between two business partners is a fuller one than that between one of them and the waiter who serves him his lunch. But in each case the relationship is essentially the same – co-operation for a particular purpose and interest in the other only for that purpose. And such relations are the rule rather than the exception: truly personal relations make up a very small proportion of the average man's life. Yet are we to condemn as wrong the profession, say, of the travelling salesman, whose contacts are bound by the very nature of the case to be almost exclusively functional?

Kant's criterion would not exclude such relationships from the moral life. It is only the 'instrumental' relation to other human beings which he condemns by his principle that a person must never be treated *merely* as a means to some other end. And yet the Christian would find it very difficult to predicate of God any but purely personal relations with all his creatures. Are we then to conclude that the difference between God and man in this respect is due merely to the latter's finitude, or is it in some degree a mark of his sin?

The answer seems to be that something of both is involved. It is quite obvious that the range of a man's capacity for knowledge of, and interest in, others is definitely limited. Life is too short for me to be able to achieve full personal relationships with every porter, chimney-sweep, ticket-collector, income-tax inspector and charwoman with whom the exigencies of life bring me into contact. It is certain that Christ, like any other finite human being, must have had numerous relationships of a similarly functional nature.

And yet a difference in the way such relationships may be regarded provides material for a genuinely *moral* judgment. The 'functional' relationship, it will be remembered, was 'proper' to organisms because it was action in terms of their nature: their nature *was* their function and could be defined in terms of it. It was 'improper' to men because in personality nature and function are not identical. Function is only a part of a man's whole being and may be isolated from it. What is wrong is that one should act towards a person *as if* it were his whole nature, treating him merely as the performer of some particular actions. It is surely possible, however, within the limitations of the functional relationship, to act towards a man by making it clear that one does *not* consider the function, which alone interests one at the moment, to be the whole man or his only justification. It is the secret of some men (one thinks of a person like Dick Sheppard), as surely it must have been of Christ, to be able to make those with whom they are brought into functional contacts feel that they are really being treated as persons, and not merely respected for what they can do. In this case, a hint is given of how an essentially 'improper', impersonal relationship may be redeemed for personality.

The modifications which we have been forced to introduce in the last few paragraphs necessarily break up the first simplicity of the pattern of the 'Thou' relationship. Moreover, the fact that we have treated what are instances of common experience as exceptions to a norm inevitably increases the difficulty which attaches to their explanation. The fact, however, that ethically they are far from easy to fit in with any general rules of judgment encourages us to think that a scheme which could include them as regular and normal phenomena would be false in its oversimplification. We remain convinced that the pattern of the 'Thou' relationship with its two separate but complementary responsibilities must form the norm of all relationships of man with his world. And towards the understanding and analysis of this relationship the two terminological usages with which we began have each contributed an essential factor.

The course of this chapter has necessarily led us on to a good deal of ground which is peripheral to our main theme. Its general necessity, however, will become clear as we proceed. Meanwhile what has been said in these pages may perhaps indicate some of the avenues of promise which the 'I–Thou' analysis of human relationships opens to us, and may also help to justify the claims made for it in an earlier connection.

Chapter Seven

PERSONALITY AS RELATIONSHIP

'O Lord, I know that the way of man is not in himself' (Jer. 10:23). It is from such a text that the opponents of the 'classical' theory of personality could well take their start. For fundamental to their position is the denial that human personality can be defined in terms of itself, as an 'individual substance'. They would begin, rather, with the fact that personality is unknown except in relationship, that I cannot be myself except as over against someone else. Their basic conviction could be stated in a passage from one of Bishop Creighton's letters: 'Life is a sum of relationships. There is no independent or self-centred existence. I am what I am in relation to others' (quoted, H. M. Relton, *A Study in Christology*, 1917, 155).

Starting from this fact of experience, they make it determinative of their whole treatment of personality. A person is the sum of his relationships. But within these relationships in general (*Verhältnisse*) they distinguish one as marking off the peculiarly personal from other forms of existence. To live only in relationship is not distinctive of personality: an animal can have no existence except over against its environment. The relationship which differentiates personality is the particular relation of 'I' to 'Thou', which Buber distinguishes from *Verhältnis* as *Beziehung*.

Inorganic substances are the sum of their relations, these being defined in terms of mechanical determination. Organisms are the sum of their relationships, these being defined in terms of the end or function they exist to fulfil. And in the case of persons the same is true, except that the situation is complicated by the possibility of divergence from the norm through freedom. In addition to the sum of the relationships 'proper' to the peculiarly personal, men can and do exist towards their world in an 'improper' fashion. Thus, although the norm of personal existence must be defined in terms of the 'I–Thou' relationship, this does not mean that everyone so exists. But the 'improper' relation is still a relation: no existence is possible outside the total relational context. There is no 'I' except the 'I' of one of the primary words 'I–Thou' or 'I–It'. Indeed, it is possible to say that in the last analysis a man cannot escape even from the 'I–Thou' relation. For the fundamental relationship which constitutes his being is to an eternal 'Thou', who can never become an 'It'. No man can ever succeed in so escaping into the world of 'It' that the word of the divine 'Thou' cannot reach him, even though it reach him in judgment. He can never finally get away from the norm of his being, however blind he may be to it or however violently he may disown it.[20] He can never sin himself out of the context of his responsibility to God. Thus the divine mercy, even though it meet him wholly as wrath, safeguards the vestige of his humanity (cf. Brunner, *Man in Revolt*, 157).

What has been said may be described in another language as a doctrine of internal relations. Every form of existence is constituted by the sum of its relationships:[21] an entity is not something that exists in itself and then, from that base, as it were, enters into external relations with other bodies. What differentiates various forms of being is not the fact that some are the sum of their relationships and some are not but rather the *nature* of the different constitutive relations. In inorganic substances these relations are those of mechanical causation: a thing is merely the sum of its determinations *a tergo*. In organisms a thing is more than just the sum of *such* relation: it can only be fully understood teleologically, in terms of its functional relations. But it is nothing over and above *these* relations: its nature *is* its function. In the case of persons a man is more than the sum of both his mechanical determinations and his biological functions. But he is nevertheless nothing out of and apart from his personal relations – here including not only all his 'proper' ('I–Thou') relations, but also the abuse of them ('I–It') which his freedom permits. He is constituted by them: he does not elect to enter upon them as something external to himself. There is no 'I' apart from them.

In the first two cases a doctrine of internal relations means determinism and no freedom. It is, indeed, a different mode of determination which governs the inorganic and the organic. In the former it is the impulsion of mechanical causation. In the latter it is what Bergson called 'the inverted mechanism' (*L'Évolution créatrice*, 1907, ET, *Creative Evolution*, 1911, 42) of teleological determination. But the cases are essentially the same (cf. Buber, *I and Thou*, 51). Both the inorganic and the organic when affected by a stimulus from without respond *automatically* in terms of their own natures, which in the former is that of the forces which meet to form it, in the latter its governing function or entelechy. But in the case of a person the stimulus comes as requiring a free and self-chosen response. The response given will be determined in terms not of the subject but of the nature of that which confronts him. From the 'Thou' point of view complete freedom and responsibility reign.

This question of freedom will be raised more fully at a later stage. Suffice it to say here that of the three sets of internal relations which comprise a person – or, rather, the three ways of regarding the one set of relations which is that person – only from the point of view of the personal 'Thou' relation is freedom to be discovered. Science can neither prove nor disprove its existence. For science necessarily views man in the 'instrumental' relation, and here the question of freedom is excluded by the very presuppositions with which one is working, namely, the abstraction which treats the object only in so far as it is a complex of mechanical causation.

But is such a thorough-going doctrine of internal 'Thou' relations the only real alternative to the 'classical' theory of personality? Might it not be preferable, in place of the extreme formula that 'personality *is* relationship', to work with some such definition of personality as 'a self-in-relationship'. In this case the fact of existence only in relationship would be an essential part of the definition of personality, and, indeed, its distinguishing mark. But the relationship would not be simply constitutive of it. A person would not be his relations and nothing more. He could not be himself without his relationships, but if, *per impossibile*, these relations were abstracted, there would not just be nothing left. There would still remain a residual 'substance', the particular subject of the necessary relations. Boethius' definition could stand, with the addition of two letters: 'an individual substance of a relational nature' ('relation' standing for the 'I–Thou' *Beziehung*). Might it not be claimed that this solution, while it still retains the idea of individual subject-hood as the centre of personality, successfully avoids the errors of the 'classical' formula?

Certainly, such a view would seem to be a faithful translation of the common-sense idea of what it means to be a person. In the same way, common sense would tend to reject the idea of internal relations as applied to things. It would be very loath to embrace the view that if all the mechanical relations which go to condition a billiard ball were abstracted there would be simply nothing left. What it would feel was being lost would be the fact of individuality – that which makes it 'a thing' – which the idea of 'substance' preserves. But if it can be shown that, in fact, all is safeguarded without it, then the lack of empirical evidence for such a 'substance' must lead to its elimination, in the same way as, in a different context, Berkeley's epistemological analysis leads to the elimination of Locke's substance.

In the case of inorganic matter it is not difficult to show that no kind of individuality is predicable of things other than that of the particular collocation of causes which make them up. Determinism, which is no more than a statement that a thing is the sum of its mechanical relations, is acceptable as an account of the material world despite the prima facie dissent of common sense. That is to say, it is an adequate *description* of it, in the sense that, if one analyses it purely from within the (deterministic) presuppositions of science, there is apparently nothing left over – as there *is* in the case of the organic – which requires some other category of interpretation. (Materialism as a *philosophy* is of course a very different matter. As Temple says, 'stark determinism is stark nonsense' (*Nature, Man and God*, 227), for the process of mutual determination could never start.)

Clearly *such* a doctrine of internal relation – that is, one expressed in terms of mechanical causes – is inadequate to safeguard the kind of individuality which experience requires us to predicate of persons. If the same were true of the doctrine of internal 'Thou' relations, then, despite the inevitable absence of empirical evidence for an 'individual substance' or 'noumenal self' over and above its relations, it seems that we should still be bound to postulate its existence. But if a genuine individuality and freedom can be established without it, then Ockham's razor must again intervene to excise a superfluous entity. The question is therefore whether the omission of the idea of 'individual substance' in the radical definition of personality as 'relationship' (*Beziehung*) is destructive of the idea of individuality. If a man is not to be defined in terms of himself, even if it be of himself in relationship, can he be called an individual self at all? Certainly if the idea of *individua substantia* were removed from Boethius' definition, we should be left with something entirely general and abstract. Can it be shown that, by the substituting of 'relational' for 'rational' nature, the excision would be any less disastrous?

There are really two questions here, which rest on two meanings of the word 'individuality'. Individuality, as its etymology indicates, may refer to the fact that the thing in question is a complete whole in itself without any division, the implication being that it really *is* divided from that which it is not. The word in this connection points to the importance of the frontier between one thing and another. This use is clearly exemplified in the 'individual fruit pies' advertised by Messrs Lyons & Co. The term simply tells me that my pie is quite detached and separate from that of the next customer: it is not just a 'cut from the tart'. But, to come to the other usage, I could with justice say that my pie had no 'individuality' at all. If I saw a number of them on a tray together they would all look *exactly the same*. I may remark that houses in a dull street possess no 'individuality' without indicating thereby that they are only semi-detached. The word here refers, not to the *separateness* of one thing from the next, but to their quantitative or qualitative *difference*.

In the 'classical' theory of personality there is no doubt about the provision made for the *first* sense of individuality. The separateness of each person is firmly stressed, at the expense indeed of the fact of his relatedness. It is safeguarded by that part of the definition which speaks of him as 'an individual substance'. 'Rational nature' is in itself a purely generic term, shared not only by all men but also, according to the Schoolmen, by the angels and God as well. Reason is a universal and contains no reference to individual boundaries and finite division.

But if we substitute the 'I–Thou' relation for 'reason' as the distinctive characteristic of the personal 'substance' the situation is altered. For this demands by its very nature a structure of existence in which individual frontiers are clearly defined and preserved. As we have seen, without a high degree of mutual isolation persons would not be capable of that relation of trust and communion which is characteristic of them. Unlike 'reason', too, the 'I–Thou' relation requires not only clear individuation but the presence of the body to supply the symbols through which this individuality can be expressed and preserved even in the act of communication which transcends it. The tendency of the 'classical' theory was always towards an idealism which would find the essence of man in 'reason' or 'spirit' alone. The body, no more than the individuality which it exists to safeguard, could not be viewed as necessarily involved in such an essence. In fact, it constituted a denial of the universalism of reason. (The Greek equivalent for individuality, significantly, was *περιγραφή* (outline), or limitation.) The idea of 'individual substance' was in no sense an implicate of that of 'rational nature'. In fact, it was necessary to introduce *individua substantia* to correct the suggestions of the other. But where such a corrective is not necessary, where in fact the idea of individuality is already presupposed, there is no need to retain the notion of substance. This is so in the case of the 'Thou' relation. There can be no such thing as a general 'nature' of *Beziehung* equivalent to that of 'rationality'. For the very idea of the 'I–Thou' relation carries with it the idea of individuation, in the sense of definition of frontiers. As far as this meaning of individuality is concerned, the idea of 'substance', as some residue over and beyond the relations, introduced to ensure their separateness, is quite superfluous.

But this sense of individuality is not in fact that which is uppermost in the minds of those who feel the definition of personality as the 'I–Thou relationship' to be inadequate. If we are not to say 'A in relationship' and 'B in relationship' but simply two relations, wherein lies the difference between A and B? If it is granted that a person is 'a "Thou" relationship' and another person a separate relation of the same kind (since, as we have seen, the idea of individuality as mutual separation is included in what is meant by such a relation), how are we to distinguish one from another? Like the 'individual fruit pies' will they not be *exactly the same*? Unless there are two different 'substances' (A and B) which are in these mutually isolated relationships, there will appear to be no qualitative difference between them. This is probably the core of the objection to the definition of personality in terms of internal 'Thou' relations.

The first thing to note is that the 'classical' theory itself is completely deficient at this point. It allows for no element of individuality in the sense in which I use the term when I ask what makes one man different from another. The Kantian Kingdom of Ends, which is the norm of society according to the rationalist-idealist theory of personality, rests on the assumption that all individuals are to be regarded as identical units of the one universal reason. Individual differences between persons are obviously there; but for the purposes of assessing the essence of personality and the true relationship which should obtain between men they can and must be ignored. The essence of personality is something universal; for all are persons by partaking of a single rational nature. In comparison with this, individual differences are contingent and insignificant. That which makes A, A, and not B, that which gives him a unique value, making it impossible to treat him as if he were B or to exchange him for B – this is of no essential importance. The introduction of the idea of an 'individual substance' makes no difference. As long as that in terms of which the substance is characterized is something universal, each individual will be qualitatively identical with the next.

We put forward the view above (Ch. 2) that the destruction of true individuality by the individualism of 'classical' rationalism was a result of its abstraction of the idea of personality from the 'Thou' relation in which alone it is given. At the risk of some repetition we may now seek to establish the connection between such individuality and the 'Thou' more closely. For it is obviously essential to our present argument.

The norm of the relationship which Kant conceived to exist between moral persons was 'respect'. Respect is called forth and required because every man is the bearer of the universal moral law. It is true that many individuals reveal little evidence of such a lofty nature and in themselves seem to command scant respect. But no man, however degraded, can forfeit what he has it in him to be: he cannot cease to be a man. The right attitude therefore is to continue to regard him for what he essentially is: I still have a duty to treat him with respect, despite his particular nature.

Respect, then, is that which attaches itself to a man *despite* his individuality. But there is another attitude, love, which fastens upon him just *because of* his individuality. This is what Kant never understood, and which the theory of personality with which he was working could never allow for. He did indeed speak of love. But the only kind of love which he could allow was what he called 'practical love', which, despite his identification of it with the *ἀγάπη* [love] of the New Testament, never succeeds in differentiating itself from respect, precisely because it is directed only to that which is universal in man. I can only love a person as an individual – not as the embodiment of some universal, but for what he is in himself, for all his peculiar uniqueness. But that is not all. It is also true that only because a man is an object of love has he value as an individual. It is love which gives that significance and worth to a person making it impossible to exchange him for anyone else. Love is creative as well as appreciative of the value of individuality. It is the knowledge that he is the object of someone's particular care and interest that restores to the object the sense of his own significance as an individual. Abstracted from this relationship he is simply one of the masses, the subject perhaps of certain universal rights but with no claim to individual consideration.

It is for this reason that the true Christian doctrine of the 'absolute value of the individual' rests on nothing inherent in the individual himself. For the individual has no such value considered in himself. Kant rightly says that only as partaker in some universal does man become the subject of rights and respect. But then he is no longer being considered as an individual; it is not his individuality which is valuable. It is only as the object of love that the individual has worth as such. Has, then, the man whom nobody loves no worth? Not so, answers Christianity, he has worth because he is the object of the love of God. This gives him a claim on the love of others and an absolute value in their eyes, even though they may not in fact love him. That claim, which attaches to every individual, is grounded solely in something outside himself – on the fact that, without any merit of his own, he is held in a relationship of loving care by God. The basis of his value as an individual rests simply in the divine word of love addressed to him.

In the case of human relationships it is the *significance* of a man's individuality, rather than the individuality itself, which love bestows. The individuality is there, and love fastens upon it and gives it preciousness. But in the case of the original word of God, love creates the individuality itself, because it can only be satisfied with an individual response. The value of individuality consists precisely in the fact that such a mode of existence is that which love desires. The word of love is always a particularizing word, and each man is precious in God's eyes because he is called to give an answer which no one else can. If, as we maintained before, 'we are what we hear from God', then we are the particular persons we are because we hear a particular word from God. Our individuality rests not in ourselves but in the particular divine word which called us into being and to which our whole life is the response we have to make. It is the 'Thou' relationship which we have with God, mediated through our relations with our finite environment, that constitutes us what we are. This is the basis of our individuality: it is not our individuality which determines the particular relations we have. The seat of individuality, then, in this sense lies, not in our own substance, but in the divine word to which our lives are, and at the same time are required to be, the answer.

The difficulty which continually attends the description of man's essence is that he is always betraying his own norm. Man is created by God to give a certain response – and he is that response. And yet equally he is not, because he refuses to give it. In this situation, therefore, it is convenient to have two terms. We may reserve the word 'response' for the actual giving back of the divine word to God by man – that which completes and fulfils the reciprocal relation of love. In contrast, it is essential to have a term to describe the norm of each individual – that to which he was created by God – which determines the nature of his responsibility, even if not of his response. For this purpose the word 'analogue' is convenient, if carefully defined. To every individuating creative word or '*logos*' which proceeds out of the mouth of God there 'corresponds' an individual who exists as its '*analogos*' – he who is called to return that particular word to the divine glory by simply being truly what he is. The essence of man is existence-as-an-analogue; and his nature can therefore only be defined by reference to God and to the particular divine word to which it corresponds. It is this that the Bible asserts by describing man as created in the image of God. Our existence is constituted in the word of God. Creation means the speaking of the divine word ('And God said . . . and it was so' cf. Ebner, *Das Wort und die Geistigen Realitäten*, 26). By the speaking of the word a relationship of 'over-againstness' is called into being: by the act of speaking the analogue, the 'Thou', exists. It is called into being to make an answer, to a free relationship of 'responsibility'. Man differs from the rest of creation in that by free choice he has to make his own the relationship in which he is created. He comes out of God's workshop not as a finished product: he comes out as a possibility which is to be fully realized only by his own response. He has to *make* the answer to God which he *is*. That answer will differ for each man according to the word which calls it forth. Individuality is constituted by the fact of a difference of divine address. The *principium individuationis* (principle of individuation) is outside man.

All the individuality, spiritual and physical, which each person betrays, represents simply the conditions of being the analogue of the particular word which created him. One of the conditions will be that which is basic to the structure of every 'Thou' relationship – the fact of individuation, in the sense of defined frontiers and mutual isolation of person from person. Of this the body is at once the symbol and the guarantee. The Christian doctrine of the resurrection of the body is simply a statement of the eternal significance of individuality in this sense. Moreover, such a structure of relationship cannot be replaced by a doctrine of absorption or interpenetration of selves without destroying personality and the significance of individuality in the other sense too – the value of the particular and unique for its own sake. And what guarantee is there that personality and such individuality will not perish? If it is sought in some inherent value of the individual *per se*, then there is none; for he has no such value in himself. The hope of eternal life is grounded not in man – as the doctrine of natural immortality asserts – but in the word which constitutes his being. It is the everlasting constancy of the caring and individuating love of God – who is not the God of the dead but of the living – not some subjective conviction that man's powers are too big to be bounded by the grace, that affords the only certain hope. 'All flesh is as grass, and all the glory thereof as the flower of grass. The grass withereth, and the flower falleth; but the word of the Lord abideth for ever' (1 Pet. 1:24–5). In himself man is nothing different from the grass. If he is to live it is not because of his glory, but solely because his being is constituted in that abiding word of the Lord. For this reason a doctrine of 'conditional immortality' is necessarily unchristian. For immortality does not depend on any condition of human attainment, but on the divine word of love, and that is absolutely unconditional. What does depend on man is whether God's relation to him, which is necessarily eternal, is to be one of mercy or of judgment, of life or of death.

The view then, that personality *is* the 'Thou' relationship and is entirely constituted by it has revealed itself quite capable of accounting for the fact of individuality. 'A man is the sum of his relationships' reduces itself ultimately to 'a man is his God-relationship', for that is the basic and determining relationship which the others mediate and embody. And there is no such thing as the God-relationship in general – it is always by its very nature individual and particular. Kierkegaard denied his 'Individual' precisely as one who knew himself to be standing in such a relation. There is hence no need to say 'a particular person in "Thou" relation': for the very fact of the existence of this relation implies that what it constitutes is a particular person. On an analysis therefore of personality in terms of the 'Thou' relationship, the idea of an 'individual substance' who is 'in' such a relation is superfluous. But from the point of view of Christian doctrine it is also destructive of its essential conviction that 'the way of man is not in himself', but always and only in God. It is just the attempt to deny this that the Bible sees as the essence of sin. Human existence is solely 'existence-in-the-word-of-God': the principle of man's being lies outside himself. And consequently also does the principle of his individuation. It is only to be grounded in the ever-particularizing, ever-individuating word of the divine love which creates the relation he is.

The new view of the nature of personality which we have been stating and advocating represents a complete break with the 'classical' theory. It is not simply a question of retaining the 'individual substance' and changing the qualities which characterize it (e.g., from 'rational' to 'relational' nature). For this whole method of analysing a person in terms of his qualities, whatever they may be, and then postulating a substance in which they can inhere, is in Buber's view just what it means to treat a man as an 'It'. The 'Thou' relation can never become one among such qualities without ceasing to be the 'Thou'. This does not mean that if the 'Thou' is treated as central, in all its 'exclusiveness', that the separate qualities are ignored in the account of personality: it means simply that they are all seen in its light (cf., *I and Thou*, 8). As Buber says in connection with the process of turning from the 'It' attitude to a tree to the regarding of it as one's 'Thou',

> to effect this it is not necessary for me to give up any of the ways in which I consider the tree. There is nothing from which I would have to turn my eyes away in order to see, and no knowledge that I would have to forget. (*I and Thou*, 7)

Similarly, there is no characteristic of the personal life which has been selected by any other definition of personality which has to be excluded. It is only that all these attributes have to be viewed as ways in which the 'Thou' relation finds expression. What they characterize is not a 'substance' but a relation. And it is possible to see them as implications of this relation which are necessary if it is to be itself, in a way in which they could not be deduced from the idea of 'substance'. That this is so in the case of individuality we have already tried to show. If we spend the remaining pages of this chapter in doing the same with the second of the two attributes of the 'classical' formula, it will at the same time assist in clarifying further the nature of the 'Thou' relation at one important point.

The fact that the 'Thou' relation expresses itself through 'reason' and self-consciousness is an essential mark in distinguishing it from the other internal relations, which constitutes the world of the organic and the inorganic. Whereas in other forms of existence a thing is what it is by the fact that it is acted upon by its environment, in the case of a person '*Ich bin durch dich*' [I am through thee] means essentially that I am constituted, not merely by the face of my relatedness to others, but by my knowledge of them as related. '*Ich werde am Du*' (Buber, *Ich und Du*, 18), 'I come into being as over against thee', implies that what I receive from the other 'I' receive consciously and deliberately. It is not just a question of foreign influences infiltrating my being: there is involved the capacity freely to accept or reject what seeks to pass the frontier of my personality. Self-consciousness and all the rational processes of thought and valuation which accompany it are integral to the possibility of the 'I–Thou' relation. (The question of the presence of large areas of unconscious influence even in the highest personal relations will be discussed in another connection in Ch. 15 below.)

But it is clear that with none of us has it been ever thus. Both with reference to God and to others (in particular, of course, our parents) must we truly say 'through thee I am' in a sense which implies no such self-conscious relationship. God has called us into being, and others have called us into being, as selves which only gradually grow to a relationship in which conscious 'answer' to the 'word' addressed becomes possible. It is for this reason that we should be slow to ascribe personality to a baby. He is not yet a 'responsible' being, and his relation to his Maker and the world around him is not the conscious spiritual relationship of the 'Thou'. The connection is in the first place entirely organic. And yet there is in this relation what Buber calls the '*a priori* Thou', which is gradually explicated by childish experimentation and first meaningless sounds into the full 'speech-situation' of conscious *Beziehung*. The essential continuity between the first organic connection of the child with its mother and the earth and the later developed 'Thou' relation of consciousness is a favourite theme of Buber's. It is brought out in the striking metaphor of the text he adopts for his *Die Frage an den Einzelnen*, 1936: '*Verantwortung ist die Nabelstrang zur Schöpfung*' – responsibility is the umbilical cord which ties us to creation (cf. also *I and Thou*, 24–8 and 96–7, where he speaks of the 'stammering of nature' at the threshold of the development from the 'vegetable security' of the animal world to the 'spiritual venture' which is man).

This same continuity between the organic connection ('*die reine naturhafte Verbundenheit*') and the properly personal relationship (*Beziehung*) must be observed in man's relation to the divine 'Other' also. Man's existence, unlike that of other creatures, in Brunner's language, is not only 'by' and 'through' the divine word of love, but also 'in' and 'for' it. He is not merely a product of that love, but is so made as to be able freely to receive and return it. The *imago Dei* (image of God) consists not in the fact that man is *more like* God in his rationality and powers than are the animals, but in the unique relationship in which he is called to employ them. 'Man is not man because he possesses intelligence and will, but because he is responsible, and knows he is responsible, for their exercise' (H. F. Lovell Cocks, *By Faith Alone*, 1943, 62). This Dr Lovell Cocks elaborates in the valuable suggestion that the inner meaning of the doctrine of the *imago Dei* is to be found not so much in the early chapters of Genesis as in those passages which speak of the 'Covenant' between God and his people. It is the ethical relation of sonship which marks the true affinity between God and man, not merely physical creation.

It is certainly true that in this filial relation and in the redeemed sonship of the New Covenant, according to the Bible, man is most fully man. The 'Thou' relation is necessarily one of conscious recognition and knowledge of the Other. The perfect state of affairs between God and his people is when 'they shall all know Me from the least of them unto the greatest of them' (Jer. 31:34). And yet there is a danger in isolating the doctrine of the Covenant from that of creation. God did not merely choose a people: he chose those whom he had created. The institution of the Covenant at Sinai is parallel to the transformation in the individual of the earliest organic relation of the infant into the conscious personal responsibility of the adult. Man is created, as he is procreated, without being consulted. Like all other beings he is completely dependent on him who calls him to be: he is 'by' and 'through' the word as much as any other creature – clay in the hands of the Potter. His capacity for standing upon his feet and addressing his Maker can only be correctly understood in the light of this fact. His utter dependence is the condition of his freedom and independence. When the call to the acceptance of conscious responsibility comes, it remains in the form 'Ye have not chosen me, but I have chosen you'. The early Genesis narratives contain the presuppositions required for the understanding of the Covenant.

Each of us has to begin with a 'Through Thee I am' which is strictly irreversible; and that formal irreversibility remains when the *durch Dich* becomes *am Du*. The absolute equality of personal 'meeting' in the conscious 'Thou' relation occurs in a context of total dependence. The 'living soul' created by the divine afflatus is the same man who is 'formed out of the dust of the ground' (Gen. 2:7). Once this connection is destroyed the truth about man's nature is distorted in one of two directions. On the one hand, the 'spiritual' relation may be exalted to exclusive pre-eminence.

Rationalism by fixing 'reason' as the core of personality obscures the fact that it is but a quality of a relationship essentially continuous with a connection of organic dependence. On the other hand, in reaction, we find Barth denying altogether the significance of the fact that man is called to confront God in the equality of reciprocal communion. The element of 'rational' nature is left out as irrelevant: the fact that 'man is man and not a cat' is 'quite unimportant' (*Nein!*, 25, 27. Quoted, Brunner, *Man in Revolt*, 95).

It is the task of a Christian theology to attempt to hold together the two elements we have been discussing in a paradox which destroys the nature of neither. On the one hand, place must be found for the everlasting fact of human creatureliness, that ineffaceable κύριος–δοῦλος (master–servant), Potter–clay relationship, which can never be altered or disturbed. 'Between God and man . . . there is and remains an eternal, essential, qualitative difference' (Kierkegaard, *Of the Difference between a Genius and an Apostle*, 1849; ET attached to *The Present Age* 1846, 151). Yet God in his mercy calls us to a relation not of sods but of sons, to the amazing reciprocity and equality of a free communion of love. 'It is indeed less terrible to fall to the ground when the mountains tremble at the voice of God, than to sit at table with Him as an equal; and yet it is God's concern precisely to have it so' (Kierkegaard, *Philosophical Fragments*, 1844, 27). Can these two facts be held together? Is it possible to assert a relation between man and God which is at the same time one of complete dependence and creatureliness *and* of complete independence and equality? And if so, what does this imply for Theology? Are we to hold equally that God is in no sense dependent on his creation, that he has no need of it whatever, and yet also at the same time that it is necessary to him who as Love yearns for the response of communion?

Such questionings arising from the nature of man drive us back to the doctrine of God, for the sake of which our consideration of human personality was undertaken. We shall have to go on in the next part to deal with just such problems as have been raised – problems which are particularly connected with the attempt to state the nature of the peculiarly personal existence of the Godhead. Before passing over to Theology, however, we propose to devote a bridge chapter to the person of him who stands between God and man, the God-man Christ Jesus. That man was found *capax Dei* (capable of God) and that the eternal God 'did not abhor the Virgin's womb', if true, cannot but be decisive for the understanding of the nature of each.

Chapter Eight

THE PERSON OF CHRIST

If to be man is to exist in the 'Thou' relationship to God, then to become man is to enter that relation. It is Christ's taking upon himself this existence-in-responsibility which is the fundamental meaning of incarnation. The ἐνσάρκωσις (putting on flesh), the assumption of that limitation of the rational nature by the body and its senses, which to the Greeks represented the most obvious fact about man, is secondary. The individuality of human existence and the physical structure necessary to its expression are to be properly understood only in the light of the peculiarly human relationship. They are simply part of what is involved in it – inevitable concomitants of its existence and conditions of its expression. For the proper understanding of the person of Christ it is necessary, then, to start, not with what were but symptoms of something more fundamental, but with the relationship which constituted his existence as a man. He was man simply because he stood in the human relation to God, other men and the world. And yet he who existed in this relation was none other than God himself. God constituted himself man by assuming the 'Thou' relation to God.

This is the heart of that astounding paradox which forms the core of the Christian gospel. In the course of a chapter it is clearly impossible to follow up more than one or two of the questions which press themselves upon the human understanding as it seeks to wrestle with such a tremendous assertion. We shall confine ourselves simply to a single point at which the substitution in Christology of the new theory of personality for the 'classical' view causes repercussions which are significant for our whole investigation of the doctrines of God and man.

It will be left to a later chapter (10) to discuss the Incarnation from the point of view of the doctrine of God; to ask, for instance, what it implies for our conception of God that he is capable of existing, without ceasing to be God, within the limitations of the human, the temporal and the mutable. On that theme we here confine ourselves to a single observation which is necessary to the position taken up in this chapter. It is this. We do not think that any Christology can fit the biblical facts which does not start from a genuine and consistent limitation of the divine knowledge and powers of the Incarnate within the bounds of the human organs as their sole channels of expression. That is to say, neither the traditional Athanasian or Cyrilline schools of thought can hope to satisfy. Both of these postulate an unlimited Logos as the subject of the Incarnate, the former attempting to explain the events of Christ's life on the hypothesis of a double and alternating centre of consciousness, while Cyril's account of his humanity cannot but ultimately pass over into Docetism. Whether this rejection commits us to a form of kenoticism, and if so in what sense, will be debated later.

Here we would merely remark that an adequate theory must be able to combine two statements. The first is that by the process of incarnation the divinity of the Second Person of the Trinity is no whit impaired and his divine attributes in no way abandoned. But, secondly, it must allow that these attributes come to expression solely through the medium of the human faculties which condition his existence. For him there could be no power but that which the human frame could transmit; no knowledge but that which his human mind could bring to him; no memory of being other than the individual he is (for to be someone else without being confined to his memories would be less than complete identification); and, above all, no awareness of God except as a 'Thou' in a polar relation to himself, an awareness which is given, moreover, through the normal processes of a developing religious consciousness. This does not mean to say that Christ could not or did not come to realize that he was in fact God and that his 'normal' relationship with the Father was not the polar relation of human communion but one of essential divine union ('I and the Father are one'). All we are concerned to assert is that even this awareness must have been mediated through the organs of human knowledge: it was not the result of direct memory or of some supernatural faculty. By becoming man God elected that the capacity of human faculties should be the measure of his knowing. His whole life was to be contained within the sum of relationships which constituted the historical existence of a single human being. Incarnation meant the will to live simply and entirely within this relational context, with no going back, no exceptions, no privilege of knowledge of any existence outside it. He did not abhor even the Virgin's womb: he elected to start human life in the only way he could if he was to be truly man – with no consciousness and no memories. All he knew – all he was – was built up out of the relations in which as a child he found himself. Like every human being he *was* his relationships. To become man was for Christ to change his status from being the subject of the divine relation to men to being also the analogue of his own word.

Now the Christological requirements set out above could in fact be combined with a view of the person of Christ based on the presuppositions either of the 'classical' or of the relational theory of the nature of personality. That is to say, it would still be possible to assert the essential difference involved in the Incarnation to be a change of relationships, even if one did not believe that such relations were wholly constitutive of humanity. This is the position adopted, for instance, by Bishop Frank Weston in his significant book *The One Christ* (1907). Adopting the 'classical' formula, he would say that Christ was a 'Self' in these relations, but that this self was the divine Logos who had become man by taking or becoming the hypostasis of the human relations. The humanity itself was 'anhypostatic', or according to the formula of Leontius of Byzantium (recently expounded by Dr H. M. Relton in his *A Study in Christology*) 'enhypostatic'. That is to say, the divine Logos himself, the Second 'Hypostasis' of the Trinity, acted as the 'self' of the human nature. This was possible because of man's creation in the image of God. The Logos contains within himself the archetype of manhood. The range of the divine and the human are vastly different, but one is contained perfectly within the other, and the centre of one is the centre of the other. The one 'hypostasis' can act as the centre of the two concentric circles of relationships. This may be expressed another way by saying that Christ became 'man' and not 'a man'. The place of the individualizing human 'self' or 'substance' was taken by the divine Hypostasis. What was assumed by the Godhead was human 'nature' – that which is shared by all men alike.

Now this position, whereas it effects a unity of personality by the admission of only one Hypostasis, cannot really sustain the claim to orthodoxy that has always been made for it. And it fails precisely because of the defects of the 'classical' theory with which it works. This can be demonstrated on two counts. There is a failure to show that Christ assumed either the *essence* of humanity in general or the individual *existence* of a particular man.

In the 'classical' theory the essence of humanity resides in the self, which, though in practice inseparable from the nexus of relationships which it enters, is logically prior to them and can be defined independently of them. The formula, as Bishop Weston himself frames it, following Illingworth, is 'I and my necessary relationships'. The ego is the core of my being and is what makes me a person: the relationships are external to myself, though required for the development of my personality and for any fullness of life.

When this is applied to Christology we get the following situation. The place of the ego is taken by the Logos, who limits himself by entering into a new sum of relationships – the human state. Since a change in the relationship in which the ego exists cannot essentially affect its being, the Christ who is the ego of the human nature is the same Christ who is the ego of the Logos in his unconditioned existence. What Christ adopts of man is an impersonal humanity. He lives in all the relationships and possesses all the qualities which characterize human beings, but he does not take on a human ego. To all appearances he is a perfectly normal human being (and for this reason this theory is able to give for the most part a perfectly adequate account of the Christ who is seen and heard in the Gospel narratives), because the sum of relationships into which a man enters constitutes everything about him which is apprehensible to the senses. But it remains true, nevertheless, that these relationships are something external to him, in the sense that they do not enter into the definition of his ego, which is what makes him a person. The formula always runs 'the ego, plus . . .' What therefore God took upon himself at the Incarnation is something other than the essence of humanity; it is the sum of external relationships in which this humanity is set. It is not thereby suggested that this theory reduces the Incarnation to a piece of play-acting. The relationships into which God entered were not simply optional extras, corresponding to the clothes a man might wear. They were the relationships through which the human ego must necessarily express itself in this world, and might be likened rather to a man's body. Nevertheless, just as in the 'classical' rationalist-idealist theory the body is not of the 'esse' of personality, so neither does the entry of the Logos into all the necessary human relationships involve for him a complete assumption of our nature. For he does not adopt that very element in man which constitutes the essence of manhood, namely, the ego or the *suppositum intellectuale* [intellectual basis], which makes a person a person.

That this criticism is not misdirected may be seen by turning to the analogies which Bishop Weston uses to clarify his meaning. It is perhaps unfair to judge a theory by the analogies adduced to illustrate it, especially when the author confesses their inadequacy. However, the specific points at which he admits that they fall short do not include the one here being stressed. Indeed, he could hardly admit a discrepancy on this point without evacuating the analogies of most of their usefulness. Since the various illustrations are much of a type, one will suffice for examination.

He pictures a king's son, who, leaving his father's palace, elects to live as a workman among workmen, sharing their life and becoming one of themselves. Despite his real position he refuses to accept any privilege or to use any methods which could not naturally be his as a manual labourer. Even during a period of acute industrial distress, though he is chosen as the leader of their negotiations with the king, he refuses to seek concessions for his fellow sufferers which any of them could not obtain. Finally, when nothing can be done, and hunger issues in rioting, he is as one of the agitators severely handled by the mob and in the end falls a victim to the strong arm of the police (*The One Christ*, 164–5).

The point of the parable is that he remains the king's son throughout, even while he chooses to know himself as such only under the conditions of a manual labourer. The real flaw in this as an analogy of the manner of the Incarnation is that in fact all that is involved in 'becoming a workman' is a change in external conditions. A man can change his social class without being essentially affected in himself. Of course, Bishop Weston would be the first to admit that what is involved at the Incarnation is much more than an alteration in anything so external as material circumstances. As was said above, it is in fact more parallel to the assumption of a human body than to the wearing of human clothes. Nevertheless, however necessary and organic the new set of relationships may be conceived to be, as long as they are regarded as something additional to, rather than constitutive of, the ego which forms the core of personality, then to enter into them will not really be to take upon oneself any new existence.

In another form, therefore, the theory of the 'impersonal humanity' of Christ repeats the Apollinarian heresy. That in terms of which man is essentially to be defined is in Christ replaced by the divine. The consequence is that we have to say that God never really became *man*, with implications for soteriology just as disastrous as those which tipped the scale against Apollinarius. The only escape from such a conclusion is to press the doctrine of the '*en*hypostasia' ἐνσάρκωσις to the point of saying that in fact Christ had always been man. As including within himself, as its archetype, the truth of human nature, Christ's manhood was pre-existent, co-eternal and co-natural with his Godhead. The Logos could act as the hypostasis of the human nature because he was essentially man already. But this doctrine (also associated significantly with the name of Apollinarius) merely cuts the knot of the problem by introducing into the premiss what the conclusion has to demonstrate. Half the difficulties of Christology would be solved if the Incarnation could be regarded as having in principle taken place from all eternity, only to be put on the screen of flesh and blood at a convenient moment in history. Incarnation would then simply be ἐνσάρκωσις (putting on flesh). And this, despite the literal words of the Fourth Gospel (Jn 1:14) is Apollinarianism. Moreover, the idea that there is a human element in the divine is only the converse of the doctrine that there is an essentially divine element in the human. And this derives, not from the Bible, but from Platonism and the mystical tradition. It is destructive of the element of that 'otherness' and polarity in the relation between man and

God which is presupposed in any truly personal, as opposed to pantheistic, world-view.

The failure of the doctrine of 'anhypostasia', or the assertion of the impersonal nature of Christ's humanity, lies in the fact that according to the theory of personality which it presupposes there *ought* to be a hypostasis. For it is that in terms of which humanity is defined. Once, however, the 'classical' assumptions are abandoned, a doctrine becomes possible which can preserve the unit of Christ's Person without falling into the Apollinarian heresies of the 'orthodox' theory. For if personality is defined wholly in terms of relationship, then the taking upon himself of the human relation, of the form of 'existence-in-responsibility', is what is meant by Christ's *becoming* man. The relations are no longer external to, but constitutive of, his essence as human. God living in a 'Thou' relation *is* man in the only sense in which he could be. To posit himself in the human 'Thou' relation, to constitute himself the analogue of his own word – that is what is meant by God becoming man. The creation of man is not the 'planting out' of an independent substance but the setting-up of a relationship. In Christ God answers his own word – and in the very process of doing so answers as man, and is man. For it is only man who 'answers'; for to 'answer' is to be a man; existence 'in responsibility' is human existence. It is only thus, in the dynamic personal terms of the speech situation, that the intensely personal union of God and man in Christ can possibly be understood. The terminology of 'substance plus nature', of 'self plus relations', can no more provide a satisfactory theory of the person of Christ than it can of the personality of man. For it is not working with distinctively personal categories at all. The attempt to combine two individual rational 'substances' is at bottom no different from the attempt to combine two impenetrable material substances. Fundamentally it is the problem of trying to place two billiard balls onto the same spot at the same time. And it cannot be done.

The 'classical' theory and the doctrine of 'impersonal humanity' which goes with it is equally unsatisfactory in facing the question of Christ's *existence* as a historical individual. According to this theory, for the 'hypostasis' or self, besides being that which constitutes the *esse* of personality is also the *principium individuationis*, in so far at least as it takes any account of the existence of individual differences. If this hypostasis is removed from Christ's human nature then there is no ground left for asserting his individuality at all. This, of course, is admitted when it is denied that Christ became 'a man' as opposed to 'Man'.

But if Christ's manhood was not an individual manhood, then it is difficult to see how it is possible to ascribe to him historical existence. For to be a particular and to exist in history are two ways of saying the same thing. The peculiar mark of the historical is what the German theologians call *Einmaligkeit* – once-for-allness – uniqueness, unrepeatability, particularity. The 'classical' theory of personality is entirely unhistorical. As we have seen, its definition is reached by 'abstracting from all individual differences'. It retains individuality only in the sense in which mutually separate identical units can be described as individuals. And an aggregation of identical units or a succession of identical events is no history. History is unrepeatability. And even that element which individualizes in the strictly formal sense of mutual isolation – namely, the substance or hypostasis – is omitted from Christ's humanity. God assumes an entirely abstract and general 'human nature'. How can the divine Hypostasis supply the basis for finite individuation, let alone the ground of the idiosyncrasies and peculiarities which must mark out any historical existent?

Again, the abandonment of the 'classical' presuppositions alone provides a satisfactory solution. For very existence in the 'Thou' relation is necessarily individual existence in every sense of the word. And to define Christ's humanity in terms of this is automatically to make him 'a man' – a man of history, a man with a uniqueness and personality of his own, loved and loving as an individual. For the Word to constitute itself its own 'Thou' meant that it must exist as an individual, as a particular man, set in the relations of a particular age and locality. What governed the appearance of one set of characteristics in Christ's personality rather than another we cannot presume to determine. We may with reverence suppose that his mental and physical make-up was determined through the more immediate 'through-thee-I-am' of heredity and environment. Ultimately, what made God elect to be one kind of man rather than another can only be referred to the infinite divine wisdom, which alone could know exactly what the 'calling' to perfect responsibility and obedience meant in terms of the contemporary human situation and of the history of the people whose 'Messiah' he came to be.

This particularizing of the personality of Christ is inevitable if only to fulfil one essential condition of any sound Christology, namely that, except to the eye of faith, there should appear absolutely nothing extraordinary about him. Only so could he be an 'offence' to his acquaintance as nothing more than a carpenter's son. This 'scandal of particularity' that God should become *an individual*, that the universal divine Word should exist as one of its particular historical analogues, is essential to the Christian gospel.[22] That 'absurdity' can never be modified or eliminated without destroying Christianity. But if we are content to leave it as a paradox and not try to explain it away, we may find help in analogous instances where the keenest individuality is not destructive of universality. Thus Professor Scott Holland wrote of the face of Bishop Edward King:

> It seemed to say 'This is what a face is meant to be. This is the face that a man would have, if he were really himself. This is the face that love would normally wear.' We felt as if we had been waiting for such a face to come and meet us – a face that would simply reveal how deep is the goodness of which humanity is capable. Oh! if all men could but be just like that! So typical was its naturalness. Yet, of course, this did not diminish its intense individuality. It was only that this most vital individuality was so whole and sound and normal and true, that it seemed to be the perfect expression of what a man might be. (*A Bundle of Memories*, 1915, 48–9)

But though an unpreparedness to face the scandal of the particularity of the person of Christ may have exercised an influence in favour of the rejection of the doctrine that God became 'a man', yet there were other and sincere reasons behind it. And if we are to assert Christ's individuality, we must be prepared to meet the objections that have historically attached to it. These are of a soteriological nature.

The chief motive for the formulation of the difficult doctrine of 'anhypostasis', by the elimination of one 'substance', was not to make possible a real unity of Christ's personality. It was rather to avoid the conclusion that he was *a* man. For the hypostasis was seen as that which separated one unit of human 'nature' from another. It was the *principium individuationis* in the sense of providing that which isolates each human being from the next, that which makes the self the self and not the not-self. What the doctrine of salvation seemed to require was that Christ should take upon him our 'nature' – that in which we all share. Redeeming that, he would redeem all who partake of it, whoever they might be and whenever they might live. If, however, he took upon himself that nature only in so far as it found expression in the circumscribed existence of a single individual, it would mean the redemption only of that particular rational substance which was himself. That is the heart of the objection we have to meet.

Before going further, however, it will be convenient to clear away *one* sense in which some have maintained that Christ was an individual, which must definitely be regarded as false and which we are not prepared to defend. This is the view which comes to expression both in the Adoptionist and Nestorian heresies, and which does inevitably carry with it the conclusion that the redemptive work of Christ was confined to the particular human being with whom the Logos entered into union.

The essence of this theory is not that God became a man, but that he united himself with an individual, who either existed as such before the union (Adoptionism) or could have existed even if it had never taken place (Nestorianism). The Word did not constitute itself its own 'other', thus bringing into being a relation that could not have been otherwise. It joined itself with an individual either already called into being or who could have been so called on his own account. At the Incarnation the Word attached itself to a particular analogue which, by a particular act, it had called into being. It did not just constitute itself its own 'other': it created another with whom it could enter into union.

It may be that historically such a theory was the only avenue open by which the individuality of Christ could be asserted. On the 'classical' presuppositions there seems no alternative to the doctrine of 'anhypostasia' except the resolute asserveration that both the human and divine natures had their own hypostasis. And then the only way of joining them is to resort to such a 'connection' or *συνάφεια* as that postulated by Nestorius. It is not proposed to put forward the objections to this theory, whether from the point of view of the person or of the work of the Saviour, which are well known. The view has only been introduced here in order to distinguish and dissociate it from what we regard as the true theory of Christ's individuality. For the abandonment of the 'classical' view, as we have seen, has made possible a third alternative not subject to the objections attaching either to the orthodox 'anhypostasia' or to Nestorian heterodoxy.

Returning now to the soteriological argument for the universal, impersonal humanity of Christ, we may restate it in St Paul's words: 'For as in Adam all die, so in Christ shall all be made alive' (1 Cor. 15:22). The solidarity of mankind in sin can only be cured by a corresponding solidarity in redemption. Now this achievement is only possible because Christ was more than an individual. He is the second Adam; and the first Adam was the type of humanity of which all partake, rather than a particular human being. If the manhood of Christ is individualized, then redemption is confined to this individual.

The first comment on this argument which comes to mind is that it dangerously imperils the historicity of the Christian revelation. Reduced to its simplest terms, the reasoning is this. The first Adam was a universal type rather than a historical individual; therefore the second must be too. What is ignored is the fact that, whereas the value of the myth of the Fall does not depend upon the actual historicity of Adam's existence, yet it is intimately bound up with the description *in the myth* of Adam as a particular historical individual. The point will call for further elucidation shortly. Here a word is necessary on the relation of myth to history.

The function of myth is to describe empirical events for which the historical evidence is either lacking or *ex hypothesi* unobtainable. Thus the events which constitute the beginning and end of the historical process itself cannot be the subject of historical judgments. The truth of a myth is determined by its correspondence and coherence with the known truths of philosophy, which in turn are derived from what is actually empirically given, that is, the historical (see, L. Hodgson, *The Doctrine of the Trinity*, 225). It is not then legitimate to argue from a myth to decide the nature of some historical event. One can only begin from a historical event, or the historical situation in general, and argue to the truth or falsity of a myth. One cannot say: Because the first Adam was such and such, therefore the second must have been too. The only defensible reasoning is: The present historical state of man is such that if we could know its origin it must have been so and so. It is always the second Adam, or the situation he came to meet, which must form the basis for judgments about the nature of the first, and not vice versa. Our later discussion will reveal that the '*fons et origo*' of sin must have been in fact *both* a historical individual *and* a type of manhood. But, in the nature of the case, actual historical existence cannot be demonstrated of such a figure. The most that can be done is that he should be depicted *as historical* in the myth. However, when another figure is proclaimed as the Saviour of mankind from this his present state, a new situation arises. The same factors in the empirical situation which required that the cause of the disease be both historical and suprahistorical will require this double quality of its reputed cure. Yet the position here is different. In the case of the former it was sufficient, because it was only possible to formulate, in Plato's phrase, a 'likely tale' which depicted a man with the two required characteristics. But in the latter case actual historical evidence is not only possible but available. Thus the Gospels must authenticate themselves, not merely, like the first chapters of Genesis, as a myth about a figure depicted as historical, but as history. If Adam, whatever more he was, was required to be at least a particular individual in the myth, so Christ whatever more he may be, must be shown to be at least a particular individual in history.

The question of course is: if Christ was a particular individual, could he have been anything more? This can only be answered by examining that nature of the actual human situation he came to meet and the quality of man's solidarity in sin. This alone will enable us to determine the kind of universality which must be postulated of the manhood both of the first and of the second Adam.

The eternal value of the myth of Genesis 3 resides in the fact that it brings out *both* that every man is his own Adam *and* that this is not the whole truth. On the one hand, Adam is depicted as the type of humanity, the ideal man. In the story that experience of every individual is recapitulated. Each man has his own Fall, and for it he must accept complete and inalienable responsibility. 'The Lord God called unto the man, and said unto him, where art thou?' (Gen. 3:9). To every soul comes that word of divine wrath demanding a response. And yet Adam is pictured not only as the ideal man, but as the first man. This does not commit us to a belief in his historical existence as a fact of anthropology. But it does give expression to the profound truth that all sin is mediated through and inextricably bound up with the historical. Each individual is not perfectly free to choose good or evil. There is an original bias, which is itself sin, that makes actual sin inevitable. The fate pronounced upon Adam and his seed for ever is an explanation in myth of an empirical situation. The complexity of the problem of sin is far too great to permit of treatment here. The one essential is to preserve the tension between individual responsibility and actual inevitability. The truth lies neither in an 'either-or', nor in a compromise between the two; but rather in a resolute affirmation of 'both-and', in which the two are held together in unashamed paradox. And it remains a paradox rather than a contradiction because, so far from being nonsensical, it is the only thing that makes sense of the intractable material of the 'given'.

It is this paradoxical quality of sin which makes it impossible to account for its origin, as theologians have always tended to do, in terms of a metaphysical or physical solidarity. According to whether the Fall is placed outside or within history man's present state has been explained on the hypothesis of some ontological or biological taint which has infected his being at its source. It is, as the Vulgate's famous mistranslation of Rom. 5:12 asserts, *in* Adam that all have sinned. The universality of sin and the inevitability of its propagation are treated as strictly parallel to the invariability of natural phenomena predicated by science. Its occurrence is determined by a necessary law of cause and effect, whether in the metaphysical realm or in the sphere of biology, psychology and sociology. The result is one of two errors. If the bias towards sin is regarded as itself sinful, then there develops an extreme Augustinianism which leaves no place for freedom. Or if it is viewed, as for instance in Dr Tennant's writings, as a merely amoral tendency to sin, then actual sin is avoidable, and the result is Pelagianism.

What is ignored in this treatment is the distinction between what Kierkegaard described as the 'objective' and 'subjective' standpoints. When he said that 'truth is subjectivity' he did not mean that there was no absolute standard beyond the relativities of the individual's judgment. He meant that 'truth' was not properly a predicate of pieces of 'objective' information, of facts and causes accumulated by the science and open to common inspection and verification. It is, rather, the way the subject relates himself to reality. It is 'existential' in the sense that only he who is prepared to live in it and make it his own can 'be in the truth'. The opposite of being in the truth is not just factual error but sin. Sin can only be understood from the point of view of the 'subject'. Its universality is not something 'objectively' automatic. There is no law governing its causes open to scientific investigation and proof. The nexus in which it appears to bind the individual is no physical or metaphysical law of this kind. Its inevitability is something 'subjective'. The sinning subject knows this inevitability; yet he knows it is of a kind that cannot be explained – or excused in terms of 'objective' causes. The solidarity of sin is such as will not for one moment relieve him of individual responsibility and guilt. Its universality is of a quality which presupposes freedom – a freedom which is always a potential denial of the universality. One reaches it, not by a process of 'objective' generalization, 'abstracting from all individual differences'; but rather by standing in the place of the subject at the moment of decision, thereby stripping off all those generalizations of heredity and environment which obscure a man's inalienable responsibility as an individual.

The 'individual' in Kierkegaard's terminology does not describe a man abstracted from the relationships in which he exists, or lifted out of the responsibilities in which he exists, or lifted out of the responsibilities which he possesses as a member of a society. Rather, it describes exactly the opposite. A man as he was called into being by the divine word, in a relation of 'responsibility' to which, as an 'I' responding to a 'Thou', is alone a 'proper' man. This relationship, and the relationship to other, finite, 'Thous' which it involves, is repudiated and obscured, though not abrogated, by sin. The attitude of being in which man stands for ever as an 'individual' before God is transmuted into an individualism, in which the centre of existence is no longer an other to be obeyed in grateful response, but a self to be gratified in proud independence. Sinful man only meets God as an 'individual' in the day of judgment. He is recalled to, and made to stand under, the original word in which he has his being. Whether that word appears to him as a word of mercy or of wrath, he must answer it as he stands alone with his conscience. In that state he faces the divine 'Thou' stripped of all the comforting screens that sin had erected to shield him from the full force of that presence and the needs of his neighbours that embody its infinite demands. Alone he confronts, or is rather confronted by, his Maker. Then there is no one on to whom he can shift responsibility, nothing he can plead in self-defence. Solidarity in sin is no excuse, its universality no explanation. Both these are real facts, and a theory of sin which ignores them is invariably Pelagian. But they are such as presuppose, and do not deny, individual freedom and responsibility.

This investigation into the meaning of solidarity in sin has been a necessary preliminary to a decision on the question of solidarity in salvation and of the quality of universality which it requires in the Saviour. For the character and quality of the diseases determine the character and quality of the cure.

Sin, like the human nature of which it is the corruption, is both rooted in history and transcendent of history. This double aspect is reflected in the two factors of individuality and universality in the myth of the Fall. Sin is something in history and conveyed through the nexus of biological and environmental events. Adam is therefore conceived as a historical figure, the first man. But it is also something which stands outside this nexus, possessing a transcendence over the temporal and historical derived from man's freedom. Adam is therefore essentially timeless; he is the ideal man, the universal, in whom is recapitulated the life-history of every individual.

The Christ, the second Adam, wears this double aspect. On the one hand, he is an individual, rooted in the particularities of history. He meets and breaks sin and its nexus in the only sphere in which this is possible – in the network of personal relations which constitute human historical existence. He knows and conquers sin 'existentially', from the only point of view from which its sting can be known or drawn, the point of view of the existing subject, the 'individual'. Only if Christ had conquered thus – as a historical individual[23] – could his victory have any relevance to ourselves. For an impersonal humanity, which is an 'objective' generalization reached by the abstraction of all individual differences, sin could have no meaning. For 'objectively' sin is not sin, but a universal phenomenon to be explained – and excused – by some metaphysical defect or sundry scientific laws.

And yet Christ is also the universal man, the Man. It is perhaps inevitable that this should be regarded in some sense as an antithesis to the truth that he is, par excellence, the Individual. Yet, truly considered, he is the one because he is the other. The universal is quite different from the general. The general is something 'objective': the universal is 'infinite subjectivity'. The universal man is he who related himself to God entirely as 'subject', he who ever stands in that complete and perfect 'I–Thou'-relation in which man is called to exist by the word of God addressed to him in creation. The universal man is the complete 'individual'. He is universal, not in the sense that he is not a particular, but because as a particular he stands where all must stand. He is the type of humanity in that he as an 'individual' does what every man must as an 'individual' himself do.

From the point of view of redemption the universality of Christ's manhood consists in the fact that he made possible this very thing for all, namely, to stand in that his 'individual' relationship to the Father. 'As many as received Him, to them gave He power to become the sons of God, even to them that believe on His name' (Jn 1:12). In the same way as the solidarity of sin was seen to be a 'subjective' solidarity, so the universality of salvation is one that presupposes freedom and faith. The truth, says Kierkegaard, if a man is to relate himself to it in the only way in which it can be the truth for him, that is, 'subjectively', must be presented, not as another's achievement for his admiration, but as a possibility for his own appropriation, as an 'ethical *requirement*' (*Concluding Unscientific Postscript*, 320). This is just what the kind of solidarity implied by Christ's 'impersonal' humanity denies. It asserts that, as in the case of sin, there is some 'objective' metaphysical connection. Because, it is argued, Christ transcends all individuality, therefore every individual in virtue not of his faith but of his humanity, not of grace but of nature, is found in his manhood – a sort of least common multiple of all humanity.

This false conception of solidarity in salvation is clearly revealed in Bishop Weston's treatment of the objection that the individuality of Christ's manhood does not necessarily exclude the race from redemption. He points out that the social and corporate nature of human existence has provided no evidence historically that the inspiration of the saint or the genius is capable automatically of raising the mass of the people. The assumption here is that, in the case of Christ, this necessary exaltation of the whole human race has been achieved. It is parallel to the emphasis of the Eastern Church on the Incarnation rather than the Atonement. By taking an impersonal manhood upon him Christ is supposed automatically to have infused some property into the human stock. This 'medicine of immortality' is of course the exact counterpart of the idea of sin as a kind of metaphysical or biological disease. Both are equally 'objectively' conceived, and both equally a denial of freedom. Christianity knows of no necessary salvation which makes faith superfluous, no universality except one which takes account of the 'subjectivity' of truth and the need for its appropriation by man as an 'individual'. This is not meant to exclude what is usually known as an 'objective' element in the doctrine of Atonement. Christ by his work has radically altered the situation: something has been achieved outside the subject which now makes possible a reconciliation not realizable before. But the 'finished work' of the Master is eternally presented, not as an object for our admiration, or even merely for our thanksgiving, but as a possibility and requirement for our seizing. He has died, not that we should not have to die, but precisely in order that we should be able to do so; that we who by nature crucify him should by him be enabled to hang with him on the Tree. Nor is this insistence upon the necessity for the 'subjectivity' of the 'individual' an advocacy of a mere individualistic and subjectivist piety which isolates from the nexus of society. There is an equally real solidarity for good as for evil, and a man cannot be saved apart from the body. It is disastrous to regard this as something parallel to the 'objective' solidarity of the masses which extinguishes individual responsibility. The solidarity of the Church is that of the 'We', not the 'They' (cf. Berdyaev, *Solitude and Society*, 107–8).

A restatement of the soteriological requirements in properly personal terms has shown that no such kind of universality is required of the Saviour as would demand a doctrine of his 'impersonal' humanity. Rather, as we saw in the passage of Scott Holland's quoted earlier, universality in this sphere is attained precisely at the point of most intense individuality.

With this we must leave the question of the person of Christ. But this chapter, apart from its connection with questions which arise later, has been introduced to point to the sort of difference which the application of a thorough-going definition of personality in terms of relation can make to the treatment of problems rendered intractable by the 'classical' presuppositions. It is the possibility of such a reopening of this and other problems we shall indicate which reinforces the conviction that the recent understanding of the significance of the 'Thou' may prove to represent the most positive and pregnant discovery of modern philosophy.

Part Two

Chapter Nine

THE DIVINE EXISTENCE-IN-LOVE

In the course of our argument up to this point we have touched upon the divine personality only in so far as it has pressed itself upon our attention as a necessary factor for the understanding of the nature of man. Human nature, we found, points away from itself to a centre outside it. Man is only one pole of a relationship, and that not the primal determinative pole. The principle of his being lies outside him: he is essentially one who is called into being by Another, and whose life from beginning to end is a *responsive* existence. His being, as constituted by his relationships, cannot be explained wholly in terms of his meeting with his finite environment of things and persons. Ever pressing upon him through these contacts is the word of another 'Thou', who, as the absolute ground of his existence, requires of him a response of total obedience, at the same time as it approves itself the final authentication of his life's meaning.

The point has now been reached at which we may direct the focus of our attention to this other pole of the divine-human encounter. We may not seek to move *outside* this relationship: all we know of God is given within its context. No more than we can know man in the solitariness of his 'I-existence' can we speak of a '*Gott an Sich*'. Each is only given in relationship to the other. As Brunner reminds us, the Bible 'always speaks of God as the God who approaches man [*Gott-zum-Menschen-hin*] and of man as the man who comes from God [*Menschen-von-Gott-her*]' (*The Divine-Human Encounter*, 31). It is with their mutual relationship, rather than with either in isolation, that the Scriptures deal. But as long as we never lose sight of the context within which alone we may legitimately work, it is both possible and necessary that, like bridge-builders, we should start from both ends of the relationship. That does not mean that we should build from one side on the foundation of a purely 'natural' examination of human experience and on the other bank from the divine 'revelation' in Scripture. If we do this the two spans will never meet. Rather we must start from the revelation in Christ where the junction is an accomplished fact, and then proceed to analyse or break up this *given* unity. Only thus will it be possible to formulate doctrines of God and man which will be in proper 'correspondence'.

Having on this principle delineated the human arm of the bridge as it reaches out to meet what comes from the other side, can we determine more closely the form of divine Being to which the responsive 'Thou' existence of man corresponds?

The final and most adequate description of this Being to which the Bible attains is the utterly simple and profound statement that 'God IS Love'. Comprehended in these monosyllables is the whole of the Hebraic conception of the one whose Being *is* a completely personal relationship to every single part of creation, who has no other existence except existence in a relation of this quality, and whose every attribute is but a way of working of a single, infinite, eternal, holy and omnipotent love. For the Bible, the attributes of God are not a sum of separable qualities definable in terms of themselves (e.g., power, knowledge, goodness, etc.) and inhering in a neutral and undifferentiated 'substance' of pure being. They are characterizations of a relation whose peculiar quality is that of the individuating 'I–Thou' relationship of perfect love. Love is not just one attribute among many; it is not even *primus inter pares* (first among equals). As Kierkegaard expresses it: 'Whereas all the other qualities that are attributed to God are adjectival, "love" alone is a substantive' (*The Journals*, ET, Entry 274). Everything else is a characterization of this love, a description of its modes of working. Thus, infinity in God *means* the utter unfathomability of this divine love; eternity, the denial that God has been or ever could be anything other than he who lives with an everlasting love; omnipotence is the omnicompetence of this love to attain its every purpose, its quality being strictly defined in terms of these ends; omniscience is nothing but 'the loving wisdom of our God' who 'overknows' all with an infinitely tender concern; his holiness and 'will to Lordship' (Brunner) are simply the expression of the absolute transcendence of this love over sinful and derived human existence.

So it would be possible to go on. But this is the theme which will be expounded and substantiated throughout the rest of this second part. By reference to some particular attributes of God we shall be seeking to describe ever more closely the form of the peculiarly 'personal' existence which marks and makes the divine Being. But in the process we shall find ourselves at the same time defining ever more sharply the difference between this, the Hebraic, approach and another, the Hellenic, which stands in large measure in direct antithesis to it. In this conflict there will be worked out, in starker contrast, the same opposition between what we met before as the 'classical' and relational theories of the nature of personality.

For the 'Hellenic' approach makes use of exactly the same presuppositions in determining the nature of the divine as does the 'classical' theory in defining the human. This approach to Theology always goes hand in hand with that conception of personality which stems from Boethius. Both work with the idea of 'substance' as their fundamental category.

In the same way the categories of the 'I–Thou' encounter have an obvious affinity with the biblical 'Hebraic' conception of the personal God. As we saw before, they have been elaborated by men who stand within the biblical tradition and for whom the distinctively personal address of the divine, together with the valuation it places on human personality, are part of the stuff of existence. This does not mean that the 'existential' 'I–Thou' philosophy is *the* Christian philosophy, in the same way as the Thomists would claim it for that of their master. There can be no one system of thought with which the Faith stands or falls. It is not that these philosophical categories are necessary to the expression of Christian truth: it is rather that they are valuable to theology because they are in fact already biblical in their inspiration and presuppositions. 'I would feel obliged to reverse Heim's statement', writes Brunner,

> that 'every theology which believes in a personal God applies ontological presuppositions to the relation between God and man', and to say: 'every philosophy of the present day which deals with the "I–Thou" relation uses, perhaps without being aware of the fact, Christian categories, while thinking that they are using purely rational philosophical ideas'. (*Man in Revolt*, 543–4)

At any rate it is undeniable that

> it was as a Christian philosopher that Kierkegaard created the 'Existential' philosophy, it was as a Christian thinker that Ebner discovered the theme of the 'I–Thou' – no Greek, however great a genius, would have ever understood such a theme – it was as a Biblical thinker that Martin Buber recognised the significance of the contrasts between 'I' and 'It', 'I' and 'Thou'. It is as a Christian thinker that Karl Heim has established his theory of dimensions which in essentials is simply the attempt to create a Christian ontology. (ibid., 546; cf. *The Divine-Human Encounter*, 57)

Reduced to its simplest terms, the essential difference of approach between the Hellenic and Hebraic is the difference between being and will. For the Greek mind the fundamental fact of the universe, the ultimate reality for which all philosophy is the search, is the fact of being, in all the purity of its immutable perfection and timeless eternity. Pure being is that which is removed *toto caelo* from all change and decay, coming into being and ceasing to be. Perfection rather than personality is its chief attribute; and perfection, in its turn, is always defined in terms of fullness of being. Imperfection, 'potentiality' and evil represent absence and deficiency of being. The *ens perfectissimum* [that which is most perfect] is by definition the *ens realissimum* [that which is most real]. Among the attributes of perfection or being are many which, in the created order, are indeed only predicable of persons. But the ascription of personality to the ultimate reality, even in the sense of mere attribution of personal qualities, is always regarded by the Hellenic mind as fraught with anthropomorphic dangers. In consequence, God is not conceived as someone who can only be known in the way we know persons. On the contrary, the road to the knowledge of God is not the way of 'meeting' and of personal encounter. True γνῶσις (knowledge) is always conceived, not in ethical terms, but in the aesthetic categories of artistic and mystical contemplation.

For the Hebrews, in contrast, the last as well as the first reality was a personal will, the subject of effective action. To the Greek, personality in God was a derivative and rather doubtful inference from his perfection. For the Jew, perfection was always an attribute of personal will (Rom. 12:2). God is essentially the one who does things, who 'works' (Jn 5:17), whose presence is to be *felt*, in history, decisively and inescapably. The assertion of God's ineffectiveness is, for the Old Testament, equivalent to the denial of his existence. 'The decisive word-form in the language of the Bible is not the substantive, as in Greek, but the verb, the word of action. The thought of the Bible is not substantival, neuter and abstract, but verbal, historical and personal' (Brunner, *The Divine-Human Encounter*, 32). This does not mean that the Hebrew mind did not think of God as subject: his 'name' is essentially the 'I AM THAT I AM'. But he is always the subject in action. The Original Word, says Ebner, is 'The verb and the personal pronoun in one' (*Das Wort und die geistigen Realitäten*, 85). This verb is not purely 'intransitive', *ziellos*. It has its *Ziel* in the 'Thou' to which it 'goes across' (ibid., 158): to 'be' is to establish a relation. And for this reason, it is not merely 'reflexive', simply the 'I am I' of the self-existent Absolute. The original sentence (*Satz*) is the 'I am' of the '*Sich-in-Beziehung-Setzen zum Du*' [putting oneself in relationship with the Thou] (ibid., 147). The quality of the divine Being as the Hebraic mind conceives it is made quite clear: the 'I AM' does not describe a timeless essence which has no reference to temporal will. The very essence itself *is* the temporal will: 'I AM hath sent thee' is the immediate sequel (Ex. 3:14). Such predication of particularizing historical inference on the part of the eternal essence of God would to the Greek mind be merely foolish and perverse. But the assertion that this very essence ('I AM' and not merely 'I') is the subject of dynamic, historical action defines the divine Being from the beginning in terms of will. Do you wish to know, the Hebrew asks, what God is like as he is in himself? Then look at him in action, in revelation. For he has no other kind of existence than the existence of 'I' in relation to 'Thou'.

The divine perfection is for the Jew essentially dynamic rather than static.

> The Hebrew mind does not dwell on the *Being* of God, but rather upon His *Activity*; God cannot be known to us in His inner being, but only in so far as He reveals Himself to us by His own activity. δύναμις, which means both latent capability of action and also power in action, represents the Being of God in His dynamic aspect, that is, in the only aspect in which we can know Him. God is pure δύνασθαι [being able to do], and only through His δύναμις [power] manifested in its effects, 'The things that are made', do we have knowledge of His 'everlasting power and divinity' (Rom 1:19f.). God is He of Whom alone it may with propriety be said: πάντα δυνατά [all things are possible] (Mk 10:27). All δύναμις is derived or delegated from God, its only source. Hence it is possible to use δύναμις as a synonym for God, and so indeed we find it used (as a reverential circumlocution) in Jesus's reply to the high priest: 'Ye shall see the Son of Man sitting ἐκ δεξίων τῆς δυνάμεως [on the right hand of power] (Mk 14:62, Mt 26:64; *cf.* Lk 22:69 and Acts 7:55f.)'. (A. Richardson, *The Miracle Stories of the Gospels*, 1941, 5)

In consequence of this his nature, God is to be known, not in aesthetic or intellectual contemplation, but in personal encounter. Unlike the *ens perfectissimum* of the Greek, he does not allow himself simply to be looked at: he intervenes – in a masterful way, in a way that demands a response from the subject. He confronts man in the narrow defile of decision – '*die andere nicht mißzuverstehende Person*' [the other person who is not to be misunderstood] (Grisebach, *Gegenwart*, 148). For the Hellenic mind, the type of all knowledge of God is *vision*. Now the act of seeing is that which we may engage upon if we have the will to look in the right direction, to open our eyes and concentrate our attention. It symbolizes what is essentially a human turning to, and search for, the divine. By the Hebrew, in contrast, the organ of spiritual perception is likened rather to the ear – the knowledge of God is the *hearing* of a word addressed. The decisive act is made not by man but by God. His is the initiative, in a revelation with authority and power. He speaks, and we cannot wholly avoid hearing. Unlike our seeing, our hearing is not dependent upon the direction in which we turn our heads, nor have we been provided with lids to our ears (cf. Farmer, *The Servant of the Word*, 50). To some degree we have to hear, though we can greatly affect the quality of reception. The call to man is always to listen purposively, to listen into decision, to obey (*ὑπ-ακούειν, ob-oedire*). The secret of the knowledge of God is to be sensitive to his touch, to hearken to his voice, to be obedient to the heavenly vision. He that doeth the will shall know of the doctrine (Jn 7:17), and the pure in heart that shall see God (Mt. 5:8).

This preliminary delineation of the familiar difference between the Hellenic and Hebraic approaches will be exemplified and expanded in what follows. Before passing to a consideration of particular attributes, however, we may look more generally at the question of the relation between nature (or being) and will in God. This is the heart of the issue between Greek and Jew, and the two attitudes can be distinguished by the primacy they give to the one or the other. Greek thought is essentially *onto*logical – 'being' is its fundamental category, and everything else, power included, is defined in terms of it. The Hebraic approach, in contrast, is characteristically *thelemato*logical (to use a word made current by the late Professor Quick). All attributes here are qualities of will, and 'being' itself is always being-in-action, existence-in-decision.

The distinction between nature and will is one that derives from the realm of human psychology. Even in this sphere it is more convenient than accurate, and if pressed too seriously is clearly dangerous. In its place, however, it is useful, as pointing to the real, though relative, distinction between (a) that part of a man's behaviour which is governed by the fact that he is a human being in general and this or that individual in particular – by the fact, that is, that he is subject to the universal conditions of human historical existence and also to the influences of heredity and environment which have shaped the particular personality that he is –; and (b) that element in conscious activity which seems at any rate to be due to the free and deliberate choice of the individual, a choice which, though conditioned by what a man is, is ultimately determined rather by what a man thinks he or his environment ought to be.

Now it would be agreed by all who have given the matter any serious thought that such a distinction, though valid of human affairs, cannot be predicated of God. Indeed, by its very nature it can only apply to finite beings. For the essence of the distinction is between those things which are under the direct control of the will of the subject and those things which he simply has to accept. The latter form, indeed, to some extent, raw material for his voluntary manipulation. But their shape and existence are, ultimately, simply 'given' and are determined by forces outside his control. And that there should be anything outside the control of God, or that his will should be determined in any way by something external to himself, must be denied by all who have an interest in the existence of a transcendent deity. Any distinction therefore between the divine nature and the divine will must, it seems, be ultimately meaningless. And this view has commanded the universal consent of Christian theologians. Thus, to take instances from quite different ages and traditions, for St Thomas '*velle divinum est ejus esse*' [the divine will is God's own existence] (*S.T.* I, 19, ii),[24] and Brunner defines God as 'the One whose will is identical with Himself' (*The Mediator*, 1937, 460. Cf. *The Divine-Human Encounter*, 101–2).

Nevertheless, a distinction between nature and will in God has made its appearance at all stages and in all types of Christian theology. God's will is not contrasted with something whose ground of determination is external to him. it is agreed that the divine will can issue from, and be determined by, nothing outside the divine being itself. But a distinction is drawn between God's absolute and eternal nature as he is in and for himself and those acts by which he relates himself to the finite and temporal.

In its most general form this distinction is expressed in the statement that the existence of the world is entirely contingent. There is *no* sense in which creation can be said to have been necessary. Not only was God's hand in no way forced from without, but the act was not grounded in any essential necessity of his being. There is no sense in which he *had* to create or in which he *needs* the world. In the words of a recent writer, 'creation, so far from being what might reasonably be expected of God, is the most incalculable and, we might even say, superfluous expression of the complete freedom and limitless fecundity of self-existent Being' (E. L. Mascall, *He Who Is*, 1943, 110). This idea is only stated in another way by Barth when he speaks of the complete 'freedom' of God over creation (*The Doctrine of the Word of God*, 426). So Brunner: 'The world is . . . not the necessary correlate of God, but it is the contingent creation of His will' (*The Mediator*, 285). To create is an act which he might just as well not have done, though, having done it, he is not able to undo it, since he cannot be mutable in purpose. St Thomas expresses the matter by saying that God has 'free will', and does not therefore will all things necessarily; not, that is to say, with any absolute necessity – for he could perfectly well exist without anything besides himself. But the divine will is necessary 'by supposition', in that if he wills anything, then it could not not be (*S.T.* I, 19, iii). Expressed in terms of the distinction between nature and will he makes the same point elsewhere by saying that, whereas creation is an act of God's will, 'the Father begot the Son, not by will, but by nature' (I, 41, ii). What is eternal and necessary is referred to the divine nature: what is concerned with God's relation to the temporal and contingent is attributed to his will.

What is precisely the same distinction appears in theological discussion not only of God's action upon creation but also of creation's action upon him. God is essentially and eternally impassible. But the idea of a voluntary passibility has commended itself to thinkers at all times. 'Impassible by nature, passible by will' was the solution of the problem posed by the Incarnation that approved itself to many of the Fathers (cf. especially, the account of a treatise by Gregory Thaumaturgus in J. K. Mozley's *Impassibility of God*, 1926, 63–72). Since then this principle of interpretation has been greatly extended. All forms of 'kenotic' Christology are based on the idea of the validity of a *voluntary* limitation of the divine. Indeed, it is safe to say that every theory of the Incarnation acceptable to English theologians today, including those who would disavow the title of 'kenotic', involves the notion that what is *essentially* unlimited became *voluntarily* confined to severe limitations in Christ's human life and death. Indeed the only alternative presented is some form of Cyrilline Christology, which leads inevitably in the end to Docetism. However it is disguised, according to this theory the situation on the Cross must be (to put it crudely) that the divine nature in Christ steps back to watch the human suffer and die. Only if the Infinite is in a real sense limited can it itself be the subject of these constricting experiences.

Moreover, the idea of voluntary passibility or divine self-limitation receives an application far outside the limits of the Incarnation. The very act of creation, and in particular the creation of free human agents, is seen to involve a very real modification of the divine omnipotence. The freedom and independence of man over against God, though delegated and limited, is something real even for God himself. It is not something which, once given, he can rescind or override. He has willed to make the fulfilment of his purpose dependent upon our co-operation: where faith is not present he can do no mighty works. Though utterly self-sufficient in his own nature, he has yet willed that even the smallest action on our part may contribute '*ad majorem Dei gloriam*' (to the greater glory of God). The divine joy, in essence infinite, is yet increased by one sinner that repenteth: for he has willed precisely to have it so. And such is the self-imposed limitation of omnipotence, that, except on the hypothesis of universalism, there is no guarantee that all, or even any, will in fact repent.

Now it cannot be denied that this distinction between what God is and what he wills has proved a useful theological device. It has been an effective way of securing the truth of his absolute transcendence over the world. By attributing creation, not to any necessity of his being, but to an act of will, Christian theology has been able to avoid that fatal correlation of God and the world which would make the Creator as dependent on his creation as creation is on him. Again, by the concept of a voluntary possibility or self-limitation, the essential omnipotence and infinitude of God has been preserved in a way which leaves room both for a respect for human freedom and for that descent into the finite of which the Bible speaks.

Pragmatically, then, the distinction has been fruitful. But this in itself does not make it true. Methodological value is no guarantee of metaphysical validity. A division between the divine nature and the divine will may be useful for our thinking, but have we any grounds for asserting that it corresponds to anything real in God? It is agreed on all hands that God's will can be determined by nothing external to himself. Its ground is therefore to be sought solely in the divine nature. The mutual relation of the nature and the will is here at issue. The very existence of a distinction between them implies that for those who make it this connection is not one of necessity. That is to say, because God is what he is, there is no *necessity* that he should do the particular things that he has in fact done – for example, create the world or enter it by incarnation. The question is, first, what are the grounds for denying this necessity? and secondly, if the connection is contingent, what governs the contingency? In other words – to take one example which is as good as another – why did God create if there was no necessity that he should?

We are here in a tract of thought in which the boundaries of meaningful statement are soon reached. An ultimate agnosticism must overshadow all our thinking. Indeed the whole idea of necessary being, though it might appear to be that about which we could have the greatest certainty, is in fact only a confession of ignorance. It is what Kant called a *Grenzbegriff* – a concept upon which the mind falls back, not because it has evidence for it, but simply to avoid the infinite regress to which the very lack of evidence would otherwise force it. The essence of what is necessary is that it could not have been otherwise. By the very finitude of our knowledge we are precluded from ever being able to say this of anything which has existence. For the purposes of thinking we may, as Kant said, have to act 'as if' this limiting concept had reality. But only as an act of religious faith does the assertion that God's being is absolute or necessary have any positive significance.

But once this act of faith has been made – one to which all religion is impelled – and once the further act of faith, to which the Bible commits us, has also been made – namely, that the universe is directly dependent for its existence on God alone – then the question we have to ask is different. We do not start from the fact of contingency and then enquire of every stage in the regress, can we say that it could not have been otherwise? If we start from that end we are bound to conclude that the whole universe possesses only contingent existence. Rather we start from God, and ask, have we any evidence that he might have made the universe otherwise, or that he might not have made it at all? Given the fact that the world is solely the expression of his will, are we in a position to say that that will is anything but the necessary expression of his nature? If we start from contingent being we shall never reach necessary being as a conclusion of reasoning: Kant has surely spoken the last word here at least. But if we start from necessary being (as religion must), is it then possible to produce evidence to show that all being is not related to it necessarily?

Leibniz declared this to be 'the best of all possible worlds'. This is purely a statement of faith: it is quite incapable of logical demonstration. But, for faith, it must be true, in the sense that he meant it. Further, a religion which attributes creation solely to the will of a perfectly good God must maintain that it is better that there should have been a world rather than no world at all. But really the whole notion of possibility is here out of place. If any other world or no world would have been inferior to the world as we know it, then these alternatives were not possibilities for a perfectly good being at all. We may say that, God being what he is, that and how the world exists could not have otherwise. Both are the necessary result of his nature. Moreover, if, with Christianity, we believe God's nature to be essentially one of love, then we can go still further. The necessity of the world is deducible not merely a posteriori, from its existence combined with the faith that it is the creation of a perfectly good being. We can also say that the essential nature of love is to be self-diffusive, to exist only in relation to an 'other' on whom it can pour itself out. God, that is to say, being love, *had* to create.

It is at this point that the challenge comes. We are told (a) that according to Christian doctrine the essential self-diffusiveness of love finds its expression within the Godhead itself in the 'I–Thou' relationships of the Persons of the Trinity; and (b) that the existence of the world, so far from being necessitated by the loving nature of God, is thereby revealed as utterly contingent. Creation is a pure act of love just because it is so 'unnecessary' to God, so 'superfluous' from the point of view of the divine glory. 'O generous love!' is the only human response to this marvel of gratuitous expense.

Before going further it will be well to clear up a confusion which is liable to cause trouble. This consists in the assumption that those who would ground creation, and all that it has involved, in a necessity of the divine Being thereby claim to show that it is something 'which might reasonably be expected of God'. The implication is that, even though they might not undertake to predict the divine action in advance, they are yet prepared to demonstrate after the event that it was inevitable, or at least 'only natural'.

Nothing could be more false. As we have said, from the human point of view there is nothing of which we can say that it could not have been otherwise. Least of all in the special acts of divine revelation can we detect inevitability or obviousness. To put it crudely, the Incarnation remains something 'we should never have thought of'. After 2,000 years it continues to shatter all our canons of what it is reasonable to expect. We can but confess in thankful adoration 'O wisest love!'. Or, again, to say that God was constrained by an internal necessity to create in no way permits us to presume upon an assumption that he needs us or to contemplate generosity of the divine love. Rather, if anything, it should increase our awe. For we see, this was not a love which might have been perfectly content not to have created or have anything to do with us, but one which was such that it could never rest within itself, but had by its very nature to expend itself on the unworthy in careless prodigality, relying on nothing in return.

After this excursus, we may now take up the two demurrers raised above. The first was to the effect that the natural self-effusiveness of love finds its expression in God within the divine Being itself. This argument is a variant of the use of the doctrine of the Trinity to answer the objection that, since a person cannot be conceived as existing except in relation to other persons, God could not exist without us. It is not proposed to enter into the validity of this answer here (see Ch. 16). It may be said in passing (a) that the existence within the Godhead of the structure of the 'I–Thou' relationship which love presupposes demands an interpretation of the Trinity far more tritheistic than the historic doctrine can allow; and (b) that no satisfactory argument has yet been produced to show the necessity for three Persons, or even, given the existence of the Third Person, how he can be fitted into the essentially dual structure of the 'I–Thou' relation.

To substantiate these statements would take us far beyond the scope of our present intentions. Fortunately, however, our argument does not seriously depend on their validity. For even if the doctrine of the Trinity provides an adequate account of the self-existence and self-effusion of the divine love, we are still faced with the question of the relation of this internal love to that which God expends towards creation. Why, if the relations which exist within God himself provide for the complete satisfaction of his nature of love, did he in fact go beyond himself? May it possibly be that there are depths of the divine love which can secure expression only when its object is *not* God? Certainly, a love which gives itself for sinners and enemies is something at least very different from anything that is possible when the Other must by his very nature return that love to perfection. And directly there is the slightest suggestion of an element in the divine Being which cannot find fulfilment except by a going out from himself, then creation is once more grounded in a need or necessity of God's nature, and the introduction of the doctrine of the Trinity (or of any tritheistic or ditheistic variant upon it) solves nothing.

Thus we are brought to the second point raised above. If the existence of the world is not to be traced to a necessity of God's nature, what is the alternative? The answer given is simply that it has no ground. Indeed there is no option. For if it is not grounded in God's nature, then we cannot look for any ground outside it – as though some external stimulus caused God to create. We should not be misled by St Thomas's statement that 'a reason of the divine will can be assigned', namely, his goodness, to which everything else is the means (*S.c.G.*, I, 86). This tells us nothing. For when we ask why creation should be necessary for the promotion of the divine goodness, we are told that in fact it is not. 'For the divine goodness neither depends on the perfection' (nor, we may add, the existence) 'of the universe nor gains anything from it.' This groundlessness of the universe, however, so far from being a source of embarrassment to its advocates, is welcomed.

> We shall never attain [writes E. L. Mascall in the passage already quoted] to that humility and wonder which are essential to the true practice of Christianity unless we realise that creation, so far from being what might reasonably be expected of God, is the most incalculable and, we might even say, superfluous expression of the complete freedom and limitless fecundity of self-existent Being.

But this cannot be allowed to pass. True humility necessitates nothing of the kind, as we have already tried to show. Indeed, it is not easy to see how the glory of God is really advanced by an argument which would require of him a purposelessness and irrationality only predicable of a human being long since confined within the walls of an asylum. It is the unsearchable riches of the divine purpose which prompt the reticence of worship, not the absence of any purpose whatsoever. In the conception of a will in God grounded in no necessity of his nature we see retained in theology that disastrous notion of a completely indeterminate *liberum arbitrium* [free will], which has with such difficulty been expelled from the field of human psychology. Complete indeterminacy is complete irrationality and complete nonsense. To call this 'complete freedom and limitless fecundity' the distinguishing sign of true love is to empty a good word of all meaning. The great value for philosophy of the doctrine of creation is that it gives a reason for the existence of the universe by grounding it wholly in a divine purpose. But if, in turn, this will is based in no necessity of the divine nature, then this value is nullified. That in which the ultimate reason for things is sought turns out to be an act of complete arbitrariness. Having been led thus far along the road the philosopher might as well turn round and go home.

It will perhaps serve to sum up what has been said as well as to introduce what follows if we ask in what sense it can be asserted that God needs the world. That there is a sense is involved in the claim that the divine will in creation is grounded in a necessity of his nature. Indeed it is just this implication which forms the motive of those who deny such a connection. That there can be any need on the part of God for anything outside himself seems to them a proposition so self-evidently false as necessarily to rule out any view which involves it. For if God really needs such a thing in order to be what he is, then he is as entirely dependent upon it as it is upon him. And this would be a complete denial of his infinitude and transcendence.

As stated, the argument is conclusive. But there is a hidden assumption in its formulation which must be questioned. It is concealed in the words 'in order to be what he is'. This assumes that the answer to the question, why did God create? is to be formulated in terms of a final clause – 'in order that he might satisfy some need, or become what it was in his nature to be'. In other words, God needed the world in order to be completely himself.

But the truly Christian, and only legitimate, argument is not that God needs the world 'in order to be what he is', but, simply, 'because he is what he is'. That is to say that the answer to the question, why did God create? is not a final but a consecutive clause. The world represents, not a filling up of something lacking in the being of God, but the overflow of the divine plenitude. Creation is grounded in a necessity of God's nature since love *must* communicate itself. St Thomas, indeed, argues that 'if natural things, in so far as they are perfect, communicate their good to others, much more does it appertain to the Divine Will to communicate by likeness its own good to others, as much as possible' (*S. T.*, I, 19, ii). But he has no conception of this self-communication as more than an optional extra for love. However, if we are to declare it to be necessary to the idea of love, we cannot reiterate too strongly that it is *because* it *is* love, rather than *in order to be love*, that it is self-communicative. Love is not any more love because it gives itself: it is simply thereby revealing itself for what it is. If it did not do so then it would not be love. There is literally a whole world of difference in this distinction between the final and consecutive clauses. Every argument here must begin 'God so loved, that . . .' his nature being what it is, his will could not have been anything different. That God created is simply an analytical proposition. It follows with necessity from what he is: it does not tell us any new thing about him, which might or might not have happened. If he had not always been a Creator-God, he could never have been a personal God.

There is no suggestion here of a mutual dependence between Creator and creature. There is no sense whatever in which we can say that God's existence depends on ours. Ultimately we all have to recognize that 'We are as clay in the hands of the Potter, and our welfare is to know it' (W. Temple, *Nature, Man and God*, 402). Our freedom is his *service* – not the knowledge that we satisfy a need of the divine nature. That would be blasphemy. God has no necessities that we can fill up, 'neither is He served by men's hands, as though He needed anything' (Acts 17:25). That is a pagan idea, and it is fitting that it should have been exposed at Athens. For was it not also one of their own poets who had represented the hands of the gods being forced by the cessation of the sacrifices on which they depended (Aristophanes, *The Birds*)?

And yet God does require the service of men's hands; he is not content to make or treat us as clay. Love finds its full expression only in a relation with beings who are themselves capable of returning it. Love's context is the reciprocity of the personal 'I–Thou' relationship. God needs other 'Thous' with an independence freely to give back what he freely gives. This is not because he lacks anything: if it is not returned he is not any the less love. ἀγάπη [love, charity] 'never fails', nor is in any way minished, if no response is forthcoming. But, nevertheless, it desires a response, and must do so from its very nature. There is thus a need in the very heart of God: yet not such as implies an imperfection, as the Greeks thought all desire must. God has made us for himself, and his heart is restless till we find our rest in him. Yet his restlessness does not indicate any lack in himself: it is entirely other-regarding. He is 'full of kind concern' (C. Wesley), not for his own welfare, but for those with whose lives as love he has identified himself. For love is such that its only joy is shared joy. It is the joy of perfect communion, and it is increased by every sinner that repenteth. And its very precondition is that the other may *freely* sin and must *freely* repent. It is thus that we know God wills it to be. And he wills it thus simply because he is what he is: being love he could do no other. It is not as though he had perfect bliss in solitude in virtue of his own nature, and then willed to make this bliss in some degree dependent upon our response. Just because it is what it is, love can only know a bliss which is bound up with the lives of others. Its fullest joy consists in the untrammelled intercourse of personal communion, for which it makes itself dependent on a response beyond its own control. But it may rejoice too in the preparations of the conditions which make this possible, and even in the suffering undertaken to win the sinner to it. If God is really love, he can have no joy outside his dealings with creation.

There is no thought here of equating 'creation' simply with ourselves, or even with the whole universe we know. But even so this must seem a shocking and presumptuous statement. But it is in fact no anthropomorphic limitation of the divine Being. It is simply one of the implications of what it means for God to be love. Creation is no *jeu d'ésprit*, which the deity could have dispensed with if he had chosen. It means everything to him if it means anything. Love just cannot abide alone. God had to create, and had, as it were, to put his whole self into it. If he had kept something back to enjoy to himself, he could not have been perfect love. For love could find no joy in that. He has willed to put everything into his relations with his creatures, to link his whole existence irrevocably with theirs, confident in the omnipotence of his love. And he has willed it, because, being what he is, he could do no other. That is what is meant by saying that the world is necessary to God, that it is a necessary consequence of his nature. This is certainly not something which we could 'reasonably expect'. In fact the naked truth of it is something which we have the greatest difficulty in accepting: we hardly dare to believe it. A love that really is like that just takes our breath away. So far from lulling us into a self-righteous complacency, the statement that we are really necessary to God is terrifying in the infinite seriousness it places upon life. It is something which no one could possibly have believed, which no one could have had the sheer courage to believe, unless it had been revealed by God himself at the Incarnation. Even now we cannot but stutter: 'Lord, I believe: help Thou mine unbelief.'

Is this then what a serious identification of God's nature and his will means? This, and nothing less. It means that everything that has in Christian theology been ascribed to God's voluntary action – from the act of creation itself down to the appalling humiliation of the death on Calvary – is really a necessity of his being. In other words, to adopt terminology employed in discussions of the doctrine of the Trinity, there is no difference between the 'economic' and the 'essential'. We cannot 'go behind' God as he reveals himself in his relations to the created and the temporal to a God as he 'really' is 'in himself', unlimited and eternal. The distinction between the divine nature and the divine will arises just because revelation is not taken seriously enough. The divine will as revealed is not made wholly determinative of our conception of the divine nature. Rather, Christian theology has on the whole started with a conception formed by purely rationalistic methods of what God's essence must be like if it is to be divine. It has then attempted to harmonize this (*a-priori*) concept with the (*a-posteriori*) knowledge of how God acts, as it is recorded in the Bible and testified to by the experience of the Church. Since the latter did not appear to follow by any apparent inevitability from the former, the convenient distinction was formulated, by which the revealed acts were attributed to a will grounded in no necessity of the nature. What God revealed himself as having *done* was fitted as best it could be into an already existent picture of what he *was*. *Will* was subordinated to *being*, and *onto*logical rather than *thele*matological categories have dominated the formulation of Christian metaphysics.

Chapter Ten

OMNIPOTENCE: THE WEAKNESS OF GOD

In the course of the next four chapters some attempt will be made to trace out the lines along which a consistent thelematology may be elaborated, and to make clear the differences between such a 'Hebraic' view of the personality of God defined in terms of the 'Thou' relationship of love and the Hellenic ontology with its 'classical' presuppositions. In order to gain in clarity and precision, it is proposed to confine our observations in the main to two divine attributes, omnipotence and eternity. These are selected for their representative character. The relation of nature and will, as we saw, is really the same as that between God as unlimited and eternal and the same God as revealed in the limitations of the finite and historical. A study of the relation of the divine power to the constrictions of its manifestation, and of the divine eternity to the temporal and mutable, will therefore afford a good field for the testing of the position put forward in the last chapter.

The idea of omnipotence, in addition, has a theological history which gives it a peculiar interest for the study of the interplay between the Hebraic and Hellenic elements in Christianity with which we are concerned. But before we turn to that history, it may be well to state in starkest form the nature of the contrast between the two conceptions of divine power with which we shall be dealing, and to indicate in advance the kind of position we shall seek to defend.

On the one hand, there is the Pauline affirmation, which, one would think, must determine the Christian understanding, namely, that to them that are called it is 'Christ crucified' who is 'the power of God and the wisdom of God' (1 Cor. 1:23–4). By all natural standards the divine omnipotence and omniscience seem, and must seem, weakness and foolishness. Here the Christian must begin whenever he seeks to know what God is really like – at the Cross. Here, as in all things, it is the final clue to the understanding of the mysteries of the divine nature. Yet what Christian metaphysic has in fact started here? On the contrary, the wisdom of Greece has been too much for the foolishness of the preaching. The attributes concerned have been defined without reference to the Cross, in terms of an infinity of potency and knowledge which has no place within it for the total constriction of both which Calvary presents. The fact that the Cross, for such a definition, remains a foolishness and a stumbling block shows that it can claim no place in a *Christian* philosophy. That at least is the contrast and that the conclusion which is forced upon us, and which the remainer of this chapter will be concerned to explain and sustain.

Turning then to the idea of omnipotence, we find that *παντοκράτωρ* [ruler of all] is a word which in origin is derived from a conception of God formulated in thelematological categories. It is the description of a sovereign will governing and controlling everything by the word of its power. It is a term coined on the analogy of the word *κοσμοκράτωρ* [ruler of the world] (C. H. Dodd, *The Bible and the Greeks*, 19); and its immediate reference is to other possible 'powers' or *δυνάμεις*, whether created or uncreated. It is not a description of God as he exists *per se*, nor does it indicate a quality of the divine nature which might be deduced without reference to the world or to anything outside him. The word and the idea which it expresses is essentially Hebraic, and is descriptive of the living, creator God of the Bible. Outside the Septuagint it is virtually unknown. When it does occur, its reference is to the deities of popular religion: it forms no part of the divine *πλήρωμα* [fullness] of Greek philosophical speculation.

In the meeting of Hebraic and Hellenic in early Christian theology *παντοκράτωρ* [Almighty] found a place in the creeds as being a scriptural word and as representing an indispensable biblical idea. But it did not come naturally to the Greek mind, which preferred negative expressions for the divine attributes – *ἄπειρος* [infinite], *ἀπαθής* [not experiencing/without emotion], *ἄτρεπτος* [unchangeable], *ἀναλλοίωτος* [unchangeable] etc. It is significant that the word *παντοκράτωρ* receives no mention in G. L. Prestige's *God in Patristic Thought*, 1936. Nor was it strangeness merely verbal. The term presupposes a view of the divine nature very different from the static, ontological conception lying behind the other expressions. The inherent tension, here as elsewhere in Patristic theology between the Hebraic and the Hellenic, was never resolved by the Fathers themselves. It was left to St Thomas, aided by the translation of *παντοκράτωρ* to *omnipotens*, to absorb the idea of omnipotence into the prevailing Hellenic ontology. This he did by making power a function, not of 'will' but of 'being'. 'God does things', he wrote, 'because He wills to do so; yet the power to do them does not come from His Will, but from His Nature' (*S. T.*, I, 25, V).

The fundamental thing which can be said about God, according to St Thomas, is that he is *Actus Purus*. He is that in which every possibility of being is realized, in whom there is no potentiality at all.[25] Power is a function of being. It is only that which is itself *in actu* which can initiate any change. *Potentia* is the state of complete passivity. It is always liable to change but never to the cause of it. It is only by being acted upon from without by something which is itself *in actu* that it can be brought to actuality. The cause of transition must itself already contain within it the state of being present in perfection. He is, therefore, the unmoved cause of all things. The exclusion of any *potentia* from his nature means that there is nothing in respect of which he can or needs to be acted upon. Just as for St Thomas goodness is a property of being (since evil is essentially a lack of some perfection, an absence of 'being'), so too is omnipotence. To say that God is *Actus Purus* and to say that his power is unlimited is one and the same thing. Whether limitation is conceived as imposed from without or is self-appointed is irrelevant. In either case it would indicate an absence of some perfection, a denial of pure actuality. Thomism is quite consistent in refusing to attribute passibility to God in any sense. He cannot be acted upon even voluntarily. Indeed the whole idea of self-limitation is impossible for this scheme of thought. God cannot contradict his own nature. He can no more will to be acted upon than he can will to be evil. For both indicate the absence of some plenitude of being in him, the lack of some perfection. Both are a denial of his very essence as *Actus Purus*.[26]

St Thomas's synthesis of Aristotle and the Bible was such that, as far as what might be known of God by reason alone was concerned, it represented a complete victory for the Hellenic over the Hebraic. The reduction of every attribute to a function of being at least produced a consistency lacking in earlier theologians. But the price of consistency was the elimination of the possibility of any voluntary limitation of omnipotence. As long as power was conceived as in some sense an attribute of will, omnipotence could be defined as the power to do anything, and self-limitation could be included in 'anything'. But now, any limitation, any passibility, must indicate an absence of being and an introduction of potentiality – an impossibility in one who is nothing if not Pure Actuality. The question is whether Christian theology can pay the price of this consistency.

The assumption underlying the whole Thomistic system is that it is possible to build a theology in two storeys out of two different kinds of material, and that the second will fit exactly on top of the first without any modification or adjustment being required. By the use of man's natural ratiocinative processes it is possible to reach a certain corpus of agreed truth, to which the body of knowledge provided by the further details of revelation can be simply added. St Thomas believed that, by using the twin 'ways' of negation and analogy, it was possible, merely from a study of 'the things which are made', to reckon among the *scibilia* [that which can be known] such facts as the existence, unity, simplicity, infinity, eternity, impassibility, immutability, omnipotence, omniscience, goodness and beatitude of God. On this substructure revelation was able to build a second storey without in any way having to relay the foundations. The doctrines of the Trinity and the Incarnation were further items of knowledge about a God whose essential character was already known without them. The *essentia* of the Godhead, as determined by philosophy, was in no way affected by the fact that the Bible showed it to exist in Three Persons or by the knowledge that one of these Persons was made man.

The facts of revelation here neither determine in advance nor modify in retrospect the categories in which the nature of the Godhead is described. These categories are simply extended to the interpretation and integration of the new material provided by the evidence of his will. Thus, in the example we are considering, the conception of omnipotence is determined in the first section of the *Summa Theologica* without any reference to the biblical revelation. And it is this conception – one of absolute potency limited only by the law of non-contradiction – which is henceforth all controlling. The manifestation of the power of God in Jesus Christ has therefore somehow to be fitted in to what is already determined by the demands of reason. It must be shown as an example of it: there is no question of modifying or abandoning the original conception.[27]

The fatal defect of such an approach is that the processes of natural theology yield a deity very different from that of the God and Father of our Lord Jesus Christ. It is not merely that the language of Scholastic philosophy seems totally remote from that of the New Testament. It is that it is impossible to see in St Thomas's theology the sort of God who must, could or would be found in Christ reconciling the world unto himself. There is no 'must', simply because the will of God in redemption is grounded in no necessity of his nature. There is no 'could', because the real limitation and passibility which alone could make the life and death of Christ the life and death of God are impossible under the definition of the divine nature from which he starts. And there is no 'would', because the whole process of dying to win men to reconciliation with himself is only intelligible on the assumption that the condition of human souls is to God a matter of infinite concern, and that he yearns for, and rejoices over, their return, in a way quite inexplicable in one who can have no unfulfilled purpose and whose nature can be touched, and whose joy affected, by nothing external to himself.

The consistency of the Thomistic ontology, then, by which everything, including power, is defined in terms of 'being', is only purchased at the expense of rendering unintelligible the revelation of the divine will. Its doctrine of total impassibility cannot allow that limitation of any kind could be a mode of expression of the divine infinity. Into such a doctrine – the product of a purely 'natural' rationalism – the facts of the Incarnation cannot be forced. The Bible testifies to an omnipotence of a very different kind – a power in God which is at its most effective in the weakness and impotence of a dying man. It is just because he has revealed himself in such facts as these, which are absolutely incapable of being fitted into the Hellenic ontological framework, that Christian theologians have found themselves compelled to work with the category of self-limitation. It was the sheer pressure of the brute fact of the revelation and experience that introduced the idea of a voluntary passibility in God. For the ontological scheme – with which all the earlier theology, whether Aristotelian or Platonic, worked – so far from suggesting it, to be consistent, must exclude it altogether.

If, then, a purely ontological definition of omnipotence is to be rejected on the grounds that some idea of revelation through limitation is necessary for the satisfactory interpretation of the course of events described in the Bible, what is the alternative? The usual solution has been to say (a) that God is omnipotent in the sense that he can do anything not incompatible with his own nature; and (b) that a self-limitation of his infinitude does not constitute an incompatibility. Why this latter proposition should be true does not appear to be clearly stated, but a counter-argument is produced to the effect that, if he could not limit himself, he would in fact thereby reveal a limitation. This line of thought is somewhat reminiscent of the familiar conundrum which asks whether God could tie a knot that he could not undo. But whatever else may be said about this conception of omnipotence, it is certain that it is incapable of establishing any necessary or reasonable connection between the infinity and the limitation. Why *should* the infinite limit itself? Even if by so doing it does not contradict itself, it is difficult to see self-restriction as a form of its manifestation which is either necessary or probable. This difficulty would be admitted and the argument used (which we met before) that creation is something which is indeed most thoroughly unlikely and entirely contingent.

The unsatisfactory nature of such a conclusion we have already sought to demonstrate. Without going into the matter again, we may simply record the fact that neither this last solution nor that of Aquinas can find any necessary basis in the divine nature for the revealed acts of the divine will. Why the power of God should stand revealed par excellence on the Cross is equally inexplicable on either theory. For the Kenoticist – and here this word is used in its broadest sense as indicating the upholder of any theory which makes use of the idea of a voluntary limitation against the background of a nature of unlimited power – Calvary represents, not the height of omnipotence, but precisely its severest restriction. The Cross, so far from being the power of God unto salvation, is the example of what happens when God sets his omnipotence aside. Christ is made impotent to save. For the Thomist, who can allow no increase or decrease of the divine infinitude, there can appear no compelling reason why this point in history, where, if anywhere, omnipotence is veiled, should be in fact the locus of its most characteristic manifestation.

The common factor which marks both these theories of divine omnipotence is their starting point. Their conclusions are very different; but they both begin by laying down as *a priori* a definition, into which particular acts of power revealed in human history are then fitted as well as may be. Though in the kenotic theory the revelation of the will is allowed to modify in retrospect the conception of the nature, in neither scheme is it permitted to determine it in advance. The result is that there is neither a necessary nor a particularly probable connection between the definition of the nature and the manifestations of the will. It is exactly such an *a-priori* rationalism, which declares in advance what omnipotence in God *must be* if he is to be God, that falls under condemnation as 'the wisdom of this world', a wisdom to which the Cross, so far from being the supreme manifestation of the divine power, is simply weakness and folly.

At this point we may ask whether it is not at least worth trying to start by defining omnipotence from the other end; that is, by taking the particular manifestations of God's power as the biblical writers see them, and forming our concept of omnipotence from the evidence thus provided. That is the Hebraic approach. And, ultimately, it is the only Christian approach. The other solutions stand self-condemned by their representations of the Cross as weakness and not power. It alone takes the revealed will of God seriously and makes it absolutely determine the concept of his nature. For it, there is no nature apart from nature revealed as will. Every statement about the nature is derived from knowledge of the will, and is therefore expressed, not in categories of being abstracted from and independent of, action, but in those of volition and personal encounter. The starting point here is not an analysis of Pure Being, but contact with a personal purpose. The fundamental statement is not that God is *Actus Purus* but that 'God is love'.

Now, as we approach the question of omnipotence from the evidence of revelation, the first point that strikes us is that we have no evidence for its existence at all. That indeed is the case wherever we start. St Thomas admitted that the divine power only manifested itself in finite effects (*S. T.* I, 25, ii, 2): its infinity is deduced, by the processes of analogy and negation, from the state of human finitude. Indeed, in the very nature of the case, any power which a finite mind could know as infinite would certainly not be so. It is *ex hypothesi* impossible for a mind whose range and categories are stamped with finitude to *prove* anything to be infinite. Thus, confronted by the love of God, the only thing of which a man has a direct experience is something finite – a love so great that it surpasses all his needs and aspirations. But a love which is so deep that we cannot plumb it is by no means necessarily an infinite love. Hume and Kant saw that argument could never establish the existence of anything more than a very great power as necessary to account for the world as we know it. The quality of infinitude is always something read into the facts, not deduced from them by rational argument. The ascription of infinity in all its forms is essentially a faith-judgment. Belief in omnipotence is the capacity of faith to perceive the infinite in and through the evidence of finite power which the world presents.[28]

But the finitude of power from which the Bible starts is not merely that which is constituted by the fact that the world, as limited effect, only requires a limited cause. It is also that the quality of the world is such as itself to present a limitation to the power that made it. The creation of personal wills with a freedom and independence to resist the will of the Creator sets up a real frontier for the divine power. But in the New Testament the power which forms the material for the faith-judgment of omnipotence is still more drastically circumscribed. For the Christian, the final constriction comes, not merely in the active opposition and rebellion on the part of men against God's purpose, but in the willingness of God to give himself over, nailed hand and foot, to suffer and die at the hands of those who oppose him. The Church's belief in 'One God, the Father, Almighty, Maker of heaven and earth' is precisely the faith that every degree of such voluntary limitation is a revelation of a single unvarying purpose of wisdom, goodness and power. Faith is that insight which can see in what to the natural eye is the height of folly and ineffectiveness the power and wisdom of the infinite God. Everything is the manifestation of one supreme omnipotence. But it takes more faith to detect it in long-suffering patience with a rebellious Semitic tribe than in the sweep and majesty of the starry heavens; more to discern it in a carpenter of Nazareth than in a conquering national hero; and still more to see in the death and humiliation of the Christ an act of omnipotence as unqualifiedly divine as the mighty acts whereby he quelled storm and demon and himself raised the dead.

That each of such manifestations, as revelations of a single unchanging purpose, should be equal displays of one infinite and unvarying power tells us much about the quality of this omnipotence – an omnipotence as potent in the still, small voice as in the storm and tempest, in the utter passivity of the Cross as in the Word that summoned universes to light. But the kind of omnipotence which the Bible reveals as belonging to God is not merely shown in its ability to express itself equally through any degree of limitation. It is also revealed in the varying significance which the scriptural writers would have us attach to the different manifestations as expressions of its peculiar quality. The collect which says that God declares his almighty power most chiefly in showing mercy and pity does not intend to suggest that these activities reveal a greater degree of omnipotence – indeed that is an unintelligible idea. But it does mean that such a personal ministry of forgiveness is the exercise of the divine power which is most expressive of its characteristic and peculiar quality. Similarly, it is the Crucifixion of Christ which is *the* manifestation par excellence of the power of God and the wisdom of God. This is not because these attributes are not manifested in equal degree in every other divine act, but because it is this fact above any other that is most revealing for the apprehension of the *kind* of power and wisdom which is to be found everywhere. It is this which is the key to the whole. As the Prologue of the Fourth Gospel indicates, the essential quality of the power through which all things came into being is to be understood in the light of the fact that this same power has actually appeared in human flesh. The quality of omnipotence is not to be determined by a survey of its cosmic functions, and the Incarnation then accounted for by some unexplained and inexplicable self-imposed deprivations of unlimited potency. Here, as elsewhere, for a *Christian* philosophy, the principle of interpretation of the totality is nothing more or less than 'Christ Jesus and him crucified'. It is the Incarnation that shows us that, though the other statements in the Prologue might by themselves be paralleled in many Greek sources, yet, in fact, St John is concerned *throughout* with a very different Logos. Though many other kinds of power might have made the universe, yet of only one could taking flesh be the supreme manifestation of its omnipotence. It is because here the divine power is shown as that of love and nothing else, that we are forced to the conclusion that, to adapt Gilbert to theology, it is 'love that makes the world go round'.

It is thus that we should seek to understand the relation between the manifestation of the power of God in Christ and in his total activity in the cosmos. It is a power whose quality *wherever it is expressed* is ultimately to be understood by reference to a single end, namely, the Cross. And, just because it is always the same power, its cosmic activities do not reveal an infinity which is different from, or somehow more unlimited than, its manifestation in the constriction of the death on Calvary. That of the being of God which was not incarnate during the earthly life of Jesus – that is, in traditional Trinitarian language, the Father – was in no way more infinite, more omnipotent (if the contradiction be allowed), or even infinite and omnipotent in a different sense, than God in Mary's womb or Joseph's tomb. Every divine activity is the manifestation of the same infinity in its totality. It is the manifestation, that is to say, of infinite love. There is no other kind of infinity, mathematical or otherwise, predicable of God. The cosmic activities of God over a sweep of millions of years and millions of miles are neither more nor less necessary in the divine wisdom than the events confined to that minute span of time in Palestine. And they are therefore equally expressions of his infinity and omnipotence, because they are equally expressions of his purpose of love. The accent of infinity is discoverable, not in the absence of any finite limitations – in both cases the power is working within severe boundaries set by itself. Rather it lies just in the quality of the love manifested alike through every limitation. It is a love which is infinite and everlasting because, whether in the amazing patience involved in the long stages of cosmic evolution, or in the cruellest suffering borne for human sin, it never fails, never lets go, but loves to the uttermost.

What differentiates the power of God as revealed in the fire or earthquake and as displayed in the still, small voice or in Jesus Christ is not anything in the quality of the power. The difference is determined by the kind of limitation required by the immediate nature of what is over against it. The infinity of love is displayed in its ability to manifest its totality within whatever bounds it must respect if it is to be love in the situation before it. The kind and degree of the limitations necessary for the final appeal to the soul of man are clearly very different from those natural laws within which the divine love elects of its own necessity to work for ordering the material conditions of life. But they are both expressions of the one loving purpose and equal manifestations of the same infinitude to those who can see them as such.

The biblical approach, then, has yielded two conclusions about omnipotence which are very different from those reached by starting with some such *a-priori* definition as 'The power to do anything not in itself inherently self-contradictory'. In the first place, we have seen that for faith – and that alone is capable of perceiving the accent of infinity in any finite manifestation of power – there is one almighty purpose revealed undeviating and undiluted, equally potent through every degree of constriction and limitation. There is here an infinity, which, so far from being negated by the finite, reveals itself in and through it. And that is what the Bible means when it teaches that God is related to the world of time and space, not as its negation, but as its Lord. No kind or degree of limitation makes any difference to his ability to make it the medium of his unrestricted omnipotence. Rather, as we shall see later, it is the very quality of the omnipotence that itself determines the degree and kind of the limitation. The omnipotence is not displayed in spite of the limitations or by ignoring them: that would make their presence inexplicable. It is in and through them that the infinity is manifested, and it is of a kind that is able to find expression in its totality and completeness in any finite situation. This possibility is presupposed in St Paul's statement that in Christ *κατοικεῖ πᾶν τὸ πλήρωμα τῆς θεότητος σωματικῶς* (all the fullness of divinity dwells bodily in him) (Col. 2:9). That is the most complete denial possible of the Gnostic tendencies he was combating. In using the phrase of his opponents he turns the tables against them. For Platonism in all its forms, as indeed for all Hellenic thought, it was absolutely axiomatic that the manifestation of the infinite and eternal in the world of space and time could be nothing more than an extremely partial and distorted refraction. And this same axiom is bound to hold for all who define infinity, omnipotence, eternity etc., in terms of the negation of the finite: the infinite cannot manifest itself as infinite in the finite. This can be seen clearly enough by looking again at each of the two cases discussed above, where an *a-priori* definition of omnipotence is adopted which does not take the fact of limitation into account from the beginning.

For Thomism, the infinity is indeed manifested; not, however, in and through the finite, but in spite of it. There is a strain of Docetism ineradicable from its Christology. It sees the flesh always as what veils, rather than what reveals, the deity. There is no sense in which the infinite is revealed *in* the finite. There is no *real* limitation within which it is genuinely constricted and which itself constitutes the actual revelation of the infinite. The suffering of Christ can never be regarded as revealing his divinity: it is only the mark of the genuineness of his humanity. *Potentia activa* could never be manifested as *potentia passiva*, power as passibility. One is the denial and negation of the other.

Similarly, any kenotic theory rests on the assumption that the finite is the negation of the infinite and is incapable of forming a vessel for the manifestation of its fullness. Whatever word is used, be it 'emptying', 'stripping off', 'abandonment', 'limitation', this theory must deny that in fact it *is πᾶν τὸ πλήρωμα* (all the fullness) which is manifested at the Incarnation. It is a mutilated deity which is revealed. There is removed that accent of unconditionality and infinity which is what distinguishes the approach of God in the human from the merely human. (The letters through which God speaks are human: it is the accent laid on them which authenticates them as the words of God – an accent visible only to faith.) The Cross is not the manifestation of *omni*potence at all, according to any definition with which such a theory starts. The idea of a 'limitation' of omnipotence is just an evasive circumlocution for its denial. To speak of degrees of omnipotence is nonsense: either a thing is omnipotent or it is not. In this theory indeed the reality of the limitation is recognized; but the infinity which was to be revealed has disappeared. In order to become manifest it has ceased to be infinite. And this is inevitable as long as the infinity is defined in its essence without reference to any limitation. When the limitation is introduced it must appear as something which, if it can be voluntarily endured, is necessarily a negation of its real nature as it is in itself.

But, secondly, the Bible teaches, not only that the infinity of God can be manifested in and through the finite and that no degree of limitation can exclude its constant presence, but that the very nature of the different limitations through which it wills to become manifest is the clue to its essential quality. Even if the other theories were capable of explaining how the fullness of the divine omnipotence *could* manifest itself in the form of a still, small voice, yet they can have no reason to give as to why a being who has the power to do anything should elect so to act. Nor, secondly, can they explain why he should declare this manifestation to be more significant for the understanding of his nature than the exercise of his power in storm and tempest. These questions obviously cannot be answered merely by an analysis of the idea of power in the abstract. And it is essentially the abstractness of the Thomist and similar definitions that is the root of their inadequacy. Power is defined with no reference to the purpose which it is to serve. But, in fact, it is only through a knowledge of the divine will that it is possible to say what kinds of power God can possess and what self-imposed limitations, if any, are required by his purpose.

The approach we are following, therefore, would presuppose a knowledge of the divine purpose as a prerequisite of any intelligible discussion of omnipotence. But this knowledge is never given in the Bible through abstract propositions. It is given in and through acts of the divine will, in the presence of faith. The divine attributes, which, in the case of a living personal God, mean the qualities which characterize his purpose, are revealed not in the form of universal statements, but in the daily encounter of God with individuals in all the peculiarities of their historical situation, individuals who yet, in faith, see in the divine dealings with them the eternal qualities of his purpose for all men. And the fact that the divine will is only thus ascertained means that actually the sequence is not so clear as we have just indicated that in theory it should be. Knowledge of the purpose of God is logically prior to the knowledge of the sort of power required for its execution. But the knowledge of the purpose is given not in propositions but in acts – acts of power. And it is through a consideration of, and response in faith to, such acts that the quality of the divine omnipotence is revealed, and through it the kind of purpose which would alone require the exercise of such a power. The acts of power throw light on the whole purpose, and the whole purpose interprets the acts of power.

This is the logic of belief which underlies all advance in the knowledge of the divine attributes. What is involved is a leap of faith from the particular and finite to the universal and infinite. It is thus that the biblical authors derive their notion of God as omnipotent. The statement that there is no power in heaven or earth capable of frustrating the divine sovereignty is not a judgment which is deducible from the facts of life by any logical process or which can be put to any objective verification. It is a faith-judgment based on the experience of Yahweh as the unfailing hope and final refuge of the individual and the nation alike, in the face of whom the powers of evil reveal themselves as impotent. The attribution to God of the ascription *παντοκράτωρ* (ruler of all) implies nothing concerning the abstract proposition that he can do anything he likes. It is an act of desperate confidence, of hope against hope, that the wages of sin really *are* death, that God will be justified in the face of his enemies, that the ultimate control of things *is* in the hands of a will which can neither be deflected nor defeated.

And it is thus that knowledge not only of the fact but also of the quality of God's omnipotence is derived. There is no general statement in the Bible that God's power is of a kind as always to respect the freedom of human personality. But there is the story of an individual, who at a particular moment of Israel's history, had the faith to detect the authentic address of the Almighty, not in the storm, neither in the earthquake, nor in the fire, but in the still, small voice. It was through this and countless other such individual acts of faith that the Hebrew mind came to the gradual realization of two things. First, that God was just as omnipotent in a voice that might possibly neither be heard nor answered, as in the processes of nature which achieve their end by irresistible force. And, secondly, that such a voice was not only an equal expression, but a more revealing expression, of the peculiar quality of the divine power – a power which was to be seen at its most characteristic in the execution of the most difficult and delicate of all purposes, the winning of men to a relation of personal love with itself.

It was noted as an inherent defect of the 'ontological' approach, which begins with a conception of omnipotence excluding all limitation, that it made the manifestation of infinity *in* and *through* the finite neither possible, natural nor necessary. It was unable to show that God either could, would or had to reveal himself in such a manner. Starting from the thelematological presuppositions that the nature of God is to be reached, not by an *a-priori* human definition in terms of the negation of the finite, but by listening to how God himself defines it in his revealed will, we have been able to return a satisfactory answer on the first two counts. We have tried to show that the divine infinity is such as *can* be manifested in its totality within the bounds of the finite, and also that it is of a quality which *would* be most characteristically itself in the observance of such limitations. Can we now take the third step, and say that is it *necessary* that the divine omnipotence, being what it is, should reveal itself through limitations? Is the very idea of finitude of manifestation involved in its being infinite, are the limitations required by the very quality of its limitlessness? In other words, can it be shown that a God with a power of the kind we have postulated (i.e., love) would be inconceivable if the idea of his definition through limitation were removed? This and nothing less must be established if all that God has done is to be grounded in a *necessity* of his being.

The initial step of the 'ontological' approach is to suppose that the real *essence* of God (the 'norm', as it were, of his divinity) is what he would be if all the limitations through which he manifests himself in revelation were thought away. In consequence, his self-definition over against creation is necessarily conceived (however guardedly it may be stated) as something less than this essence – *an* expression of it, but a contingent expression: not the revelation of it in all its necessity and totality. But a God who could be himself apart from any such self-definition could not be a God of love. For an infinite love *must* reveal itself through limitation, since to respect the frontier of the 'other' is involved in the very idea of love. The only way to escape this conclusion about God would be to say, either that in his essential being he has no 'other', or that this 'other' has no limits requiring limitation of himself. In the first case he would not be love (for love except in relation is impossible): in the second he would not be God (for there could not be a *second* infinite being). The idea of self-definition through limits, therefore, is essential to the idea of a God of love. That does not mean that he himself is limited by the presence of such limits: rather, it is precisely through them that he reveals the quality of his infinity, namely, as one of love. Limitation would consist precisely in the incapacity to express his infinitude in and through the finite. For if it could not be so expressed, it would be the infinitude, not of love, but of a power which could only be itself by the negation and destruction of the frontier of finite personality. Such a power would not win men but overwhelm them – and that would not be a victory but the defeat of love. Love as love would be powerless – and God has no power but that of love.

Without the presence of limits, therefore, the divine omnipotence would not be omnipotent. The limits do not limit God – that is just the error of the kenotic hypothesis – they are what enable him to express his infinity. They are necessary to him: he could not be himself without them. Yet, once again, it must be stressed with all possible force that he does not need them *in order to be* what he is, but *because he is* what he is. He expresses himself in and through the finite because, being what he is, he cannot help it: he does not require the finite in order to enable him to be God. Without the finite, it is true, he would not be the God of love; but (if we may so put it) it would be the case of the finite not being there because he was not God, rather than he not being God because the finite was not there.

If, then, a limitlessness which expresses itself through limitations is the only type of infinity we can predicate of God, then the constriction of the Cross, for instance, is not to be viewed as a voluntary self-limitation against a background of 'essential' unlimitedness. The idea of self-limitation, except to make the rather obvious point that every action of God proceeds from himself alone, is both otiose and false. God is never limited by Himself any more than by others. His nature is infinity, and limitation would just destroy it. In this the Kenoticists are wholly wrong and the Thomists are wholly right. But what the Thomists fail to see is that the infinity of love is such that it can and must show its limitlessness only in and through the finite. The Logos in Christ is unlimited, as it always must be; but it revealed this infinity, not in the fact that the boy saviour ruled the world from his mother's knee, but in the acceptance of worldly impotence and ignorance. The divine 'nature' of his Person authenticates itself, not by being impervious to his suffering, but by the very entry of the iron into his soul and his steadfast refusal to forego it. For it was these things – his weaknesses – that showed the absolute infinity of his love, which is but another way of stating the essence of his divinity. This is the only Christology which fulfils *both* the conditions set out in Ch. 8, namely, that the divine attributes should be in no way abandoned, limited or curtailed, and yet at the same time that they should come to expression in all their infinitude only in and through the limitations of the human. And for the same reason it is the only Christology which is true to the Pauline estimate of Christ crucified as the power of God and to the Johannine identification of the Cross with the throne of glory.[29] And the attainment of such a genuinely biblical – and, therefore, Christian – view is possible solely because of the abandonment of the 'classical' ontological assumptions which underlie the definition of omnipotence, and of all the other attributes, by both the Thomistic and kenotic schools. Once again, distinctively personal categories are alone adequate for the determination of the peculiarly personal mode of existence, whether in man or in God.

Chapter Eleven

OMNIPOTENCE: STRONGER THAN MEN

In the last chapter we were considering the nature of the divine omnipotence, that 'weakness of God', as St Paul calls it, by which he effects his will. We saw it to be a power of a kind, not merely *capable* of revealing its infinity by the very act of respecting the limits of the finite, but such as to declare its peculiar and characteristic quality most unmistakably in so doing, and even, by its very nature, to *require* a finite manifestation. For love, if it is to be a power at all, must respect the integrity of the will on which it hopes to act. Otherwise, as such, it has no power. Its potency is entirely bound up with the fact that the other is free to reject it. If this is not so, then as love it is impotent. I cannot move a chair by loving it, but only a person who is at liberty to refuse to be moved.

But it is not sufficient that love should respect the freedom of the other. That in itself does not make it effective. It is also necessary that in the very act of respecting its freedom it should be able to overcome its resistance. For power expresses itself in the mastery of opposition, and love is potent in the degree to which it is able to effect its designs in the face of contrary powers. To describe it as *omni*potent means that it can and will overcome *all* resistance. There is nothing that can ultimately stand in its way or frustrate its purpose. To designate the divine love *παντοκράτωρ* is to say that it has the measure of all *κράτη* (rules). It means that it is omnicompetent to be itself in a world where its purposes are continually challenged. And it is thus that the divine omnipotence must be defined – not as the power to do anything not logically self-contradictory, but as the complete capacity of love to fulfil its will and purpose.

What, then, is this purpose? The author of 1 Timothy expresses it by saying that 'God willeth that all men should be saved and come to the knowledge of the truth' (2:4). This is elsewhere described as the *ἀποκατάστασις πάντων* (the restoration of all) (Acts 3:21), when, at the end, the world shall be restored sinless to that relationship to God in and for which he made it. In Rom. 8:19 St Paul conceives the purpose for which creation exists as 'the revealing of the sons of God'. Otherwise expressed, it is the final vindication of the divine kingship, when every lower power which enslaves the hearts of men shall be abolished, and love shall be solely regnant in a perfect mutuality of communion and knowledge. Or, put perfectly simply, God's sole will of love is to be loved by all whom he has created for love.

To call this will of love omnipotent (which is the same as to call it divine) is to assert that this its purpose will most surely come to fulfilment. Its consummation is as necessary as its initiation, for both are grounded in the necessity of God's nature. If there was anything that could prevent it, then that power would be stronger than the divine love, and God less than παντοκράτωρ (ruler of all). But at once a problem arises. For this very statement seems to throw doubt on the reality of freedom, which love presupposes in order to be a power at all. Is it not a contradiction in terms to say that all men must be saved by love? For if they must be saved, then salvation would appear to mean something other than free response to love. What becomes of the power to reject if all must accept? To ground the initiation of the world plan in a necessity of the divine being, with whatever other difficulties it may be attended, can at any rate hardly be regarded as an infringement of human freedom. But to fix its completion in a similar necessity is clearly a very different matter.

The dilemma may be stated thus. *Either*, love is omnipotent (this is a necessary statement if God is to be God, i.e., infinite): in which case it *must* conquer. But this 'must' involves the elimination of the very thing which makes its victory a victory of love – that is, freedom. By the very fact, therefore, that he *is* omnipotent and does necessarily fulfil his purpose, God contradicts himself and works his own defeat. *Or*, freedom is absolutely inviolable (this is a necessary statement if God is to be God, i.e., love): in which case there can be no *necessity* in his victory. And this means there is no necessity that God can be himself – infinite and unbounded. But the very possibility that he could not be what he is once more involves him in self-contradiction. Thus the inevitable conclusion to be drawn seems to be that the ideas of omnipotence and love are themselves mutually contradictory. God cannot be omnipotent love. As we saw in the last chapter, he may manifest his power in such a way as never to compel. But in that very act he puts outside the bounds of possibility the *necessity* that he will draw all, or even any.

Now if we are not to rest in this position, which would cut at the heart of the whole Christian doctrine of God, there are two courses open to us. *Either* we must be prepared to show that the possibility that all are not saved is compatible with the divine omnipotence: *or* we must establish that the necessity for all to be saved involves no infringement of human freedom, and therefore no denial of God's love. The former course has been taken by traditional orthodoxy; the latter, the doctrine of universalism, though favoured at different stages of the Church's history by some of its greatest thinkers, has generally been regarded with suspicion, even when not condemned as heresy.[30] We shall consider the two in turn.

The first position is defended by St Thomas Aquinas in his *Summa Theologica*, I, 19, vi, 1. He supports the thesis that 'God's will is always fulfilled' in the face of the scriptural assertion that God 'willeth that all men should be saved and come to the knowledge of the truth', of which he says simply '*hoc non ita evenit*' (this has not happened thus). He offers three interpretations of the text which might bring it into line with what he regards as observed fact. The first two are merely sophistic, and he rests nothing on them. The third, which he cites from John of Damascus, is the following. A distinction must be made between the antecedent or absolute will of God and his consequent or conditioned will (without implying by this any idea of temporal antecedence or change of mind). Absolutely, God wills all to be saved, in the same way that a just judge desires in general that each man should live rather than die. But in the same way as the judge must will that a homicide should be hanged, so God's consequent will is that some should be damned, since his justice demands it ('*secundum exigentiam suae justitiae*' (in accordance with the requirement of his justice/righteousness)). What, therefore, God in general does will to happen may not take place, since there are circumstances in which to will it would mean that he would be willing something evil or unjust. But what God does actually (i.e., consequently) will in any given situation always come to pass. In this way St Thomas seeks to combine the possibility of damnation with the complete fulfilment of the divine will. The exercise of freedom to reject salvation does not destroy the omnipotence of God.

The essential contention of this argument, which, in some form or other, must be that of all who would wish to defend the same position, is that what is apparently a 'change' of will (from saving to damning) is based, not in any external inhibition of the divine power but in the internal constancy of the divine nature itself. There is no contradiction of this nature in the condemning of those it created to save: rather, this is the expression of its very consistency. The contradiction would be that God should save those who by their sin have made themselves worthy only of punishment. For he would be being false to his own nature of *holy* love.

But let us analyse this contention a little closer. The assumption underlying the foregoing statement is that in his love God wills all men to be saved, but that his justice requires many to be damned. Attempts would be made to cover up such a bald antithesis, but it is, nevertheless, ineluctably present in some form. St Thomas, indeed, would have no objection to the statement as it stands. But it could be altered to present a more acceptable appearance, in which case it would run something like this. The divine power is not defeated by the fact that God's antecedent will of love is not fulfilled. For it is a power which is equally one of justice. A failure to convert is not really or finally a failure: the divine nature is still vindicated in condemnation. God's glory and power are always perfected, whether in the life or the death of the creature, whether in mercy or in judgment. If men will not be drawn by his love, they shall bow to his justice. In each case he is omnipotent: he has not failed.

But under whatever form or disguise it appears, this solution cannot satisfy, because it cannot preserve the absolute identity of the divine love and the divine justice. For, ultimately, these two are not parallel attributes, each of which stands for a different requirement of God's nature. Rather is his justice a quality of his love, a characterization of its working. His is a love of cauterizing holiness and of a righteousness whose only response to evil is the purity of a perfect hate. Wrath and justice are but ways in which such love must show itself to be love in the face of its denial. If it appeared in any other form, it would be less than perfect love. It is most important to hold to the fact that justice is in no sense a substitute for love, which comes into operation when the other has failed to be effective. The impression is often given that God has reserves of power upon which he could fall back if the power of love were to fail; that souls who cannot be won to a free response fall under a judgment condemning them to an involuntary destruction. (Cf. Brunner: 'He wishes to make Himself known as love, as far as this is possible; but He must also make Himself known as the holy righteous Judge when this is inevitable' *The Mediator*, 551.) But God has no power but the power of love, since he has no nature but the nature of love. If that fails, he fails. Justice is no second line of defence: it has no power of its own. For it is none other than love being itself, love in the face of evil continuing to exercise its own peculiar power.

Unless this is understood, not only does love become sentimental and forgiveness immoral, but justice becomes sub-Christian. A view of the divine justice is introduced which can be satisfied with a purely negative assertion of its rights in the condemnation of a sinner. It is regarded as *in no sense a failure* on God's part if some men are committed to eternal punishment or death, because therein the divine justice is fully vindicated. Rather, we must say that, precisely because justice is always the sternness of his *love*, such an issue can never be its vindication, or indeed anything but its hopeless defeat. For death or a purely retributive punishment (which *eternal* punishment must be by definition) is the completest contradiction and denial of love. Simply because justice is in no sense antithetical to love, but a very way of its working, it is impossible that it should ever be content with a purely negative assertion of itself. Judgment can never be God's last word, because, if it were, it would be the word which would speak his failure. Judgment is, indeed, absolutely necessary, as being that through which alone sinful man can hear the word of mercy. But the sole possible function of judgment can be to enable men to receive the mercy which renders it superfluous. God is the eternal 'Yea', and if his last word is any other than his first – a creative, affirming *Bejahungswort* – then his love is defeated and his love is not omnipotent. But that word can only be pronounced upon a creation which is in every respect 'very good'. Only if and when all men respond with that 'yes' which they are called into being to give (*cf.* p. 83), can God utter the final consummation.

The same point can be made in another way by saying that the position adopted by St Thomas presupposes that, in the last resort, we can rest content with the attitude of the just judge he cites in illustration. The judge does not regard the condemnation of a homicide to hanging as in any sense a failure; rather, it embodies the entire satisfaction and complete fulfilment of his pure will to justice. Without going at length into the Christian doctrine of punishment, we may register the conviction that, whatever it may be, it does not stop there. No Christian could acquiesce in such a *purely* retributive theory or regard the sending of a criminal to the gallows as reflecting no failure except in the man himself. It would be impossible for him to derive entire satisfaction from such a 'vindication' of justice or to say that he wills the man's death *simpliciter* (St Thomas's word) – without, that is, any qualms or reservation or sense of frustration. So, neither, could any Christian ascribe such an attitude to God. Just as every verdict of condemnation in the courts is at the same time a confession of failure on the part of the society which pronounces it, so every final damnation on the part of God would be an admission of the frustration of the omnipotence of his love.

According to the Christian view, justice is only finally vindicated in forgiveness. In the common mind forgiveness is the antithesis of justice: a recommendation to mercy in the courts necessarily wears the aspect of a reversal of the verdict of justice. That is so because justice is defined, not as a quality of love, but in independence of it. The pronouncing of forgiveness, therefore, always appears to come, in Luther's expression, as '*noch eyn ander wort*' [yet another word], and a word, in consequence, which can never clear itself of the suspicion of immorality.[31] Only if justice is firmly held throughout as a quality of love does forgiveness reveal itself, not only as other than intrusive and disruptive, but actually as necessary to it. For if justice is a way of love's working and nothing else, then it cannot stop at anything short of forgiveness. Only if God's justice is defined independently of his love can it find any fulfilment in consigning to damnation. And if his power is the power of his love, anything less than the salvation of all is a mark of its defeat.

In the last resort, there is no way of avoiding the conclusion that any modification of the antecedent will of God to save all implies concession to a power outside himself. One may work in terms of the demands of justice and love and thus persuade oneself that the modification is compelled by an internal rather than an external necessity. But the idea of a 'consequent' will cannot succeed in clearing itself of the suspicion of being in some degree a falling away from the antecedent, simply because the justice which it embodies is but one element abstracted and isolated from God's holy love. The will to forgive is quenched, and God satisfies himself with stopping at the point of condemnation. And what is the reason? None other than that his power to forgive is limited by the recalcitrance of the sinner. There could be nothing in God himself which would induce him to be content with this second best. The assertion that the divine power is completely vindicated as omnipotent in negative judgement is simply an attempt to cover up and justify what is really a disastrous failure. For antecedently, God's will extends beyond judgment to life. His power is his omnicompetence to fulfil this great purpose of love. And if it should not work out exactly as it was planned, the modifying factor must be sought, not within God's nature, but outside it. Nothing *in God* would make him will anything but life for all in any circumstances. The slightest modification would be a monument to the power of human self-will to resist the divine love even to the uttermost. This power would have shown itself to be stronger than God and thereby have reared a final disproof of the omnipotence of his love. Whether he had to condemn to extinction one or millions, God would have failed and failed infinitely. For love could not will such a thing, nor contemplate the prospect of it with anything but abhorrence. Whether this failure is represented simply as a bounding of his omnipotence of love or as a resort to a power of compulsion other than that of love makes no difference. In either case a complete contradiction is set up within the divine being: God would just cease to be God.

It will be recalled that we set ourselves to examine the two answers which have been propounded in face of the dilemma occasioned by the apparent irreconcilable ideas of divine omnipotence and divine love. The first was to the effect that the omnipotence of God's love is in no way frustrated or unsatisfied, even though not all come to that state of salvation to which in general he wills to bring the human race. This solution we have found to be profoundly unsatisfying. It involves a resignation on behalf of the divine forgiveness in face of the intractability of the human will. Being unable to show mercy, God is forced, it is true by the requirements of his own holiness, to condemn. But his justice, if it could rest in such a final negative, would show itself to be no longer part of the holy love whose function it is. That love, once omnicompetent unto salvation, would have been shattered on the reefs of human sin, and the negative assertion of abstract justice be all that remained to witness to a nobler lordship.

What, then, of the second alternative, namely, the thesis that the necessary salvation of all is not a denial of human freedom, neither, therefore, of God's love? Can we hope for anything more from an attempt to make sense of a love which works by necessity? If all *must* be saved, can any be *saved*, in the only sense which makes the operation a work of love? If freedom and the ultimate capacity for refusal is infringed, what profit is there in such a work of salvation for a God of love? To repeat Kierkegaard's warning, 'It would help very little if one persuaded millions of men to accept the truth, if precisely by the method of their acceptance they were transferred into error' (*Concluding Unscientific Postscript*, 221).

This warning must be taken to heart with all possible seriousness. Any solution which in any way compromises the fact of freedom stands self-condemned. For without freedom love could not be love; without its exercise by man God would not only not be omnipotent, he would be utterly powerless. For though love for its purposes may operate through those secondary causes and determinations which control the world of matter and of organism, yet it can only achieve that ultimate end which characterizes it as peculiarly and unmistakably itself in the relationship where the response given is not automatic. I may act upon another for his good through forces which ignore his co-operation. But ultimately, I cannot love him if I confine myself to doing this. Such actions cannot, and ought not, to be eliminated: their necessity is obvious, for instance, in the bringing up of children. But they only authenticate themselves as dealings of love if they lead the 'other' to the point at which he can, if he wishes, reject them *in toto*. Love is only peculiarly love and its power only purely that of love when this capacity to flout it is presupposed in all its integrity. Depreciate this in the least degree, and love is impotent. Nothing is so helpless as love which can enlist no co-operation. If it cannot draw out men's will to free response, then it has no other alternative: its day is over.

This unswerving insistence on the inviolability of freedom must be maintained from beginning to end if what follows is not to fall away into self-contradiction and futility. But, taking our stand on this fact, can we see any possibility of its reconciliation with the divine necessity that all shall be saved? If God's omnipotence is to work upon men that all ultimately must acknowledge it, is there any way it could work that would not be destructive of freedom?

Now it is evident, if we may say so, that God has as much interest in the preservation of our freedom as ever we have ourselves, even in our most self-assertive moods. For if his omnipotence is to be *acknowledged* (and that is the only way in which an omnipotence of love could become effective and victorious), then the freedom required for the acknowledgment must be preserved right to the very end. For the very act of submission is an act of freedom and embodies the assertion of its eternal inviolability. But to say that, if God were to be omnipotent, then an ultimate compatibility of absolute freedom and absolute power, so far from being impossible, would be an essential prerequisite, is very far from saying that such a reconciliation of freedom and necessity actually exists or could exist.

Now it is, of course, impossible to prove that God is omnipotent. Such an assertion, like all statements involving the ascription of infinity in any form, is necessarily a *faith*-judgment, in the sense explained above (see Note 28). But such judgments, though involving an alogical jump, are not simply irrational leaps in the dark. The Hebrew mind, experiencing no place where God was not already there to meet it, no hour when one was not anticipated by his presence, concluded that God was *omni*present, at every point of space and moment of time (cf. Ps. 139). St Paul, conscious of the victory of Christ's love over the apparently intractable material of his own soul, asserts that there is *nothing* that can defeat or separate from it: its very conclusion of all in unbelief can only be instrumental to the final universal victory of the everlasting mercy (Rom. 8; 11:25–36). Such inferences are neither explicit nor logical. There is here no analogical induction, only an *analogia fidei* (analogy of faith). It was such experiences of personal encounter with God that were the means by which the biblical attributes of God became recognized. They did not prove them: but they provided the indispensable material for the faith which grasped them.

Now is it in like manner possible from the realm of personal encounter to draw out material for the faith that God's power is such that, while all will and must acknowledge it in the end, yet such acknowledgment need involve no surrender of their freedom and personal integrity? Can we, in other words, find indications of love's power freely to compel which enable us in some measure to grasp the idea of a love omnipotent to conquer?

The mental picture conjured up by most people of the relation between divine omnipotence and human freedom is probably that of two irresistible forces each pulling in opposite directions. If, *per impossibile*, one were to gain a painful inch here or there, it could only be at the expense of the other's loss: submission to the power of God must involve the abandonment of the freedom of man. But there is no reason to think that this is at all an accurate picture of what happens when will meets will in the personal relationship of love. On the contrary, it is false and misleading.

When a man or woman really shows his or her love for us, whether it be in some costly manifestation of forgiveness or self-sacrifice, or in some small act of kindness or consideration, we feel constrained to respond to it – we cannot help ourselves, everything within us tells us that we must. Our defences are down, the power of love captures the very citadel of our will, and we answer with the spontaneous surrender of our whole being. Yet at the same time we know perfectly that, if we choose, we can remain unmoved; there is no physical compulsion to commit ourselves. Everyone may point to instances in which he has been constrained to thankful response by the overmastering power of love. And yet, under this strange compulsion, has any ever felt his freedom to be infringed or his personality violated? Is it not precisely at these moments that he becomes conscious, perhaps only for a fleeting space of time, of being himself in a way he never knew before, of attaining a fullness and integration of life which is inextricably bound up with the decision drawn from him by the other's love? Moreover, this is true however strong be the constraint laid upon him, or, rather, it is truer the stronger it is. Under the constraint of the love of God in Christ this sense of self-fulfilment is at its maximum. The testimony of generation is that, here as nowhere else, service is 'perfect freedom'. In throwing ourselves into an action on behalf of someone we really love in Christ, our whole personality can become united, our intellect and emotions fused, in one all-subordinating purpose of the will, in that complete self-determination in which we know, as at no other time, that we are truly free. When faced by an overpowering act of love, we realize how absurd it is to say that the freedom and integrity of our moral personality is only safeguarded if we set our teeth and determine not to allow ourselves to be won to its service. If, then, we do not lose but rather find our freedom in yielding to the constraining power of love, is there anything to be gained for the cause of liberty by demanding that, when it is under the control of self-will, it shall in the end be stronger than when it is under the control of love? May we not imagine a love so strong that ultimately no one will be able to restrain himself from free and grateful surrender? If the miracle of the forcing of pride's intransigence, which is no forcing but a gentle leading, can be achieved in one case (St Paul would say, in *my* case), who are we to say that God cannot repeat it in all? One by one, each will come to the point at which he finds himself constrained to confess in Wesley's words:

> I yield, I yield, I can hold out no more:
> I sink by dying love compelled
> To own thee conqueror.[32]

But, it will be said, in all this there is still presupposed the real possibility that the power of self-will could be the stronger, even though we may admit that a universal victory of love would not in any degree imperil freedom. At the end of the process it would not be the fact that all have been saved, but that all had to be saved, which would throw doubt on the validity of what had been achieved. The knowledge that, since God is what he is, the result could not have been different, seems to cut at the very root of freedom. A very powerful love which in the end carried the day by winning all to the service of itself – yes. But an omnipotent love which knew from the beginning that it could not but conquer – where does that leave room for reality of decision?

Let us go back once again to our human loves, and let us call to mind how it has been with each one of us. We have known what it is to be confronted by a love too strong to resist. We had no intention of yielding one whit of our proud independence. And yet we fell: it was too much for us. It forced us to a free acknowledgment of its power. And how wonderful that moment of surrender was! We felt that that was the moment for which we had been born for just such an act as this. And yet, as the weeks passed, there still seemed so much of us that was not bound over and committed, so much that we would far rather surrender to the other's keeping, but which we could not bring ourselves to part with. At intervals we felt that love overmastering here a little more, there a little more. But the process appeared so slow – and so uncertain. What ground was there for supposing that that complete surrender for which we yearned would ever be made possible for us? Supposing that other love, though so much greater than anything we could command, was just not powerful enough ever finally to win the last fastnesses of our resistance and selfishness? Could we ever be certain that we should attain that which we knew to be the purpose of our life, but which we realized equally we could never reach except we were drawn from without? What if that other power might prove not quite equal to it – should we be faced with the prospect of life's meaning frustrated at the last great encounter? Thus we reflected. And we knew that others too, if we could but penetrate to their deepest anxieties, must also be standing before this possibility, looking into it and wondering. And then we seemed to hear a voice, which told us we need have no fear. It spoke of another love, which, though we knew it not, had all the while been meeting us in that love we knew. It was this love that had really been drawing us to itself and imparting to us that sense of coming back to our long lost home. For it was that from which we had come, and in which, all unknowing, we had been living, and which now at length had begun to reclaim us for its own. And when we heard this, we took courage and put away our fears. For then we knew. We knew this love, that it was none other than the infinite love of God; and we laughed that we had ever allowed ourselves to think that there might not be a power without us great enough to conquer those last shreds of our pride and independence. For we knew that the power of *this* love could experience no bounds at all. Sooner or later, as we let it, it would bring us back to the haven where we would be. We rejoiced to know we could not stop it, though we could not always trust ourselves not to want to stop it. But in the end we knew that even this wish that it should not conquer would be taken from our willing hearts. That this would be so we were fully assured, and we remembered how it was said that 'the godly consideration of predestination and our election in Christ was full of sweet, pleasant and unspeakable comfort'. And with this assurance we were brought to the knowledge that with those others too, of whom we had thought before, it was in the same case. For even though they might be men who, like ourselves, thought not to know anything of the love of God, and who might meet but little love in those around them, yet we were persuaded that all of them would at last come to desire that same love as that by which we had been found. For we saw in the love, crucified for every man, a power which could not but draw all to itself, so gracious was it and insupportable for sinful men to behold. And with this vision of the sureness of the victory of God's love, when all would freely own its sway, we returned to the world content. The knowledge that it must needs take place did nothing to disturb the certainty of our freedom. For we knew that this surrender was in no way contrary to it, but that, rather, in it alone could we discover our true liberty. And our assurance of it did but establish our hope, and the hope of all men, beyond the power of anything whereby we sinners might be able to prevent it.

It is in some such experience or vision as this that most of us perhaps have come, if we have come at all, to the knowledge of the strange compulsion of God's love and to the assurance that its necessary victory would not abrogate, but simply release, our freedom. But in a theological treatise it is necessary to try also to set out the truth in more careful, philosophical language.

The doctrine of predestination – and universalism simply means a doctrine of a single universal decree – is only fatalistic and morally debilitating if it is viewed 'objectively' (cf. pp. 129–33). When it is sought to fit the fact of freedom within the scheme of 'It' knowledge, it is inevitably subsumed under the categories of cause and effect whereby this knowledge is ordered. When this happens, the meeting of two wills in love is pictured in terms taken from the contact of two physical substances. The one can only move by eliminating the resistance of the other. Thus the omnipotence of God is regarded as being able to prevail only at the expense of the freedom of man. But, as we have seen, this is a completely misleading representation. From the point of view of the 'subject'-in-meeting, the knowledge that the divine victory of love is necessary brings joy and peace in believing. For this necessity is in no way inimical to freedom, but its very substantiation and fulfilment.

Reference to the doctrine of predestination may serve to introduce a further point.[33] It is a common observation about both Calvinists and universalists that their actions do not appear to follow logically from their theories. If one is bound to go to heaven (or hell) in the end, why trouble further about anything? That would seem the natural conclusion. Yet neither of these classes of men appears to be characterized by any less moral earnestness. They reveal a concern for converting and improving the world at least as serious as that of other Christians. This is usually regarded merely as a notable and inexplicable fact, although the corollary is sometimes added that it indicates that they cannot really believe what they profess.

But the divergence is not in truth so very strange. It simply marks the difference between the 'subjective' and the 'objective' standpoints. From the point of view of the logic of the 'It', the exercise of the divine omnipotence renders superfluous, even if it does not eliminate, any effective human action or co-operation. Looked at 'objectively', therefore, the consistent line of conduct would be simply to let things take their course, with no effort to alter them, except in so far as the passage of this world can thereby be rendered more comfortable or agreeable. But to the 'subject' in the 'Thou' relation of decision, the matter looks very different. The reality and significance of human responsibility is heightened rather than diminished. The knowledge that one is the object of another human being's love, who, whatever one may do, will continue to love and to cherish, is not the signal to seize the opportunity for careless and thoughtless living. Rather, the knowledge brings with it an overwhelming constraint to pursue precisely the opposite course. It is only he who does not really love, who looks at the matter 'objectively', to whom the 'logical' course of action could possibly suggest or approve itself. So it is in our dealings with God. It is only those who do not know grace, in the only way in which it can be known, that is, 'subjectively', to whom the exhortation to 'sin that grace may abound' can have the least plausibility. There is not the slightest need to treat seriously the objection to universalism that it is morally or spiritually debilitating. The objection rests upon a misunderstanding into which no one who makes an 'existential' profession of the belief is in any danger of falling.

For the 'subject', the 'individual', in moral decision the possibility of hell is an ever-present reality. There is a dimension of seriousness which Christianity introduces into the question of existing which, as Kant once stressed, is bound up with its uncompromising dualism between heaven and *hell*, and not merely between heaven and earth. There are the two poles between which every choice has to be made. The blessed assurance of universalism, that, ultimately, hell can be an actuality for none, in no way removes its relevance for decision. Here again an 'objectivized' logic falsifies. In human relationships, the possibility of failing a loved one, even unto the destruction of the relationship itself, always remains terribly and relevantly alive, even though one is confident that the claim of the other will always be too strong to allow one to fall away completely. In the God-relationship, where, through faith in the absolute omnipotence of the divine love, this confidence is translated into certainty, the possibility of an ultimate denial is existentially just as real. That is why the New Testament, in many passages clearly universalistic in its doctrine of God, is, in other passages which relate to the consequences of decision, as strongly insistent on the reality and relevance of ultimate damnation. It is futile to attempt to prove that Christ taught no belief in hell or eternal punishment, though much, it is true, may be said by way of modification. Nor is it at all necessary to a sound doctrine of universalism to establish that such is the case. Hell is eternally a live option: the assurance that no one will in fact reach it does nothing to belittle the reality and significance of the ever-present 'either-or'. That is what the logic of the 'It' can never comprehend. For the fact of freedom cannot be contained within the simple disjunction of the law of non-contradiction: it registers its presence in the irritating appearance of the paradox – that resolute assertion of 'both-and' by which it protests against every attempt to contain it within the categories, or plot it by the co-ordinates, of 'objective' knowledge. Within the 'It' language the paradox – that disturbing indication that all has not been fully resolved – stands as an ever-present reminder that such language is inadequate to the only things that are ultimately real or significant. For the final, decisive reality is existence in the 'Thou' world – and that is always existence-in-freedom.

But it must not be concluded that the presence for decision of a genuine, living alternative in any way throws doubt on the primacy of heaven over hell. To us, both are equally real possibilities. Indeed, if one was not to be realized, it would be far more reasonable to expect it to be heaven rather than hell: the doctrine of man provides not the least ground for a universalistic hope. But the point of view of man *in via*, of the sinner-in-decision, is not the ultimate standpoint. For us, as Berdyaev says, there are always two voices.

> One of the voices that speaks in my soul tells me that all are doomed to hell, because all more or less doom themselves to it. But this is reckoning without Christ. And the other voice in me says that all must be saved, that man's freedom must be enlightened from within, without any violence being done to it – and that that comes through Christ and is salvation. (*The Destiny of Man*, 1937, 353)

But of these voices only the latter will ultimately abide; for the Cross of Christ is a more final fact than human sin. This is the sheet anchor of the Christian hope. Without it the universalistic belief would not be more than a defiant cry, a desperate asseveration of a final theodicy in the face of all appearance.[34] With it there is substituted a quiet confidence in the absolute control of the divine omnipotence. God has exposed the strong right arm by which he has declared he will curb the nations. And, lo, it is pierced with nails, stained with blood and riveted in impotence. Is it to us also an offence and a foolishness? Yet that is the authentic quality of love's omnipotence. 'The weakness of God is stronger than men' (1 Cor. 1:25). For 'I, if I be lifted up from the earth, will draw all men unto myself' (Jn 12:32): that is the divine promise; and who or what may stay the course of its fulfilment?

Chapter Twelve

ETERNITY: THE NEGATION OF TIME

It is generally accepted among philosophical theologians that, however eternity is to be conceived, there is one way in which it cannot be represented. It cannot be represented as an endless duration of time. That is a naive and unphilosophic account, which will not bear serious scrutiny. Rather, we must say that God is outside time: duration cannot be a 'form of intuition' of the divine experience. His apprehension is not successive like ours. His eternity is to be expressed, after the haunting words of Boethius' famous definition, as an '*interminabilis vitae totum simul et perfecta possessio*' [perfect possession of unending life all at the same time] (*De Consolatione Philosophiae*, v. 6).

In this matter of the nature of time and eternity Christian theology has been almost exclusively Hellenic in its thought and expression. The tradition, with but minor developments, has run unbroken from Plato and Plotinus through Boethius and St Thomas down to modern times. For this tradition eternity is strictly the negation of time. It is not merely that duration cannot be used in the same sense (*univoce*) of men and God: it cannot even be predicated analogically of the divine existence. For in the Greek view, reality, as opposed to phenomena, is essentially static, changeless and timeless. God is absolutely immutable, and temporal succession or duration cannot enter into his experience. To postulate a real 'not yet' in his apprehension would be to ascribe 'potentiality' to him. To one who is *Actus Purus* there can be nothing that is not fully and completely present. The divine state must be represented by some such phrase as a *Totum simul* [all at the same time] or a *Nunc stans* [permanent present]. In it the panorama of time is spread out to view as one eternal and immutable 'Now', in which there is no past, present or future. The most we can say is that God sees things as happening one after another. Thus, he sees the Battle of Waterloo as really occurring after and not before the Battle of Blenheim. But he does not experience them one after another: he has seen all events in a single Now from all eternity. An element of successiveness enters into the object but not into the mode of his apprehension. So, a man on a mountain-top may see one village as more distant than another; but he sees them both at once. Thus St Thomas writes: '*Licet contingentia fiant in actu successive, non tamen Deus successive cognoscit contingentia prout sunt in suo esse, sicut nos, sed simul*' (Although contingent things become actual successively, nevertheless God knows contingent things not successively as they are in their own being, as we do, but simultaneously) (*S. T.*, I, 14, iii: cf. *De Veritate*, 2, xii).

It may be stated at once that it is the purpose of this and the following chapter to challenge and, if possible, to refute this view. The ground of accusation on which we intend to take our stand is that it is unbiblical. And that, at least in any Reformed Communion, should be sufficient to exclude it from a place in a *Christian* theology, a place which it has long claimed and too easily enjoyed.

It is not proposed to begin, as might seem natural, with an examination of the meaning of αἰώνιος (eternal) and its equivalents in the Bible, and to compare this with the signification of 'eternity' just set forth. Little would be gained from this, since the conclusion we should reach is already admitted on all hands. Any dispute that can arise over the biblical use of the word αἰώνιος has reference to the question whether it always strictly involves the idea of 'endlessness'. It has never been doubted that it implies that of 'duration'. On the basis of a careful study of the Hebrew and Greek terms employed, Mr F. H. Brabant gives as his conclusion that 'the Biblical use of the phrases under discussion implies *duration*, of whatever length; there seems no reference to the *Totum Simul*, the changeless perfection of the philosophers' (*Time and Eternity in Christian Thought*, 1937, 45. Italics his). It is safe to say that the English translators were right in regarding 'eternal' and 'everlasting' as interchangeable in biblical usage. If further authority were required, there is that of the the late Dr Edwyn Bevan. 'So far as the language of the Bible goes', he writes, 'there is nothing to show that the eternity of God is understood in any other sense than that of unending time' (*Symbolism and Belief*, 97). 'I will remember the years of the right hand of the Most High', says the Psalmist (77:10). God for the Old Testament is characteristically 'El Olam', the One from of old (Gen. 21:33). The Eternal is he who 'endures', he 'whose goings forth are from ancient days' (Mic. 5:2, RV mg.) and who 'sitteth king for ever' (Ps. 29:10). 'Before the mountains were brought forth, or ever thou hadst formed the earth and the world, even from everlasting to everlasting thou art God' (Ps. 90:2). So too in the New Testament, the One that 'inhabiteth eternity' is 'the Alpha and the Omega . . . which is and which was and which is to come' (Rev. 1:8). There is nothing to suggest an idea of eternity which is the negation of time, nothing like a *Nunc stans* or a *Totum simul* where the reality of duration is obliterated. Even in those books of the New Testament which are most influenced by Greek thought, the quantitative aspect of *αἰώνιος* is not superseded by the increased stress on the qualitative. Thus, in the Fourth Gospel, the eternal food is contrasted with the water whereof a man may drink and thirst again and with the bread whereof he may eat and still die (4:13–15; 6:48–58). 'Work not for the meat which perisheth, but for the meat which abideth unto eternal life' (6:27). In the Epistle to the Hebrews the antithesis throughout is between the permanence of the New and the temporary nature of the Old Covenant. Christ is a priest *εἰς τὸν αἰῶνα* (for ever) after the order of Melchisedek 'according to the power of an endless life' (Heb. 7:16). It is noteworthy that each of these two books contains more instances of the word *αἰών* [Age, eternity] with its inevitable durational reference (whether in the sense of 'the ages' (*οἱ αἰῶνες*) or 'for ever' (*εἰς τὸν αἰῶνα*)) than any other New Testament writing.

This conclusion concerning the durational nature of the scriptural idea of eternity cannot be gainsaid; nor indeed is any attempt made to do so. There is no suggestion that the terminology of the Bible and of the Schools is anything but different. But the Schoolmen would not for this reason admit that their theology was unbiblical. And they would be right in their refusal. For in matters of this nature, where any words we use cannot but be symbols of a truth ultimately inexpressible in human terms, the claim to be true to Scripture is not founded merely on approximation to biblical terminology, but on faithfulness in interpreting the real heart of biblical doctrine. And this the Scholastics and their modern followers would claim to be doing. The symbolism of the biblical authors, they hold, is too naively anthropomorphic. The Hebrews were not a philosophical people. There were many problems they did not see, and for an answer to which their categories are inadequate. A theory of eternity which is to bear the criticism of philosophical thought must be differently conceived. If the real biblical teaching about the eternity of God is to be safeguarded, then it must be expressed in language, not of endless duration, but of absolute timelessness.

It is some such defence as this which would be urged in justification of the interpretation of time and eternity in Christian theology in Hellenic rather than Hebraic categories. And it is at this level that the question of its biblicity must be decided. The actual terminology is in itself unimportant. One does not necessarily propound a scriptural doctrine of the afterlife just because one's measurements of the furniture of heaven are drawn from the

Book of Revelation. What one has to be sure is the same is not the symbol but the thing symbolized.

But we may not change our symbolism too freely; it is to some extent determined for us by the reality it represents. Thus, it would generally be agreed that an element in the Christian hope expressed, however inadequately, in the idea of the resurrection of the body is lost by substituting the philosophically more acceptable 'immortality of the soul'. In the same way we are bound to ask whether the ascription of real duration to God, however anthropomorphic, may not represent an essential element in the Christian doctrine which is destroyed by conceiving him as outside time altogether. No one will pretend that the biblical authors were thinking or writing in philosophical language. Their phrases cannot be lifted from their context and employed as they stand as counters in metaphysical debate. But it may be that by adopting and adapting these Hebraic categories, rather than by discarding them for others, the true biblical doctrine of God can alone be preserved. Some of the problems for which they are not adequate may turn out to be problems that only arise when the conception of God is entertained which is not that of the Old and New Testaments. And, equally, it may be that there are other problems – the *Bible*'s problems – which are shelved or rendered insoluble by the adoption of the notions of time and eternity so congenial to the wisdom of the Greeks. These suggestions we purpose to expand, and if possible to justify, in the course of the ensuing pages.

At this point, it may be convenient to indicate our general scheme of procedure. First, in this chapter, we shall attempt, by direct assault, to show the incompatibility of any doctrine which places God outside time with the notion of the personal, 'living', purposive God who speaks through the pages of Scripture. Then will follow an exposition of the peculiar contribution of the treatment of time – God's time – made by the New Testament writers. Finally, we shall seek to answer some of the objections to the inclusion of an element of duration in eternity which have caused Christian theology generally to discard biblical symbolism in favour of a more 'philosophic' set of ideas. In the process it is hoped to be able to show that the Hebraic categories can provide the basis for a doctrine of God just as philosophical as the Hellenic, and for a philosophy, moreover, which alone is Christian, because it alone is biblical.

We have already discussed at some length the nature of the two attitudes to our environment which have been characterized as the 'I–Thou' and the 'I–It' relationships. It will, therefore, have become evident that the distinction is one that has an obvious relevance to the problem of time. But the measure of its importance still requires to be brought out. For it is not too much to say that the question whether time is regarded from the point of view of the 'I' or of the 'I–Thou' relation or of that of the 'I–It' always determines, and always has determined, every theory of its nature and status. At the risk of some repetition, therefore, we shall attempt to restate the difference between the two attitudes in their special reference to the time-process. Buber's terminology, which we found reason to adopt before, will be followed. Indeed, nowhere is its superiority more evident than here. For the use which would locate the difference between the relationships in the nature of their objects (persons and things) has no particular contribution to make to the problem of time at all.

The 'I–It' attitude – to take first for convenience of exposition what is really a secondary product or deposit of the primary 'I–Thou' relation – is essentially that of the detached spectator. It is the attitude of the analyst or critic standing back from his subject and viewing it objectively as the effect of its causes, of the the sum of its parts. The object thus regarded is always something which is fixed and settled, taking its place in the continuum of experienced events, and bound up in the nexus of ascertained or ascertainable causes and consequences. This does not mean that the object of apprehension may not be what appears as a present process. The political theorist may be studying current events, the scientist an actual chemical change, a father the immediate conduct of his children. All these things, however, are presented to the spectator as something past and unalterable. This is obvious in the case of the astronomer, engaged, say, on the analysis of the composition of a distant star. What is presented to his retina is in fact the condition of the star many thousands of years ago. Similarly, in very different degree, by the mere fact that light and sound take time to travel, everything of which we are or can be spectators is something which has been, something which is fixed and settled, and which takes its inevitable place in the continuum of events before and after it.

From this point of view we cannot but see all events, including the actions of persons, as the necessary outcome of what preceded them and as the determining condition of what follows them. In this world, the world of the scientist, there is no freedom. If we study any epoch of history, as, for instance, Tolstoy studied the decline of Napoleon, we are bound to admit the legitimacy of his presuppositions, if not the accuracy of his conclusions. As historians, we study any event with the assumption that the future is as really existent as the past: we view it in the context both of what followed it and of what preceded it. For us, whatever they may have appeared to Napoleon in 1812, the years 1811 and 1813 possess precisely the same historical status. Time, whether past, present or future to the historical agent at any given moment, is viewed by us as a continuous and indivisible whole, any part of which possesses the same status in reality as any other. Whether time is represented as a stream which flows by a particular fixed point, which is the individual; or whether it is the subject himself who is regarded as moving through time, directing his awareness upon one bit of it after another, as a policeman (to use a simile of Professor Broad's quoted by Edwyn Bevan) might go along a street at night lighting up each house successively with his bull's-eye lantern – the precise metaphor is unimportant. What is relevant is that each part of the stream or street is regarded as real and existent as any other, whatever section of it the individual may happen to be seeing at the moment.

It is equally possible to view the period through which one is actually living from exactly the same point of view. The spectator attitude to the present is that which regards it as though from the vantage point of the historian of tomorrow. What will be the judgment on us then, it asks, when the scroll is unrolled and our period can be viewed as a whole? That is to say, it treats the present as if it were the past, regarding it as it will look when it is just part of a sequence between last year and next year. It is only when one can stand back and view the period in its context both forward and backward that one is capable of pronouncing an 'objective' judgment. This judgment can never be final, as the years yet to be unrolled will in some degree always continue to modify it. From the point of view of the spectator, from the point of view of the scientific historian, the future is as important as the past for the understanding of the present. That is to say, both have for him equal reality-status. He can work only when this assumption holds; only, therefore, when his subject matter is past, or is regarded as such.

Science, in any field, is bound to treat everything on the assumption that it stands as an item in a sequence of events, equally real and existent whether after it or before it. That is to say, it makes of universal application a presupposition valid for the study of the past. That is perfectly legitimate, since, as we saw, the objects of its observation are always in fact fixed and past, by the very fact that it takes time to observe them. But when it transfers this fixity and determinism to events not yet observed, it does not say anything about the nature of the events themselves. It only tells us something about itself. Looking from the scientific point of view, that is, regarding things *as though* they were events in the past, it pronounces them fixed and determined. This only informs us that events in the past, and all events so regarded, are fixed and determined – and this we knew before. It cannot tell us anything about events when they are not so regarded, for example, as they are, not to the observing spectator, but to the agent in the act of creating them. Science can no more say of the present and the future that they are determined than that they are not determined. For it only deals with the past, and things as if they were past; it does not deal with the present as present.

Now against this spectator attitude – which is by no means confined to the scientist any more than a man who happens to be a scientist is confined to it – there is set the radically different perspective of the 'I–Thou' relation. This is the point of view of the personal agent at the moment of decision. It is a moment which gives to the notions of freedom, choice and responsibility a validity which the combined efforts of all the scientists and philosophers who ever have lived or ever will live can never persuade us is illusory. There are, indeed, times when they seem to convince us 'at the top of our minds'. But they have never yet persuaded anyone to act on that conviction with any consistency. That is because, from the point of view which we adopt at the moment of action, the conclusions derived from viewing life as 'It' are just not valid or applicable. This does not mean that the results of scientific investigation are of no use when we come to do anything. That, of course, would be patently absurd. But it does mean that we act on the belief that, whereas science may be able to tell us what to expect from two lines of action chosen, yet it cannot tell us what we shall choose, let alone what we ought to choose. If I knew that anyone could predict with complete certainly what I should do in the next five minutes I should be forced to conclude that my freedom was illusory. But as I know there is no one who can, I feel justified in not allowing myself to be shaken from the conviction that I really am free. I admit the possibility that, if any scientist or scientists had the requisite knowledge – which they have not, and do not appear to be likely to have within any foreseeable period – then they might be able to demonstrate to my satisfaction that my conduct of the *last* five minutes was *completely* explicable in terms of the thousand and one causes – chemical, biological, psychological, sociological, economic – which have determined its course. But that would not disturb me in the least. For that is an analysis of the fixed, past world of 'It'. And that is not where freedom lives. Freedom's world, the 'Thou' world, is quite unassailable by the most potent assaults of the scientific determinist.

This antinomy – to use a word of Kant's, whose treatment of freedom is still the most profound in the history of philosophy – cannot be resolved, if by resolution is meant the breaking down in thought of what Karl Heim has called the 'dimensional' difference between the two worlds. It is, however, an antinomy which causes us no disturbances or even astonishment in the ordinary business of living. If a very homely example may be excused, the following experience of the writer will serve to explain what is meant.

Engaged upon a game of table tennis, I found myself, somewhat to my surprise, winning 10–4. At this point my opponent, exasperated at losing so many rallies, made the prediction that I should not gain another point. Whereupon, true to his word and despite my full intention to prevent him, he proceeded to win the game 21–10. Now if I had really thought that he knew with certainty all the strokes I should make for the rest of the game and that they would all be losing strokes, I should have felt not a little perturbed. In fact, of course, his prediction was nothing more than a rash boast backed by an increased determination to win. His failure to fulfil a similar prophecy in the succeeding game provided sufficient confirmation, had I needed it, that it was based on no scientific calculation. If, however, *after the event*, he had been able to show me exactly why it was that I did in fact lose all the strokes I made, and that the combination of eye and wrist and everything else required to make a winning shot was each time superior in his case than in mine, so that the result was inevitable, I might well have marvelled at his analysis of the determining causes, but I should hardly have felt that my freedom had been abrogated.

It may be objected, 'Yes, given the fact that you made those particular strokes, the result was inevitable; but you *might* have made other ones'. This must be granted. It is certainly true that if I could not have done anything else, then my freedom was illusory, even though I might have felt free at the time. But, be it observed, this saving possibility that I *might* have done otherwise is not derived in any way from the analysis of the chain of cause and effect. From the spectator attitude, looking back on it as a past event, there is nothing that would afford any evidence of a real choice. There is no break in the chain at any point, at which some mysterious act of freedom has to be postulated to bridge the gulf. Whether there was in fact a real choice or not cannot be determined, either negatively or positively, from an analysis of the course of events in the past, from the 'It' point of view. For whether there was a real choice or not, the chain of cause and effect would look *exactly the same*. If, therefore, after the event, someone could point out such a chain unbroken at any point, it could do nothing to affect my belief in my freedom one way or the other.

What makes me say, 'I could have done otherwise', is not any inference from the past, from a study of the 'I–It' world, but simply the conviction that at the time of action, in the sphere of the 'Thou', I *knew* I could. And this is a piece of knowledge around which the whole of my existence is organized and which possesses a reality-status which no considerations drawn from the dead, past world of the 'It' can shake. This judgment of the supreme reality of the 'Thou' world is ultimately indemonstrable. It cannot, without ceasing to be itself, form the conclusion of an argument based on inference from other 'facts' (*facta* – *past* participle passive) already 'established' and organized within the framework of 'It' knowledge. Either a man sees that, in Buber's phrase, 'real life is meeting' (of 'I' with 'Thou'), or he does not. It cannot be proved to him. This ultimate 'irrationality' (the very phrase betrays the bias which identifies the rational, that which possesses and bestows meaning, with the 'It' world) or freedom is not just the theory of a particularly anti-intellectualist philosophy. It is an inescapable truth; or, rather, a truth which can only be escaped by a system of thought which denies freedom. Freedom, literally, 'does not bear thinking about'. Directly one does think about it, directly one puts it on the analyst's table, it disappears, and leaves behind only the dead bones of an unbroken sequence of cause and effect. It cannot be the subject of any scientific verification. In Mr M. Jarrett-Kerr's words, 'we really have no guarantee that the relation, the "I–Thou" exists at all' (*Theology*, July 1944, p. 154). The purport of these words is to demonstrate the epistemological insecurity of Buber's whole position. But Buber would be the first to admit their truth – though he would say that what they demonstrate is simply the restricted applicability of any such scientific 'guarantees'. In all the decisive things of life we can give no proof that must convince: we cannot even describe the 'Thou' relation without turning it into an 'It'. We cannot describe freedom. We can only point to a conviction which we find others share. To one who knew it not, we could no more make it intelligible than we could describe the colour of a rose to a blind man.

From the point of view of the 'I–It' relation, as we saw, the future has to be treated in exactly the same way as the past and given an equal reality-status. This is inescapable. For just as from this point of view there is no evidence for suggesting that the past is anything but inevitable and determined, so, from this point of view, there can be no evidence which would lead to a different conclusion about the future. The future is in fact already settled and, in a true sense, exists, although I may not have reached it yet. The gramophone record of the whole is there complete, though the needle on its track, which is the subject in time, has only reached a certain point and can only see backwards.

But, just as, in contemplating the past, we cannot, without denying the reality of the 'Thou' world, admit that it could not have been otherwise, so too, unless we are to be false to ourselves, we must revolt against this conception of the future as existent and determined, just waiting for us to get to it.

We know that the last word on history is not that it is a determinism. We know that to treat the year 1812 as part of an unbroken continuum of determined sequence from 1811 to 1813 is to leave out the point of view which is really decisive for its interpretation and which is alone a sufficient ground at the time for the events later to be pronounced inevitable. The decision of Napoleon at the moment of his action is the important thing, a decision characterized by the absolute freedom and responsibility of the 'Thou' world. Of course, it did not come as something out of the blue, completely unrelated to his past existence or present environment. In fact, it is so related to them that, to one looking back on it in the 'It' relation, there is nothing that could not appear, in theory at least, explicable in terms of them alone. There is no gap left when the element of freedom is not taken into account. But to look at history from the point of view from which this element is necessarily invisible is, in a simile of Professor Dodd's, like beginning by sterilizing the culture one intends to test for bacteria. The only way to a proper understanding of the year 1812 is to regard the events from the point of view of Napoleon deciding, at the time of his action. And, at the time of his action, the year 1813 *simply did not exist.*

If the reality of the 'Thou', of freedom, decision and responsibility is to be maintained, this absolute non-existence of the future must at all costs be insisted upon. It is not just that it is not yet existent *for me* at the time of action. It cannot exist at all. For if anyone – God or man – could see me already doing what I have not yet done, then my future would be as unalterable as my past, and all choice illusory. However the phenomena adduced by Mr Dunne in his *An Experiment with Time* (1929) are to be explained – and Bevan offers an alternative explanation (*Symbolism and Belief*, 92–3) – it is certain that Mr Dunne's own theory is completely destructive of the reality of the 'Thou'. If we are to have a simile to express the nature of time, it must be one in which the absolute, metaphysical difference between the 'already' and the 'not yet' is made clear. Neither the stream nor the street[35] is any good. Bevan's image is that of

> a comet or rocket shooting through the void, the luminous head symbolising the present, and the tail of light behind it the past. In front of it, there is nothing but emptiness and blackness, though as it moves onward, more and more of that emptiness is changed into its line of light. (*Symbolism and Belief*, 88–9)

Between the 'already' and the 'not yet' there is an absolute difference. The former is 'there', fixed and done with, open to inspection, analysis and explanation, and patient of interpretation in terms of cause and effect. The latter is non-existent, fluid and undetermined. The moment which separates them is the creative moment of 'meeting', of action, of decision. This is not the so-called 'specious present' of the psychologists, which is said to vary from half a second to four seconds. For this is only another way of saying that percepts possess duration, and that we are aware of them as such for a short period before they pass into mere memories. It does not mean that we do not perceive them within the specious present as past. 'Percept', like 'fact', is a past participle passive. No, the 'now' of the 'Thou' world – the *Gegenwart* which signifies both the presence of personal meeting and the present of temporal duration – may not be assessed in terms of seconds or any such measurement. It is not an interval like that. Indeed it cannot be conceived as an interval at all. 'The span of time which demands our investigation', writes Grisebach in the passage quoted before, 'lies at the point where that succession which is apprehended as a continuous process is interrupted; where the man whose knowledge is concerned with the past is forced to come to a halt' (*Gegenwart*, 148). It is not an interval, because it is not a point between anything. It would only be so if it *were* part of a 'succession apprehended as a continuous process', of which the future was a real constituent on the same level of existence as the past. From its very nature, the moment of decision, of creative action, is indescribable. But there is no one who does not know what it means. And, against the closed and logical system of the 'It' world, it must be affirmed as the crucible of reality – unless we are to rest content with a theory of time which denies the most inalienable fact of our personal existence.

That the realm of the 'Thou' is the realm of the distinctively personal, that personality *means* the capacity and responsibility for this relation to one's environment, finite and infinite, is the thesis we have been propounding throughout. It is not proposed to argue this position again. At any rate, it could hardly be doubted that the capacity for the 'I–Thou' relation is *included* in what we mean by personality. For freedom, responsibility and the choice which lies at the root of purpose are on any analysis essential elements in personal existence. And these, if they are to be found anywhere, are to be found in what we have called the sphere of the 'Thou'.

This enables us to draw the conclusion that any theory of time which does not allow for the 'Thou' is *ipso facto* incompatible with a philosophy which preserves a place for the peculiarly personal form of existence. If time is treated as an unbroken continuum, if there is not a radical and metaphysical difference between past and future, if there is any being, or the possibility of any being, for whom the future is as the past and for whom the absolute 'not yet' of real duration is not a final fact, then the whole realm of personality and personal values is but the unsubstantial fabric of a dream.

This, then, is our quarrel with the Thomistic view of eternity, as with all theories which treat time from the point of view of the 'It'. By postulating an eternity for which the future is as actual as the past and for which there is not a real 'not yet', they inevitably depersonalize both God and man. They do admit, of course, that time is real and important for us and therefore, in that sense, real and important for God. Time is God's creation, and if he has any concern for our moral and spiritual existence, he must also respect the conditions which make it possible. But this alone is not adequate to the biblical idea of God. In Scripture not only do we have purposes which are gradually fulfilled, implying a real 'not yet', but God does too. He is a person in action, a living agent at work in the world, at every stage of whose activity there is a creative 'now' which fashions things really new, and 'calleth the things that are not' – really are not – 'as though they were' (Rom. 4:17). The Bible lends no countenance to the idea that history is but the playing out in time of a gramophone record laid up in heaven, whose end is as determined as its beginning – the theory which St Thomas only states in other language in his doctrine of the *Ideae* on God's mind. '*Cum omnia sunt a Deo, non a casu facta, necessarium est in ejus mente omnium ideas praeexistere objective, ad quarum similitudinem omnia condita sunt*' (Since all things are made by God, not by chance, there must pre-exist in His mind the ideas of everything in whose likeness all things were established) (*S.T.*, I, 15, i, conclusio). If reality is, as the Greeks thought it to be, static and motionless, if eternity is a *Totum simul* for which there is no difference between past, present and future, then decision is not real. Nothing that persons do is decisive, nothing is *really* happening, nothing really new, nothing that makes any *difference*. To treat past, present and future as if they were one and the same for God is to treat time purely from the point of view of the 'It'. And this is what St Thomas does. God's eternity is not regarded from the point of view of the 'I' at the moment of action, of the 'I' confronting the 'Thou' and calling for response. It is the *Nunc stans* of a static 'It' world, not the creative *Gegenwart* of the decisive 'Thou' relation.

In consequence, the fact that God's being is that form of *personal* existence which is constituted by this relationship is missed. The peculiar significance of what is meant by calling God a personal, living God is not understood. The fundamental fact about God is, certainly, one of 'being', as the Thomists assert. But it is 'being' in this personal relationship – the 'I-existence' which makes man's nature 'Thou-existence' or, as Brunner expresses it, 'being-in-responsibility'. Nothing is more significant than the different treatment accorded to the biblical statement about the ultimate name and nature of God – the 'I AM THAT I AM'. It is the foundation both of Hebraic and of Hellenic theology. But for the latter, it is transformed into a substantival impersonal, timeless 'It-existence'. The original 'I am', that primal word of deep calling unto deep, is transposed into the third person, into the relationless 'He who is' of Professor Mascall's title, into the objectivized *Ewigseiende* [eternal identity] against which Ebner directed his polemic (*Das Wort und die geistigen Realitäten*, 163; cf. also the references given above, p. 54). For the Bible 'being' is the 'infinite subjectivity' (Kierkegaard) of the 'I' in the decisive, purposive relation to a 'Thou', acting and calling for action. The 'I AM hath sent thee' is what defines the biblical meaning of the essence of God, a meaning which is totally foreign to the Hellenic metaphysic.

Thus, even if the reality of freedom and decision and personality were retained for *man* in the Thomistic scheme, by emphasis on the genuineness of duration for us, the fact of *divine* personality is completely mutilated. But, inevitably, failure here means that human personality is also robbed of its reality. The Bible represents God's purpose as one for *persons*, a purpose of fashioning *sons* in freedom unto himself. That is to say, it is a purpose which respects personality, which treats persons as they really are, as beings in a 'Thou' relationship. And one of the conditions of 'Thou-existence' is the reality of temporal duration, which involves a true 'not yet'. The future cannot exist in any form previous to my making it. If it is literally true that, in St Augustine's phrase, '*futura jam facta sunt*' (the future is already made), then nothing I do can make any difference, the decisiveness of decision is gone, and freedom is a myth. The reality of this 'not yet' must be absolute, even for God himself. If the future is really to be non-existent, then it cannot exist for him, and consequently he cannot know it. Any theory which says otherwise depersonalizes not only God but man. A real objective 'public' time is a prerequisite of freedom and personal existence. If anyone could see me doing a thing before I do it, even if it be God himself, then my actual doing of it is not that which brings it into existence – it is not decisive or creative. If the 'It' point of view, the spectator attitude, were all that we had to consider, then there would be nothing objectionable in the idea that different observers could at some other point see things happening that had not yet occurred. But if the reality of the 'Thou' is to mean anything, then any such possibility must be ruled out.[36]

Numerous attempts, of course, have been made to show that there is no real incompatibility between freedom and foreknowledge. On careful examination, however, it is difficult to see that all these are anything more than varyingly impressive pieces of logical legerdemain. Boethius' classical attempt, which had such an appeal for St Thomas, and which appears to have satisfied very many, including, recently, the author (C. S. Lewis) of *The Screwtape Letters*, 1942, is surely nothing more. Put briefly, the argument is this. God sees everything, past, present and future, in one eternal 'now'. He does not therefore foresee the future: he sees it. And to see a man doing a thing is not to make him do it.

> If thou wilt weigh His foreknowledge with which He discerneth all things, thou wilt more rightly esteem it to be the knowledge of a never-fading instant than a foreknowledge as of a thing to come . . . Why, therefore, wilt thou have those things necessary which are illustrated by the divine light, since that not even men make . . . those things necessary which they see? for doeth thy sight impose any necessity upon those things which thou seest present? . . . As you, when at one time you see a man walking upon the earth and the sun rising in heaven, although they be both seen at once, yet you discern and judge that the one is voluntary, and the other necessary, so likewise the divine sight beholding all things disturbeth not the quality of things which to Him are present, but in respect of time are yet to come. (*De Consol. Phil.*, v, 6; ed. Stewart and Rand)

Boethius distinguishes between an absolute and a conditional necessity in things. If a man is doing something, then he cannot not be doing it. To see a man walking means that he cannot be doing otherwise. But it does not mean that he could not have done otherwise, that he was bound to do it. Since future things, therefore, are the objects of God's present sight, they are necessary '*per condicionem divinae notionis*' with a conditional necessity. But they are not necessary *per se*: they might have been otherwise in so far as they are contingent events.

> But thou wilt say, 'If it is in my power to change my purpose, shall I frustrate providence if I change to alter those things which she foreknoweth?' I answer that thou mayest indeed change thy purpose, but because the truth of providence, being present, seeth that thou canst do so, and whether thou wilt do so or no, and what thou purposest anew, thou canst not avoid the divine foreknowledge, even as thou canst not avoid the sight of an eye which is present, although thou turnest thyself to divers actions by free will. (ibid.)

Boethius' position may be summarized in the words of W. R. Sorley: 'Universal determination contradicts freedom; universal knowledge does not' (*Moral Values and the Idea of God*, 1921, 472; cf. Lotze, *Outlines of the*

Philosophy of Religion, 1885, 120: 'A knowledge of what is free is possible, but a foreknowledge of it is inconceivable').[37]

But this specious solution cannot survive an obvious dilemma. Either the man has done the thing which is being seen or he has not. If he has, then it is an action in the past, and is irrelevant to the question of God's foreknowledge of the future. If he has not, then to see him doing it is to see it as something determined beforehand, or, in the case of God, to have determined it. Whatever the position of the divine observer, whether he sees it as happening or as going to happen, *the fact that he sees it at all means that it is there to see.* It is not something brought into being for the first time by the man's creative decision at the moment of action. If freedom is real, then it is simply not there to see, whatever the capacity of the divine observer to see it if it were.

Exactly the same applies to St Thomas's illustration of the same point. 'He who walks on a road does not see those who come after him, but he who looks at the whole road from some height, sees at one all those who are walking on the road' (*S.T.*, I, 14, xiii, 3; cf. *De Veritate*, 2, xii). Here again, the fallacy simply consists in the assumption that the later men are there to see. If they were, we cannot deny that God could see them. But if the future is really non-existent, he can only see it as such. The 'not yet' is a 'not yet' for him, or it is illusory for all.

What is fatal to the reality of freedom is just this assumption that the future is there to be seen. It does not help in the least to be told that 'to some things God has fitted necessary causes that cannot fail, from which effects proceed by necessity; but to other things He has fitted contingent defectible causes, from which effects proceed contingently' (*S.T.*, I, 19, viii). This indeed acquits St Thomas of a determinism of mechanical causation. He does not regard all future events as inevitably contained in the present: 'for the contingent is in its cause in such a way that it may not result, or may result, therefrom' (*S.c.G.*, I, 67). This does not mean to say that God cannot see all future events '*prout sunt in suis causis*' (as they are in their causes) (*S.T.*, I, 14, xiii). For, 'since God knows all things . . . He knows not only the cause of contingencies, but also that which may possibly hinder them. Therefore he knows certainly whether contingencies be or not' (*S.c.G.*, I, 67). However, he regards it as an inadequate account of the divine foreknowledge to say merely that God sees the future in its present causes. He knows it '*non solum ea ratione qua habet rationes rerum apud se praesentes, ut quidam dicunt; sed quia Ejus intuitus fertur ab aeterno supra omnia, prout sunt in Sua praesentialitate*' (not only because He has the types of things present within him, as some say; but because his glance is carried from eternity over all things as they are in their presentiality) (*S. T.*, I, 14, xiii). He sees them as completely actual now in eternity as he ever will when they become present in time. If this is the case, if the future is fully there to be seen, then the fact that it is reached in the time process by causes which might have been otherwise is irrelevant. For, in fact, they will not be otherwise than God knows they are. To say that God knows and wills that they happen contingently does not obviate an ultimate divine determinism: it only eliminates a proximate necessitation. St Thomas admits that everything is necessary '*secundum modo quo subsunt divinae scientiae*' (according to the mode in which they are hidden in the divine knowledge), even if not '*secundum quod in proximis causis considerantur*' (according to what are held to be their immediate causes) (*S. T.*, I, 14, xiii, 3). It is a solution which can fully satisfy neither the moral agent nor the scientist. From the point of view of the 'Thou' there is no freedom: from the point of view of the 'It' there is no determinism.

The inherent inadequacy of all such images to represent eternity as those employed by Boethius and St Thomas lies in the fact that they are *spatial* metaphors. They treat past and future as if they were exactly similar to left and right. That is to say, the difference between them is made to depend entirely on the position of the observer. For one who is outside space altogether there can be no left or right. In the same way, God is treated as outside time, and for him, therefore, there can be no past and future. He sees the whole of time at once as he sees the whole of space at once. But to treat time as thus comparable with space is to treat it purely from the point of view of the 'It'. For it is only from this point of view that it can be regarded as an unbroken continuum in which past and future possess precisely the same reality-status.

That the Thomist theory of time and eternity involves a doctrine of God which is unbiblical may be restated by way of summary by noting how completely destructive it is of the biblical valuation of *history*.

This world and human history is for the Bible the scene of real, decisive, *metaphysical events*. The Incarnation is the climax and the type of all such events. In it something happened which really made a difference – such a difference as to render it unrepeatable. The Crucifixion is a metaphysical event in being, as it were, part of the stuff that makes up eternity and reality. It is not simply part of 'a moving image of eternity', to use Plato's famous phrase (*Timaeus*, 37 d), just the reflection on the historical scene of another, timeless reality in heaven. It is in itself the reality. This is made clear when, as in the Epistle to the Hebrews, an attempt is made to express the Cross in terms of the Platonic metaphysic. The metaphysical status of this event in history is asserted by its representation as a timeless sacrifice in the heavenlies. By this the author did not mean that the historical event was a mere copy of a more ultimate, static reality. The event, an occurrence in the phenomenal world, was itself the reality: no one insists so much on the ἐφ' ἅπαξ (once and for all) as he does. Yet in order to signify its metaphysical quality, he has to transpose it into the timeless, and represent it as being enacted for ever in the noumenal world. For that is the key to the Real in this philosophy.[38]

Nothing could be more significant than this attempt at their combination for revealing the absolute incompatibility of the Greek and Hebrew assessments of time and history. On the one hand, the whole framework of the Greek theory is destroyed by the introduction of a particular piece of temporal and phenomenal existence into the ontal ('Real'), eternal realm. While on the other hand it can be shown, though here it would take us too far from our purpose (cf. Ch. 17 below), that the view of the nature of Christ's eternal priesthood, to which the attempted fusion commits the author, and of the nature of the faith which apprehends it, omits that necessary backward reference of Christian πίστις (faith) to a historical event in time, which the parallel Pauline doctrine of 'justification by faith' preserves. Faith is viewed as the assurance that Christ's sacrifice is perpetually being enacted in an eternal 'Now' in a world as yet invisible to us. By making its reference 'perpendicular' (from the 'now' in history to the 'Now' of heaven), this view leaves out what Kierkegaard in his *Philosophical Fragments* described as the 'Absolute Paradox' of Christianity, that our eternal happiness depends upon an event in time. Faith in the New Testament contains an essential reference to the particular and temporal – it is that which sees and adores the infinite and eternal in all the 'offensiveness' of the *einmalig* [once]. Its function is not to translate us into timelessness but to make us contemporaries of the past, to make the word of love spoken out on Calvary as 'present' to us in the 'now' of the 'Thou's' converting challenge, as it was to the centurion and the thief.[39] We are 'found in him' in so far as we make our answer to the *same* word, spoken once and for all, and yet ever availing, because ever capable of becoming 'present' to the believer. The particular form of the doctrine of Christ's eternal sacrifice which the Epistle to the Hebrews propounds cannot but be regarded as an unhappy compromise. By attempting the fusion of incompatibles, it fully satisfies neither the wisdom of the Greeks nor the foolishness of the Preaching; though, of course, at the decisive point – the metaphysical status of the particular and historical – it leaves us in no doubt as to where it stands.

Finally, it is only a doctrine of God's relation to time which has a place for this eternal seriousness of history that can give any real answer to the question: why, if the divine will is good and almighty, did it not make all things perfect from the beginning? Only if the perfection is of a kind which is impossible except as the culmination of a process, only, that is to say, if it must come at the *end* of something, can the apparent 'slackness of God concerning his promise' be explained or justified. Unless past and future are really different for God, there is no meaning in talking of a perfection in connection with him which derives its peculiar quality from the fact that it is an *eschatological* perfection. The realization that God cannot enjoy this perfection yet, that there is a real 'not yet' for him, is the ground of the biblical ascription to him of the quality, anthropomorphic though it may be, of *μακροθυμία* (long-suffering) – an attribute for which no place can be found in the Thomistic scheme. Because God is a Person dealing with persons, the tempo of the fulfilment of his purpose is in large degree dependent upon other wills than his own. To force the pace – the 'rend the heavens' and 'come quickly down' – is to force personality. And that he will not do, because, being love, he cannot. On the Thomistic analysis, however, there is no good reason why he should not increase the speed of the recording at will; or even, indeed, why he should trouble to play it at all, since he knows it all anyhow in a non-successive, and therefore presumably superior, manner.

Chapter Thirteen

ETERNITY: THE LORD OF TIME

In the previous chapter we completed the first of the tasks we set ourselves in relation to the problem of time. We attempted to show that the Hellenic-Thomistic view of the nature of eternity is strictly incompatible with the biblical doctrine of God. For, in treating time solely from the perspective of the 'It', it leaves no room for that distinctive mode of being – existence as an 'I' in relation to a 'Thou' – which the Hebrews implied when they spoke of God as the 'living' God and which we mean when we refer to him as personal.

We may now go on to look at the peculiar positive contribution to the notion of time made by a people who *did* regard the 'I–Thou' relation as the point of view from which alone its nature could truly be understood. It does not appear to be generally recognized that the Hebrews *had* a doctrine of time. Such is the bias which refuses to recognize philosophy in a source whose categories and conclusions are not those of Hellenic philosophy. But a brief examination of the words for 'time' in the New Testament may do something to dispel this error. These have received far less attention than those which connote 'eternity', and, in consequence, the conclusion that αἰώνιος means 'endless *time*' tends to be misleading in the absence of a closer analysis of the meaning of the latter. As a result of this analysis the biblical idea of 'eternity' may perhaps reveal itself to be less crude than it is usually considered.

The New Testament has two words for 'time': χρόνος and καιρός. The difference in their meaning corresponds exactly to the difference we have drawn between the 'It' and the 'Thou' viewpoints. There are a few passages in which the distinction is not clear-cut (thus we should expect καιρός in Lk. 1:57; Acts 3:21 – but cf. v. 19 – and Gal. 4:4 – but cf. Eph. 1:10), but this is to be expected in any living usage, especially among a people who were not careful about philosophical distinctions. But the general difference is quite clear.

The first point of note is that χρόνος is the less common of the two terms. This is in contradistinction to non-biblical usage, where it is the normal word for 'time'. The reversal in frequency might have been expected, since χρόνος describes time from a point of view which, for the New Testament writers, is not the 'proper' viewpoint, one from which its true nature cannot be understood. χρόνος is time out of relation to decisive action. It is neutral time, time abstracted from the 'Thou' relation and the personal purpose which gives it meaning. It is indeterminate time; time when nothing in particular happens; time which hangs heavy because it is not seen to have reference to any purpose; apparent delay (cf. the use of the verbs χρονίζω (prolong/delay) (Mt. 24:48; 25:5; Lk. 1:21; 12:45; Heb. 10:37) and χρονυτριβῶ (waste time/loiter) (Acts 20:16)). This comes out in the contrast of Heb. 4:7: 'Again, he defineth a certain day, saying in David, after so long a χρόνος, To-day'. For the most part it indicates an interval of time whose length is strictly irrelevant to the decisive events. Thus, in the parable of the vineyard, the owner planted it and let it out, and then went abroad χρόνους ἱκανούς (for a long time) (Lk. 20:9). In Rev. 20:3 we read that the Devil is shut up and sealed in the bottomless pit till a thousand years should be fulfilled: and after that he must be loosed μικρὸν χρόνον (for a short time). The exact period is undetermined. What is important is that, whatever it is, he only enjoys it by God's sanction. Similarly, in Jn 16:16ff., the duration of the 'little while' is unimportant: it is not relevant for determining the nature of the actions which follow it, and can therefore be treated freely. χρόνος is indeterminate because it determines nothing and nothing is determined in it.

καιρός[40] (which occurs in all the 27 books of the New Testament except Philippians, Philemon, James, 2 Peter, the Johannine epistles and Jude) is the word which reflects the peculiarly biblical way of regarding time. It is time in a positive relation to action in the 'Thou' relationship. This relationship, unlike the 'I–It', involves a real reciprocity, in which the 'I' and the 'Thou' both have a necessary part to play in mutual give and take. When the 'Thou' is also a person, this reciprocity takes the form of word and answer, claim and response, '*Spruch und Widerspruch*'. There is therefore a double reference in καιρός, according as to whether it is considered from the point of view of the address of the 'I' or of the appropriate response on the part of the 'Thou'.

In the former case it indicates the time at which the 'I' speaks or acts, or may be expected to speak or act, the time at which some event may be awaited. It is the ordinary word for the 'season' of fruit etc. – the time when one may look for it (Mk 11:13; Mt. 21:34 *et passim*). At a certain 'season' the angel could be expected to come down into the pool of Bethesda (Jn 5:4).

In due 'season' we may look for the reward of our labours (Gal. 6:9). What is significant is that in every case it is the time when *someone*, that is, God, may or will do something. What is expected is not regarded merely as some neutral event, out of relation to any particular personal purpose. It is not just a case of a thing happening, but of a person doing it. To talk of *καιροί* (times) for harvest, childbirth etc., implies for the biblical authors that it is *God* who gives the fruit of the earth, the fruit of the womb and the fruit of our labour. The use of *ἄχρι καιροῦ* (until the time) in Lk. 4:13 suggests that even the activities of Satan come within the compass of the overriding divine governance: the *καιρός* when he returns will be chosen, not by him, but by God (cf. Acts 13:11).

Secondly, and obversely, God's *καιρός* is man's opportunity, man's hour. Because the 'season' is not just a neutral event, but God speaking, so it is also at the same time the moment for our response. It is not something we can afford to ignore, as having no particular reference to action. The *καιρός* is the 'now' of the 'I–Thou' relationship. And the 'I' cannot speak without a claim being laid on the 'Thou' for an answer. *καιρός* is then for the New Testament authors, not only the time at which God acts or may be expected to act: it is also the time at which we have to act in response. In non-biblical usage this time for action, this opportunity, is as often as not self-determined. It is not, that is to say, a response to something given from without; it is chosen by the self, or at any rate freely selected from various fitting occasions. This sense does occur once in the New Testament, significantly enough in the mouth of the pagan governor Felix. 'Go thy way for this time', he says to Paul; 'and when I have convenient season (*καιρὸν μεταλαβών*), I will call thee unto me' (Acts 24:25).

But because the Bible takes the 'Thou' context of *καιρός* seriously, it believes that in all matters of any significance the time for action cannot be settled solely to suit our convenience. To manipulate events according to our own wishes is the mark of the 'It' approach. Rather, we have to answer *when* God calls: the *καιρός* is determined for us, and we must seize it while it is there. Just as there is a too-soon and a too-late for looking for the harvest, so there a too-soon and a too-late for gathering it in. Action has to be taken when the time is ripe or not at all. This explains the note of urgency which attaches to the biblical use of *καιρός*. It is something that a man must seize before it escapes him. 'The time is short' (1 Cor. 7:29) is the typical warning. The *καιρός* is like something which is to be bought up quickly before it goes off the market (Col. 4:5; Eph. 5:16). (So Lightfoot, though Armitage Robinson prefers to take *ἐξαγοραζόμενοι* (redeem, buy back) as meaning 'redeeming the time out of the possession of the evil one'.)

The assertion that the *καιροί* are not determined by us but for us is the Hebrew way of expressing the fact that we are *in* time. They are not ours to choose: they are God's to be answered and obeyed. The *καιρός* is ordained and given by God: there is nothing we can do to hasten or defer it. What we have to do is to await it, to expect or watch for it (Mt. 24:42 etc.), and to be able to discern it when it comes (Mt. 16:3). And when it does come we have to act upon it – before it is too late. In every *καιρός* there is something given and something required. God gives the time of harvest: we have to reap. In each case the divine word comes to man demanding a decision, a decision which must be taken then or never. The 'now' of the Bible, which is the 'accepted' time (2 Cor. 6:2), the 'today' (Ps. 95:7, as expounded in Heb. 3), is contrasted, not with the past and the future, but with the 'too-late' and the 'too-soon'. It is always 'now' in relation to personal action and response – the 'now' which is the narrow sphere of the 'Thou' relation.

This interpretation of time covers everything that happens. There is nothing that falls outside God's purpose. Every thing and person has its *καιρός* or *ὥρα* (hour). The words are used in respect of the occurrences of the natural order (the fruits of the earth, Mk 12:2 etc.; a woman's delivery, Jn 16:21), of the historical order (Jerusalem, Lk. 19:44; the Gentiles, Lk. 21:24; all nations, Acts 17:26), and of the supra-historical (the destruction of evil spirits, Mt. 8:29; the appearance of the Antichrist, 2 Thess. 2:6; the judgment of the dead, Rev. 11:18). Above all, there is the *καιρός* or *ὥρα* of Jesus himself (Mt. 26:18; Jn 7:6; 12:23; etc.). This is the climax of the whole time-process (*τὸ πλήρωμα τῶν καιρῶν* (the fullness of time) Eph. 1:10) and what gives it its meaning. 'The *καιρός* is fulfilled' (Mk 1:15) is but another way of stating the gospel of God's good purpose.

But of whatsoever or whomsoever these *καιροὶ* are predicated, they have one thing in common: they are God's own (*καιροὶ ἰδίοι* (one time, proper time) 1 Tim. 2:6; 6:15; Titus 1:3). Everything that happens happens in his good time. If the mills of God appear to grind slowly, it is not because he is 'slack concerning his promise'. It is rather the sign of his 'long-temperedness' (a translation of O. C. Quick's, whose unpublished lectures provided the seed of many of the ideas in this section): whether it takes a thousand years or one day, it is all the same to him (1 Pet. 3:8–9). This does not mean that time intervals are unreal to God. It means that the true measure of time is God's *καιρός* and not man's *χρόνος*. Time must be reckoned long or short by what there is to do in it, or by what God is doing in it – not by counting the hours and days. 'The time is short (*συνεσταλμένος* (contracted, shortened))' entails no implications as to the immediate end of the world. If the New Testament usage is understood, it is not so 'very strange that the last days should last so long' (A. R. Vidler, *Christ's Strange Work*, 1944, 30). Time can and must be reckoned only in reference to God's purpose.

God is the Lord of time, and all time is his. It is entirely subordinate to his purpose of love, which is gradually unfolded in and through it. Though we may not know them, the times and the seasons are in the Father's own power (Acts 1:7). History is God's καιρός, not mere human χρονολογία (records of time). He 'appoints' times for all things, times which are moments of κρίσις (cf. Eccles. 8:6: παντὶ πραγματί ἔστι καιρὸς καὶ κρίσις (to every matter there is a time and a season)), when his love is accepted or rejected, his purpose hastened or retarded. No time is unrelated to this one overarching purpose. All things and events are included in it, and everything is working towards one supreme consummation – to a final καιρός which is the final κρίσις (Mk 13:32–3). Christians are living in the 'last times': the hour for decision is short. For *the* καιρός is at hand (ἐγγυς, Rev. 1:3; 22:10). Indeed, it can even be said to have begun to break (ἤγγικε (is at hand) Lk. 21:8). Then will come the final 'too-late' and the doors will be shut. With the consummation of his purpose comes the consummation of time, which has no significance, and therefore no existence, except in relation to it. χρόνος – time considered without reference to God's action – cannot go on when the purpose is fulfilled; for it is a mere abstraction without self-existent reality. χρόνος οὐκέτι ἔσται (the time is not yet) (Rev. 10:6).

After this survey of the peculiar biblical understanding of time, we may now go on to substantiate the view that this understanding provides the basis for a perfectly tenable philosophical theory of the nature of eternity and of God's relation to temporal duration. Indeed, we hold that it provides the only basis for a theory which is consistent with the Christian doctrine of God. These statements may best be justified by undertaking an examination of the various objections which philosophers and theologians have felt to the ascription of real duration to the eternal God. These objections must be taken seriously. For it is not for nothing that Christian theology has discarded the Hebraic categories for the Greek. When we think, for instance, of the almost slavish literalism with which St Thomas incorporated into his system the biblical symbolism of angels, we cannot accuse him of lightly regarding the *a-priori* claim of scriptural language to be the medium of expression for his philosophical thinking.

Some of the objections are set out by Edwyn Bevan in the Gifford Lectures already quoted. Two of them he shares, but another he states only to dismiss. This is the familiar one, that the conception of eternity as endless durations is, to say the least of it, a most depressing thought. Now he is perfectly justified in pointing out that the inevitable association for us of indefinitely prolonged duration with fatigue and tedium derives from the conditions of our physical existence, and cannot therefore possess any validity in reference to such prolonged activity in heaven. But there does seem to be something more in the objection. For the duration is described nor merely as indefinitely prolonged but as 'endless'. Now, literally understood, endlessness involves purposelessness and meaninglessness. For if eternity is really endless, it means, either that God's purpose is never fulfilled, or that time goes on after it has been fulfilled. In either case eternity loses its significance. And such a meaningless eternity could not be ascribed to God.

This is probably a final objection to the interpretation of eternity as 'endless duration'. If *αἰώνιος* (eternal) means this in the Bible, then this biblical category at any rate cannot help us. But there is no *necessary* reason for supposing that this is what the biblical writers did mean by it. They, no more than we, could have rested content with a concept possessing implications such as have just been drawn; it may be said that this *was* their meaning, and that they did not see the implications. But such a conclusion is not forced upon us by the facts. For there does not appear to be any direct and positive suggestion in the term *αἰώνιος* of a time of which we can say definitely that it has no end. Indeed there are examples of its use to mean an indefinitely long period which, in fact, is not strictly endless. The word seems to embody a judgment of ultimate nescience, rather than any positive assertion of endlessness. It is applicable to something to which *we* can put no bounds: it may be endless for all we know, but that is not necessary to the idea. We may have to speak of it as endless, since to suppose an end would be to destroy the notion of eternity. Thus, in the case of God's existence, we may not assume any end. But to say positively that it is endless involves us in the attribution of meaninglessness explained above. We may say that it has not got an *end*; but not that it has *not* got an end.

The reason why we may assert with fair confidence that, to the biblical writers, *αἰώνιος* did not imply a positive assertion of endlessness, for the question only arises on a view of time in which they were not interested. It is only in terms of *χρόνος* that the problem can be discussed as to whether or not time goes on for ever. A mathematical infinity such as this is meaningful only out of relation to decisive personal purpose. For a time that really only exists in relation to purpose must cease at the culmination of the purpose – and such a time could not be strictly endless. Only an indeterminate and indecisive *αἰώνιος* could literally go on for ever. For such a time must either continue after the purpose is completed – and in this case its existence would obviously not be constituted by its relation to purpose; or it goes on for ever because the purpose does. Now a purpose which never ends can never be fulfilled, and a purpose which by definition is doomed to frustration from the beginning is as purposeless and futile as no purpose at all. Unending *χρόνος* is an impossible description of eternity. But, then, for the Bible *αἰώνιος* does not mean unending *χρόνος*.

For the scriptural writers, *αἰώνιος* is only really another way of saying that God is 'incomprehensible' purpose. Eternity here *means* that God 'loves with an everlasting love'. There was never a time when God was not God, personal purposive love. The ascription *αἰώνιος* is just the assertion that the conditions of this quality of 'Thou' existence have always been and always will be, as long as God himself has been and will be. Of this existence we cannot say that it began or will have an end. But neither can we make the opposite assertions. The categories of human *χρόνος* just do not apply. To ask, for instance, what happens after God's purpose is completed is an illegitimate question. It is attempting to judge God's *καιρός* by man's *χρόνος*. The assumption is that the divine purpose is something that takes place in a *χρόνος* which extends at either end of it. Whereas in fact *χρόνος* is just an abstraction from the purpose and has no existence apart from it.

Of course, to assert that God's being has always been this form of 'Thou' existence (which is only to assert that he has always been personal) is to make time (his *καιρός*) and creation (his 'Thou') co-eternal with himself. This would be denied by Thomism and, in fact, by traditional theology generally. This controversy, however, we have already had occasion to discuss in a previous chapter and we shall here add no more than a few words on the strictly temporal issue.

It should be noted that the co-eternity of God and the world is only objectionable on the ground that it implies their mutual interdependence. To say that God existed *before* time or the world is, after all, just a symbolical way of stating their dependence on him. But a convenient symbol is not a metaphysical truth. It is noteworthy that Boethius only objects to the idea of co-eternity if the word 'eternal' is used univocally of God and the world (as in Plato). What distinguishes the two for him is not that the world has a beginning and an end whereas God has not, but that the eternity of each is of a different quality ('*Neque deus conditis rebus antiquior videri debet temporis quantitate sed simplicis potius proprietate naturae*' (And further, God should not be regarded as older than his creations by any period of time, but rather by the peculiar property of his own single nature.) (*Consol. phil.* v, 6)). The eternity of the one is that of interminable duration, of the other that of an all-embracing simultaneity: God is *aeternus* (of eternity), the world *perpetuus* (long-lasting). As long, then, as eternity is not conceived univocally of

Creator and creature, Boethius has no objection to the idea that no beginning in time can be postulated of the world. And although we must conceive the distinction he makes somewhat differently, we, for our part, as will appear later, are just as interested in denying a univocal ascription of duration to God and man.

Even St Thomas can find no grounds, apart from the statement of 'revelation' in Gen. 1:1, for asserting definitely that the world is not eternal: '*Dicendum quod mundum non semper fuisse, sola fide tenetur, et demonstrative probari non potet; sicut et supra de mysterio Trinitatis dictum est*' (To say that the world has not always existed is only a statement of faith, and it cannot be proved by demonstration just as was said above about the mystery of the Trinity) (*S. T.*, I, 46, ii). Given the assertion of the Bible, we may indeed see the fittingness of a temporal beginning. For though in action (such as the act of creation) which is not successive, or 'by motion', the cause need not precede the effect (*S. T.*, I, 46, ii, 1; *S.c. G.*, II, 38), nevertheless, 'the world leads more evidently to the knowledge of the Divine creating power, if it was not always, than if it had always been; since everything that was not always manifestly has a cause; whereas this is not so manifest of what always was' (*S. T.*, I, 46, i, 6). But that is all it comes to; and now that the Genesis myths may no longer be regarded as an infallible storehouse of philosophical and scientific truths, there seems to be remarkably little basis for the assumed orthodoxy of 'creation *post nihilum*' (after nothingness).

Directly a little thought is given to it, the most obvious and insuperable difficulties are seen to attach to any idea that God was at some time different from what he is now – that is to say, something other than a Person, speaking and working out a purpose of love. The assertion of co-eternity only claims that God has always been what he is 'from everlasting'. *Because God is what he is* he could never have had being except in this 'Thou' existence, that is to say, existence ἐν καιρῷ (in time): being love, he had from all eternity to create, to utter his word to which the universe is the answer. This does not mean that he needs the world, or ever needed it, *in order to be what he is*: it does not make created existence anything but dependent, responsive existence. He is no more dependent on the world than is the question on the answer or the giver on the gratitude returned.

So far we have been concerned with the problems connected with the phrase 'endless duration' as a description of eternity. We have agreed that if this means 'endless χρόνος', it will not do. But there is not the slightest ground for supposing that the biblical usage of αἰώνιος contains such a signification. It always includes the idea of temporal duration, but that is because personal 'Thou' existence always includes the idea of καιρός. God is the One for whom it is ever the present. It is in this sense in which he is the eternal 'Now'. His mode of existence is ever present because he is ever in the 'Thou' relation. This is not the *Nunc stans* of timeless contemplation, for which the distinction between past and future is unreal; but the *Nunc agens* of him who ever 'works' (Jn 5:17), confronting and challenging the world with the love which is himself – a 'now' which leaves the future open for the exercise of freedom. It is the *Gegenwart* which calls for response and decision 'while it is called Today' (Heb. 3:13).

But, and this brings us to the second objection, it is not only the idea of endless duration which causes offence, but the idea that God is 'in time' at all. Against this idea Bevan brings forward two considerations which he believes to be fatally damaging. The first is that to be 'in time' means in fact to be subject to it. There is a helplessness in face of the inexorable beat of time's tread, that 'unperturbèd pace' (F. Thompson) which we can do nothing to hasten or retard. The clock of the years ticks on. In vain may Ovid cry '*O lente, lente, currite, noctis equi*' (run slowly, slowly, horses of night) as he lies in his mistress's arms. 'To think of God's experience as Time prolonged', Bevan concludes, 'is to think of time as stronger than God' (*Symbolism and Belief*, 111).

All this is perfectly valid against any theory which would postulate of God a temporal existence exactly the same as human temporal existence. But this has never been suggested, and certainly such a thought is strongly opposed to the biblical view. Psalm 90 is a sufficient refutation, if one is required, of the idea that such a suggestion could be entertained for one minute. There can be no such univocal attribution of duration to the finite and infinite. To ask, is God 'in' or 'out of' time, is to frame a false disjunction. If these were the only alternatives, then Bevan's conclusion of ultimate agnosticism would be the only one possible. For to answer either question in the affirmative is attended with insuperable difficulties.

The third, and biblical, alternative, if we have to continue the spatial metaphors, is that God is 'over' time. He is the Lord of time – neither its negation nor its subject. It is only we who are 'in time', we who cannot determine and chose our *καιροί*. But in the case of God they are *his own καιροί*: 'the times and the seasons are in the Father's power'. A fixed and regular calendar-time, in which the days and years (themselves *καιροί* for the Bible) go on in steady sequence, in which the 'horses of the night' do not slacken their pace to suit an individual's whim – this regularity is as essential for the moral personal life of his creatures as is the regularity of all the natural processes. But this uniformity is his servant, not his master: it is what his purpose uses for its ends. It is not these temporal measurements which control his actions, as to a large extent they do ours. He may come at any hour, late or soon, 'as a thief in the night', summoning the soul, challenging its response. 'One day is with the Lord as a thousand years, and a thousand years as one day' (2 Pet. 3:8). Such measures are not the ultimately determinative ones. They are not the standards by which we are to evaluate the universe or to judge whether God is slack concerning his promise. For his purpose is greater than these; he is the Lord of the years.

The second objection which Bevan advances against the ascription of real duration to God is again conclusive against any theory which places him 'in time'; but it cannot touch the biblical view. Time to us, he points out, means continual deficiency and loss. Each instant as it passes slips back into non-existence.

> Only the moment in which we feel and act is real, exists; as soon as we reflect on our feeling or action, it is already a bit of the dead, unchangeable past. We cannot keep our own being more than a moment. (*Symbolism and Belief*, 111–12)

This is the same experience which Buber has described as 'the exalted melancholy of our fate, that every "Thou" in our world must become an "It" ' (*I and Thou*, 16).

But for Buber, as for the Bible, God is 'the eternal "Thou" ', 'the "Thou" that by its nature cannot become an "It" ' (ibid., 75). Not only can he never become an 'It' to us: nothing can ever become an 'It' to him. Everything that has been remains 'real' to him, remains, that is to say, in the 'Thou' world. It is always 'now' for him, as when it first occurred. This is where the analogy of the *Totum simul* may legitimately be introduced to help our imagination. As we listen to a tune or phrase of music, we apprehend it as a whole. The earlier notes are retained, so that we do not hear them as isolated chords, but as integral parts of the complete tune: they affect the way we hear the later ones. As each new note is struck it takes its place in an ordered whole. The amount we can so apprehend at once in a single 'now' is, of course, small, though it varies with musical sensibility and training. But it is not impossible to imagine a being for whom the whole past is thus retained in a single 'now', so that none of it is 'dead', but each part affects what happens after it and forms its living context. The important point – that which distinguishes this from the illicit use of the analogy – is that what is included in the present 'now' is only the past and not the future. Even if the future did exist to be viewed now, this analogy from our experience could give us no indication that in fact God does see it. For the experience as we know it has reference solely to the retention in the living present of what has *already* occurred.

But, rightly used, the analogy can help us to a conception of an eternal 'Thou', in whose sight, to adapt the Psalmist, 'a thousand years are but as today'. As Lord of time he is one for whom nothing is ever lost, because nothing ever falls out of the one purpose to which everything that happens is integral. It is because we see the notes of a tune as forming together a single 'meaning' that we can retain them in a single 'now'. They lose 'Thou' existence when they become too many or too distant for us to see each of them as parts of a purposive whole. For him to whom everything is always a part of such a whole, nothing can cease to be a 'Thou'.

Finally, there are two further points, two further possible sources of objection, on which our position ought perhaps to be made clear. They concern the effect of our view of the nature of God's eternity on two other attributes of the divine being.

The first attribute is that of immutability. On this point there is little that needs to be said, though there is a prima facie difficulty to be faced. For the Hellenic-Thomist tradition, immutability and timelessness go together. God is the negation of every kind of change. Once, therefore, time and duration are made realities for God's own existence, it might seem that an essential quality of divinity had been excluded.

But all that in fact has been discarded is the Greek version of immutability. The Bible is ever insistent on the changelessness of God. But it is not the static immutability of still life, from which all motion is excluded. It is the assured constancy of an inflexible purpose. Once again, God is related to change, not as its negation, but as its Lord. In and through it he steadily brings to fruition a purpose, which, though infinitely adaptable to the ever-varying conditions introduced by human freedom is yet as certain in its aim and as unswerving in its direction as the arrow shot at the mark. That purpose is the one reliable thing in a mutable world: 'I the Lord change not; therefore ye, O sons of Jacob, are not consumed' (Mal. 3:6). God is not 'in change', any more than he is 'in time'; but neither is he 'out of' it. For reality of duration, and therefore of change, is a condition of personal 'Thou' existence. He is 'over' change. Nowhere is the biblical view of God as the sovereign Lord of change more magnificently stated than in the words of the Psalmist:

> Of old hast thou laid the foundations of the earth; and the heavens are the work of thy hands. They shall perish, but thou shalt endure: yea all of them shall wax old like a garment; and as vesture shalt thou change them, and they shall be changed: but thou are the same, and thy years have no end. (102:25–7)

God is the same 'yesterday, today and of ever', not because he is entirely unrelated to change, but because, amidst all the vagaries and mutabilities of life, he is the one element which stands above them and directs and controls them. He is the 'faithful' God, whose promises fail not, who keepeth covenant and mercy for ever. 'I will be that I will be' (Ex. 3:14, RV mg.): 'If we are faithless, He abideth faithful; for He cannot deny himself' (2 Tim. 2:13). That is the biblical affirmation of the divine immutability. The ἀναλλοίωτος (unchangeable) beloved of the Fathers is lifted from Aristotle's *Metaphysics*: the New Testament is content with πιετός (faithful).

The second attribute whose existence might seem to be threatened is that of omniscience. The conviction that God must know everything, and that 'everything' includes the future, has been one of the strongest motives for the formulation and retention of the view which regards God as the timeless surveyor of all time, past and present and to come. The postulation of a real 'not yet' for God necessarily involves the assertion that God does *not* know everything that is going to happen. God does not even know exactly what I am going to do in the next minute. If he did, the future would be already in existence, and free choice illusory. If God does not know all, how then can he be omniscient?

It is possible to give some answer to this question without moving outside the criteria propounded by St Thomas himself. For, in dealing with the subject of omnipotence, he lays it down as a rule of interpretation that God can do everything that does not involve an inherent contradiction (*S. T.*, I, 25, iii). To treat being as if it were non-being, or vice versa, would involve such a contradiction. This is the reason why he cannot treat what has happened as if it had not – he cannot undo the past (*S. T.*, I, 25, iv). (We may ask in parenthesis, why the *past*? For God the whole of time has equal reality-status and is equally fixed and irrevocable. In emphasizing the unalterability of the *past*, St Thomas would seem to imply that the future is somehow different, and that, after all, there is a distinction between them for God.) But just as undoing the past is to treat what is as if it were not, so, on our theory, to know the future would be to treat what is not as if it were. That would be equally impossible for God, and not, therefore, to be included in the concept of omniscience.

But such a way out is not possible for the Thomist. He cannot agree that the future is in fact strictly non-existent. The only things which are impossible for God are those which are intrinsically self-contradictory. And the present existence of the future for God is not intrinsically self-contradictory. It is only contradictory if human freedom is to be a reality. In other words, the contradiction is constituted, and the resultant limitation placed on God's knowledge, by something outside God himself. But in Thomism there is no place in God for any external limitation, voluntary or otherwise. There is nothing which can act upon him or affect him, or to which he can even stand in a *real* relation. He is absolutely impassible. Any limitation or passibility immediately introduces an element of *potentia* into one who is by definition *Actus Purus*. He cannot will a limitation in himself. For that would be to will an element of non-being into himself – which really *is* an intrinsic impossibility. *Any* limitation is an absence of being, an absence of perfection. Therefore God must know everything that does not involve intrinsic impossibility. Since such an impossibility is not constituted by respect for human freedom (the only reason why he should *not* know the future), God must know everything that is going to happen, in exactly the same way as he knows everything that has happened.

As long as we hold to the Thomist presuppositions and the Thomist methods of determining the divine attributes (by which any denial of power not intrinsically self-contradictory is an attribution of non-being and imperfection), then there is no alternative to postulating in God complete omniscience and complete prescience. Our theory of time would then involve a denial of one of the necessary attributes.

But there is not the slightest reason why we should be bound to this method of determining the divine attributes. It is not the Hebraic method. The Bible does not start from God as pure being, being in the abstract. It starts from God as being-in-relation, the 'I' confronting the 'Thou'. God's being is the personal, purposive existence of loving will. The attributes of the divine being are the nature and requirements of this loving purpose. They are all simply the qualities which must be postulated of God if this will is to be itself. They are the ways by which love must work if it is to be love. Any qualities which are either rendered irrelevant or excluded by this criterion cannot be ascribed to God. This is the real nature of the 'contradiction' which makes any attribution impossible. Thus, in determining the answer to the question, can God know the future? we ask whether this is required by, or compatible with, his nature of love. And the answer is, no. For love implies the reality of, and the respect for, freedom in its 'other'. And this freedom would be illusory if God knew everything this 'other' was going to do. Therefore God does not know the actual course of the future. This is no 'limitation'. It is simply the condition of his being what by nature he eternally is. The fatal limitation would consist precisely not in not knowing but in knowing. If he did know, then he really would be limited; so limited that his nature of love would be completely mutilated and destroyed. He would contradict himself if one of the conditions of his being love were denied by his own knowledge.

In the light of these considerations we may try to state what knowledge it seems that it *is* legitimate to attribute to God. This will be the meaning and scope of his omniscience – the knowledge of all that it is necessary for him to know in order to be himself and to fulfil his purpose of love. It is an omnipotence which may come to expression equally in the incredible wisdom which orders and disposes the milllionfold processes and contingencies of the cosmic scene, as in the complete nescience of the child Christ in his mother's womb. In neither is the knowledge in any degree 'limited', though in each case it manifests itself only through the finite. The divine omniscience was not laid aside by the Incarnate – it was exercised in the provision of just that knowledge, and no more, which would secure the triumph, and not the defeat, of love working in human form. What Christ knew in the flesh was determined by his human limitations, the observance of which was required by infinite love in order to be itself in the purpose it was seeking to achieve. Omniscience *is* all the knowledge God requires in order to be love. What in any situation is the precise measure of this knowledge will differ according to the particular end in view. The Incarnation represents one exceptional set of conditions which determine the form of its manifestation. Here the 'absolute offence' is presented, when omniscience *expresses itself* as total nescience. But it is also possible to state in more general terms the marks of the divine omniscience which are determined by the fact that it is always an omniscience of *love* dealing with *persons*. What knowledge can we, and should we, always ascribe to God? We may, for convenience, seek to state this under two heads, though it will be seen that ultimately it is but a single knowledge.

In the first place God must know his love for what it is. He must know, that is to say, that it is infinite and eternal, bounded by no limits external to itself, and possessing a power which no creature is ultimately able to resist. It is a love which can and will fulfil its purpose, a triumphant love, confident of victory – not a struggling power which makes for righteousness, uncertain of itself and of its ability to win a hostile and indifferent world. Even when it is on the Cross, at the moment of its greatest constriction and apparent defeat, it must know that the very same Cross is the means whereby all will ultimately be drawn in free and willing obedience. God must know, as, in the well-known simile of William James's, the master chess-player knows, that he will win, whatever the other may do (*The Will to Believe*, 1896, 181). And to win means for God that love shall be triumphant by love's methods. The forcing of any to salvation or the abandonment of any to destruction or eternal hell would not be love's victory but its defeat. For love cannot have made man for that. Divine omniscience means at least this; that God knows the power of his love to be such that, sooner or later,[41] there is no one who will not willingly and joyfully own its sway. If any one could in the end hold out against its freely persuasive constraint, then human self-will would have proved itself stronger than divine love. That love would not be infinite, and God would not be God.

The mention of W. James's simile brings us to the second sense in which we must say that God is omniscient. It is indeed really but the obverse of the first. The master player knows that, whatever move his novice opponent makes, he will win. He does not know what move the other will in fact make; but he knows the possibilities, and he knows that he possesses an answer to them all. In the same way God does not know exactly what we shall do. But he knows all about us that can be known. 'There is no creature that is not manifest in his sight: but all things are naked and laid open before the eyes of him with whom we have to do' (Heb. 4:13). He is the one 'unto whom all hearts be open, all desires known and from whom no secrets are hid'. He knows all the raw materials of our choices. He understands us through and through, because, in order to be absolute love he must. We know how so often our best intentions are frustrated by an insufficient knowledge of the true nature of the person with whom we are dealing. The consequence is that we frequently do out of love what turns out to be ultimately detrimental to the other's true good. How often a father must long to be able to know his boy's character through and through, so that he could be sure what was the best way of treating him, what was in fact the loving act, each time he went wrong. Ought he to overlook it, or ought he to punish? And if so, how much? All this God knows; and he knows it because, unlike knowledge of the future, it is knowledge which, so far from contradicting his nature of love, is presupposed by it.

In the course of this section an attempt has been made to adumbrate some of the lines along which an adequate conception of the personality of God can be wrought out. The traditional theology, with its categories of substance and causality, its analysis of pure being and its attempted 'proofs', has left us with an 'It'-God, a 'God in the third person', between whom and the 'Thou' of religious faith an impassible gulf is fixed. It has equipped this being with a number of personal attributes, but it has not given us a personal God. For a being with every personal attribute who yet stood only in a distant, impersonal relationship to man would not be what is looked for in a personal God. That he should ever face each individual in a truly 'personal' relationship – this is a prerequisite that we cannot afford to relinquish: it must form part of the definition of his personality. And it is because it occupies no such place in the idea of personality with which the traditional theology of 'substance' works that this theology fails, and ever must fail, to satisfy our most fundamental requirements.

'Existence as a substance' and 'existence as a person', said Ebner, stand in irreconcilable antinomy. No amount of variation upon, or refinement of, a theory of existence which builds on the wrong foundations can do the least good. It is only by a complete reversal of basic presuppositions, by going right back to the beginning and starting again on another path, that any real progress can be achieved. This involves a philosophical revolution, beside which that of Descartes is insignificant. This 'Cartesian *faux pas*' (W. Temple) was still a step in the same direction as before: its effect was simply to establish even more impregnably the philosophy of substance in terms of which the interpretation of personal existence had been cast.

The achievement of an alternative philosophy of personality must naturally be a slow process. It will mean learning to work with a whole new set of categories, derived, not (like those of substance and causality) from things standing in external connection with each other, but from persons in the reciprocity of internal 'Thou' relations, (e.g., word and answer, claim and responsibility). In the development of the philosophy of the 'Thou' a beginning has been made in this direction. It has succeeded in delineating a form of existence which may at last be called truly personal. This is an existence which cannot be translated into the objectivity of the third person, but which lies in the relation between the 'I am' and the 'Thou art'. All human existence is being-for-the-Thou, being-in-responsibility; it is relational existence, grounded, not in the self-contained substance of the individual, but in the address of an 'other'. And, in the last resort, this 'other', in response to whose word of gift and claim the self has its being, is for every man the divine 'Thou' of God, the unconditional Person. In and through the nexus of historical personal relationships, and uniquely in the relationship to Jesus Christ, its very incarnation, is met the Word of one who is pure 'Thou', through whom, and in whom, and unto whom are all things. God's existence is given as 'Thou' existence or not at all – though awareness of it immediately forces the recognition that its absolute priority demands that it be called more appropriately the 'I' existence over against which all human life is but a 'Thou'.

The doctrine of the personality of God means simply the assertion that this peculiarly personal existence, in which alone he is known, is that which characterizes him as he essentially is; in other words, that he possesses no other mode of being than that of existence-in-relation-to-a-Thou. It means that God *is* love, that a relation to an 'other' constitutes the very essence of his being – an 'other' who, nevertheless, is utterly derivative and dependent and is in no way a presupposition of his own existence or a complement of his own insufficiency. God as he is in himself is never God as he is for himself, but always God as he is for another. Creation and revelation and the whole relational structure brought into being by the existence of the finite 'Thou' are just part of what it means for God to be a Person. If they are not conceived as issuing from a necessity of his being, then that being is not personal existence. It is this existence-in-love, rather than a concept of pure being divorced from relation to anyone or anything, which must form the ground of the divine 'attributes' and determine the manner of their predication. The attributes of God are not so many 'perfections' characterizing his being per se, without reference to the relations in which he stands or the purpose he exists to achieve. They are rather the conditions of his existence as love and the presuppositions of the victory of its purposes. They are to be determined, therefore, by the fact that the being they predicate is nothing other than the divine will. Anything less than a consistent thelematological interpretation reveals a lapse into the view that the real essence of God is something other than, or beyond, the will of his love, and this *ipso facto* involves the ascription to him of an ultimate form of existence which is *not* that of the personal.

The elaboration of such a consistent thelematology is again something which must take time. It means that the Christian philosopher must be prepared to be biblical with a seriousness which was not so urgent when God's 'will' in revelation was regarded as no more than a non-essential expression of a 'nature' determined independently of it. St Thomas was able to reach a definition of omnipotence and eternity (to take the two illustrations with which we have been especially concerned) without making any reference to how that omnipotence had defined itself in the Cross of Christ, or to the quality of that eternity as the biblical writers had always conceived it. And, on his presuppositions, he was justified in so proceeding. But, for us, this is impossible. If it is the divine will which is to be absolutely determinative, then it is the Hebraic rather than the Hellenic insights into the nature of God that must form the starting point for any theology which regards the Bible as final for the revelation and understanding of that will.

What must make progress so slow is that, here too, the new approach demands of us that we shall work with a wholly different set of categories than those which have served theology hitherto. According to the traditional view, the essence of God was 'ontologically' defined and the revealed facts of his will fitted in as best they might into this scheme. The fact of apparent discrepancy, say, between an omnipotence which could admit of no limitation and the biblical assertion that 'the power of God' was supremely to be seen in the constriction of Christ crucified, was not fatal to a theology which claimed no necessary connection between being and will in the divine. But it soon becomes evident that, for the purposes of interpreting the will as determinative of the whole, the ontological categories, deduced from a conception of the essence which ignores the will, are likely to be grievously inadequate. This we have discovered to be very clearly the case in the matter of the nature of eternity. If we start from the Hebraic insights, we find that, in order to be expressed at all, they require to be formulated in their original biblical categories. The ontological presuppositions which underlie the Hellenic thought-forms cannot be applied to these insights without destroying them. St Thomas thought merely to smooth away the anthropomorphic and unphilosophical elements in the biblical conception of the divine eternity by transposing it into the key of Greek thought. But by dropping the peculiarly Hebraic idea of *καιρός*, and radically changing the signification of *αἰώνιος* by the elimination of its durational content, he effected, in fact, a fundamental alteration in the scriptural doctrine of God and made his eternity a quality, not of a Person, but of a Substance.

St Thomas, of course, was correct in regarding the biblical notions as unphilosophical as they stand. No one would wish to pretend that the Bible was philosophy. Moreover, the contribution of Hellenism, with its discipline of metaphysical thinking, its analysis of the structure of Being, and its purgation of human ideas of Reality of a false anthropocentrism, must never be disparaged. Without that we should certainly not be where we are now. But the time has come when we are being forced to recognize that it is only by applying the critical approach it has taught us to the Hebraic ideas themselves, rather than by discarding them for its own set of categories, that we may reach a conception of the personality of God adequate to the religious awareness of the Hebraeo-Christian tradition. Until recently there was no philosophy available whereby the insights into the structure of personal relations reached by an unspeculative race could be worked up into a systematic view of God and the world capable of challenging the imposing edifice of Thomism. In this matter the 'I–Thou' philosophy has proved itself a true 'handmaid of theology'. Without making any extravagant claims for it as a new *philosophia perennis*, one may fairly claim that is has enabled the Hebraic categories of personal encounter to become recognized as a legitimate basis for a genuinely independent and self-existent theological structure. And because it is biblical in its inspiration (and only in so far as it is so) it may claim to present at least *a Christian philosophy* – and this in a sense that the self-styled *philosophia perennis* cannot, for the reason that it does not ascribe to the Deity a form of existence which is the same as that of the dynamic, 'living' God who speaks through the record of the scriptural revelation. In these chapters, only a small beginning has been made in the direction we have indicated. What is needed is, indeed, a new *Summa* – one which will interpret the biblical revelation in terms of a philosophy that has allowed the Bible's categories to come to their own. But this is something for which we may have to wait many years, perhaps generations. We stand as yet only at the opening of the vista that lies ahead.

Part Three

Chapter Fourteen

THE PLACE OF THE DOCTRINE OF THE TRINITY

The two preceding parts, either directly or indirectly, have been occupied with working out a doctrine of the divine personality adequate to the experience given in the Hebraeo-Christian tradition. In other words, our task has been one of biblical philosophy. We have sought to start from the general biblical assumptions concerning the nature of God and his relation to the world and build them up into a philosophy of personality, human and divine, capable of interpreting the sum of our experience. To a large extent this method has justified itself, and the Hebraic presuppositions have afforded categories of interpretation philosophically in no way less valuable than those of Hellenic ontologism. It is a method, however, which raises questions at the same time as it answers them. The most fundamental of these questions now requires our attention.

The ground from which the stronghold of Hellenism has been assailed has been the Bible as a whole rather than the New Testament in particular. That is to say, it is Hebraism rather than Christianity which has been set against the wisdom of Greece. When Tertullian uttered his famous rhetorical question, 'What is there in common between Athens and Jerusalem?' (*De Praescriptione Haereticorum*, 7), he was in fact contrasting 'the Academy' with 'the Church'. Nevertheless, the words might form the text for much of what we have been saying. For 'Jerusalem' is a symbol of the continuity between Judaism and Christianity, being the centre both of the Old and of the New Israel. This continuity has been stressed against Hellenism. It has been asserted that a view of God and of the knowledge of God underlies, and is common to, all the books of the Bible from Genesis to Revelation. The unity of this witness is not disturbed by the specifically Christian elements introduced as a result of the events which the Gospels record. Though reached in its fullness only after a slow and faltering process, there is a single view of God's nature with which, if it were presented to them, all the biblical writers would concur. It is the awareness of God as holy will, dealing with men in mercy and judgment through the historical processes in which they are set. The quality of God's purpose is seen at its highest as the love of a father for his children. Having created men, he suffers them, though they have rebelled against him, guiding, pleading, chastening, forgiving – to the end that they may be drawn back to that state of complete personal communion with himself for which he made them, and to which in his mercy he will raise eternally those who respond to his call. This, in terms of individual experience, may be described as the awareness of God as an eternal personal 'Thou', meeting the soul in inescapable, absolute demand at the same time as he freely offers himself as its sole refuge and only true fulfilment.

But while the unity of the biblical view is granted, and its validity as an alternative to Hellenism acknowledged, there remains the question of the relation of this Hebraic position to the Christian faith. In the preceding chapters we have, indeed, drawn upon material which is peculiar to the New Testament. Taking the will of God as historically revealed as the equivalent of his essence, we naturally have not neglected what we should regard as both the culmination of that revelation and the key to its understanding. Thus, on the question of the quality of the divine omnipotence, we did not hesitate to begin with the Cross of Christ, where the New Testament asserts God most chiefly to have declared his almighty power. Again, our general statement of the Hebraic doctrine of God as pure love was clearly dependent upon the 'completion', the 'clarification' and the 'correction' (Niebuhr) which even the highest Old Testament insights in this matter had to receive in the life and teaching of our Lord. But none of these peculiarly New Testament elements in any way affected the formal structure of the Hebraic doctrine of God as personal will. Rather, they presupposed it and took their place within it, whether by way of addition or modification.

But another consideration introduced by the fact of the Incarnation is of a different kind from any of these. This is not some particular corrective to our doctrine of God contained in the teaching or example of Jesus Christ, but, rather, the whole challenge of the fact of his Person. He claimed – and the assertion is the most central article of the Christian faith – to be, not simply another, or even the final, teacher *about* God, but to be very God himself. The Jews of his time regarded this claim as shattering the whole framework of their doctrine of the divine unity. Whether they were right or wrong, it is clear that this fact – and the doctrine of the Trinity which emerged from it – is of a very different nature from the other considerations with which we have been occupied. It is a potential challenge to the whole structure of the Hebraic view of God as a single personal will. In other respects it may be possible to speak of a general 'biblical' view of the 'living'

God, presupposed by and controlling every fresh insight into his nature and purpose. But does not the claim of the Person of Christ and the assertion of God as a Trinity threaten to disrupt the essential structural framework of the 'Thou' relation between God and man? Is the fact of the divine triunity to be regarded as an additional differentiation within the same formal unity of personal will: is it the same one 'Thou' now revealed under three modes? Or does the fact of triunity itself constitute a new framework within which all else is given: is it now a question of three 'Thous', instead of one, being the form under which God is known?

Though the form of the questions may be new, the problem at bottom is the same as has agitated philosophers and theologians for centuries. It is true that the contrast, historically, has been stated in the form of the antithesis between faith and philosophy, revelation and reason. Here, rather, it is between views based on one set of revelatory events and experiences (the Bible generally) and others grounded in a special set of such events and experiences given within the larger context of the same revelation (the New Testament). The contrast is drawn between a more general and a more special revelation, rather than between reason and revelation as a whole.

But the difference in the form of the question is not of great importance. The hard distinction between reason and revelation is breaking down. The claims of natural theology to constitute an autonomous science are being challenged from all quarters. There is a return to the real Pauline position, which attributes 'that which may be known of God . . . through the things that are made', not to the operations of men's unaided reason but to the fact that 'God manifested it unto them' (Rom. 1:19–20). The names of Emil Brunner, John Baillie and William Temple, amongst others, may be cited for the view that the distinction which used to be drawn between natural and revealed knowledge ought rather to be made between two kinds of revealed knowledge, general and special – a distinction grounded only in the fact that, though all are equally expressions of a personal will, some actions are more 'revealing' than others (see: Baillie, *Our Knowledge of God*, 35–43; Temple, *Nature, Man and God*, Lect. XII; E. Brunner, *Offenbarung und Vernunft* (ET *Revelation and Reason*, 1947); *Natur und Gnade*, 1934 etc.).

Much, therefore, of what was said in the older controversies concerning the 'relation' of natural and revealed is relevant when discussing the connection between the two degrees of revelation we have called the Hebraic and the Christian. Having transposed them, as it were, into this new key, we may briefly consider the different answers which have historically been given. As representative of two recurrent views within the Church, the attitudes of St Thomas Aquinas and John Calvin may be contrasted and compared.

In Art. 1 of Qu. 32 of Pt. I of the *Summa Theologica*, St Thomas declares that knowledge of the Trinity is not something which can be reached by the reason alone. The unity of the Godhead can be demonstrated to all and sundry, and that on three grounds: (a) '*ex ejus simplicitate*' (from his simplicity) (b) '*ex infinitate ejus perfectionis*' (from his limitless perfection) (c) '*ab unitate mundi*' (from the unity of the world) (11, iii). But the fact that this unity exists in three Persons cannot be known to natural reason. For the only knowledge of God which this faculty affords is knowledge derived *ex creaturis* (from created things). The power manifested in creation is something which belongs to the Godhead as a whole, and its effects therefore do not afford evidence of the activity of any separate Person or Persons. All that reason can yield is statements concerning the one divine essence, '*non autem ea quae pertinent ad distinctionem personarum*' (not those things which concern the distinction of the persons) (32, i).

St Thomas's position, then, is that reason can take us far in the knowledge of God. It cannot indeed reveal the fact that the unity of the divine being exists in trinity, but of that unity it leaves us in no doubt. The function of revelation is just to disclose an additional fact about this unity.

And, for him, the case is essentially the same with the relation of the Old Testament to the New. As Augustine before him had confessed, it is impossible to attribute the theophanies vouchsafed to the Patriarchs and Prophets to any one Person of the Trinity or to use them as positive evidence for any division within the Godhead. But the New Testament came to fulfil the old dispensation by showing the already cognized unity to be in fact a triunity. Christ revealed that to be also three which was already fully understood to be one.

The assumption lying behind the Thomistic approach is that the doctrine of the Trinity is an additional revelation to complete an already existent corpus of knowledge about God. Without it, a perfectly consistent Theological structure can be erected, and the superimposition of the Trinitarian coping stone in no way modifies the original building. The unity of the Godhead is taken as certain; and, without in any way affecting this unity of essence, a division of Persons is then introduced.

Calvin will have none of this presupposition. Apart from the Trinity there is for him no knowledge of the unity. Of God he says,

> While He proclaims His unity, He distinctly sets it before us as existing in three Persons. There we must hold, unless the bare and empty name of Deity merely is to flutter in our brain without any genuine knowledge (*nudum et inane dumtaxat nomen sine vero Deo in cerebro nostro volitat*). (*Institutes*, I, 13, ii)

It is not here a question of the knowledge of tri-Personality being added to an already true and self-complete Theology. The doctrine of the Trinity gives us the 'name' of God; or, perhaps we might say, the Christian name of God. As A. Calov says,

> *qui non addunt mentionem trium personarum in descriptione Dei, eam nequaquam genuinam aut completam sistunt, quum sine iisdem nondum constet, quisnam sit verus Deus* (Those who do not make mention of three persons in their description of God do not make that description either genuine or complete, since there is not yet in it who is the true God). (*Systema loc. theol.*, II, 182; quoted Barth, *Doctrine of the Word of God*, 347)

There is here a tension between Dogmatics and Philosophical Theology. St Thomas could spend the first two-thirds of what he wrote on the doctrine of God in the *Summa Theologica* without mentioning the Trinity, and then, having introduced it, never allow it to modify or affect what had gone before. Karl Barth, in contrast, has put the doctrine of the Trinity in the very forefront of his *Dogmatik*. He criticizes those who 'reserve the question to which the doctrine of the Trinity is the answer (namely, *Who* God is) and deal first with His *existence* and His *nature*, as if this That and What could be determined otherwise than on the presupposition of the Who' (*Doctrine of the Word of God*, 345).

Is there any mediating between these two positions – between those who would see in the Trinity the coping stone and those who would regard it as the foundation of the doctrine of God? And, in particular, what of the notion of a 'Hebraic' view which claims to give an account of the fundamental conception of God's personal nature and will as revealed in the Bible without introducing any of the notions of tri-Personality derived from the New Testament?

The course of our argument in previous chapters would seem to have committed us to what might be called the Thomistic approach.[42] We have analysed and adopted the Hebraic position as affording the only doctrine of God which can take seriously the constitutive significance of the 'I–Thou' relationship for the nature of personality. Starting *ex creaturis* (or, rather, in particular, from *persons* in relationship to each other, the world and God), we have been led, as St Thomas says is inevitable, to a conception of the Godhead which in itself does not contain any internal differentiation of Persons or Hypostases. Hitherto our only mention of the Trinity has been to dismiss it as the answer to the purely philosophical problem of God's 'other'. Now, it seems, it is to be introduced very much as a coping stone to an otherwise complete and self-consistent structure. Our method seems to have been that of Philosophical Theology rather than of Dogmatics. But the situation in fact is not so simple. For a closer analysis of this Hebraic position reveals influences to have been at work which cannot be understood from the standpoint of pure Judaism.

Now it is not argued by its advocates that there is nothing in the Hebraic position which does not go beyond the teaching of the Old Testament. The term in fact refers to the Judaeo-Christian tradition as a whole. They do assert, however, that there is nothing in this position so dependent upon the fact of the Incarnation, and the doctrine of the Trinity to which it gave rise, as to be inexplicable without them. Thus, the final affirmation of the Hebraic view that 'God is love' is not to be found in the Old Testament *simpliciter*. God there is, indeed, 'loving unto Israel', but the point is never reached at which it is possible to assert that the words 'God' and 'love' are interchangeable, and that everything in God, his creative and sustaining power, his omniscience, justice, wrath and all the other attributes are in fact but qualities and ways of working of this one holy love. But it would be maintained that this conclusion was already logically present in the Old Testament, and that, although the Incarnation may have provided the occasion for its full realization, it was in no sense the indispensable condition of it. In other words, the knowledge of the unity of God as the knowledge of the unity of a single loving purpose is not dependent upon the knowledge of God as triune. The presupposition of the Thomistic approach holds; namely, that the knowledge of the oneness of the divine essence is neither effected nor affected by the knowledge of the threeness of the divine Persons.

But this presupposition cannot survive a closer analysis of what awareness of the unity of God really means. For what does the credal assertion 'I believe in one God' actually imply? It implies a faith that, despite all appearances to the contrary, *everything* in experience is either the direct expression, or can be made the instrument of, a single all-embracing purpose of love. And, just as nothing can be separated from, or be regarded as lying outside, this love, so its power is such that ultimately there is also nothing that can separate from it. The faith in one God is the faith that, in the last resort, there are not many forces at work in the universe but one only, and that 'all things work together for good to them that love God' (Rom. 8:28). (This and what follows owes much to unpublished lectures of Professor Farmer.)

This can be expressed in another way by saying that monotheism means 'reconciliation' to the whole of one's environment – in respect of one's own inner life, of one's relationship to others, and of the chances and appointments of the material universe, and, in and through all these, reconciliation to God. It is true that for us *in via* this reconciliation can be 'in principle' only. That is to say, it is 'by hope' that we are saved. For monotheism is an act of faith, not a statement of objectively verifiable fact. Yet, though it is reconciliation only in principle, as far as it goes, it is total. For if there is any sphere of existence which is not viewed as the locus of love's working, then a theoretical monotheism remains a practical polytheism. An internal disharmony of the soul, a grudge against a neighbour, a resentment at life's circumstances, all belie any intellectual assertion of belief in one God. For in each case there is some tract of existence which is subject to another law than that of God's will of love. Mere assent to the unity of the Godhead without this total reconciliation is knowledge shared with devils (Jas 2:19). 'If a man say, I love God' – and this is what the confession of unity means – 'and hateth his brother, he is a liar' (1 Jn 4:20).

This is a hard saying. But then it must be remembered that for the Hebrew mind the unity of God was the subject not of a self-evident proposition but of a divine commandment. It stood as the first of the Ten Words pronounced from Sinai, and is to be regarded as the basis of the whole Law. For the sin of pride, the root of all disobedience, is nothing but the denial of the one absolute sovereignty of God. The commandment 'Hear, O Israel, the Lord our God is one Lord' is but another way of saying 'Thou shalt love the Lord thy God with all thy heart, and with all thy soul and with all thy might' (Deut. 6:4–5). Similarly, 'Thou shalt love thy neighbour as thyself' (Lev. 19:18), like all the ordinances of that chapter, is grounded in the words 'I am the Lord'. As St Thomas says, '*omnis actus peccati procedit ex aliquo inordinato appetitu alicujus temporalis boni*' (Every act of sin proceeds from some inordinate appetite for some temporal good) (*S. T.* II, 77, iv). And the inordinate desire for a temporal good is nothing but idolatry, which is polytheism.

It is a revelation of the spiritual depths of Judaism that its basic article of faith (belief in one God) is also the ground and sum of its commandments. For paganism (and, to a degree, for Pharisaic legalism) religious belief issues in ethical injunctions which are separable from it. Religious belief is not in itself a matter of ethical injunction: it is something natural to the soul. And ethical injunctions are not simply another way of stating the religious belief: they are little informed by it, and they can be detached from it and observed for their own sake. Such was the Hebrew understanding of the human situation, that the Old Testament sees that for man the sinner sees belief in the one God of love is the exact equivalent of the command to love the one God of belief. To 'man in contradiction' what in one light is belief in another is commandment. The religion of the Jew was a matter of ethics, because his monotheism meant that belief in one God was nothing less than that total reconciliation which is love of one God. If the belief is meant seriously it *presupposes* the commandment of love; otherwise it is merely belief with 'the top of the mind' (J. Baillie). And again, if it is meant seriously, if it does indeed affect 'the bottom of the heart', then it also *issues* in the commandment of love. The commandment is first and last. But with equal truth it could be said that the belief is first and last. For the Jew religion and morality were but two aspects of the same thing.

Judaism alone of ancient religions produced a genuinely ethical religion and a truly religious ethic. That is its glory. But that is also its despair. It saw that genuine confession of the oneness or unity of God, with all the heart and soul and might, so far from being an elementary and demonstrable proposition, is in fact an ultimate moral ideal. But, humanly speaking, it is also an unattainable ideal. Unattainable, because no one could dare claim to fulfil the Law, which is but the equivalent of its attainment. For the Jew, just because he saw what the assertion of monotheism really meant, the unity of God remained to the end a subject of commandment. He knew 'with the top of his mind' (and indeed with much more) that God is one, but he was unable to make this belief operative 'from the bottom of his heart', and unable therefore to make it sincere. There was always, as St Paul found, a law in his members which warred against the law in his mind – and, where the authority of two laws is admitted, there is for that man no longer in any reality one God. The throne is shared with Mammon.

St Paul here exposed the predicament of Judaism and the source of its bankruptcy. It could not provide the power to fulfil its fundamental commandment, which was also its basic article of belief. But the Apostle also had an answer to this predicament. He asserted the one love, from whom nothing, internal or external, could separate, to be a matter, not merely of commandment, but of experience. Every dualism and discord was for him swallowed up in an overriding conviction of unity. 'We *know*', he said, 'that all things work together for good to them that love God' (Rom. 8:28). Here is the full act of faith in monotheism for which Judaism strove, and strove in vain. And it was achieved, not by extending a dialectic of thought already immanent within Judaism, not by drawing out the logic of ideas contained in essence within the Old Testament itself. It was something that 'the Law could not do in that it was weak through the flesh'; it was unattainable, because the commandment though 'holy, righteous and good' was incapable of making its adherents so. Monotheism could only become assured because the righteousness of man was annihilated, in face of the righteousness of God. Without ceasing to be ethical, religion was no longer a matter of ethics. The total reconciliation which belief in one God means could be achieved, not by works, but only through justification by faith in Christ. It is sin which is the focal point of the 'enmity' which blinds to a vision of the unity and all-sufficiency of God's love. It is only through the atoning work of the *Son* for sin that the rule of the *Spirit* can take that sole possession of the soul, which, after the distractions of warring loyalties, brings 'life and peace' and over the whole field of experience enables a recognition of the ordering and guiding hand of a single loving *Father* from whom nothing in heaven or earth can separate.

It is highly significant that Romans 8, in which this line of thought comes to most complete expression, should be at once the most uncompromising statement in Christian literature of the absolute unity and all-inclusiveness of the divine love and at the same time the *locus classicus* in the New Testament for the roots of the doctrine of the Trinity. For there is no tension or antithesis between the two emphases. It is precisely in the assertion of the fact of the Trinity that Christianity makes possible for the first time a genuinely monotheistic faith. The Godhead can in reality only be confessed as one as it is known as three. Monotheism is reconciliation. But without redemption there is no reconciliation. And apart from justification in Christ and sanctification in the Spirit, there is no redemption. That is the logic of the Christian faith. It is its gospel of a divine Trinity which enables it to speak of a love from which and through which and to which are all things, not simply as an article of injunction, but as a fact of assurance and experience.

We may thus see in the relation between the doctrine of the Trinity and the knowledge of the unity of the Godhead the same dialectical connection as St Paul traced between the Old and the New Covenants in general. As in all respects, so in regard to its basis, the doctrine of God, Christ comes as the τέλος (completion, goal) of the Law, in both senses of the word. He is the fulfilment of the monotheistic command and makes possible the vision of what prophets and kings had longed to see. Yet he is this only because he is the end or abolition of the righteousness that comes by the Law. The Thomistic approach is right in that the revelation of the Trinity presupposes all the striving and all the progress towards a monotheistic conclusion of which nature and Law are capable. Without a prior demand for and insistence on unity, the revelation of three Persons means three Gods. Nor must the achievement of Judaism ever be minimized. It had brought men nearer to what monotheism really means than any other faith or philosophy – certainly nearer than the Hellenic tradition with its entirely abstract and purely intellectual conception of τὸ ἑν (the One (thing)).

Yet at the point at which it stood nearest its ideal, it also stood furthest away. It was a *praeparatio Evangelia* (preparation for the gospel) only because it drove men, as it drove St Paul, to despair at its complete ineffectiveness. Unitarianism as an achievement of human righteousness is fulfilled only as it is negated in a trinitarianism as the revelation of a righteousness which is of God. It is possible to say much about the unity of God and to analyse the experience of a 'Thou' who is infinite love – and never mention the Trinity. But it must equally be recognized that the value of such statements and of such analysis is in itself precisely nothing. Apart from the Incarnation and the doctrine of the Trinity, monotheism is neither worth establishing nor capable of establishment. There is a double failure.

In the first place, there is, as we noted, even in Judaism a falling short of the fullness of a conception of God wherein everything is seen as evidence of the omnipotent control of a single love. Only the love of the Cross could possibly bring men to the point of daring to believe that. The simple identification of God with love had to await the Incarnation. The true content of monotheism as total reconciliation at that level had not been fully grasped even by Judaism. And, of course, for the Greek mind, this content was infinitely less full than it was for the Jew. By isolating the intellectual faculty in man, it arrived at a concept of unity which, for the intellect, was as complete and as satisfying as could ever be desired. But, from every other point of view, such an entity as, 'the One' of Plotinus was utterly abstract and bloodless. It provided no unifying principle by which any of the manifold tensions and conflicts which militate against wholeness of life could be resolved or reconciled. On the purely intellectual level a unity from which all differentiation and discord are absent is attainable easily enough. But this is not a personal unity capable of integrating the thousand distractions and disharmonies of everyday historical existence. It has nothing at all to offer in face of the fundamental need of man for reconciliation in a sinful world. In the same way, St Thomas, under the influence of the intellectualistic bias of Hellenism, also had no difficulty in reaching by reason alone what, for him, was a completely satisfying conception of the divine unity. But it is not the rich concrete unity of personal existence; it is simply an abstract and impersonal entity containing within it no inherent logical contradiction. It is for this reason that Barth is so insistent that it is necessary first to establish *who* is one before it is any use trying to prove *that* he is one. Only if the unity is the unity of the Christian God, of the love that was displayed at Calvary, is monotheism in the last resort worth establishing. It must be the God of the Incarnation and the Trinity or nothing.

And, secondly, there is at any stage short of the full Trinitarian dogma, a failure not only in content but in effectiveness. Not only, without Calvary, is the unity of God not *worth* establishing, but, equally, without Calvary, it is not capable of establishment. The incapacity of Judaism to make belief in one God effective for the life of its adherents lay, as we say, in the impossible burden of attendant ethical demand which it placed upon them. And the more complete and inclusive the conception of this unity, the more impossible became its achievement. Jesus proclaimed a view of the omnipotent fatherhood of God which carried with it ethical requirements which, *as law*, are utterly unattainable. As an achievement of human righteousness the Sermon on the Mount is 'an impossible ethical ideal' (Niebuhr). But in the very act of making belief in the unity of God thus quite unattainable and, therefore, ineffective and irrelevant, Jesus proclaimed a righteousness of God which was capable of translating it into an assured fact of the believer's experience and making it really effective for all his living. By the justification which comes through Christ and the indwelling presence of the Spirit, belief in the unity of God – and a belief in this unity as its richest, personal and ultimately only satisfying level – is at last removed out of the realm of struggle and demand into that of achievement and grace. After Easter and Pentecost it emerged from a state of ineffectiveness and haunting irrelevance as a directive, decisive power. Thus Calvin is justified in his saying that, apart from knowledge of the Trinity, '*nudum et inane dumtaxat nomen sine vero Deo in cerebro nostro volitat*' (the bare and empty name of Deity merely flutters in our brain without any genuine knowledge).

There are, therefore, in the approaches both of Aquinas and of Calvin elements of truth which must be carefully preserved. It is only by holding the two insights securely together that the place of the doctrine of the Trinity in the Christian scheme can rightly be estimated. It can properly be introduced neither simply at the beginning nor simply at the end. Not simply at the beginning, because the Trinity presupposes the unity: in the divine economy, the triune name of God was not revealed except to a people already well established in a monotheistic faith. And yet, not simply at the end, for the unity presupposes the trinity: when the revelation came it claimed to be the truth of what was known before; and, now it has come, it would be a denial of that claim to treat it as less than the interpretative principle of the whole *from the beginning*. Of course, for the purposes of exposition we are forced to select one or the other of the two places, and to introduce it *either* at the beginning *or* at the end. But this is an instance of the disadvantage under which every consecutive exposition of the organic body of Christian doctrine must labour. The fact that we have chosen to place it at the conclusion of our treatment reflects the nature of this work as an essay in biblical philosophy rather than in Christian Dogmatics.

Finally, we may translate this conclusion into the terms which have been employed throughout, the conclusion, namely, that the truth of the matter lies in the resolute combination of the approaches of both John Calvin and St Thomas Aquinas. On the one hand, it is justifiable to speak of a single general 'Hebraic' position, only if it is already admitted as Christian in its conclusion. Before it can acquire a complete content in the human mind or a really effective expression in human life, the doctrine of the Trinity must be presupposed. Just as, in idea, the conception of a single universally sovereign love as the source and end of all things had to await the Christian revelation for its genesis, so, in experience, the total reconciliation which alone can make it sincere and operative was, and is, impossible without the justifying power of Christ mediated to the believer by the Spirit.

Nevertheless, while the doctrine of the Trinity makes all the difference, there is a real sense in which St Thomas is right in saying that it makes none. For him the unity was unaffected by the fact that revelation showed it to exist in trinity. The trinity does not destroy or change the unity or make our knowledge of it false: it fulfils the unity by showing it for what it really is. It is the old unity which is newly revealed. The doctrine of the Trinity, like the commandment of love to St John, represents something which at the same time is both new and old (1 Jn 2:7–8).[43] It is new in that it is a genuinely fresh revelation. It tells us what God is really like, *who* he is (the 'name' of God) in a way that could not be known prior to the Incarnation. And yet it is old, for this name it reveals is no strange or new name, but the very God who was the God of Abraham, of Isaac and of Jacob. The trinity makes known the unity – the same unity which was there before, but which could never be known as really one – the unity, that is to say, of a single, almighty love. It does not reveal a different 'I AM', a different 'Thou'. It is the same which was from everlasting, the name of love, of the 'I' in relation to a 'Thou'. It tells us the true meaning of the old relationship: it does not set forth an entirely new structure of relationship. It does not render our previous analysis of the divine-human encounter irrelevant. Buber the Jew can make a contribution to Christian theology, simply because the doctrine of the Trinity is a statement about the name of the old 'Thou' and not of another.

Chapter Fifteen

THREE 'THOUS' OR ONE? (1) THE EVIDENCE OF IMMEDIATE EXPERIENCE

The previous chapter was spent in remarks of a largely introductory character. They were concerned with the place which the Trinity should rightly occupy in an exposition of the Christian doctrine of God. But they have already posed the form and, as we shall see, to some extent determined the answer of the questions we are going to have to ask of the doctrine of the Trinity. For our treatment of the subject must necessarily be selective. We have approached the doctrine from the point of view of the idea of the personality of God in Christian theology. The following examination of it is undertaken, not for its own sake, but for the fuller understanding of the nature of the divine 'Thou' and the relation in which he stands to the world. What is the connection between the idea of the personality of God and the doctrine of the Persons of the Godhead? What difference does the doctrine that the unity of the divine essence or personality only exists in threefold form make to the understanding of the eternal 'Thou'? Have we now three 'Thous' instead of one? Or are the Persons of the Trinity something different from persons as we have defined the term, as beings in a 'Thou' relationship?[44] And, if so, what are they, and what is the connection between them and the one divine personality?

Now, if what has been said in the preceding pages is correct, it affords at least a presumption upon which we can work in answering these questions. If it is legitimate to speak of a single biblical or 'Hebraic' view of God, albeit one which is already Christian in its presuppositions, then this argues a continuity of structure in the divine-human 'Thou' relation throughout the Bible which the recognition of a tri-Personal manifestation does not affect. If the doctrine of the Trinity is the true 'name' of the God of the Old Testament and not of some fresh divine unity, then it is the truth about a single divine 'Thou'. If this were not so, if the fact that there were three Persons or Hypostases meant that there were three persons or 'Thous', then the structural continuity would be so seriously impaired as to make it impossible to speak of a single 'biblical' account of the relation of God and man at all. It is the single essence of God, the I AM of the divine being, which is meant by the personality of God. The 'Persons' are the three ways in which this personality subsists, and in and through which its unity is known. They are not themselves separate 'Thous' or personalities entering into distinguishable relations with the Christian believer.

This at least is the conclusion to which our examination of the place of the doctrine of the Trinity in Christian theology would naturally lead us. But it is a position that has not yet been established on only independent grounds, for example, by appealing to the actual witness of Christian religious experience or by adducing the support of the New Testament evidence. This must now be done. And there are reasons why it will be necessary to substantiate what is said with some care.

It is probably true to say that, until recent times, the conclusion we have reached would not have been seriously challenged; the conclusion, namely, that the doctrine of the Trinity means that one divine 'Thou' meets us under three forms and not that three distinguishable 'Thou'-relations are set up with the three Persons of the one God. Of course, the matter would have been expressed in different language. The question of the relation of the personality of God to the Persons of the Godhead could not have been raised in this precise form at a time when the whole idea of the divine personality was so little developed. But, whatever may have been true of the past, there are today many who would openly question this conclusion. It is asserted that Christian experience can only be described as that of three distinguishable personal relationships, the terminus of each of which is divine. Each of the 'Persons' is in fact a separate personality or centre of consciousness and will confronting the believer as a distinct 'Thou'. One of the most common forms in which this analysis comes to light is in the reproof which emanates from many a page and pulpit chiding of Christians for an allegedly defective experience of the Holy Spirit. It is assumed that the ordinary believer has a firm and clear sense of what it means to enter into particular relationships with the Father and the Son, but that for some reason his peculiar awareness of the Third Person as a person requires constant stimulation and exhortation. This is a point which will receive further attention later. Here it is only introduced as an illustration of the presuppositions of much popular Theology.

But such a Theology is not confined merely to popular writers and speakers. It pervades, either explicitly or implicitly, a great mass of modern thought on the subject of the Trinity. The burden of proof, wherever it may have lain in the past, now rests on him who would show the Christian experience of God to be uni-personal rather than tri-personal.

Consequently a challenge to the current mode of thinking requires to be backed by a fairly careful critique of the views in question. This may perhaps best be done by an examination of two of the most recent and scholarly contributions to the subject: Dr K. Kirk's essay in *Essays on the Trinity and the Incarnation* (1928) and Professor L. Hodgson's book, *The Doctrine of the Trinity*. The latter to a certain extent is dependent on the former, but it will be useful to draw quotations from both.

What is under consideration at present is solely that Trinity of the believer's immediate experience. We are not concerned at the moment with the metaphysical status or mutual interrelation of the Persons, nor with the special relationship of men with the Second Person of the Godhead established during the period of Christ's life in the flesh. Our data therefore will not be drawn from the speculations of the theologians and philosophers, whose interest is in the nature of the 'essential' Trinity which may be inferred from the Trinity of revelation and experience, nor, again, from the Gospels, whose first concern is the impact made on man by Christ during the thirty years of his earthly life. We must look rather to the records of the experience of the Church as recorded in the rest of the New Testament and in the testimony of Christians from the first Pentecost to the present day. The question at issue is how men, from the Apostles onwards, have described their experience of God; whether they have known in it a single 'Thou' under three forms of manifestation, or whether the impression is such as can only be accounted for by speaking of relations with three distinct 'Thous'.

The question immediately frames itself in the form: 'Is it *necessary* to assume three "Thou's"?' The first Christians approached the problem of the Trinity from within the presuppositions of Jewish monotheism. Trinitarianism presented itself as a potential *challenge* to those presuppositions. If the new experience of the divine was to be conceived as the distinct awareness of three persons, then this could only be because its nature was such as to be *incapable* of any less 'offensive' interpretation. And the fact that the Church started from these presuppositions cannot be regarded as a mere historical accident. The Trinity was only revealed and, so far as we may see, could only have been revealed to an existent belief in a single personal God. Without that belief, and except as a differentiation of a unity already, to some extent at least, assumed for thought and life, the doctrine of the Trinity can be nothing else than tritheism. There is no road to Trinitarian faith from the presuppositions of Olympian polytheism. The Trinity necessarily presupposes that unity within which it is a differentiation, although, indeed, it is also that which, for the first time, really makes it possible. In all questions about the doctrine we must always start from the one and ask 'why three', but never from the three and work towards the one. In the light of this, we may turn to examine the view of those who regard the supposition of three 'Thous' as indispensable.

According to Dr Kirk (*Essays on the Trinity and the Incarnation*, 226–37) the Father, Son and Holy Spirit represent the termini of three distinct human relationships with God. As such, each must be given hypostatic existence as a centre of consciousness and will; for that is the form of being under which it is alone possible to be a participator in a reciprocal personal relation. The three relationships are respectively (1) that of *κύριος–δοῦλος* (master–servant), of Creator over against creature, (2) that of 'communion' between two intimate personalities, (3) that of 'possession', 'a relationship in which the human spirit is wholly controlled, if not superseded by the divine' (ibid., 228).[45]

There are two questions which at once present themselves. (a) What is it that makes it necessary to describe these relationships as taking place with three separate centres of consciousness, rather than as different and complementary aspects of a single relationship with one 'Thou'? (b) Is not the inevitable effect of Kirk's division the depersonalization of the Holy Spirit?

(a) The only justification, it would appear, for insisting on three termini rather than one is that the quality of each relation is such that they cannot be conceived as existing together with one and the same being. That is to say, the being before whom man cannot but be a *δοῦλος* (servant) is of a kind that makes it impossible for him to exist towards him also as a *φίλος* (friend), in the reciprocity of an equal personal communion. Or, again, the being who 'possesses' a man or unconsciously inspires and guides him cannot be the same as either of the other two.

In the case of men there are two, and only two, reasons which would lead us to postulate a new or hitherto unrecognized personality as the terminus of any given relationship or the cause of any set of personal manifestations. These are (1) because we see these manifestations to be connected with or to proceed from a different physical organism or body from those previously observed; or (2) because their character and quality are not compatible with the actions of any agent we already know.

Now, in the case of experiences or manifestations of the divine, the former reason does not apply. It is only, then, if we had an experience of a divine activity of a kind or quality which could not be predicated of God in conjunction with some other such experience that we should be forced to postulate two termini for the relationships established with him. But to admit that there was experience of such activity would be to abandon the conviction of the unity of the Godhead altogether. For it would be an admission that some manifestations of the divine nature, or some 'characters' in which he reveals himself, were incompatible with others. From the point of view of religious experience, the only valid reason for predicating more than one personality in God would be to avoid the conclusion that his was a split personality.

The process of thought lying behind Kirk's view seems to be something like this. He starts by adopting an analysis which sees in the human relationship with God three facets or moments: (a) the awareness of one who is 'wholly other'; (b) the experience of an intimate personal 'I–Thou' communion of reciprocity and apparent equality; (c) the recognition of the presence of what John Oman calls 'impersonal operations' of grace. He then proceeds, first, to treat these as three distinct relationships, and, secondly, to claim that they are relationships of a kind which could only be established with three different persons. The truth is rather that, so far from requiring different termini, they are not really different relationships. It is only by holding together in paradoxical union the elements of 'ultimacy' and 'intimacy' (not forgetting those operations of God upon the soul which are not consciously apprehended till after the event, if at all) that the true character of the divine-human relationship can be understood. Unless it is constantly kept in mind that it is precisely the same being who can only be known both as wholly other and as infinitely near – and both at the same time – then the peculiar *quale* [character] of religious experience is lost.

(b) The second objection, that the designation of the relationship of the Third Person as 'possession' has the effect of depersonalizing the Spirit, is faced and answered by Kirk himself. The question remains, however, how far this answer can be regarded as satisfactory.

Kirk's argument is that the Old Testament and early New Testament association of the Spirit with some sort of semi-physical *ruach* (Hebrew: spirit, wind), which acts on men without their co-operation or conscious volition, does not necessarily imply that it was, or is to be, conceived as impersonal. He says, truly, that to call a thing 'semi-physical' is not to say that it is impersonal. Both personal and impersonal influences are mediated alike through the senses, and it is not the characteristic of the personal to be non-physical. But it is when he comes to say what he *does* think the peculiar feature of the personal to be that his analysis is inadequate. He holds that it is the 'selective initiative' of the Spirit that distinguishes his working from that of a drug – the fact that he chooses the recipients of his gifts, 'dividing to every man severally as he wills' (1 Cor. 12:11). This is true as far as it goes. But something more is required to characterize the distinctively personal relation. When Oman speaks of the 'impersonal operations' of grace he does not mean that either the subject or the object of this activity is not a person. 'Experiences', he points out, 'are not personal merely because they happen to a person, any more than they would be nautical merely because they happen to a sailor' (*Grace and Personality*, 1917, 72). And what holds of a person's experiences holds, too, of his actions. The late efforts of Messrs Goebbels and Himmler to coerce the minds and bodies of their subjects certainly exhibited an adaptability and selectiveness only predicable of persons. But that did not make them personal operations. For the methods of the concentration camp and the propaganda machine are only successful in so far as they treat persons exactly as if they were not persons but things, as material for exploitation or manipulation. The fact that a tyranny may be completely benevolent in its intentions does not prevent it bringing about a depersonalization of the relationship between ruler and ruled. A relationship only remains fully personal when the freedom of the 'other' to accept or reject my will for him is preserved inviolate. That is what the physical and mental coercion of Nazi methods sought to override. What was looked for was that the desired response should be given automatically, whenever the appropriate stimulus was applied. This ideal situation would be realized if success could be made independent of the co-operation of the other's conscious choice. The application of drugs or hypnotic techniques would be the most efficient method, were it not that they cannot be used either continuously or extensively. Moreover, the responses desired include acts of cerebration and will which the employment of such methods would preclude. Propaganda and suggestion, though less sure, are ultimately more effective. However, the success of any such attempts to treat persons as if they were something else is bound to be only partial; and the appeal for voluntary co-operation in the achievement of high ideals constituted a dominant element even in Nazi techniques of suasion. However, in so far as a man can be manipulated as though he were simply an organism whose responses to given stimuli are inevitable, all the devices of modern totalitarianism were applied to see that he was. And in so far as these methods are deliberately employed, their effect is always to depersonalize human relationships.

Now, the fact that the ends which the Holy Spirit has in view are diametrically opposed to those we have been considering does not make his work any the more personal if, as is maintained, it is confined to those activities in which our conscious co-operation and acceptance is not required. The history of the Church – and in particular of the Jesuit movement – has provided too many examples of attempts at compulsory salvation by physical or psychological manipulation for us to be ignorant of the depersonalizing effect of the use of such methods.

At this point it is necessary to remove a misunderstanding which may easily arise. We shall be told that much of what is known as grace achieves its effect upon us without our conscious acceptance or even our awareness of its presence. The recognition of the hand of Providence almost inevitably takes the form of a confession after the event that God was in this or that situation, moulding and guiding its course and our response to it in a way that we could not know at the time. Similarly, there is testimony beyond measure in the history of Christendom to conversions in which the subject would confess that his own will and powers had been aided to the extent of being superseded by a will and power possessing and impelling him from without. The doctrine of the irresistibility of grace, partial and erroneous as it may be, was suggested to the Church by facts which confronted it. It was not merely the reflection of an age in which human creativity was lightly valued and human liberty little regarded.

Again, it does not require the conclusions of modern psychology to convince an observant person of the enormous extent to which his life is controlled by influences affecting him well below the level of his conscious self. Even in the highest and most intimate personal relationships these factors are not absent, or even diminished. Rather, it is probably true to say that in the intimacies of a relationship such as that between a man and a woman the effects of unconscious influences are to be seen at their maximum. There are here impulsions at work, forces which take a person out of himself and lead him to acts for good or evil of which he would otherwise be incapable and which he cannot hope to explain.

But – and this is the important point – under none of these pressures and impulsions of love does he feel his personality to be violated or his liberty infringed. Every lover knows the difference between the unconscious influences he may exert on his beloved and the deliberate manipulation of these influences to force her into accepting him or his will for her. Such influences, though impersonal in themselves, only become depersonalizing if isolated and utilized for non-personal ends. The human personality is something which has its feet as surely planted in the physical and biological as with its head it transcends them. Man is an animal organism, and his existence is to a large extent governed by the action and reaction of stimulus and response initiated by purely organic mechanisms. But these operations become the organs of a personal activity only in so far as they are taken up into, and held within the context of, a relationship where the controlling factor is absolute respect for the freedom of the 'other' to give if he will a final 'No' to all such influences.

It is not the fact that we are subject to influences over which we have no immediate control that depersonalizes us. That would be to define personality purely in terms of spirit – a definition which has proved as unrelated to facts as it is gratifying to pride. What depersonalizes is the manipulation of these influences to prevent their becoming the data for free and untrammelled judgment, to prevent their being taken up into a relationship where respect for personality is regnant. What differentiates the methods of God from those of Goebbels is precisely that, in the former case, the ultimate object is the making possible of a free personal acceptance of what is offered, whereas to the latter this was both superfluous and dangerous.

God treats us as whole men. Since we are what we are, since, in other words, we are *not* pure spirit, pure consciousness, he cannot achieve his will in us by acting as if we were, however much it may minister to human conceit to think that he could and does. He approaches us by ways of which we may at the time or even now know nothing. But these manifestations of grace have only power to save, only, that is to say, to initiate that personal relation to himself which is his will for us, if they become the data for the free acceptance and willing obedience which is faith. A man may be converted apart from himself, but apart from himself he cannot be saved.

What, then, are we to make of Kirk's statement that God's grace can possess an irresistible compulsion without ceasing to be personal, and that in experience of 'possession' 'we have the differentia of the Spirit's approach to man' (*Essays on the Trinity and the Incarnation*, 234)?

We have seen that the 'impersonal operations' of one personality upon another only depersonalize when they are isolated and removed from that context of relationship whose structure is the meeting of 'I' and 'Thou' in claim and counter-claim, freely given and freely received. That is to say, irresistible workings are only personal in so far as they are ultimately resistible, and the unconscious only so far as they are taken up into consciousness for free acceptance or rejection.

This implies that the approach of God to the conscious and unconscious mind is really but one approach. Both ultimately are only revelatory or saving in that they are not differentiated. To isolate the unconscious, and in themselves impersonal, operations of God's love and to attribute them to the activity of a separate Person who is 'the terminus of a distinct and recognisable relationship' (ibid., 236) is at once to make complete shipwreck of the faith. This Person immediately becomes entirely impersonal, and in his effects as depersonalizing as anything that proceeded from the *Reichspropagandabüro*. Once again, as in the case of the experiences of the 'ultimacy' and 'intimacy' of God, so, here, any attempt to divide what are indissoluble aspects of a single relationship into awarenesses of separate and distinguishable personalities is as disastrous as it is arbitrary.

In conclusion, it may be added that the identification of the 'κύριος–δοῦλος (master–servant) relationship', 'communion' and 'possession' with the Persons of the Father, Son and Holy Spirit respectively no more fits the usage of the Bible than the data of experience. A detailed demonstration would take us too far afield. Suffice it to say that, first, the type of perfect 'communion' set before us in the New Testament for our imitation is that of the Son with the *Father*. Secondly, so far from the κύριος–δοῦλος relationship being the distinctive relationship with the Father, St Paul (if the Pastoral Epistles be omitted) never once speaks of himself or anyone else being a bond-servant of God or of the Father, whereas δοῦλος Ἰησοῦ Χριστοῦ (servant of Jesus Christ) (or its equivalents) is one of his commonest appellations. Lastly, it is indemonstrable, either that the operation of the Spirit is confined to possession (which would make present experience of him either non-existent or solely abnormal and ecstatic) or that every instance of possession or impersonal operation is the work of the Spirit.

Even Kirk himself is not very confident on this latter point.

> It would be mere academic pedantry [he writes] to attach this experience (of irresistible operation) rigidly to the doctrine of the Spirit; and it is true that it would be impossible to analyse the New Testament or the Fathers and show that all the passages which refer to this type of the divine action are associated with the name of the Spirit, and none of them with the name of the Son.

And he adds, somewhat ingenuously, 'a living theology cannot be tested by canons as rigid as this' (ibid., 234). But why not, we may ask, if there is this 'distinct and recognisable relationship'? All that a study of the New Testament can reveal is that, while there are some instances of the Spirit possessing men, there are just as many others where relationship with him is one of personal communion. Although ἡ κοινωνία τοῦ ἁγίου πνεύματος (the communion of the Holy Spirit) certainly cannot mean 'communion with the Holy Spirit', is the constant association of communion with the Third Person accidental? All we can say is that the New Testament speaks of the three aspects of the one divine-human relationship that have been mentioned, as it also speaks of the existence of three Persons. But a rigid identification of the two is more than any honest exegesis can extract.

The discussion above has occupied itself largely with the peculiar characteristics which Kirk and Hodgson see as marking the distinguishable relationships with the three divine 'Thous'. It is clear that those who claim to be able to differentiate three such relations within their experience must be prepared to state what in each case is the *proprietas incommunicabilis* (to use a phrase of Calvin's) which distinguishes them. And it is of the most scholarly of such statements that we have made examination. But it can further be shown, not only that some particular attempt to demonstrate that the unity of religious experience demands description in terms of three 'Thou' relations is unsuccessful, but that any such efforts must be so in the nature of the case. For Professor Hodgson himself admits that such a description is always in the nature of an interpretation of the experience in the light of facts brought in from outside; it is not demanded by the experience itself, which is equally patient of interpretation as the awareness of a single 'Thou' in three aspects. Our concern at the moment is not with the facts that may be adduced from without: they may, or may not, compel us to reverse the judgment based solely on the evidence of religious experience. That must be considered at a later stage. Here we are concerned only with the nature of the 'Thou' relation to God as the evidence of the immediate experience of the Christian believer requires us to see it.

Hodgson, in discussing the question of the personality of the Spirit, makes a distinction of his own between what he calls 'He-ness' and 'It-ness'. By 'It' he has no intention of implying that the Spirit is in any way impersonal. Rather, it has reference to that view which (as in Old Testament usage: 'the Spirit of the Lord God is upon me', Is. 61:1) would see the Spirit as a personal manifestation of the one God, a way of working of the divine love. The ascription of 'He-ness' means more than this. It means that that which is experienced is not simply a manifestation of the single 'Thou' of the divine personality, but a separate centre of personality with whom it is possible to enter into a distinguishable 'I–Thou' relation.

In the light of external considerations, which will have to be examined presently, Hodgson concludes that, on balance, the New Testament pronounces in favour of the attribution of 'He-ness', or separate personality, to the Person of the Spirit. What is important here is not his conclusion but the way he reaches it. For although he considers the evidence provided by the experience of the Apostolic writers, it becomes clear that it is the presuppositions with which he starts, rather than the bare evidence itself, which determines his findings. For in the course of his argument he makes statements which must rob the evidence of experience of any weight in settling the question by itself. He admits that experience of the Spirit's working cannot in itself tell us whether the Third Person is himself a person (a 'He') or a manifestation of the single personality of God (an 'It').

> When we approach the subject from the human end, it makes no difference whether the immediate cause of the χάρισμα (grace/favour) is a 'He' or an 'It'. The effect might have been produced equally well by the Father or the Son by an output of love or power which would be 'It' in the same sense as a man's love or power is an 'It' as contrasted with the man himself. (Hodgson, *The Doctrine of the Trinity*, 82)

Again, if the Spirit were eternally 'It', then 'It-ness' would have served the revelatory purpose equally well' (ibid., 83). If this is true of our experience of the Spirit's revelation – and it must be, from the nature of the case; for at the level of the immediate data of experience alone we can never distinguish a personal manifestation ('It') from a manifestation of personality ('He') – then it must have been true also of the experience of the New Testament writers. What justification is there then for the statement that 'the "He" character of the Spirit may be taken as revealed in the New Testament experience of God's redeeming activity' (ibid., 82)? For experience in itself cannot decide. As was made clear above, it is only if we had experience of a divine activity of a quality which could not be predicated of God as manifested in the Persons of the Father and the Son that we should be required to infer that the Spirit was a separate personality and the active ground of these phenomena. To admit that there was experience of such activity would be to abandon the conviction of the unity of the Godhead altogether. For it would be an admission that some manifestations of divine revelation are incompatible with others. Once again, the only valid reason for predicating more than one personality in God would be to avoid the conclusion that his was a split personality.

The statement that there is no evidence, from the point of view of present experience, demanding the existence of the Spirit as a separate personality inevitably commits one to the position that there is equally no evidence, from this point of view, requiring such an existence for the other two persons. For such evidence, if it were there, could only be evidence for tritheism. But it must not be thought that, by the reduction of all experience of God to the level of 'It-ness', any depersonalization is implied. For in his definition Hodgson, as we saw, is careful to insist that by this word he in no way means to deny that the phenomena so described are manifestations of a personal working. All he is asserting is that these modes of manifestation are not themselves separate centres of consciousness and will.

This distinction between 'He-ness' and 'It-ness', though necessary when discussing the metaphysical grounds of experience, is, as Hodgson recognizes, irrelevant for experience itself. Hence it should cause no surprise that the Epistles, which are essentially the record of an experience controlled by an event, are not careful in making it. They describe the approach of the Spirit both in terms of 'He' and in terms of 'It'. The conclusion to be drawn from this is not that the two usages are incompatible and that one must be explained away as 'expressing an apprehension which is partial and incomplete, but true as far as it goes and historically explicable' (Hodgson, *The Doctrine of the Trinity*, 82). Both are equally valid descriptions of the facts, and it is indeed a pity from this point of view that any distinction between the two classes of passages has been drawn.

We may perhaps sum up Hodgson's position by saying that, while experience alone could never have given us the conviction of 'He-ness' (or the conviction that the Persons were also persons), yet other considerations make it not only permissible but also necessary to view our awareness of the Hypostases of the Godhead as relations with separate personalities. Leaving aside at present the nature and validity of these other considerations, we could agree that this would be a perfectly tenable position if it could be verified in experience. Without other facts we could not deduce merely from our experience of the Father, the living Christ and the Holy Spirit that each of these must be separate personalities and not simply three manifestations of one personality. But having, as it were, learnt that they are, can we confirm in our experience the existence of distinct 'Thou' relationships?

Dr Kirk admits the necessity for this empirical verification. 'For the recognition of distinct hypostases within the Godhead' (each of whom is a personality) 'there must be, on the part of man, a conviction that he also has, or is competent to have, "personal relations" with each one of them'. For:

> no human mind would have been capable of, or content with, the continuous and unprecedented effort of believing in the several existence of three persons within the One, unless it had clear and convincing evidence of those three persons. (*Essays on the Trinity and the Incarnation*, 168)

But when he comes to the question, 'What quality in this experience is it which enables the Christian to say that his intercourse is with three "persons" in one Godhead, and not rather with one God in three aspects?' (ibid., 17), his answer is hardly convincing. He distinguishes between the *characteristics* or attributes a man possesses and the *characters*, or complex of characteristics, he may assume (e.g., guide, philosopher, friend; or, in God, Creator, Redeemer, Sanctifier). He goes on:

> If we could recognise three activities of the Godhead towards ourselves, each sufficiently universal to be the expression of a whole personality summed up in one activity, and not a mere attribute, 'characteristic', or even (in the human sense) 'character', allowing room for other attributes alongside itself; and could recognise, moreover, that these activities, so far from being intermittent, transitory and successive, were contemporaneous and continuous, we should have empirical support for a belief in three persons in one Godhead, as distinct from a belief in three attributes or aspects of the Godhead only. It would be mere hardihood to say that the content of any single Christian's experience gives him grounds for such a recognition; but unless the Church as a whole had such grounds in her experience, we should have to pronounce the Christian doctrine of the Trinity to be either a temerarious hypothesis, or (if it be preferred) an unmeaning and useless revelation. (ibid., 171–2)

This is indeed a curious 'argument from experience'. No single individual has, or, presumably, has had, the experience in question; but Holy Church teaches a doctrine which would be nonsense without the experience; therefore she must have, and have had, the experience. Quite apart from what is meant by an experience of 'the Church as a whole' which is not the experience of 'any single Christian', we may note that this is a purely *a-priori* argument. It is a justification of the experience from the doctrine and not vice versa. And unless that form of the doctrine, which it is the purpose of the argument to establish (namely, that the three Persons represent three personalities), is already assumed in the premiss, then the conclusion does not follow. It is a completely unproven, and, to say the least, an extremely questionable, assumption that the Church has historically taught a doctrine of the Trinity which involves its members in the claim to have distinguishable relationships with each of the Persons. For the Church of England at least, Hooker may be allowed to speak:

> Dare any man unless he be ignorant altogether how inseparable the Persons of the Trinity are, persuade Himself that every one of them may have their sole and several possessions, or that we, being not partakers of all, can have fellowship with any one? (*Eccl. Pol.* V, lvi, 6)

And Hooker is here firmly grounded in the Bible. Without entering into the extremely vexed question whether the New Testament identifies the Spirit with the risen Christ, we may say that neither in the Johannine nor in the Pauline writings – where, if anywhere, we might expect to find it – is there a *consistent* separation of the Holy Spirit or Comforter from the Person of Christ.[46] Thus, Romans 8 shows the experience of the unity of love's working to be so overmastering that St Paul does frequently 'confuse the Persons'. It is impossible to say, this is the work of the Father, this of the Son, and this of the Spirit: all is the manifestation of a single personal dealing. Yet this is not to minimize the significance of the three Hypostases or Personae. Rather, the whole of God is given in each: in every action or revelation of God there is the one creative, reconciling, sanctifying love at work. That no hard-and-fast lines can be drawn is to be seen in St Paul's use in consecutive verses of the words 'the Spirit of God', 'the Spirit of Christ', 'Christ' and 'the Spirit' to mean one and the same thing (Rom. 8:9, 10).

That Romans 8 is not untypical of St Paul's thought in general can be seen from a study of the evidence of the Epistles as a whole. In discussing the benediction of 2 Cor. 13:14 ('The grace of our Lord Jesus Christ, and the love of God, and the communion of the Holy Ghost, be with you all'), perhaps the passage which at first sight suggests the greatest differentiation of the Persons, H. Wheeler Robinson says, 'There is certainly no warrant in the New Testament for the interpretation "fellowship *with* the Holy Spirit" as a personality here distinguished from the Father and the Lord Jesus Christ' (*The Christian Experience of the Holy Spirit*, 1928, 232). Indeed, it is doubtful whether St Paul would have attached any meaning to experience of the Spirit apart from the Father and the Son. Rather, like Jesus, he conceives the work of the Spirit to be the taking of the things of Christ (that is, the revelation of the Father and his own saving acts) and showing them unto us. It is a making available to us of the whole of God's activity.

> There is a gathering up of all that has been or is being done outside our consciousness and a bringing of all this into our consciousness. God as Holy Spirit, therefore, may be conceived as present in all his activities, creative, redemptive and sanctifying. The Holy Spirit in fact repeats within the human life the whole work of God without the life. By the further transformation of personality he works a 'new creation'; by in-dwelling human life as his temple, he repeats the mystery of the Incarnation, *mutatis mutandis*; by taking human life into the inclusive fellowship of the divine, he appropriates man for God. This is the justification for that transference of function, the Pauline interchange of 'Christ' and the Holy Spirit, which was later to be reflected in the ecclesiastical doctrine of *perichoresis*, the 'going around' of the activities

> and attributes of the 'Persons' of the Godhead. Wherever we begin we find God; where God is, there the whole of God is active. (ibid., 238)

In no experience is it possible to meet any one of the Persons in a peculiar or distinct relationship.

At this point it may be well to take stock of the position we have so far reached in this third part. Starting from the conclusion to which our analysis of the 'Thou' relation to God had led us, we began by enquiring how this was affected by the notion of threefoldness which Christian theology introduces into the unity of the divine nature. The mere fact that the work of Buber the Jew has been acclaimed and assimilated by numerous Christian theologians might have led us to suspect that the fundamental structure of the relation to God as he analysed it would not be rendered simply irrelevant, or even radically affected, by the doctrine of the Trinity. This supposition has been shown to be correct. Starting from an examination of present religious experience, we have seen the failure which must meet any attempt to describe the Christian awareness of God as the apprehension of three 'Thous', as distinct from that of a single 'Thou' in three aspects. We have tried to show, first, that the Christian experience provides no evidence for an awareness which sees in each Person 'the terminus of a distinct and recognisable relationship'; secondly, that attempts to find the basis of three 'Thou' relations in any several aspects of God's work or of our relationship to him must result in a splitting of the divine personality whose only end is tritheism; and, thirdly, that even if it be admitted that experience alone provides no ground for the ascription of separate personality to each of the Persons, it is still more than doubtful if Christian experience, whether of the New Testament or later writers, provides any confirmation or substantiation of such an ascription based on other grounds.

It is important to recognize exactly what has, and what has not, been debated and concluded. There have been two limits governing our argument, the one determining our point of approach, the other defining the content of our discussion. In the first place, the standpoint has throughout been that of the experience of the Christian believer as a member of the Church. The limitations of this standpoint must be recognized. It cannot of itself decide the question as to whether the Persons of the Trinity exist as persons. It is not merely, as Hodgson admits, that the experience would be the same whether it was one of 'He-ness' or 'It-ness'. It may be also that other facts which are not the objects of present experience (such as, e.g., the fact that Christ in the flesh did indeed live as an independent personality), demand an interpretation of *Persona* in terms of personality which otherwise would not be justified. But within its limits the voice of present experience is authentic. That it fails to yield of itself evidence for three distinguishable 'Thou' relations may not be fatal to the doctrine that the divine Hypostases are persons. That it cannot be said even to confirm such a doctrine is, however, as Kirk would admit, a very serious matter. This means that when the time comes we must give very special scrutiny to those other factors which are reckoned to require it.

In the second place, the *content* of our discussion has been confined to the differentiation of the Persons as personalities or termini of separable 'Thou' relations. The issue has been whether Christian experience provides the basis for *such* differentiation. Now another question, rather like it, is concerned with the location of the *incommunicabilis proprietas* of each Person. To this there are some (e.g., St Thomas, K. Barth etc.) who would say that in virtue of which the Persons are distinguished as Persons is not to be sought in any manifestation of the Godhead that forms part of our experience, but in the eternal invisible relations of origin of generation and procession. Others (e.g., Kirk, Hodgson, Raven etc.) would find it in different aspects of God's revelation, in different 'characters' of the divine being, requiring from us different responses and initiating different relationships. What it is important to grasp here is that this question and that with which we have been concerned are not the same. It is possible to say that the answer to the Augustinian question '*quid tres*?' (What is it in virtue of which the Godhead is three?) lies beyond the range of our experience, without thereby committing oneself in any way to the question whether the Persons are or are not persons. Again, while Hodgson and Raven agree in seeking the *proprium* of each Person *within* the field of religious experience, the one would see it as constituting the possibility in each case of a separate 'Thou' relationship, the other as a mode of manifestation of a single divine 'Thou'.

These two statements of the limitation in the scope and content of our discussion up to this point will have served to indicate how it must now move on. Our ultimate end will be, within the one personal 'essence' of God, to determine more closely the meaning of that form of existence to which the names *ὑπόστασις* and *persona* have been given. This is now, as it has always been, the central issue involved in Trinitarian debate. We hold out no hopes that we can advance beyond the position of St Augustine, who confesses that the precise meaning of *persona* is beyond human formulation. If we use the expression *tres personae*, he says, this is done '*non ut illud diceretur, sed ne taceretur omnino. Non enim rei ineffabiles eminentia hoc vocabulo explicari valet*' (not in order to say something but in order to not be completely silent.

For the ineffable eminence of the matter cannot be explained with this vocabulary) (*De Trin.* V, 10; cf. VII, 11). St Anselm likewise speaks of the *ineffabilis pluralitas* of the '*tres nescio quid*' (ineffable purity of the three I know not what) (*Monol.* 38). With this confession of ultimate ignorance always in mind, theologians, however, have essayed to indicate more positively the peculiar connotation of Personhood in God. And to this we must also now address ourselves.

Chapter Sixteen

THREE 'THOUS' OR ONE? (2) THE EVIDENCE OF THE INCARNATION

At the close of the last chapter we indicated two points from which our discussion might move on with a view to determining more exactly the meaning of Personhood within the Godhead. The first concerned the *form* of Hypostatic existence and the grounds, outside immediate experience, which might require us to describe this as that of a person in a 'Thou' relation. The second had reference to the *locus* of differentiation between the Persons and to the question, what is it in virtue of which God is three? Discussion of these two points will occupy the next four chapters.

First, then, what is it, beyond the range of the Christian's present experience which is held to necessitate an interpretation of *persona* in terms of personality in the modern sense of the term? Why do some theologians feel themselves obliged to speak of the Persons of the Trinity as beings capable of distinguishable 'Thou' relations with each other and with the human believer, when the evidence of immediate experience seems to lend no support to such a requirement?

In a word, the fact which is regarded as decisive is the Incarnation. Then at any rate, it is argued, there can be no doubt that the Second Person of the Trinity possessed full independent personal existence, marked by a perfect 'I–Thou' relationship to God and man. Whatever may be true of our present experience, to his historical contemporaries Jesus presented himself as a separate 'Thou', and not merely as a manifestation of the single 'Thou' of God: there was a real polarity of relationship between him and the Father. Now, it is stated, the doctrine of the Trinity represents simply 'the projection into eternity of that relationship between Christ and the Father which was revealed in the incarnation' (Hodgson, *The Doctrine of the Trinity*, 121). If, then, the Second Person was revealed there as possessing personal existence in a 'Thou' relationship, this must hold of him essentially and eternally. Such a projection does, indeed, involve a process of 'thinking away' those conditions of Christ's human existence which cannot simply be transferred into eternity. But when this is done, the essential 'Thou' relationship remains unaffected, and with it the personality of the Persons which is constituted by it. In its complete form the doctrine of the Trinity represents the positing of three beings facing each other as persons in the reciprocity of mutual 'Thou' relationships. The personality of the Spirit follows automatically, by analogy, from the relation of the Incarnate Christ to the Father (on this, see pp. 261–5 below).

With the general validity of the method whereby the earthly life of Christ is transposed into the key of eternity in order to give us a picture of the life and nature of God, there can be no quarrel. It is only taking seriously the conviction of the New Testament that 'God was in Christ', and that Jesus was the express image of his Person and the final revelation of his nature of love. Nor, again, can we doubt the necessity for thinking away those conditions of bodily confinement which flesh is heir to. To arrive at the nature of God we shall have to discount any changes and limitations to which Christ subjected himself in order to become man. It is not intended to raise at this point the question as to how far these conditions have been retained, if, as the doctrine of the eternal humanity of Christ asserts, manhood has been taken up into the Godhead. This is a complicating factor which at this stage can be left out of the account (see Ch. 17). At any rate, before the Incarnation the nature of the Second Person was not subject to the conditions of manhood. And if the mode of existence of the Son is to be of any value as an analogy for understanding that of the Spirit, the picture which we have to consider must clearly be that of the Son stripped of those special human limitations which made him also man. For the Spirit was never incarnate.

The only criticism which we have to make of this method of arriving at the doctrine of the Trinity adopted by Hodgson and others is simply that they do not apply it thoroughly enough. For among the elements in Christ's incarnate life which have to be 'thought away' we would put the very structure of the 'I–Thou' relation itself which existed between the Father and the Son. The love relationship is just one of those things whose transference into eternity as it stands is illegitimate. We cannot argue that, because Christ in history existed as a personality in such a relation, therefore he does so eternally. Rather, such a mode of existence was his in virtue, not of his divinity, but of his manhood.

The basis for this assertion is the doctrine of the nature of man expounded in the earlier sections of this work (cf. especially Chs 7 and 8). It is not intended to argue this anthropology again. Suffice it to state that we found the essence of humanity to consist, not in any intrinsic qualities or powers man may possess in himself, but in the mode of his relatedness to

God. Definition of personality is in terms of relationship; and the basic relationship upon which all depends is the relationship of 'responsibility' to God and his Word. The fact that God and man are related as 'I' and 'Thou' is the distinguishing mode of existence which makes humanity what it is. To be man is to live in this relation: to cease to be man is to cease to do so. For God to become man means that God must relate himself to God in the way that man does, or, rather, in the way that man ought to. For though sinful humanity still lives its life in a relation of 'responsibility' to God, it is a situation where the response is required as a matter of law rather than given as an act of love. The Incarnation means that the norm of the human response, of love answering the Word of love, was only made because it was made by God. God was on both sides – the 'I' and the 'Thou'. But yet it was a fully human response, because it was a man that made it. For one in the human relation to God, even though he be God, is by the very fact that he is in that relation, in the fullest and only sense of the word, man. The 'I–Thou' relationship is the specifically human mode of existence. Christ in the flesh was in this relation to the Father because he was man. In fact it was this and this alone which constituted his humanity. The *ἐνσάρκωσις* and the limitations of the flesh were but the necessary external conditions of this relationship. If we are to think away the factors in the Incarnation which were connected with the temporal assumption of manhood, then it is with the whole form of the relation of sonship that we must begin. For sonship is just another name for the relation of loving obedience which is the norm of the human relation to God.

At this point, a word is required to protect what has been said from being misunderstood. At the Incarnation the Son became a person, took upon himself personality and the relationship it involves, for the first time. There was then a new element introduced into the Godhead – a polarity of will confronting will and a love relationship of which this polarity is the necessary condition. But there is no suggestion that the Person of the Son only came into existence at the Incarnation, as Sabellius asserted. That he existed as a person, in an 'I–Thou' relation, for the first time at the Incarnation is no denial of the pre-existence of Christ as a Person. As the express image of God, the Second Person of the Trinity is a real embodiment of the nature of the Godhead and therefore eternal. But he who is eternally the subject of the divine love became also at the Incarnation its object. In the strict sense of the word he could then first be spoken of as the Son; because only then did he live in that relation of which sonship is the type. It was of himself in that relation that Christ used the term. To extend the appellation to his pre-existent and eternal state is a convenient way of indicating that it is the same Person who was and is 'with God' (Jn 1:1) eternally, who also confronted and communed with him in Palestine. But, the extension becomes dangerous directly it implies a transference of filial relationship to eternity. He is always the Son in that he is the 'express image' and 'Word' of the Father. He is not always the Son if the strict implications of the relationship of sonship are pressed. The distinction may be made by reserving, as the Fourth Gospel does the term 'Logos' for the pre-existent Christ, while using 'Son' when the reference is to the Incarnation.[47]

Failure to make this distinction reveals itself in a notion which has appealed to theologians of every age (e.g., out of many, John Pearson, *An Exposition of the Creed*, 1659, I, 47–8 (ed. Burton, Ox., 1847), and B. F. Westcott, *St John*, 216), namely, that there is a certain 'fittingness' that it should have been the Son rather than the Father who became Incarnate. But any such demonstration is merely a piece of circular reasoning. The Second Person of the Trinity is called 'the Son' in virtue of the fact that he lived in a filial relationship to the Father at the Incarnation. It is impossible to go on from there to say that it was he who became incarnate because he was the 'Son' and therefore more suitable to be 'sent' than the Father.

It may be objected that such statements reveal a dogmatism concerning the inner nature of the Godhead for which there is no justification. But in fact the dogmatism is on the other side. We are making no attempt to define positively the mode of existence of the Persons, which is exactly what the others are doing. And their definition is nothing but a colossal piece of anthropomorphism. For they are reading into the interior life of God relations which, as far as we can know, only obtain between man and man and between man and God (the former term of each pair including God when he was man).

If it is said that the charge of illegitimate anthropomorphism only holds if our anthropology is accepted, we may admit it, but add in reply two considerations. First, the definition and interpretation of humanity in terms of the 'I–Thou' relationship has been adopted for reasons which we believe can be shown to shine in their own light and, independently of all Christological considerations, to provide a more genuinely satisfactory theory of personality than the traditional 'classical' view. Such a demonstration has already been undertaken to the best of our ability and need not be repeated here. Secondly, it is legitimate to point to the Theological consequences of the view that the 'Thou' relationship obtaining at the Incarnation can be postulated *simpliciter* of the eternal relations within the Godhead. These we would regard as inescapably tritheistic and destructive of any orthodox doctrine of the Trinity.

The most usual form in which this view finds Theological expression is in the doctrine of the existence of love relationships within the Trinity. Now not all writers who have used the word 'love' to describe the mutual relations of the Persons would accept a 'social' doctrine of the Trinity which attributes personality to the three Hypostases. This is true, for instance, of that writer who first showed the way in describing the divine life as that of the lover, the beloved and the love that passes between them. St Augustine has no intention of asserting here that the Trinity is anything like three persons in love. He dismisses the analogy of the family in this connection as 'in truth so absurd, nay indeed so false, that it is most easy to refute it' (*De Trin.* XII, 5). Apart from its inherent deficiencies, he declares it to be contrary to Scripture, which has it that it is the individual man who has been made in God's image (XII, 6). The analogy which he actually adopts, though admitting its inadequacy (XV, 42, 43), is that of the co-existence of memory, intelligence and will within a single personal centre. His illustration of the lover, the beloved and their love is perfectly compatible with this. For it is essentially the answer to the question 'But what if I love none except myself?' 'For in that case to love and to be loved are not two different things, just as he who loves and he who is loved are not two different persons. But even so, love and what is loved are still two things' (IX, 2).

The idea of love within the Godhead has historically been held independently of the doctrine of a 'social' Trinity, and we have no wish to find ourselves in disagreement with those doctors of the Church who, while equally agreed in rejecting the latter would still retain the former. It may be true that the doctrine of a social Trinity is the logical implication of the idea of love between the Persons. But the usage of 'love' here is parallel to the extension given to the application of the term 'Son' noted above. We have seen how this word could and, in the absence of any more accurate term, had to be used of the eternal nature of the Second Person, even though the actual form of relationship which occasioned its suitability, and which strictly its use implies, was confined to his temporal life. In an exactly similar way, the same inevitable poverty of thought and expression occasions the use of the word 'love' of the eternal Trinity. Love necessarily implies, if it is to retain any clear and defined meaning at all, the structure of that 'personal' 'I–Thou' relationship, of will over against will, of which it is the most perfect and complete instance. It is but another name for that relation of free and spontaneous 'responsibility' to God and man which is the norm of the peculiarly human mode of existence. Love, therefore, is strictly predicable of the Son towards the Father only in so far as he is really living in the filial, human relation to God. But the inability of man to picture the relations of the divine Persons except in anthropomorphic terms (namely, as those of persons) requires him to use the word 'love' to describe that complete union of Persons of which the unity of personal communion on the basis of a polarity of wills is the earthly analogy. The fact that the Fourth Gospel (17:24) uses the word love of the eternal relation of Father and Son no more commits us to the literal philosophical implications of the term for their status as persons than any of the other word-pictures of the heavenly places, constructed by the biblical writers out of materials drawn from this world, force upon us a particular metaphysic of eternity. As myth such usage is true and valuable. What is disastrous is that what represents, after all, simply an admission of failure on the part of human knowledge and imagination should be taken as the basis of a serious philosophical doctrine of the nature of the Persons and their relations. It was just because St Augustine and others treated the idea of the lover, the beloved and their love as a useful picture rather than a serious philosophical analogy that they were not driven to the doctrine of a social Trinity which logically it would entail.

The use of the idea of love relationships within the Trinity is no more philosophically accurate than the Book of Genesis is a scientific description of the origin of species. The place of myth lies in the interpretation, in terms of known symbolism, of that for which we have or can have no direct evidence. Its truth consists in providing a 'likely tale' of what has happened, is happening or will happen in 'the heavenly places'. When it ceases to do this, or when it is more misleading than helpful, then it must be discarded in favour of some other. Perhaps much of the traditional picture of heaven and hell comes under this condemnation. We may ask whether the same might not be said of the notion of love relationships within the Godhead. It is not as if the truth to be expressed had in any way changed. But progress in the analysis of the 'Thou' relationship of love has made us far more conscious than were our predecessors of the emphasis on individuation involved. We cannot so easily use the word and ignore the structure of relationship it implies.

At the risk of repeating what has been said above in an earlier connection (Ch. 5) we may point to the fact that the precondition of the existence of a *personal* relationship and of real *communion* (as opposed to some organic or sub-personal connection or union) is, paradoxically enough, a high degree of individual isolation. In man the isolation of the individual and the definition of the frontier which divides one psychical existence from another has reached its most advanced stage of development. Yet, corresponding to this increasing isolation of the individual and his psychic states, there goes, as we mount the scale of life, an increasing ability on the part of individuals to communicate these states to one another. There seems no doubt that a bird knows more of its fellows than do infusoria, a dog more than a bird, and two friends infinitely more than either. Yet these two facts – increasing isolation and increasing power of communication – are not mutually incompatible. Thus on the human level the isolation of mind from mind is overcome by a method of communication which not only does not override but also pays deference to the personal integrity of the other individual. The use of symbols in general and of speech in particular secures the other person against that direct exercise of manipulative control which constitutes an abuse of personality by denying him the right, as it were, to close his frontier against what he does not want to admit. It is just when this opportunity is not given, as when the attempt is made to influence the mind of another by suggestion of propaganda, that the human relationship becomes depersonalized. The retention of a polarity between will and will, of a respect for the other's frontier, is thus essential for all personal relations. And in their highest form it is more, rather than less, important. For love involves absolute consideration, absolute respect for the other's right to exercise his choice contrary to one's own wishes. No one will put a person he really loves in a position in which the desired response is in any way forced. It is because the frontiers of individuality are so clearly defined at the highest level of personal relationship that the love which overcomes them is so much the more valuable and so much the more precarious. When love is suddenly removed, the depths of misunderstanding and mutual isolation uncovered disclose the yawning gulf over which it has been holding the two persons. It is because it is ever thus suspended above '70,000 fathoms' (Kierkegaard) that love is so precious in its achievement and so tragic in its failure.

Turning to the relations between the Persons of the Trinity, we should expect, if they are not to be conceived as lower than the highest kind of personal relation we know, that the individuality of each Person would at least be as well defined as our own. Indeed, we should surely picture it as much more so. This is not an argument from analogy. It is not being suggested that, because human relationships are such, therefore the divine are the same, *eminentiore sensu*. We only mean that *if* we are to apply the word 'love' in any sense to the divine relations then we must be prepared honestly to transfer to them, at the same time, that structure of relationship without which love as we know it would not be love. In other words, if we think of love-relations within the Trinity, we must be prepared to accept the fact that the implication for the status of the persons must be one of increased rather than diminished individuation. They must each be separate personalities, existing as independent volitional centres, in spanning whose potential mutual isolation love can alone exist. But such a Theology is nothing short of polytheism, however harmonious the wills may be in their common purpose of love.

It is this increased awareness of the nature of the structure of the relationship which it implies that makes the use of the term 'love' definitely misleading where this structure would be disavowed. The danger lies in the fact that, however carefully it may be stated that the use of the term as an imaginative picture to describe the relations between the Persons of the Trinity carries with it no philosophical implications as to their status as persons, yet this is the conclusion that will be drawn. A supreme instance of the reality of this danger is the frequent use we noted in an earlier connection of the doctrine of the Trinity as a solution of the problem as to how God can exist as personal love without other persons. The idea that the 'Thou' relations required for God's existence as personal are to be found *within* his own being seems a heaven-sent solution to what is otherwise an extremely perplexing difficulty. But this solution does exactly what it is not legitimate to do. It takes the idea of love within the Godhead as if it were a philosophically accurate account of the structure of relationship between the Persons and proceeds to draw out all its implications. What the problem requires is the proviso of a real 'Thou' for God confronting him as a will, with all the independence, freedom and inviolability which belongs to any other individual in this highest personal relationship. Nothing less will suffice. But to postulate such a mode of existence of any of the Persons of the Trinity is pure tritheism and goes far beyond what historic orthodoxy has ever allowed.[48]

The tritheistic tendency of such argument has, of course, often been recognized by theologians. But they have sought to retain the idea of love within the Godhead as a philosophical truth, and even to use it as a solution of the problem discussed above, by employing a line of reasoning fundamentally opposed to that which has been our principle of interpretation. The argument they use is that the degree of individuation, instead of increasing in the higher forms of relationship, does in fact rapidly diminish. At the level of the Godhead it is possible to conceive a form of love-relationship in which the various selves so interpenetrate each other by mutual coinherence, that 'the divine hypostases, though still distinct subjects and agents, may, or rather must, be conceived as much less individual than human persons' (Tennant, *Philosophical Theology*, ii, 171. For a similar argument, cf. H. R. Mackintosh, *The Person of Jesus Christ*, 1912, 1913 2nd edn, 524–5).

By means of this assumption, which seems entirely unproven, namely, that the increasing power of self-communication in the higher relationships is due to an increasing penetrability and transparency of the selves to each other, theologians have tried to have it both ways. They have sought to retain the idea of love within the Godhead while denying the only conditions under which love in any meaningful sense is possible. Love presupposes the meeting of will with will, the standing of one free, inviolable and independent personality over against another. There can be no compromise in this point: either the conditions are there in full or there is no love at all. Dr Tennant, indeed, is prepared to admit that any theory of a divine 'society', his own included, involves an abandonment of the historic Trinitarian formula in the direction of tritheism. But others whose interest is more doctrinal than philosophical are indisposed to admit that a genuinely orthodox doctrine of the Trinity cannot be so formulated.

The crucial point is the legitimacy of the assumption of decreasing individuation. No argument which includes this line of reasoning can seem to us to be valid. But certainly, no argument which does not include it can hope to escape tritheism. Its indispensability may be shown by a glance at two theories which do not make it explicit.

These do not start, like Tennant's, from the fact of human individuality and proceed to show that this is less marked in the case of the Trinity. Rather, they begin with an assertion that individuation is not the fundamental fact even about human personality. Thus R. C. Moberly (*Atonement and Personality*, 157) says that our normal view of personality is too individualistic, that we define a person in terms of the fact that he is *not* someone else, thereby minimizing the more fundamental fact of mutual relatedness. This is a perfectly sound criticism, and is in fact the point from which Buber begins, when he insists that a person is essentially one who stands in an 'I–Thou' relation and only exists in that relation. But it is hard to see how it helps here. Surely the point which requires demonstration is that, however mutually 'inclusive' human persons are, the Persons of the Trinity are considerably more so. Otherwise the result will be tritheism (i.e., three personalities), *however* one defines human personality.

Wheeler Robinson (*The Christian Experience of the Holy Spirit*, 274–7), whose general position as regards the degree of individuation with the Trinity is more acceptable than that of either Tennant or Moberly, argues from the experience of the religious man, who, by a surrender of his own will, is enabled to live in God and to know God in him, in such a way that his individuality is in no way diminished or absorbed, but rather enriched and fulfilled. His own personality is so integrated into the divine that he can say with St Paul, 'I live, yet not I, but Christ liveth in me' (Gal. 2:20). He then proceeds to argue, citing Christ's relation to the Father as the supreme earthly example, to the existence of a perfect 'inclusiveness' (without less of individuality) among the Persons of the eternal Trinity.

The structure of experience of which Wheeler Robinson here speaks is not peculiar to religious experience, but is in a very real degree to be found also in human personal relationships. A genuine 'losing' of one's own will in that of another, so that his personality permeates one's own without destroying it, is realizable by two friends or lovers. In other words, it is a normal feature of *any* personal 'Thou' relationship at its highest. But we have seen the corollary of this real transcendence of individuality to be a high degree of individual isolation: the two increase and decrease *pari passu*. Robinson himself admits that

> if . . . it is necessary to the Christian values of Father, Son and Holy Spirit that we should base them ultimately on a conception of Divine personality possessing three distinct centres of consciousness, it seems doubtful whether we ought to speak of Christian *monotheism* at all. (ibid., 269)

And again: 'If our theology has issued in the doctrine of three distinct "persons" with the modern connotation of personality, it is certainly true that no metaphysical dexterity will ever avail to combine them into a convincing unity' (ibid., 271–2). But his own analogy depends for its soundness on the fact that the relations between the Persons of the Trinity are thought of as continuous in structure with human 'I–Thou' relationships. There is here no *μετάβασις εἰς ἄλλο γένος* (changing over to another kind. The very fact that he can use Christ's earthly relation to the Father as the type of the eternal relations within the Godhead shows that he is in fact thinking in terms of 'three distinct centres of consciousness' and using the word 'Person' with precisely 'the modern connotation of personality'. For no one could deny that the Incarnate Christ was anything but a fully independent centre of will and personality.

The inevitable tritheistic consequences of the conception of the Trinity as a communion of three persons in the 'Thou' relationship of love points to a dilemma for modern Trinitarian theology, which only the abandonment of the 'classical' theory of personality can solve. If we devote a small space to elaborating this dilemma we may see another instance of the contribution which the adoption of the philosophy of the 'Thou' can make to problems of doctrine apparently peripheral to it.

It will be remembered that the ground for the assertion of internal love-relationships within the Godhead was the necessity of seeing in the relation of the Incarnate Christ to the Father a pattern of the eternal divine relations. All turns on the legitimacy of the transference of the personality of Christ in the flesh, and of the 'I–Thou' relation then established, to the essential nature of the Son and the other Persons.

Unless there are sound reasons for showing such a transference to be impossible we should be bound to make it. Anything in Christ which is not clearly connected with the temporary conditions of his manhood must for the Christian be regarded as the express revelation of the eternal Godhead. Unless the 'I–Thou' relation can be regarded as a peculiar feature of his humanity, then, like everything else, it must be taken as a manifestation of the divine. On the presuppositions of the 'classical' view of personality, for which this relation does *not* form part of the definition of humanity, the course of an argument such as Professor Hodgson's is unexceptionable and inevitable. He claims to be following in the footsteps of tradition, and especially to be representing the true mind of Augustine, Aquinas and Calvin. This claim is justified in that the method of his argument, though not always theirs in detail, yet works with a principle of interrelation endorsed by them and the whole Church. But – and this is where the modern dilemma arises – whereas earlier authors could use the idea of love within the Godhead (which this method of interpretation must yield, as long as the 'Thou' relation is not regarded as peculiarly human) without implying anything definite concerning the personality of the Persons, this is now no longer possible. The same method must now produce different results. The development of the concept of personality in the modern era has made it impossible to ignore the fact that a necessary implication of love within the Godhead is a 'social' Trinity of highly individualized Hypostases. In this respect Hodgson's conclusion, though reached by methods to which they would have no objections, would be repugnant to the three authors with whom he especially seeks to align himself.

The present situation may be stated thus. *Either* the idea of love within the Godhead, and the apparently necessary interpretative principle which yields it, must be given up *or* the doctrine of the full personality of the Persons, which the love relation entails, must be introduced. In each case there is a serious breach with tradition. The development of the idea of personality, though the essential 'classical' framework within which it was cast has until recently remained the same, has yet had profound repercussions on the doctrine of the Trinity. It is impossible to ignore this, and to continue speaking as if the problem which faces us is the same as that of the Fathers, the Schoolmen or even the Reformers.

As long as the presuppositions of the 'classical' view of personality are accepted, there is no escape from the dilemma propounded above. Given the fact that the 'I–Thou' relation itself is not part of the condition of Christ's humanity, then it must be a divine relation eternally subsisting between the Persons. From which it inevitably follows that the status of the Persons is the only one which would make possible this structure of relationship – namely, independent personalities, such indeed as Christ was in the flesh, but without the peculiarly human mode of consciousness and individuality of which the finitude of the body is the symbol. The only way of avoiding this conclusion is to deny that the relation of the Father and Son at the Incarnation is in fact a manifestation of the eternal relations of the Trinity. But, since on this theory such a relation is not a specific characteristic of what was temporary and human, such a denial amounts to a statement that the divine as manifested in Christ is not a picture of the true nature of the Father. And the abandonment of a principle of interrelation so fundamental for Christianity has implications even more disastrous than any of the tritheistic consequences which attend the other view.

Only if humanity is defined in terms of the 'I–Thou' relation is any satisfactory doctrine of the Trinity possible. It alone enables the all-important distinction to be made between (a) the relation of Christ to the Father at the Incarnation, which was the human, filial relation and (b) the eternal relations of the Persons, who, since they are not human, cannot be conceived as confronting one another as 'I' and 'Thou'. Only thus can be avoided the attribution of the most completely independent and individuated personality to each of the Hypostases – an attribution inevitably fraught, as we have seen, with the most disastrous tritheistic consequences. The rescuing of the doctrine of the Trinity from this its fatal modern dilemma is probably the greatest contribution which the 'I–Thou' philosophy has to make to the subject.

Before closing this chapter on the evidence of the fact of the Incarnation for determining the status of the divine Persons as three 'Thous' or Persons, we must return to take up a point left behind at p. 251. The question at issue hitherto has been the legitimacy of the transference to eternity of the relation at the Incarnation between the *Son* and the *Father*. But the doctrine of the Trinity speaks of *three* Persons. In the previous chapter we found no ground in immediate experience for supposing the Third Person to exist as a separate 'Thou'. But is there nothing in the historical revelation of the Incarnation which might provide independent evidence? And if so, what relation does this bear to the evidence concerning the Second Person recently under consideration?

It is a commonplace of the history of doctrine that the status of the Spirit within the Godhead was fixed in a comparatively casual manner. The decisive struggles were waged on other issues, and the full divinity and equality in substance of the Spirit was introduced into orthodoxy, not by any discussion of the merits of the case but purely by analogy of the status of the Son. The Macedonian controversy was in fact ended before it began. The issue had already been decided on other grounds before it was raised in the case of the Third Person. The conclusions which had emerged from the conflict with the Arians were transferred without further examination to the Person of the Spirit.

A precisely similar line of procedure is adopted in modern arguments used to establish the personality of the Spirit. It will be remembered that by his own confession Professor Hodgson acknowledges that experience alone is unable to decide this question. What in fact determines him in the preference he gives to the 'He' passages of Scripture is not any direct awareness of the Spirit as a person, but the pressure of analogy. Having concluded in favour of the eternal existence of an 'I–Thou' relationship between Father and Son, he is bound to postulate similar relations between Father and Spirit and Son and Spirit. For the basic assumption of his whole treatment of the subject, both in his own theory and in his historical review, is that there is no difference in status between the Spirit and the other two Persons. If they are Persons, then he must be too. This is perfectly sound; and if the Augustinian formula means that the Father and Son are Persons while the Spirit is merely a relation between them, then it is false. But Hodgson's premiss requires him to go further than this, and he proceeds to the position: since they are Persons, he must be too.

But is this argument from analogy, from the general principle of the equality of the Spirit with the other Persons, the sole ground for the assertion of the personality of the Holy Spirit? If there is no certain evidence to be deduced from the direct experience of Christian believers, is it not possible to base it on the relationship of the Incarnate Christ with the Spirit parallel to that which he had with the Father?

When we come to examine the Gospel narratives, however, we find that they are curiously silent on the subject of such a relationship. And the fact that Professor Hodgson makes no use of it in establishing the personality of the Spirit, but, like the Church before him, argues indirectly by analogy from the Father–Son relationship, is a tacit admission that it cannot be found in the New Testament. But if this is so, how is this situation to be accounted for? Why do the Gospels witness to a continuous relationship of prayer and communion between the Son and the Father, but apparently have little to say of any such awareness by the Incarnate of the Third Person as a 'Thou'? What we might expect is one of two alternatives. *Either*, it would seem, Christ knew the Godhead, like other human beings, as *one* 'Thou' under different forms (in his case two, instead of three, as he himself, as one of the Persons, stood on the opposite side of the polar relationship); *or*, conceivably, since he was also God, he might have had a 'Thou' relation (in itself a mark of his humanity), in a way that was impossible to human beings, with *each* of the Persons (i.e., the Father and the Spirit). The latter alternative is not indeed one that we should independently expect: but it could not be ruled out, should the evidence of the Gospels require it. The difficulty lies in the fact that this evidence actually appears to fit with neither alternative. There is certainly an awareness by Christ of the Father as a 'Thou' indistinct personal relationship with himself. But of the Spirit we cannot say the same. There are many signs of Christ's recognition of the existence and activity of the Spirit in connection with his own ministry. But the evidence cannot be said to yield the conclusion that this existence and activity is only describable for Christ as that of an independent 'Thou'. Fortunately the value to be assigned to the Johannine Paraclete discourse as evidence of Christ's own consciousness need not here be argued. For there the hypostatization of the Spirit has reference not to his relationship with himself but to the Spirit's relation to the Church as Christ's *Alter Ego*.[49]

The problem on which we have touched is one that has extensive implications for the doctrine of the Trinity as a whole. It is concerned with the gulf, or at least the difference, between the way in which the New Testament refers to the different Persons of the Godhead and the presuppositions of the doctrine of the Trinity as it later came to be formulated. It is well known that the New Testament never calls either Christ or the Holy Spirit 'God' simply and unambiguously.[50] 'God' both for the Gospels and the Epistles is synonymous with 'the Father'. Without necessarily any denial of the equality of the Persons, this element of subordination (of the Son and the Spirit) is present throughout the New Testament. It finds its reflection in the account given of the human experience of the Trinity. This is perhaps most concisely stated in St Paul's phrase: 'Through him (Christ) we have our access in one Spirit unto the Father' (Eph. 2:18). On these words Wheeler Robinson comments:

> This means that Paul did not conceive Father Son and Spirit as three 'hypostases' and one 'ousia', three centres on one plane equidistant from the believer. Paul conceived a line of intensive approach, always in the Spirit, always through Christ, always to the Father, even though he may not always express this as explicitly as he does in the passage quoted. (*The Christian Experience of the Holy Spirit*, 231)

And what is true of St Paul in this matter is true of the New Testament writers as a whole. For St John, no man can come to the Father except by the Son, and no man can come to the Son except the Spirit lead him. There is the same intensive approach corresponding to the same subordinationism within the Godhead. The goal of such a pilgrimage is always the Father. For St Paul it is because of our adoption through Christ and our life in the Spirit that we are able to call God, Abba, Father (Rom. 8:12–17). For St John 'this is life eternal' to 'know Thee the only true God, and him whom thou didst send' (Jn 17:3). It is only of the Father that the New Testament could ever use the expression *ὁ μόνος ἀληθινὸς θεός* [the only true God].

It is Sabellius whom Harnack credits with being the first to treat the other two Persons as on the same formal level as the Father (*History of Dogma*, III, 87). It is probable that Sabellius' temporal modalism was the price of this step. As long as the Persons were regarded as co-eternally present to the believer, the idea of subordination and of an intensive approach was perhaps inevitable. But whatever may have been the cost in orthodoxy which its introduction required, it is certain that it was an idea which orthodoxy was to find indispensable. No genuine doctrine of the Trinity could have developed unless it had become possible to say of the Son and the Spirit that they were God as unambiguously and in the same sense as the Father.

We are not here concerned with the relation of the earlier intensive approach to the fully developed doctrine of the Trinity as three equal Hypostases in each of whom the whole *οὐσία* (being, substance, reality) subsists. We do not ask whether a synthesis of these two standpoints is either desirable or possible, or what implications are involved for a doctrine of the Trinity which claims to be true to Scripture. Some of these questions will have to be raised later in connection with the locus of differentiation of the Persons.

All we have to do now, in fact, is to note the difference of standpoint, and to be on our guard against treating as valid of the biblical authors distinctions which rest on presuppositions they never shared. When the New Testament speaks of the relation of Christ or the Christian to 'the Father', it is not thinking primarily or at all of a relation to one of three parallel Persons of a Trinity. The reference is to the Godhead as a whole, to the fount of deity, the one and only 'true God', the God of Abraham, of Isaac and of Jacob in these latter days manifested as the Father of our Lord Jesus Christ. When therefore the Gospels speak as though Christ stood in an 'I–Thou' relation to the Father in a way in which he did not to the Spirit, they are saying nothing that need cause difficulty for a theologian of the Trinity. In their terminology 'Father' stands for God as a whole, and corresponds with what later writers called *οὐσία* or *essentia* and what we should describe as the one divine personality. To this Christ, as man, stood in a relation of 'I' to 'Thou'. The Spirit, in contrast, corresponds with what was later to be distinguished as one ὑπόστασις (actual existence, reality) or *persona* (character, actor's mask). He is definitely not God absolutely, but God in a particular mode.[51] With such the Incarnate Christ, like every other man, does not enter into a different or separable 'I–Thou' relation. The personality over against whom he stands is the one divine 'Thou' (God, or, as the New Testament has it, the Father). The Spirit is not an independent personality, but a mode in which God defines himself. He is 'the Spirit of God' (Rom. 8:9), or, as St John puts it in more dramatic terms but meaning the same, he is 'sent' by or from the Father (Jn 14:26; 15:26). In view of the close connection between the 'Thou' relationship and the 'speech situation', there is a special interest attaching to the words, 'He shall not speak of himself; but whatsoever he shall hear, that shall he speak' (Jn 16:13). They might well stand as an expression of the truth that the Spirit is not a separate pole of an 'I–Thou' relationship but a mode of self-definition of the one eternal 'Thou' (similar phrases are of course used also of the Son – e.g., Jn 15:15; cf., 5:19, 30).

In the light of all this, it is therefore clear, from the point of view of the Gospels, as before there was not from the point of view of the Epistles, there is not anything that could of itself require us to believe in the Spirit as an independent 'Thou'. The only safe assertion is that the general New Testament teaching about the divinity of the Spirit would demand this conclusion by analogy, *if* it could be shown that the other two Persons eternally so existed. Now we have argued that this latter statement cannot be demonstrated: even if Christ's relation to 'the Father', as the New Testament speaks of it, referred to a relation between two Persons (and not to that of the God-man with the Godhead as a whole), it would be illegitimate to transpose the 'I–Thou' form of the Incarnational relation into eternity. Since, then, the Person of the Spirit introduces no independent considerations, it can do nothing to disturb our previous conclusion that belief in the Trinity as three divine 'Thous' is no more required by the evidence of the Incarnation than it was by that of immediate experience.

Chapter Seventeen

THREE 'THOUS' OR ONE? (3) THE EVIDENCE OF CHRIST'S ETERNAL HUMANITY

There remains to be examined one further consideration which might be advanced in support of the attribution of separate 'Thou' existence at any rate to one of the Persons of the Godhead. The form of the 'I–Thou' relation we argued before to be the peculiar characteristic of *human* existence. It could not, therefore, simply be transferred to the eternal relations of the Godhead as such. But what is the situation if, as orthodoxy asserts, the Second Person of the Trinity *retained* his manhood after his Ascension, and, therefore, also the form of existence in the 'Thou' relation which constitutes it? Are we not here at least faced with the necessity, before denied, of attributing personality to one of the Persons of the Trinity? And is not this disruptive of the simple conclusion at which we had previously arrived?

The doctrine of the eternal humanity of our Lord is one that historically has had little connection with Trinitarian controversy. Discussion of it, on the whole, has fallen within the Christological field. Even here it has not received the serious philosophical treatment which has been accorded to the manner of the *historical* Incarnation. Too often this doctrine has been treated in devotional or Eucharistic writings in a way which has isolated it from the rest of Christology. F. Weston (*The One Christ*, 1919, 175–9, 287–90) has shown how neither the Alexandrian nor the kenotic theories of the Incarnation make full allowance for the significance of the perpetual humanity of Christ. In the former case the state of glorification is so conceived that the humanity and any limitations it may possess are simply swallowed up in the deity. It is held that Christ is still man, and stands before God as our eternal High Priest; but the manhood cannot be said to affect or make any real difference to the Godhead. This criticism, indeed, holds of this theory of the Incarnation in general, wherein the impassible God is incapable of any genuine limitation by the human. But in the heavenly places its effect is that any real distinction between the human and divine disappears in what is in effect deification. Monophysitism is triumphant.

Again, the result of the kenotic theory is, surprisingly, not very different.

According to this view, the state of self-limitation and self-abandonment ceases at the Ascension. Clearly Christ cannot be regarded as permanently deprived of those attributes of omnipotence, omniscience, omnipresence, of which, according to the kenotic theory, he emptied himself at the Incarnation. These are therefore conceived as restored to him in his glory. But with this restoration disappear what kenoticism regards as the condition of real humanity. The manhood may be retained in name, but, as in the Lutheran doctrine of its omnipresence, its attributes are now no longer human but divine. The humanity is once more absorbed by deification. The *communicatio idiomatum* is entirely one-sided, and the result again is monophysitism.

In theory at least, it would be perfectly possible to construct a satisfactory Christology of eternity wherein human consciousness, though no longer limited by physical organic conditions, was still the form of our Lord's apprehension of God and the measure of his activity on behalf of men. Omnipotence and the other attributes would be there, as always, but, as in the flesh, they would be exercised through limitations, which, though not identical with those of historical human existence, would not be qualitatively different from them. But the details of such a Christology are not our concern here. Rather its implications for the doctrine of the Trinity must be examined.

These implications have tended to be minimized in proportion as the effects of the humanity of the ascended Christ on his divinity have been ignored. As long as the manhood is regarded as exercising no genuine limitation on the Godhead and as making no essential difference to it, the consequences for the doctrine of the Trinity are not serious. But if there is a real and noticeable distinction in the form of consciousness and activity of one of the Persons when compared with that of the others, then the implications cannot be ignored.

On any theory, therefore, which takes the meaning of Christ's eternal humanity seriously there are difficulties raised for the doctrine of the Trinity which have to be squarely faced. The mere absence of such discussion from Trinitarian literature is sufficient evidence that the problems concerned have not been seen or wrestled with. This too will be our excuse for giving what would otherwise be a disproportionate amount of space to this topic.

It is important to recognize that these difficulties are involved *whatever* theory of the nature of humanity is accepted. For it will be argued that on the theory we have adopted the problems are very great. And it is well to see that, however serious, they differ only in degree from those attaching to any other theory.

The 'classical' view of personality would require us to see the Second Person of the Trinity as eternally, in some sense, 'an individual substance of a rational nature'. This note of individuality is difficult enough to introduce into the doctrine of the Trinity; but nothing less will do. Without it the peculiar form of consciousness which is the human is absorbed in one which is not human because it has no finitude.

On the view on which we have been working, however, this and more is involved. The old problems are still with us. That individuality and self-consciousness are essential marks of personality is not denied. What is asserted is that they do not constitute the distinguishing element in terms of which personality is to be defined. This is, rather, a type of relationship, of which these and other qualities are but the necessary marks and modes of expression. Not only, therefore, are we faced by the problem raised by the introduction of permanent human limitations into the divine. The essential thing for us about the eternal humanity of Christ is that these limitations are to be viewed as the necessary conditions of a permanent 'Thou' relation to God. The fundamental problem, therefore, is how we are to fit into the doctrine of the Trinity the notion that one of the Persons exists as a person in an 'I–Thou' relationship to the Godhead as a whole.

Now this, of course, is no problem at all for those who do not regard this relationship as the mark of the peculiarly human, but in any case postulate it eternally of all the Persons.[52] But if we have reason to deny it of all, then to postulate it of one brings consequences which must be squarely faced. There is thereby introduced into the Godhead a polarity of relationship wherein one of the Persons stands on the opposite side to the other two, not in themselves possessing such separate existence as persons. Such a situation is far more complicated than that allowed for by any traditional doctrine of the status and relationships of the Hypostases of the Trinity. That in itself is not a decisive argument against the idea of the eternal humanity of Christ. But if this is to be retained, its full implication must be faced. Certainly there must be no thought of throwing over the doctrine just because it is inconvenient for our own particular scheme of thought or for any other. That would be a glaring example of that *a-priori* rationalism (what Protestant scholasticism called the 'legislative' use of reason) which pre-judges the evidence of revelation. If the Bible and Christian experience demand its retention, then it must be retained whatever the Theological repercussions.

However, the existence of such a problem as has here been encountered does justify a re-examination of the evidence for, and the religious value of, the doctrine of Christ's ascended humanity. And we are forced to ask again what is the philosophical status of any such assertions as we may be required to make.

'It is Christ Jesus that died, yea rather, that was raised from the dead, who is at the right hand of God, who also maketh intercession for us' (Rom. 8:34). This is a sequence of events to which the New Testament testifies. The exaltation and heavenly session of Christ are treated as one piece with his Resurrection. Indeed, in many passages these appear to be distinguished as but two aspects of the same event. The glorification of the man Jesus was part of the earliest κήρυγμα (proclamation) (Acts 2:33; 5:31), and formed an integral element in the catena of Old Testament passages cited as *testimonia* (proof texts) (Ps. 110:1). The lifting up and exaltation of the Suffering Servant (Is. 52:13) was essential to the significance of that song. So too, it must be the same Lamb who was slain for the sins of the world who appears before the throne of glory (Rev. 5:6). This element of continuity is necessary to the idea of the vindication before men of Christ and the divine purpose he served. At times the close connection of the Cross and the Resurrection suffices for its establishment. At other times (e.g., Phil. 2:5–11) the chain of events is extended both backwards and forwards into eternity to show Christ Jesus as 'the same yesterday, and today, and forever' (Heb. 13:8).

This, then, is one of the biblical motives for the exaltation of Christ's humanity even to the heavenly places. But it is doubtful whether the necessity for continuity would have been, or, from the doctrinal point of view, is, sufficient to explain the insistence on the retention of the *manhood*. After all, all the analogies of contemporary Hellenistic religious speculation would have pointed not to its retention as a separate and inviolable element but to its absorption by deification. Doubtless the emphasis on continuity, aided by the natural anthropomorphism of the imagination, would cause men to speak of a deified *man*. But there would be no special significance attached to the retention of the humanity, which, if it were taken seriously, could not but be conceived as a liability and a limitation. Had the New Testament writers been challenged with some of the philosophical difficulties involved in a serious preservation in the Second Person of the Trinity of a manhood that cannot be violated by the divinity to which it sets real bounds, then, from the evidence so far examined, there is no reason to believe that they would have insisted upon it as more than a convenient representation or myth. That is to say, it would be an expression in picture language of a truth which is religiously, but not philosophically, exact. In the same way, the narrative of Genesis 1–3 can claim an accuracy of religious insight which is in no way destroyed by the fact that it cannot be taken precisely at its face value by the scientist or philosopher. We might say that the idea of Christ's session at the right hand of God no more carries with it for philosophy the implication that there is manhood in the Godhead than that there is space in heaven.

It is doubtful, then, if the idea of the retention by Christ of his humanity would have been exalted into dogma had the notion of continuity been the sole ground for its insistence. The important thing here is that 'Christ lives'. *How* he lives – whether as a personality in a 'Thou' relation, or in the same mode of existence as the other Persons – is really irrelevant. After all, the continuity of his life is in no way broken by the fact that he *assumes* the form of humanity (Jn 1:1–14; Phil. 2:5–8); it could not therefore be impaired if he were to relinquish it.

But there remains another set of considerations which finds expression in parts of the New Testament, where the emphasis is very definitely on the significance of Christ's manhood in eternity. In St Paul's words, Christ not only lives, 'but also maketh intercession for us' (Rom. 8:34). The reference to the intercessory role of the ascended Christ is not in itself a proof that the writer would regard the retention of humanity as essential. After all, he has made exactly the same statement of the Holy Spirit only a few verses previously (Rom. 8:26–7). But by another writer – the *Auctor ad Hebraeos* – this theme is developed in a way in which the emphasis on the humanity of the exalted Christ is made as important as the fact of his divinity.

Christ, for him, is the heavenly High Priest, the eternal Mediator between God and man. For this it is necessary that he should have been a partaker in our flesh and blood (Heb. 2:14), wherein he was tempted in all points like as we are and showed that he could be touched with the feeling of our infirmities (4:15); wherein too he learned obedience by the things which he suffered (5:8) and was thereby enabled to make the perfect oblation of himself to God (5:9; 7:27). But this is not enough. It is also necessary that as man he should have passed through the heavens (4:14) and sat down on the right hand of the Majesty (8:1; 10:12). Only if Christ is still man as well as God can he exercise his priestly function of intercession (7:25) and mediation (9:15) and keep open that new and living way which he dedicated for us through the veil, that is to say his flesh (10:20). What he did as man in Palestine, he now does eternally in the heavens. The retention of the manhood is no longer here an unavoidable anthropomorphism: it is an essential element in the economy of atonement and sanctification.

This is the solid core of the doctrine of Christ's perpetual humanity. Other considerations may in a peripheral way enter in, but it is by this that it must be judged. Moreover, the importance of the idea of the heavenly priesthood of Christ is not to be assessed merely by the space which it occupies in the pages of the New Testament. It is a theme which has received a prominent place in the Eucharistic doctrine of the Church from the earliest times. The assurance that we 'have with us him that pleads above', the presentation by Christ of the prayers and oblations of the faithful before the throne of heaven, the knowledge that we and our offering can be well-pleasing to God only in so far as we are 'found in him' and incorporate in his ever-living sacrifice – these and similar themes fill the hymns of Charles Wesley as of William Bright, and control the expression of Reformation as of Roman piety.

What are we to say to these things? First this: whatever conclusion we come to must in no way minimize or obscure the fundamental religious truth enshrined in this line of thought. The doctrine that only in the perfect human offering of Christ have we any plea before God is central to the whole of Christianity and might, without exaggeration be called the heart of the gospel. It is what St Paul is constantly expressing in other terms as 'justification by faith'. Only in Christ, in his prayer, in his obedience, his sacrifice, can we be clothed upon with a righteousness not our own, and thus be made fit to approach the throne of heaven.

This reference to the Pauline doctrine of justification by faith raises an interesting comparison, which it will be useful to follow out. Reference was made to it above (Ch. 12) in connection with the problem of time. Expansion of what was there said will be instructive for discerning the essential religious significance of the idea of the heavenly priesthood of Christ. It is probably not possible in the distinction that follows to say that St Paul stands wholly on one side and the author to the Hebrews wholly on the other. That would be an oversimplification of the evidence. There is, however, a genuine difference of approach between them, and their names may conveniently be used as labels to mark the distinction that we have in mind.

This can best be expressed in terms of the different accounts given by the two writers of the nature of faith. In the Epistle to the Hebrews there is a careful definition of the term. Faith is there 'the assurance (or substance) of things hoped for, the proving (or evidence) of things not seen' (11:1). For this writer, the point of reference is always a reality which is eternally present in a world for the moment hid from our eyes but which we have sure confidence will be ours to enjoy after this earthly pilgrimage. Faith is the translation of the invisible present of eternity into the here and now of historical existence. It 'lifts us out of the time series, in which the past has ceased to be and the present is not yet, and exalts us into the eternal world, in which the future is as real as the present' (W. R. Inge, *Personal Religion and the Life of Devotion*, 1924, 41–2, commenting on St Chrysostom's exegesis of

Heb. 11:1). It is that which enables us to pass through the veil which hides the unseen from the seen, the noumenal from the phenomenal, and transforms the eternal reality from a hope laid up in the heavens to an energizing factor in earthly living. The idea of faith, like the whole of the Epistle, is set within the framework of a Platonic thought-structure.[53]

The Real for this philosophy is essentially the timeless, the eternal, the unseen: it is something which is always present behind the *σκίαι* (shadows) of this world. It is true that this framework is completely shattered in the Epistle to the Hebrews by the assertion that the most real thing of all is an event which took place 'once and for all' in history. For Platonism nothing that happens in history can have any effect on eternity, let alone an absolutely decisive effect. Here the Platonic scheme is shattered. But, like St John, whose *σὰρξ ἐγένετο* (became flesh) has equally disruptive consequences for the Hellenic framework within which he expresses himself, the author to the Hebrews continues to employ Greek categories of thought. The event which took place *ἅπαξ* (once only) on earth, just because it possesses this ultimate noumenal reality, takes place also eternally and timelessly in the heavens. For the key of the Real for this scheme of thought is the timeless. It is in virtue of the fact that it has this eternal quality of Reality that the sacrifice of Christ is an object of faith, not because it was a historical event. The reference of faith, as of true *ἐπιστημή* (knowledge, understanding), is rather upwards to the ontal ('Real') world than backwards along the plane of phenomena. The lifeline of faith is vertical. It joins the *Nunc stans* of eternity with the *hic et nunc* of actuality. It is not horizontal, drawn from the 'now' of one historical moment to that of another.

St Paul's use of *πίστις* (faith) is far more complex and varied, and he proffers nothing corresponding to the definition of Hebrews. Our intention here is very far from attempting an exhaustive account of this treatment of the subject, and what we have to say is more to point the contrast with the line of thought we have just examined than to put forward an independent statement of an aspect of Pauline theology.

As for the Synoptists, the opposite of *πιστεύειν* (to have faith) for St Paul is essentially *σκανδαλί]εσθαι* (to take offence, to fall away). Kittel's now famous phrase, 'das Ärgernis der Einmaligkeit', 'the scandal of particularity', sufficiently sums up what all *σκάνδαλον* is. It is essentially something particular, individual, historical. The true function of the particular and historical is to be transparent and sacramental of the eternal and infinite. It is the belief of Hebraic, as opposed to Hellenic, religious thought, that the infinite and eternal can and does reveal itself in its completeness in and through the finite and temporal. The organ by which the infinite is discerned in any finite situation is faith. But at any time anything in experience may become a stumbling block, which bars rather than mediates the approach of the infinite 'Thou'. The *σκάνδαλον* is something which prevents the situation becoming revelatory (either to oneself or to others), something which stands between a man and God. It may be the 'offence' that the infinite should be revealed decisively in the particular at all. Or it may be that the divine majesty should be revealed in some particular things (e.g., riches, the 'right hand') are themselves being elevated to the level of the eternal, absolute, and conditioned, instead of pointing to something beyond them which stands in judgment over them. Faith is that which overcomes the stumbling block, which sees the gift and demand of the infinite and eternal in all the offensiveness of the particular and temporal.

For St Paul the supreme offence is Christ Jesus and him crucified. *τὸ σκάνδαλον τοῦ σταυροῦ* (the scandal of the Cross) (Gal. 5:11) is an integral element in his gospel. In the Cross is focused at its most intense the contrast, nay the contradiction, between the *einmalig* and the eternal, between the total constriction of finitude and the infinity of omnipotence it mediates, between the wisdom of this world and the 'foolishness' of God, between all human ideas of power and the divine 'weakness'. The life, death and Resurrection of Christ is the decisive moment in history, the invasion of the temporal by the absolute and eternal, the locus of the world's judgment and the world's salvation. Faith is that which discerns this 'absolute paradox' (Kierkegaard), that our eternal blessedness hangs upon a moment in history. This moment is faith's point of reference. What faith makes possible is that over and again we become contemporaries of this moment. It is that which enables us to 'stand where Moses stood', to hear the Word of God speaking to us at the same time as it spoke to Amos and Jeremiah, to see the very vision that Isaiah saw 'in the year that King Uzziah died' (cf. Dr George MacLeod ' "The year that King Uzziah died" was, to be more precise, this year', *The Coracle*, February 1944). But, above all, it places us in Bethlehem, in Galilee, on the road to Jerusalem, in Gethsemane, on Calvary, at the empty Tomb, on the mount of Ascension. The act of faith is that which abolishes time and space so that the eternal and the infinite may be seen in the very particularities of time and space. Faith can never bypass the historical. The revelation has been given in and through the historical, in a decisive manner, in a way that can never be repeated. If we want to see it we must ever return to the time and place it was given: there is no other way. It is not as if the revelation were a revelation of ethereal truths, first manifested, indeed, in historical form, but now perceptible independently of that particular occasion. That is Hegelianism, not Christianity. Christianity is ever a pilgrimage of faith to the foot of the Cross and to the Garden early. There are no short cuts to eternity. The lifeline of faith is here horizontal: it is a line back to a point in history. In faith we may meet the eternal and the infinite in everything around us; but – and this is the 'scandal' of Christianity – it is only by going *there* that we can meet him decisively, savingly. In the same way, we live in a 'sacramental universe': but Christians are still bound to foregather in that 'upper room'. This is the true significance of the 'memorial' of the body and blood of Christ. It is not 'the bare remembrance of his Passion'. It is the deliberate placing of oneself back at the point in time and space which is the eternally appointed trysting-place between God and man. 'Faith must be as true a subsistence of those things past which we believe, as it is of the things yet to come which we hope for' (Dr D. Brevint, Preface to John and Charles Wesley's *Hymns on the Lord's Supper*, Sec. II).

The movement of faith is not vertically upwards to an eternal present – a timeless world of reality always objectively 'there', if we could but apprehend it. The movement of faith is rather backwards, to a point in the historical process, where in absolute 'subjectivity' God can become present to us in a saving manner. Christ only lived and spoke and died and rose *once* (ἅπαξ). If we are to see and hear him and to share in his passion and Resurrection, we have to become his contemporaries. To effect this is the work of faith.

This distinction between the two views of the function of faith – between the 'Hellenic', whose point of reference is the *Nunc stans* of eternity, and the 'Hebraic', which ever directs one back to the *Gegenwart* of a historical 'meeting' – this distinction throws light on the true significance of the doctrine of Christ's perpetual humanity. For it is now possible to see the ideas of 'eternal priesthood' and 'justification by faith' as but treatments of a single theme from these two different approaches. For the former, the point of reference is something which is now, and ever, happening in the heavenlies: for the latter, it is an event 'under Pontius Pilate' in AD 29. The statement that 'Jesus lives', in the first case, is an assertion about an 'objective' metaphysical fact: the humanity of Christ is 'there' in heaven acting on our behalf. This fact is now, indeed, a matter of faith, but some day it will be capable of verification in a mode parallel to that to which the Apostle Thomas resorted.

In the second case, the statement is equally a faith-judgment, but in a different sense. It is the assurance that the sacrifice and Resurrection of Christ are ever valid for those who by faith become its contemporaries. For those who stand at the foot of the Cross, for those who visit the Empty Tomb, it is possible, from whatever land or age they come, there to meet

Christ, to die and rise with him, and thus to be presented incorporate in him, a sacrifice well-pleasing to the Father. We are justified by the faith that through grace can make that pilgrimage to Calvary. Christ's sacrifice is ever-living, not because it is ever-availing to those that claim and plead it. His manhood is eternal, not because it now exists in some form that in another existence we might be able to touch or see; it is eternal because the act he wrought once as man on Calvary can be as contemporaneous to us and to all generations as it was to the Apostles. In fact they are in the same position as ourselves. For the Cross to them was not at the time the locus of the power of God and the wisdom of God. After the event, they too had to make the same journey of faith back to the place without the gate. The 'other disciple' entered a second time within the tomb (cf. Kierkegaard, *Philosophical Fragments*, chaps IV, V).

Christian theology has to find a means of expression for the fact that, to faith, the historical is supra-historical without ceasing to be history. It has to find a way of combining the belief that 'Christ suffered for sins once' (1 Pet. 3:18) – that the earthly life of Jesus is finished and over and done with, like any other past event – with the belief that this death is an eternal fact, a sacrifice 'as to grace and mercy, still lasting, still new, still the same as when it was first offered for us' (D. Brevint, Preface, II). The doctrine of the eternal humanity and heavenly priesthood of Christ is one way of giving representation to this paradox of the eternal present significance of a past event. It pictures the crucial event of Christ's atoning work as 'fixed' and prolonged for all time – or rather, taken out of time altogether, so that it never grows old or passes away. It happened once and for all – no writer is so insistent as the author to the Hebrews on what P. T. Forsyth happily called 'the ἅπαξ λεγόμενον [a word that only occurs once] of the Cross' (*The Person and Place of Jesus Christ*, 1909, 166) – it need never and can never occur again in history. Yet, at the moment of its occurrence, it was (as it were) translated into the eternal and lifted out of the power of time's effects.

> The instruments that bruised Him so
> Were broke and scattered long ago,
>   The flames extinguish'd were;
> But Jesu's death is ever new;
> He whom in ages past they slew,
>   Doth still as slain appear.
>
> The Oblation sends as sweet a smell,
> Ev'n now it pleases God as well

As when it first was made:
The Blood doth now as freely flow
As when His side received the blow
That shew'd Him newly dead.
(John and Charles Wesley, *Hymns on the Lord's Supper*, 3)

That is one way of representing the truth of the religious paradox. But it remains a 'representation': it is a 'mythological' statement, not a metaphysical one. To picture the eternal validity and availability of the Atonement in terms of an everlasting priesthood involving an actual retention or prolongation of Christ's manhood beyond the Ascension is legitimate myth: but it provides no basis for philosophy. The status of the two statements that 'Christ is eternally God' and 'Christ is eternally man' is different. The first forms the keystone of Christian metaphysics and of any philosophical doctrine of the Trinity. The second is a mythological representation of a paradox of the religious consciousness. It may be religiously accurate, but it can lay no claim to philosophical exactitude.

As a matter of fact, it may be doubted if it is the most satisfactory representation even of the religious fact. The Platonic view of reality as essentially static and timeless hardly makes it the best system of thought to do justice to a religion for which the most real thing is an act of the divine *δύναμις* (power) in history. By making the work of the Spirit the fixing or perpetuation in a timeless existence of the things of Christ, it tends to obscure the fact that the journey for faith is continually back to a historical event. The work of the Spirit is not (as it were) to elongate the Incarnation, so that at whatever time we live Christ is still man. It is rather to make us contemporary with the Incarnation; though not in any merely temporal sense (as if there were some particular advantage enjoyed by the inhabitants of first-century Palestine), but with the contemporaneity of faith, which 'sees his glory' even though it cannot touch and handle. The present humanity of Christ is not to be conceived as the *Nunc stans* or an 'objective' *Gegenstand* (object) but as the '*hic et nunc*' of a 'subjective' *Gegenwart* (presence). The heavenly intercession is an ever-present fact, not because it is somehow going on all the time 'objectively' in a realm of existence as yet beyond our vision. It is ever-present because what Christ pleads – his perfect self-oblation of obedience – ever avails for those who, in the infinite 'subjectivity' of faith, die and rise with him.

If what we have said is correct, if the essential religious truth of the eternal priesthood of Christ is in no way minimized when his perpetual humanity is treated as a mythological representation rather than a metaphysical fact, then the problems with which we were confronted in connection with the doctrine of the Trinity have disappeared. We need not and cannot hold that anything like an eternal 'Thou' relationship is introduced into the Godhead which gives to one of the Persons a mode of existence entirely different from that of the other two. The human life of Christ really did end at the Ascension. That event was, as it were, the outward and visible sign that the peculiar relationship to the Godhead which obtained at the Incarnation was now at an end. As the God-man, Christ was, so to speak, both the subject and the object of the divine love: now he returned to be once more simply its subject. The polarity was at an end. Christ's status as a Person of the Trinity remained, as always, unchanged; but he was now no longer a person. It is the same Christ who reigns in heaven as was found in fashion as a man on earth: there is the continuity which is essential. But the mode of his existence is different: he no longer lives towards God and men in the peculiarly human relationship.

We have sought to show that nothing of any religious significance is lost by such a metaphysic. Indeed this is the only interpretation possible, unless mythological representation is to constitute philosophical data, in a way no one would allow were we dealing with the myths of Genesis. There are, however, two further objections which might be levelled against the solution propounded above, which demand brief attention before we pass on. The first is religious, the second philosophical in its nature.

The former could be stated thus:

> I see [the religious man might say] the distinction you are drawing between mythological and philosophical truth; and I am prepared to grant that, as far as the doctrine of Christ's heavenly priesthood is concerned, the central core of religious truth is unaffected by the fact that His eternal humanity may be regarded as the mythological representation of a faith-judgment rather than a philosophically accurate description of a metaphysical state. There is, however, something else which I feel would be irretrievably lost on your interpretation. The Jesus we know and love from the pages of the Gospels, the Jesus who was made at all points like unto ourselves, who was touched with the feeling of our infirmities – has he ceased to exist as such a personal centre and independent subject, and become once more just one mode of existence or form of manifestation of the eternal Godhead, a Person and not a person? And if so, is not the content of faith thereby impoverished?

This is the kind of objection which we cannot afford to treat lightly. If a philosophy is to be a Christian philosophy, then it must be determined at all points by the dictates of the unsophisticated religious consciousness. It cannot dismiss the postulates of a simple faith, after the manner of Hegel, as beneath the dignity of what is essentially a higher form of knowledge. If a philosophy which claims to be Christian is not an honest transcription of what every true believer requires for his religion, however unlearned he may be, then the wisdom of this world has begun to judge the foolishness of the Preaching.

But, like everything else, the postulates of the simple religious consciousness need to be sifted and tested. And we venture to suggest that the postulate here required of us is in fact a spurious one. It may be said to belong to that form of heresy to which uninstructed faith is perhaps most prone, namely, what may be called 'Jesus worship'. This is heretical, because, by fastening upon the historical Jesus as the centre of adoration, it in fact denies that he is in the fullest sense the express image and complete revelation of the nature of God. The Father is pictured, in deistic fashion, as somewhat distant and unapproachable, King of kings and Lord of lords, the only ruler of princes, who beholds from his throne all the dwellers upon earth with a magnificent impartiality. In contrast, the Son is one who really knows our estate, who feels and suffers for us – a God who can really walk in our midst, sup at our tables and dwell in our hearts. Naturally, on these presuppositions, much, if not all, in Christianity is felt to be jettisoned, if the warmth and closeness of the personality of Jesus is exchanged for mere Personhood in the eternal Trinity.

But on a true doctrine of God such a feeling of loss is non-existent. If Christ's earthly life is a true manifestation under human form of what God is really like; if God is such that he can, and even must, be manifested in manhood; and if he is of a nature that, to be truly represented as man, he has to choose the form, not only of a servant, but of a suffering servant; then the Father, or the ascended Christ, even though not in human guise, will yet be exactly the same, exercising the identical individual care and suffering love which we see placarded in human lettering in the life and death of Jesus of Nazareth.

The assumption which underlies the heresy of Jesus-worship is that God has to be incarnate in order to be the sort of God we see in Jesus Christ. Not only is the Father set in contrast to the Son as somewhat removed from man and his most intimate needs, but the Son too, unless he retains his earthly personal form of existence, is regarded as losing that proximity to, and identification with, the human situation, which the gospel asserts of God.

The reasons for this assumption, which has no basis in the New Testament, are various. There is, indeed, one that deserves scant respect. It derives from the desire of man to make God in his own image, to have a deity who is thoroughly human, a being with whom he can feel at home and be on terms of comfortable equality, a being from whom all disturbing tones of wrath and justice and overawing transcendence have been excised. Such a deity, again with no justification, many have sought and found in the Christ of the Gospels and have set in opposition to the God of the Old Testament.

But there are other reasons, which, though they command more respect, yet cannot be said to merit more acceptance. They are bound up with the Greek idea of a wholly transcendent Godhead, removed from the commerce of human affairs, outside history and the changes and chances of temporal events, whose contact with actuality is maintained only through the offices of a mediator or of a series of mediatorial beings. In such an atmosphere of thought the message of a God who had actually *become* man and has been made 'a partaker in our flesh and blood' was indeed a gospel. The possibility of personal union of the divine, infinite and eternal with the human, finite and historical was to the Greeks 'foolishness', because it was too good to be true. But it was in fact the solution of their search, religious and philosophical. And, consequently, it was the Incarnation rather than the Atonement which was set forth as the chief content of the gospel by the Greek Fathers. This was indeed *the* miracle; and to deny its permanence was to destroy the heart of the Christian message. God except in the form of humanity was not the God who could be human or who could satisfy humanity's deepest needs. Unless Christ retained his manhood, he could not remain for faith the Christ of the Gospels: mere Personhood in the eternal Trinity was something very different.

This line of thought comes to its clearest expression in the question of suffering in God. Impassibility of the divine was an unshakeable conviction of the Greek mind. Only as man could God have been touched with the feeling of our infirmities or borne consequences of our sin. The gospel declares that he was so touched and did thus bear. And if this passibility is to be more than something transitory and temporary, then the manhood, which could alone be its subject, must be eternal. 'Sympathy in God: suffering in Christ': this is the conclusion which von Hügel proffers in his well-known essay in defence of the doctrine of impassibility (*Essays and Addresses*, II, 1926, 209). And this conclusion, which epitomizes the furthest concession Hellenic thought can make, demands that the personal form of existence enjoyed by Christ in the flesh is never rescinded or altered to mere Personhood.

But if the Greek view of God, and with it the Greek requirement of impassibility, is rejected as unbiblical, then there is no ground for this insistence on the retention of Christ's humanity. If Jesus Christ could not be the same in character without his manhood, then Jesus Christ could not be the same in character as the Father. That is the crux of the matter. The idea that the alteration in form of existence from personality to 'mere' Personhood implies a loss of warmth and intimacy is only tenable on the assumption that there is a difference in character between the love of God the Father, who is a 'mere' Person, and that of God the Son. Personhood, whatever else it may mean, is a mode of God's loving wherein the whole of the divine essence confronts the believer. This is the love of the Father and the Son and the Spirit for all men always. So deep and intimate is it, that in terms of humanity it could only be expressed in the communion of love between two personalities. The love of the man Jesus for every individual is not something different from, or less remote than, the love of God for men; it *is* that divine love defined in humanity. That is how God loves always. It is how Christ loves always, even though it be not always in the human mode. The change of mode destroys nothing. Jesus Christ is 'the same yesterday, and today, and for ever' (Heb. 13:8). The disciples at first thought to lose much or everything by the removal of the presence of their Master. But Christ taught them otherwise. To desiderate the humanity of Jesus is to crave an illegitimate knowledge of the 'Christ after the flesh'. The ground of our present knowledge of God in each of his modes of loving is the 'Christ *according to the flesh*'. This is the canon of all revelation and of all knowledge: 'Every spirit that confesseth not that Jesus Christ is come in the flesh is not of God' (1 Jn 4:3). The flesh is the locus of the revelation. But it is not the revelation itself. It points ever away to the eternity of the divine love, which is the same, whether in the Father or in the Son, whether in the flesh or out of it.

The first objection, therefore, which was raised to our treatment of the doctrine of the eternal humanity of Christ, may now be said to have been answered. The change in form of existence from personality to Personhood implies no more loss of personal intimacy on the part of Christ than can the reverse process which began the Incarnation be said to have constituted an increase. Throughout it was and is the one omnipresent and omnipotent love of God which breaks in upon man in mercy and judgment through different modes of existence.

The second objection, which is of a more philosophical than specifically religious nature, is this. If every, or even any, human personality survives death and lives with God for ever, then surely this must be true a fortiori of the one perfect human personality, Jesus Christ. How then can we deny his eternal humanity in the most literal sense? Or, by reversing the question, we may put it in a more arresting, if somewhat crude, form: what happened to our Lord's human personality?

The first point to note is that, on what is usually regarded as orthodox doctrine, such a question could never arise. For those who hold the view of the 'impersonal humanity' of Christ and say that God became 'man' but not 'a man', there can be, as it were, no individual human remains of which to dispose. If there was no human subject whose place was taken by the divine Logos, then there can be no question of its independent survival. On this view there is no difficulty – though neither, of course, can it provide any argument for the opposite case, as it is implied that it does.

But the situation is not quite so simple. For elsewhere we have argued (Ch. 8) that the doctrine that the incarnate Christ was not *a* man, like every one else, in the sense of a highly individualized centre of consciousness and personal relationships, is untenable, except in one specialized connotation. It is not proposed to go again into the reasons advanced for this conclusion, especially as they are not immediately relevant. For in fact it is the specialized sense in which 'personal' or 'hypostatic' humanity must be denied that is alone at issue here. We have only raised the other point in order that it may be understood that there is no contradiction between our general assertion that Christ became 'a man' and our present contention that his human personality was not eternal.

The specialized sense in which it is possible and necessary to deny that Christ was 'a man' like anyone else had reference, it will be remembered, to the Adoptionist and Nestorian errors. What must be repudiated is a Christology which would picture God uniting himself to a human individual who might have existed anyhow, even if the Incarnation had never taken place. The idea of the Virgin Birth is valuable as a symbol of the fact that it was not a question of God having to wait until a perfect human personality appeared in the normal course of generation. The Incarnation then would have been either impossible or superfluous. Either the all-pervasiveness of sin for which it was the only cure would have prevented its happening. Or its happening would have proved that the human situation was not such as could only be redeemed from without.

Christianity has an essential interest in asserting that God did not come together with a human being that either could or did not exist apart from that fact. He constituted himself man by taking upon him the human relationship: he did not join himself to a man. The human personality brought into being by the relation was the human personality of God, not that of a man united to God. At the Ascension the relation ceased, and with it the human personality. Just because there was no already existent man to which he joined himself, so there could be no still existent man, who had either to be left or taken up with him. When Christ ceased to live in the human relation, there could, as it were, be no residue, since he brought nothing but himself to it. Christ the perfect man lived on, but once the relationship was altered, when he stood once more on the other side of the divine-human encounter, he was not man any longer, but God. There was nothing left on the human side of the relationship, and therefore nothing to be eternally man.

As a result of the foregoing discussion it appears that the doctrine of the eternal humanity of Christ, in its essential truth so necessary to faith, need not, and indeed cannot, be regarded as enjoying the same philosophical status as the doctrine of the Trinity. The latter is the ground of Christian metaphysics, the former a mythological representation in terms of certain, by no means indispensable, categories of thought of the everlasting contemporeity of the saving events of the gospel to him who by faith can stand among them. It is not a question of one sort of statement, the metaphysical or the mythological, being more true than the other. Both are true in a different way. The myths of Genesis 1–3 are neither more nor less true than the attempts to explain the beginning of things made by the scientist or the philosopher. Of course, there may be bad or inadequate myth just as there may be bad or inadequate science or philosophy. But one cannot be more true than the other *because* it is science or *because* it is myth. And just because the two are dealing with different aspects of the truth, the conclusions of the one cannot overturn or affect those of the other. If this had been seen more clearly in the Darwinian controversy there need not have been that acute conflict between religion and science which Professor Raven has characterized as 'a storm in a Victorian tea-cup' (*Science, Religion and the Future*, 1943, Ch. 3). Similarly, it is possible to assert all that can be required of us about Christ's eternal humanity without in any way affecting the discussion of the doctrine of the Trinity or forcing us to postulate of the Second Person a form of personal existence which we have found reason to deny on every other ground to the Persons in general.

With this conclusion we have said all that need be said by way of demonstrating the impossibility of identifying the meaning of *persona* as it has come to be applied to the Hypostases of the Trinity with anything corresponding to personality, in the sense of which we have been using it of men and God and their mutual relations. Whatever the relation between the Persons is, it cannot be interpreted in terms of the categories derived from the 'I–Thou' relationships, which characterize men's contact with each other and God. But such a conclusion, though it requires affirming in face of current interpretations of the doctrine of the Trinity, provides us with little positive. Perhaps there is little positive that can be said. But at least some attempt must be made to examine the difficulties before they are judged insuperable. We have tried to show what we believe *persona* does not mean. Can we do anything towards ascertaining what it does? This may be undertaken by turning to answer the second question propounded above (p. 250). It was concerned, it will be remembered, with the locus of the differentiation between the Persons. Is what gives to each its peculiar and incommunicable quality something which lies within the sphere of the immediate experience of the believer? Or is it something which we know, either from the words spoken by Christ or from necessary inference from the events of the New Testament, to exist within the nature of God, but of which we have no direct cognizance? If we can answer this question concerning the location of the differentiation, we may have gone some distance towards determining its nature. And this, in its turn, may lead to a clearer understanding of the connection between the Persons of the Godhead and the personality of God, for which our whole examination of the doctrine of the Trinity was undertaken.

Chapter Eighteen

THE GROUND OF DISTINCTION OF THE PERSONS (1)

It is essential to any doctrine of the Trinity to establish the differences between the Persons as distinctions grounded in the being or action of God himself.[54] That is to say, statements about the Father, Son and Holy Spirit in every sense must be statements about God and not about our experience of God. This applies, whether the distinctions are conceived as inhering in the 'economic' or in the 'essential' Trinity. Thus, whether what distinguishes the Father is that He is Creator or that He is 'unbegotten', it is essential that this distinction should rest in some peculiarity of the Person concerned and not in our way of looking at the matter. In this respect, the Persons must differ from the divine attributes. Of the latter we have to confess that ultimately they are inseparably one. When we say that God reveals now his mercy, now his wrath, we do not really mean to imply that God changes or 'repents'. We mean that the one constant fact of the divine love must be revealed to the sinner as different, according to whether he is penitent or not. And it is the same with all the other attributes. Power, eternity, infinity, holiness – these are but human distinctions necessary for characterizing the boundless richness of the one supreme and never failing love of God. Like a diamond it sparkles differently in different lights: it itself is always the same. Wisdom, goodness and power, as St Thomas insisted (*S. T.* I, 28, iii, 2; 30, i, 2; 40, i, 1), are the same thing in God. To conceive the distinctions between the Persons as comparable with those between the attributes is in fact to deny that they are *real* distinctions at all.

All this is only expressed another way by asserting that there must be a *proprietas incommunicabilis* (incommunicable quality) (Calvin, *Institutes*, I, xiii, 6) by which each Person is differentiated. If there is to be a *real* distinction between them, each has to be characterized by something that the others do not, and cannot, possess. There must be an element of relative opposition between the Persons, arising from the fact that the Father would not be the Father if he possessed certain characteristics which belong properly and exclusively to the Son or the Holy Spirit. Thus it is impossible to designate the Persons as certain attributes, not only because there is no real opposition or distinction between, say, power, wisdom and love in God, but also because we cannot ascribe any attribute exclusively to one Person, as though the others did not possess it.

If it is agreed, then, that we must find an element of 'incommunicability', wherein are we to seek it? Where is the *locus proprietatis* (location of the property)? There have been, historically, two answers to this question. Some have placed it in the 'economic' Trinity, in the sphere of revelation and experience, in the *opera Trinitatis ad extra* (external works of the Trinity). Others have sought it rather in the 'essential' Trinity, in God as he is in himself, in the eternal relations of 'generation' and 'procession' which obtain between the divine Persons, apart from all reference to the world. On account of the extreme difficulty and apparent unintelligibility which attends any exposition of the latter position, popular theology has always tended to rest in the former solution. This, however, is a position which found little favour with any of the systematic theologians of patristic or scholastic times. But in recent years there has been a leaning towards it, because of the strong reaction against its alternative, which is regarded as a doctrine completely unrelated to the experience of the believer. The locus of incommunicability tends now to be sought and found in the Trinity of revelation, within the sphere of the Christian's knowledge of God. This reaction claims to be more than popular theology, and it must be taken seriously. When we hear a Regius Professor of Divinity rejecting bodily the doctrine of relations within the Godhead with the remark that he has 'not the least idea of what is meant either by filiation or procession in respect of the divine Being' (Hodgson, *The Doctrine of the Trinity*, 144), it is clear that the reaction has gone far. This at least is an honest statement; but it is possible to sympathize and even to concur with it without agreeing with the alternatives the professor has to offer.

In what follows there will be much in the way of criticism of both the positions here outlined. But it will be maintained that the 'traditional' solution, as it is found in Augustine and in Scholasticism, in both Catholic and Protestant, has many merits, in that it sees and deliberately avoids pitfalls into which the other school fearlessly treads. It may appear unintelligible – though this is by no means the most serious charge that can be brought against it – but to point this out does not by itself commend the truth of its alternative. To advocate one's view by challenging one's opponents to produce a clear definition of the ideas of 'generation' and 'procession' is reminiscent of a delightful story quoted by Professor E. H. Carr (*The Twenty Years' Crisis*, 1941, 12, n.). It concerns a gentleman, who, during the Lisbon earthquake of 1775, lighted upon the idea of vending anti-earthquake pills. When someone intimated that the pills could not possibly be of use, the hawker replied: 'But what would you put in their place?' The strength of the position of those who would find the distinctions between the Persons in a Trinity of revelation must be shown to rest on its own merits and not in an appeal to the inadequacies of any alternative. When so regarded, this position does in fact reveal a serious weakness. This can be stated quite shortly. In whatever particular characteristic the distinction is regarded as inhering, a *real* differentiation (in the sense explained above) can only be secured at the expense of the destruction of the unity of the Godhead. That is to say, the element of relative opposition would be introduced where there should be a unity differentiated only to our way of looking at it. If power, wisdom and love were the distinguishing properties of the three Persons, an opposition would be set up within the Godhead between the attributes: each Person would be characterized by one attribute, just because the others did not and could not possess it. We should then have three Gods of a different character, not one God characterized by a single love of many facets. Trinitarianism would have been abandoned in favour of tritheism.

Exactly the same is true if, instead of three attributes, three 'characters' (to use Kirk's term) of the divine activity are taken as the distinguishing properties of the Persons. 'Creator', 'Redeemer', 'Sanctifier' represent the commonest collocations of such groups of attributes or facets of the divine work. We could only say that God the Father was distinctively characterized by being Creator if such activity could be denied of the Son or the Spirit. This is clearly impossible. The Nicene Creed, reproducing the testimony of the Bible, ascribes creative activity to all three Persons – the Father is the 'maker of heaven and earth and of all things visible and invisible'; the Son is he 'by whom all things were made' and the Holy Ghost is 'the giver of life' (*τὸ ζωοποιοῦν*), the Creator Spirit.

It is now possible to see the logic which drives authors like Dr Kirk and Professor Hodgson, who locate the differentia of the Persons in the 'opera ad extra', to suppose the existence of three distinct 'Thou' relationships between man and God. The only way in which they can establish the fact of *real* differences between the Persons is by saying that there is something in our experience of each of them which cannot be predicated of the others. It is not enough to say that there is one divine 'Thou' which meets us in various operations (e.g., creating, redeeming, sanctifying) or in various relationships (e.g., *κύριος–δοῦλος* (master–servant), communion, possession). We have to be able to say that each Person meets us *exclusively* in one of these operations or relations. This comes to the same thing as saying that we are dealing with three 'Thous', with 'God the Father, who hath made me and all the world', with 'God the Son, who hath redeemed me and all mankind', and with 'God the Holy Ghost, who sanctifieth me and all the elect people of God' (The Church Catechism), and that we meet them as the termini of three distinct relationships, of creatureliness, communion and possession respectively.

There are many who quite reasonably object to going so far towards tritheism, and yet, like H. Rashdall or Professor C. E. Raven, place the differentiation of Persons in three 'characters' or 'modes of manifestation'. But it is difficult to see how they can establish any *real* distinction between the Persons, grounded in an *incommunicabilis proprietas* of each. Certainly the biblical evidence (cf. Note 46) is against any exclusive appropriation to each of different functions in the economy of creation and salvation, and the isolation of the particular Persons in Christian religious experience, as we have seen, is impossible. And yet the establishment of a genuine 'peculiarity' of each Hypostasis is absolutely necessary if the doctrine of the Trinity is to stand for a threeness in God which is really 'essential', 'irremovable' and 'ineffaceable' (Barth, *Kirchliche Dogmatik*, I, a, 380; ET *Doctrine of the Word of God*, 414).

The conclusion is that any attempt to place the differentia of the Persons in the *opera Trinitatis ad extra* is bound to fail. It must issue either in modalism or in tritheism. For this reason the classical authors all avoided this solution (see, G. L. Prestige, *God in Patristic Thought*, 256–64. The doctrine that God in his relation to the world is one in operation or 'energy' goes back to Athanasius, *Ad Serap.* i, 19). Before going on to examine the answer they gave, however, a word may be said about what they called the doctrine of 'appropriations' or attributions. Although they never sought to make the different attributes or 'characters' of God the basis of the Personal distinctions, they did regard it as legitimate and even necessary to appropriate different functions or qualities to the different Persons. One of the most familiar is that made in the Church Catechism quoted above. But there are a host of others: *Aeternitas, forma, usus* (eternity, form, use) (Hilary, quoted by Augustine, *De Trin.* VI, 11); *unitas, aequalitas, connexio* (unity, equality, connection) (Augustine, *De Doctr. Christ.*, I, 5); *potentia, sapientia, bonitas* (power, wisdom, goodness) (St Thomas, *S.T.* I, 45, vi, 2); unity, truth and loving-kindness (Bonaventura, *Breviloqu.*, I, 6); *principium, sapientia, virtus* (beginning, wisdom, power) (Calvin, *Institutes*, I, xiii, 18); goodness, wisdom and power (Hooker, *Eccl. Pol.*, v, lvi, 5); etc. Again, many have seen the fittingness for the purposes of appropriation of the threefold ἐξ αὐτοῦ, δι' αὐτοῦ, εἰς αὐτόν (from him, through him, to him) of Rom. 11:36 (see, K. Barth, *Doctrine of the Word of God*, 428–9 for these and similar attempts).

Such appropriations, it was insisted by their authors, can never be exclusive. As Augustine clearly saw, it is impossible to designate the Son as wisdom or the Spirit as love in any sense which would involve a denial of these attributes to the other Persons. Nor, they said, must they be arbitrary – though it is sometimes difficult to see that this condition is observed. There must be some analogy between the qualities appropriated and the actual distinctions which do mark the real differences between the Persons (the 'relations of origin' of *paternitas* (being the Father), *filiatio* (being the Son), *spiratio* (being the Spirit – lit. breathing)). St Thomas's definition clearly explains the grounds of appropriation: '*Appropriare nihil est aliud quam commune trahere ad proprium . . . non ex hoc quod magis uni personae quam alii conveniat . . . sed ex hoc quod id quod est commune, majorem habet similitatem ad id quod est proprium personae unius quam cum proprio alterius*' (To appropriate is to make something common one's own . . . not because it is more suitable for one person than for another, but because what is common has greater similarity to that which is proper to one person that what is proper to another) (*De Veritate*, 7, iii). That is to say, if 'love' is to be appropriated, for instance, to the Holy Spirit, it is not because the Third Person is more loving than the others but because the attribute of love is claimed to have a particularly close connection with the mode of the Spirit's 'procession'.

The legitimacy of this analogical deduction from the 'relations of origin' proper to each Person will call for further examination later. It is only necessary to say here that some sort of doctrine of appropriations seems to be required for Christian dogmatics. If the ground of the threefoldness of the Godhead lies beyond any direct experience of ours, then we are indeed required to say with Barth of the distinctions of attributes and operations found in Scripture:

> The limit of our conception lies in the fact that in *conceiving* these distinctions we do *not conceive* the distinctions in the divine modes of existence. These do not consist of such distinctions in the acts or attributes of God. If that were our assumption, we should be assuming three Gods or a tripartite essence of God.

Nevertheless, even though it is true that 'in *these* distinction cannot rest the distinctions in God *Himself*', 'we must *believe* that those distinctions in the operation of God really *take place* within the sphere and limits of our conceivability' (*Doctrine of the Word of God*, 427). There *is* a threefoldness of operation in God's dealing with us, grounded in the historical manifestation at the Incarnation. Unless this were so there would be nothing remotely to suggest or commend the views of those who find here the *real* differentia of the Persons. The division of creation, redemption and sanctification and their appropriation to Father, Son and Holy Ghost are neither arbitrary nor unscriptural. We could not equally well apportion the operations differently or divide them between two or four Persons. Though we may not base a doctrine of the Trinity on these distinctions, no doctrine can be considered satisfactory which ignores them or fails to relate them integrally with what it does treat as the *real* differences.

Having thus given notice that we must return to the distinctions in the '*opera ad extra*', we now pass to consider the solution of those who trust not to them but to the relations of 'generation' and 'procession' to provide the element of 'incommunicability' required.

There is no need here to recount in detail the history of the idea that mutual relations of origin are the Person-constituting elements in the Godhead. Barth (*Doctrine of the Word of God*, 419) traces it back to Tertullian (*Adv. Prax.*, 25). Alexander of Alexandria stated that to be ἀγεννητός (uncreated, unborn) was the only ἰδίωμα (unique property) of the Father (Theodot., *H.E.*, I, iv, 52). In the Cappadocians the doctrine becomes explicit. (Dr G. L. Prestige has collected the relevant passages in his *God in Patristic Thought*, 244–8). Basil speaks of the γνωριστικαὶ ἰδιότητες (characteristics that can be known) of the Persons (*Ep.* 38, 5; *Contra Eun.*, 2, 29) and they are identified by him and Gregory Nazianzene (*Orat.*, 25, 16) with the modes of origin. Pseudo-Cyril (*De Sanc. Trin.*, 9) has 'ἀγεννησία (without origin) and γέννησις (begetting) and ἐκπόρευσις (coming forth): in these hypostatic peculiarities (ἰδιότητες ὑποστατικαί) alone do the three holy Hypostases differ from one another'. The same doctrine is clearly stated in Augustine (*De Trin.* V, 6) and Boethius (*De Trin.* V). When Augustine says the Son 'is understood to be the Word relatively, but wisdom essentially' (*De Trin.*, VII, 3), he states the principle which later became universal, that 'only terms belonging to relation may be applied singly to each' (Boethius, *De Trin.*, VI); the substantial or essential attributes must be predicated of the Godhead as a whole. But this principle, like everything else, is stated with greater fullness and precision by St Thomas. Without spending further space, therefore, on the history of the identification of *persona* with *relatio*, we may turn to the exposition of the whole theme given by Aquinas. This occurs in his treatise on the Trinity in the *Summa Theologica*, Pt. I, Quests. 27–43, to which extensive reference will be made.

The first statement to which St Thomas commits himself on the subject of the Trinity is to the effect that 'the Divine Persons are distinguished from each other according to the relations of origin' (27, introduction). That is to say, the Three Persons are differentiated by the fact that the Son is related to the Father as being generated by him, and the Spirit to the Father and the Son as proceeding from them. It is this opposition of relation – *generans* (begetting) and *generatus* (begotten), *spirans* (breathing) and *spiratus* (breathed) – which gives to each Person his *proprietas incommunicabilis* (incommunicable characteristic). And, apart from this, there is no distinction to be drawn between them. St Thomas would subscribe to what one of his editors (Ludwig Guerin, ed. 1873) calls '*illud theologorum vulgare axioma*' (that common axiom of theologians), namely, that '*in divinis omnia unum sunt ubi non obvia relationis oppositio*' (in divine matters all are one where there is no manifest opposition of relationship) (cf., *De Veritate*, 7, iii). '*Appropriatum non est proprium*'. Rather, the fittingness of the attribute appropriated (e.g., wisdom to the Son) is determined by the particular relation of origin which distinguishes the Person (thus, the Son, according to St Thomas, proceeds 'by way of emanation of the intellect' (34, ii). Similarly the Holy Spirit is Personally and properly called Love, only because love is something which like the Spirit proceeds 'according to the will' (36, i; 37, i). '*Opera Trinitatis ad extra sunt indivisa*' (The works of the Trinity are outwardly indivisible): the distinction of the Persons rests, not on any experience on our part of a differentiated revelation of the divine nature, but solely on the distinctions of internal relations within the Trinity itself.

But these relations are internal not only in the sense used above, but also in the more strictly philosophical meaning of the term. That is to say, they are themselves not merely distinctive but also constitutive of the divine Persons. The relations are the Persons and the Persons are the relations (29, iv; 30, i). Abstract and concrete are in God one; 'when we speak of paternity in God we mean God the Father' (32, ii; 40, ii). Another way of putting the same thing is to say that, if the relations of origin were mentally abstracted from the Persons, then there would be nothing left; '*abstractis personalibus proprietatibus non remanent hypostases*' (if the personal relations are abstracted, the hypostases do not remain) (40, iii, *conclusio*). If this were not so the relations would be external to the Hypostases, '*assistentes sive extrinsicae*' (accidental or external), as in the heresy of Gilbert de la Poré (28, ii).

But relations can be their own hypostases only if they are themselves substantial or subsistent. In creatures this is never so – they are always accidents, externally adjoined to the substance. But, 'whatever has an accidental existence in creatures, when considered as transferred to God, has a substantial existence; for there is no accident in God; for all in Him is His essence' (28, ii). Thus 'relation in God is not an accident in a subject, but it is the Divine Essence itself; and so it is subsistent, for the Divine Essence subsists'

(29, iv). In man it is possible to make a distinction between what he is and the way in which he acts, between him and the various modes of his existence. But in God this is not permissible, since it is destructive of the 'simplicity' of the divine nature. '*In Deo non differt "quod est" et "quo est"* ' (In God there is no distinction between what he is and whereby he is) (29, iv, 1). To say that relations are essential or substantial in God is not merely to say that they are not accidental; it is to say that they *are* the Essence itself (28, ii; etc.). Their substance or subsistence *is* the one divine substance or subsistence; 'relation really existing in God has the existence of the Divine Essence in no way distinct therefrom' (28, ii). When St Thomas defines Person in God as '*res subsistens in natura divina*' (a thing subsisting in the divine nature) (30, i), he is in fact saying the same thing. For 'that which subsists in the Divine Nature is the Divine Nature itself' (29, iv).

But if it is true that 'in God Essence is not really distinct from Person', then the problem immediately arises as to how it is possible to say that there are three Persons and only one Essence. For an answer it is necessary to go more fully into the precise use of the terms which St Thomas employs. This he is himself careful to define himself in 29, ii–iii.

The statement above, that the substance or subsistence of the Persons and of the Essence is the same, is true as regards what they are (*quod sunt*) but not as regards the mode of their existence (*quo sunt*). For although the two are in being the same, the Essence subsists, as it were, as a species, the Person as an individual within a species. The 'Essence' is what is expressed by definition, that is, the general principles of the species: 'Person' adds the individual principles to the idea of Essence. We may say that both are *substantiae*, for they are both in fact the same substance. But the Person is what Aristotle called *πρώτη οὐσία* (*substantia prima*), the Essence *δευτέρα οὐσία* (*substantia secunda*). The latter signifies the 'quiddity' of a thing, that in terms of which it is defined, and corresponds to what the Greek theologians called *οὐσία*. The former is an individual subject or *suppositum*, which subsists in the species 'substance', and is what the Greeks called *ὑπόστασις*. This second is given various names, according to the different aspects from which it is viewed: (a) *subsistentia* – as being something which exists '*per se*'; (b) *res naturae* – as underlying some common nature; (c) *hypostasis* or *substantia* – as underlying accidents. *Persona* is the proper equivalent of this individual substance in the genus of *rational* substances; although *hypostasis* has also, by common usage, become confined to the individual of a *rational* nature. Moreover, as the word *substantia* is ambiguous, the word *subsistentia* is generally used to signify *substantia prima* (*ὑπόστασις*) to distinguish it from *substantia secunda* (*οὐσία, essentia*).

This terminology is directly applicable to Theology, although a few modifications are required. Thus, if God is to be called a 'substance' or *hypostasis*, it is not because he is to be thought of as underlying any accidents, but simply as signifying self-subsistence. Again, he is only spoken of as an 'individual' in the sense which implies incommunicability – for normally the principle of individuation is matter. Thus St Thomas adopts Richard of St Victor's emendation for Theological purposes of Boethius' definition of *persona*: '*naturae rationabilis individua substantia*' becomes '*divinae naturae incommunicabilis existentia*' (incommunicable existence of the divine nature).

With these definitions it is possible to return to the relation of the divine Persons and the divine Essence. It was made clear above that there is in God no real distinction between *quod est* and *quo est*, between Essence and Person. They are both the same and both subsistent. But they are the same thing subsisting in different modes, the first absolutely or indeterminately, the second 'with the determinate mode of existence of singular things' (30, iv). Or, as Ludwig Guerin comments on 29 iv, *persona* '*significant essentiam non absolute, sed quatenus habet conjunctam relationem seu proprietatem individualem*' (*Person* signifies essence, not absolutely, but to the degree that it has a relation or an individual property). Thus, St Thomas can speak of the Son as 'the begotten "Who Is", and for as much as "God begotten" is Personal. But taken indefinitely it (i.e., "Who Is") is an essential term' (39, viii). Again, he is 'the Creator begotten' (34, iii, 1), or, in St Augustine's phrase 'begotten wisdom', 'begotten knowledge' (34, i, 2). In other words, he possesses all the essential attributes, in fact *is* the Essence, in exactly the same way as the Father and the Spirit are, 'but with another relation' (42, vi, 3). 'Relation really existing in God is the same as His Essence, and only differs in its mode of intelligibility' (28, ii). Each Person is the whole Essence, and the three are not more the Essence than one (39, vi). It is not as though there were three things or parts in God which taken together make up his Essence. It is not legitimate to speak of the Persons as '*aliud, aliud, aliud*' (31, ii). Rather, we must say '*alius, alius, alius*', interpreting this as 'speaking', in Barth's words, 'not of three divine "I's," but thrice of the one divine I' (*Doctrine of the Word of God*, 403).

But if relation differs from essence 'only in its mode of intelligibility', what has become of St Thomas's assertion that there are *real* distinctions within the Godhead? For the difference between relations and attributes is that, whereas the latter are also subsistent – as is everything in God, in that everything is essential – yet they are not really distinguished from each other, the divine goodness and wisdom, for instance, not being mutually opposed (30, i, 2). Relations of origin, however, *are* mutually opposed and thus really distinct. What, therefore, is meant by saying that the difference between them and the Essence is 'only in mode of intelligibility'?

The answer lies in recognizing that there are two ways of looking at relations. We may consider them with reference to the one Essence or with reference to each other. Now it is fundamental to St Thomas's position that 'relation as referred to the Essence does not differ therefrom really, but only in our way of thinking (*non differt re, sed ratione tantum*)' (39, i). Consequently, 'the relations themselves are not distinguished from each other so far as they are identified with the Essence' (39, i, 1). In other words, 'The Divine Persons are not distinguished as regards Being (*esse*), in which they subsist, nor in anything absolute, but only as regards something relative' (40, ii, 2); for otherwise 'it would follow that there would not be one Essence of the three Persons' (36, ii).

Nevertheless, this 'something relative' is not merely something which exists only to our way of thinking. Compared with essence relation is indeed distinguished 'only in mode of intelligibility', *ratione tantum*; but 'as referred to an opposite relation, it has a real distinction by virtue of that opposition' (39, i). It is this real opposition, this element of incommunicability, that distinguishes the Persons from the essential attributes of God. For the latter, 'although they subsist, nevertheless are not several subsistent realities (*quamvis . . . eis conveniat subsistere, non tamen sunt plures res subsistentes*)' (30, i, 2). Persons are *res* not because they are mutually independent substances, but because, relatively to each other, they differ *re* and not *ratione tantum*. The balance between the essential identity and the relative distinction between the Persons is well kept in the editorial comment on 29, iv, the first part of which was quoted above. Ludwig Guerin writes of the term *Persona*:

> *Significat essentiam non absolute, sed quaterus habet conjunctam relationem seu proprietatem individualem; quam tamen distincte significat.* ('Person' signifies essence, not absolutely, but to the degree that it has a relation or an individual property; this, however, means distinct.) Or, finally, we may quote the *conclusio* of 39, i: '*Cum persona sit relatio subsistens in divina natura, idem realiter est quod divina essentia; distinguuntur tamen personae inter se realiter, ratione oppositae realis relationis.*' (When a person is a relation subsisting in the divine nature, the same naturally has a divine essence, however, the Persons are really distinct from one another by reason of an opposite real relation.)

By way of summary of the relation which St Thomas conceived the Persons to bear to the divine Essence, we may perhaps attempt to state the matter diagrammatically, bearing in mind the dangers of oversimplification and of expressing a personal unity in mathematical terms. In the diagram following the three Persons are represented by three triangles standing on the same base and of equal area. The area of each is also the area of the Essence. Apart from them the Essence has no subsistence, and vice versa. They are in fact the same as the Essence, being three different modes of its existence. In so far as they are compared with it, they differ only '*secundum intelligentiae rationem*'. Between themselves, however, there are real differences constituted by the relations of origin, the Son being generated by the Father, and the Spirit proceeding from the Father and the Son. Finally, as far as man's experience of the revelation of God is concerned, *opera Trinitatis ad extra sunt indivisa*. He only perceives the single divine Essence. It is true that that Essence has been manifested historically in three forms, and that different attributes may therefrom be appropriated to the different Persons. But neither of these facts constitutes the ground of the real distinctions. On the contrary, both the 'missions' of the divine Persons and the 'appropriations' assigned to them derive from the internal, invisible relations of origin. Thus, neither is Rashdall right in saying that St Thomas distinguishes the Persons merely as three attributes of a unipersonal being – power (or cause), wisdom and will (or love) (*Philosophy and Religion*, 183–4). And still less Professor Hodgson, who in his *Doctrine of the Trinity*, 157–65, interprets them as three separate personalities or centres of consciousness and volition, with each of whom it is possible for the believer to enter into a distinct 'I–Thou' relationship.

With this exposition of the nature of the Persons in the Godhead, Karl Barth is in virtually complete concurrence. It is true that there are two

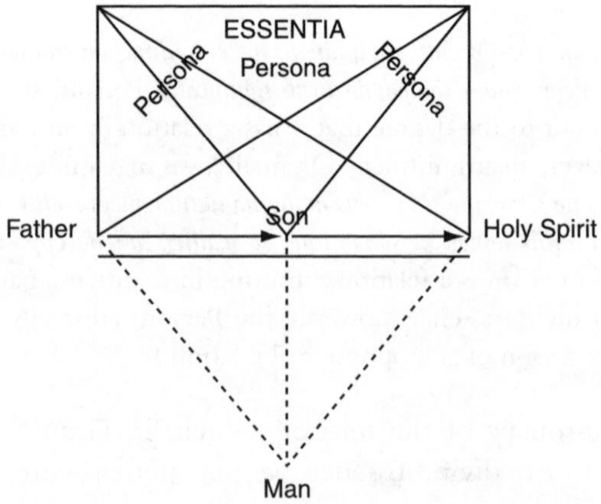

modifications which he wishes to make, but these do not alter the substance of the Thomistic position. In the first place, he argues that the word 'Person' should be dropped altogether in favour of 'mode of existence'. The wisdom of this will be discussed later. Suffice it here to say that the change intends no alteration in St Thomas's conclusions. It is rather regarded by Barth as the logical result of these conclusions. Secondly, he takes objection to the duplication implied in the description of Persons as '*res subsistentes in divina natura*' (30, i). He insists that it is the *natura* or *essentia* itself, or more correctly, *God*, who *proprie subsistit*. The individuality of the Persons can be 'sufficiently described only by adverbs (*proprie*, etc.) or ablatives (*proprietate*) describing the word *subsistere*, while the subject of this *subsistere* and therefore of the *proprie subsistere* as well cannot be a *res* or *subsistentia* different from the one essence, but only this one essence of God itself' (*Doctrine of the Word of God*, 414–15). By the use of the word *res* St Thomas seems to Barth to make the Persons additional subjects of the verb '*subsistere*' instead of adverbial qualifications of the subsistence of the one divine Subject.

This, however, is not at all St Thomas's intention; though it must be admitted that his language gives colour to such a misunderstanding, and would for that reason be better avoided. St Thomas's meaning can be explained by an expansion of something that has already been touched upon. This is the important distinction he makes between the attributes and Persons of the Godhead. 'The absolute properties in God, such as Goodness and Wisdom, are not mutually opposed; and hence, neither are they really (*re*) distinguished from each other. Therefore, although they subsist' (since nothing is 'accidental' in God), 'nevertheless they are not several subsistent realities – that is, several Persons (*Quamvis ergo eis conveniat subsistere, non tamen sunt plures res subsistentes, quod esse plures personas*). But the absolute properties in creatures do not subsist' (they are accidents of the substance), 'although they are really distinguished from each other, as whiteness and sweetness; on the other hand, the relative properties in God' (i.e., the relations of origin) 'subsist, and are really distinguished from each other. Hence the plurality of such properties suffices for the plurality of Persons in God' (30, i, 2). From this it is clear that what constitutes the Persons as *res* is not the fact that they possess subsistence in any form – the attributes do that. It is rather on account of the form in which they possess it – because they differ from each other *re* and not *ratione tantum*. That is to say, the distinction of Persons has nothing to do with the subject which subsists but with the way in which it subsists: it has to be expressed not in the nominative but in the ablative. The definition of *persona* as '*relationem, ut rem subsistente in natura divina*' [a relation, subsisting in the divine nature as a thing] is a shorthand way of stating the two characteristics of the relations of origin which make them capable as acting as the ground of threefoldness in God. They are subsistent, that is to say, they are ways in which the divine substance or nature exists. And, secondly, unlike the attributes, they are, in respect of each other, *really* (*re*) distinct. In what they mean to say at this point, therefore, there is no quarrel between Barth and St Thomas; though we must agree that the latter's condensed expression is unfortunate and misleading.

There is thus a general and essential agreement between these two writers in their treatment of the Trinity. This agreement is the more remarkable between men who on other matters disagree so profoundly, and its significance should be noted. It is not without justification, despite Professor Hodgson (*The Doctrine of the Trinity*, 229), that the first half of Vol. I of Barth's *Kirchliche Dogmatik* has been described by its translator as 'undoubtedly the greatest treatise on the Trinity since the Reformation'. And when we see such a measure of concurrence between the two most important authors on the subject on each side of the great historical and theological divide which has rent the Church, we are bound to take notice of the fact and to attach the greatest weight to their combined conclusions.

Nevertheless, it is necessary to consider some of the objections which have been brought against such a position. It is not relevant here to discuss those which are aimed at particular points in the exposition of St Thomas or Barth. Although we would wish to say that these are the two most satisfactory statements of the traditional position which have been evolved, it is not with particular elaborations that we are here concerned, but with the general view that the ground of the Personal distinctions in the Godhead is to be found in the eternal relations of origin. It is against this general statement that the most recent English work on the Trinity directs an attack, and though we may disagree with Professor Hodgson's alternative solution, we are bound to weigh his criticisms.

As already stated, Hodgson finds the ideas of generation and procession entirely meaningless. He does not deny that they may be true, but he prefers not to waste time in discussing distinctions which he does not understand, and to which anyhow he attaches no value. Now the fact that they are strictly unintelligible, in the sense that we cannot describe what we mean by the divine relations, is really no conclusive argument against them. St Thomas, indeed, does attempt to explain the difference between generation and procession, by analogy from the way that thought and actions issue from a man. But this does not get us very far, and if pressed he would have been quick to admit that the ideas are really beyond human comprehension. This, of course, would be even more readily conceded by Barth. For him the revelation is given in Scripture and that is the end of it. It is useless to seek an explanation for what is by its very nature beyond the grasp of our understanding.

That we do not understand the distinctions is, then, in itself no final argument against the idea of relations of origin in the Godhead. And this is, in fact, not the real reason why Hodgson discards them. It is rather that he fails to see in them any value. He does not need them for marking the distinction of Persons. His grounds for finding this distinction elsewhere are quite independent: they do not derive from his criticism of the relations of origin. Rather, he criticizes the doctrine of relations because he has already found another *locus proprietatis* which renders it superfluous. And if it is superfluous, the fact that it is also unintelligible is sufficient reason for rejecting it. But it is not merely that he considers it superfluous to his particular theory: he finds in it the relics of an older approach which he regards as definitely false.

In the first place, he traces in the doctrine what he calls a 'relic of subordinationism' (Hodgson, *The Doctrine of the Trinity*, 156). By this he means that there is still retained in a Trinity of Persons, of whom 'none is afore or after other: none is greater, or less, than another' (The Athanasian Creed), the idea of the Father as the *principium* (origin) of the Godhead or the πηγὴ θεότητος (fount of divinity), from which the other Persons proceed. He regards the retention of this idea as directly due to the 'mathematical' conception of simple unity with which all the classical writers worked. Unless of the three Persons there was one who was the underived *principium* of the others, then there would be three *principia* (origins); and that would be destructive of the undifferentiated, inorganic unity, which alone they knew. That is to say, Hodgson traces the retention of a relative, though not essential, subordinationism to the presence of a *philosophical* presupposition concerning the nature of unity. This conception of unity he gives good reasons for rejecting, as inadequate to describe the unity which characterizes organisms, let alone persons. So far we may follow him.

But though this philosophical presupposition was one of the reasons for the retention of the doctrine of procession, it was by no means the only one. It is extremely doubtful whether, even if these writers had arrived at a philosophically more satisfactory notion, they would have seen fit to reject the old element of subordinationism. For as we have seen (pp. 282–3), the New Testament throughout assumes an 'intensive' approach to God – to the Father, by the Son, through the Spirit. To this fact on the human side there corresponds a subordination in the Godhead. The Father, 'the only true

God', 'sends' the Son, who, in turn, with the Father, 'gives' the Spirit. As St Thomas says at the very beginning of his treatise on the Trinity, '*divina Scriptura in rebus divinis nominibus ad processionem pertinentibus utitur*' (the Holy Scriptures, when speaking of God, use words relating to procession) (27, i). This is his starting point. Although metaphysical presuppositions may have conditioned his thought, it is primarily as a faithful exposition of the *Bible* that he presents his doctrine of divine procession. This can only be dismissed if it can be shown that it is his exegesis and not his philosophy which is at error.

After all, Barth, whose thought cannot be said to be dominated by Greek, or, he would claim, by any, philosophical conception, sees fit to retain and emphasize the whole doctrine of the relations of origin. Not only does he regard it as biblical: he finds in it the only basis for a real differentiation of the Persons. Statements which purport to assure us what dead authors would have written had they lived today always tend to reflect more of the mind of their maker than of the authors themselves. But Professor Hodgson commits himself to a judgment which of this kind is perhaps more than usually naive. 'I am of the opinion', he writes, 'that if St Augustine, St Thomas and Calvin were alive today they would be glad in this respect' (the doctrine of relations) 'to revise what they had written' (*The Doctrine of the Trinity*, 157). We may surely assert with equal confidence that it is unlikely that men of this stature would have allowed a new (? Was it so unknown to Aristotle?) philosophical conception of unity of itself to move them from what they regarded as the one divinely given key to the understanding of the threefold nature of God. It is not just a question of one philosophical notion giving place to another. The statement whereby Hodgson makes out that his divergence on this point from Augustine, Aquinas and Calvin is 'not a serious matter' (ibid., 144) reveals an extraordinary misunderstanding of the significance they attached to the doctrine. His claim to be following in their teaching is unfortunately completely vitiated by his abandonment of the idea of the relations of origin, and by the consequent tritheism to which he is forced by the substitution for them, as the differentia of the Persons, of personal 'Thou' relations within the Godhead.

Hodgson does indeed recognize that it is biblical evidence as well as recalcitrant Greek metaphysics with which the classical authors were struggling. But he seems to suggest that there is no more that need be said, once they have been shown to be working with an outworn principle of interpretation, by which revelation is regarded as the purveyance of divinely guaranteed propositions about heavenly truth. We may entirely agree with his views on the nature of revelation given in the first lecture of his book.

But this does not alter the fact that, as St Thomas says, 'in reference to God Holy Scripture uses words which have to do with the idea of procession'.

The interpretation we bring to the New Testament may be different, but the evidence which speaks of subordination still remains the same. What are we to make of it?

Chapter Nineteen

THE GROUND OF DISTINCTION OF THE PERSONS (2)

In assessing the biblical support for the doctrine of relations of origin as the differentia of the divine Persons, we may for the sake of convenience divide the relevant passages into three groups. The first are those in which the subordination of Christ is implicit in the very fact that ὁ θεός is used absolutely of the Father alone. The second contains those words spoken by or about Christ which have primary reference to his subordination *as incarnate*. The third are passages which provide evidence for and against eternal subordination.

The first group is impossible to isolate from the corpus of the New Testament, and to attempt to do so would in any case be unnecessary. For there can be no dispute about the type of Trinitarian theology which implicitly or explicitly pervades the whole. It may be summed up in the familiar words of St Paul: 'The grace of the Lord Jesus Christ, and the love of God, and the communion of the Holy Ghost' (2 Cor. 13:14). This Theology is definitely subordinationist, in that the Father is identified with God *simpliciter* (directly), in a way in which neither of the other Persons could be. There is here no denial of the divinity of Christ or of the Spirit: of this the New Testament is quite sure, even though it may not express it in so many words. The furthest point to which any biblical writer goes is the statement of the Fourth Gospel: θεὸς ἦν ὁ λόγος (the Word was God) (Jn 1:1). But ὁ θεός (The God), no. Similarly, St Paul can write: 'God was in Christ reconciling the world unto himself.' The biblical writers acclaim Christ as 'the Son of God': they never go so far as to speak of 'God the Son'.

Now, if we are to say that this further transition is not only legitimate but necessary; if the full Trinitarian dogma of the Church is not merely a permissible interpretation of the New Testament but an inevitable conclusion from it; if, in fact, it is impossible to stop at the position at which the biblical writers leave us; then reasons must be given for the necessity for the doctrine to pass through a slow evolution at all. Why, if the complete equality of the Persons is the real truth of the matter, was it not immediately grasped? Only if some answer can be given to this question, can the New Testament evidence be shown not to conflict with the final position of the Church.

The answer is familiar to all students of the history of doctrine. There is no need to retrace it here, except to point out its relevance for the understanding of the true significance for dogmatics of the 'subordinationist' texts included under our first heading. The first Christians were Jews. They started with a settled monotheistic faith. To them Christ first appeared as one who had come in word and deed to proclaim the mercy and judgment of the God of their fathers – the one God they knew, or thought they knew. Here was a man doing in their own age what the prophets had done for theirs. 'A great prophet is risen up among us' (Lk. 7:16) was the reaction of the majority of Christ's contemporaries who were prepared to give him a favourable hearing. For those who understood the real significance of what he was and did, the verdict of 'a man sent from God' did indeed soon change into another – 'the Son of God'. The message he brought was seen to be not merely good news *about* God: he *was* his own gospel. So we have the ambiguity in the first words of the earliest Gospel: *ἀρχὴ τοῦ εὐαγγελίου Ἰησοῦ Χριστοῦ* (The beginning of the Gospel of Jesus Christ/concerning Jesus Christ). Here, in the possibility of taking the second genitive as descriptive and not merely possessive, is the first crude raw material of Trinitarian theology. The problem is now posed. But it is the form in which it was posed that is of significance to us. To the early disciples it was always a question of how the fact of the divinity of Christ (and the, not always distinguished, fact of the divinity of the Holy Spirit) was to be introduced into *an already existent monotheism*. The simple identification of the Father of whom Jesus spoke with the God of Abraham, Isaac and Jacob went without saying. How, then, were the other two facts to be accounted for without destroying the unity and supremacy of this God? Wherever it might lead it, there was only one road by which the Church could set out. The Logos speculation of contemporary Hellenism and the Old Testament language about 'the Word of God' and 'the Spirit of the Lord' – these both pointed the same way. The accommodation of the belief in, and worship of, 'Jesus as Lord' to the unity of God could only be achieved, if it were to be achieved at all, by some doctrine of subordination. What exercised the early Church was not the fact of subordination but its degree. It never doubted that Christ was 'begotten': but it was determined to establish that he was 'not made'. It was *γεννητός* (begotten) or *γενητός* (born): there was no third alternative.

It is true that, reading back, the New Testament authors were able to see the work of Christ in functions ascribed to the God of the Old Testament. The immediate identification of the Person of the Father with the God revealed in the former dispensation received some modification. On the one hand, Old Testament statements about Jehovah κύριος (the LORD) could be applied directly to Christ, apparently without exciting comment, or requiring defence (e.g., 1 Pet. 2:3–4). On the other, Christ could be seen as the true agent of the divine economy long prior to the Incarnation. Through him were all things, and he was the life and light by which the world lived, though it knew it not (Jn 1:1–13). It was he who was with Israel at the Exodus (1 Cor. 10:4); it was his spirit which inspired the prophets (1 Pet. 1:11). Yet in all this we are not *in principle* beyond the statement that 'by the word of the Lord were the heavens made' (Ps. 33:6) or the confession of the prophet that 'the spirit of the Lord God is upon me' (Is. 61:1). The divine agent might in each case now receive a capital letter; but he remained still the *agent* of 'the one true God'. That the Logos was πρὸς τὸν θεόν (with (the) God) and even θεός (God), was not among the statements which St Augustine failed to find in the Platonists. *In principle* nothing is added until we can say ὁ θεός (The God). The Logos doctrine hindered the transition from 'Son of God' to 'God the Son'. We may agree with Professor Hodgson that the doctrine is really incompatible with the Hebraeo-Christian conception of God and that its usefulness ended at the Council of Nicaea (*The Doctrine of the Trinity*, 113–22). However, its historical utility, and even indispensability, must be stressed. At the beginning some form of subordinationism was inevitable. The history of Trinitarian doctrine can be read as the gradual purging away of the subordinationist elements which were necessary for its early growth.

The question remains: may we dispense with these elements altogether? From the larger historical perspective we enjoy we are bound to read much of the biblical evidence somewhat differently. Just as the Church could not remain content with the παῖς (servant/child) Christology of the early chapters of Acts (3:13, 26; 4:27, 30), so we may surely see much of that other somewhat less crude subordinationism as historically inevitable but not doctrinally determinative. For the Jew of the first century there was no other way of preserving both the divinity of Christ and the unity of God. As long as we are sure we can retain these together are we bound to the method of subordinationism, which was forced upon the Church more by the inevitabilities of history than the inescapability of evidence?

But what of the evidence? Was there in fact none? Granted that we may legitimately discount much of the subordinationist element, can we discard it all? Can we attribute the whole of it to the method required for the working up of the Trinitarian data into Trinitarian dogma? Or is there something of it in the data itself? If we kicked away the ladder altogether, could the worst accusation be one of ingratitude to history – or would it be also disloyalty to truth?

This brings us to the fact of the subordination of the Son to the Father involved in the Incarnation and to the second and third classes of passages distinguished above. It is clear that whereas the form of subordinationism was derived from the thought-categories of the time, both Hebrew and Greek, the matter was provided by the obvious fact that the Son was revealed historically as living in a relationship of subordination and obedience to the Father. He was presented to the eyes of his contemporaries 'in the form of a servant'. He spoke to them of one from whom he had been sent, whose will he was on earth to fulfil, and to whom he would eventually return. There could be no doubt that, as he was, the Father was greater than he. It was natural then that the first Christology should build from this filial or even servant relationship.

But the question could not but arise whether this relationship was not peculiar to the Incarnation. What of Christ in his glory? What of his eternal relation to the Father ἐν μορφῇ θεοῦ (in the form of God)? Christ might have come forth from God, and the Spirit been given by him and the Father; but did this temporal mission imply an eternal subordination and procession? It is the possibility of making this distinction that justifies the separation of our second and third classes of passage – of those that have reference to the subordination of Christ *qua* incarnate and those which extend this to the eternal relations of the Persons in heaven. Those who are to make use of the idea of eternal relations of origin in their doctrine of the Trinity must be prepared to establish that there *are* in fact passages of the third type.

The passages that have to be considered for this test fall naturally into two classes, Johannine and Pauline. There is another set which we shall not consider here. These are those which treat indeed of the glorified Christ, but which regard his relation to the Father from the point of view of the retention of his humanity. Among such passages may be included those that speak of his session at the right hand of God; the allusions to the Lamb in the Apocalypse; the references to the priestly function of the ascended Christ, particularly in the Epistle to the Hebrews. The peculiar problems raised by these passages have already been considered; and they can, in any case, have no bearing on the question of the relation of the Persons outside the Incarnation, since they presuppose the conditions of manhood to be in some form operative.

Of the Johannine passages, there are those which, in St Thomas's phrase, 'use words which have to do with the idea of procession', and there are those which assert, explicitly or implicitly, the superiority of the Father to the

Son. Of the former it is possible to speak with fair confidence. The only conclusion which an impartial exegesis permits is that there is no ground for the assertion of an eternal procession above and beyond the temporal mission of the Persons. There is nothing on which a doctrine of eternal relations within the Godhead can be directly based. On this point the commentaries are unanimous (see, e.g., Westcott, Bernard, Hoskyns and Davey). Even with the distinction which Westcott finds between ἐκ, (out of), παρὰ, (from the place of), and ἀπὸ τοῦ πατρός (from (implying separation)), the *locus classicus* for the procession of the Spirit (Jn 15:26) is decisively against any reference to non-temporal relations. But any real distinction between the use of the prepositions cannot, in fact, be sustained; and the attempts to base anything on the differences in Jn 8:42 and 16:27–8 are hopeless.[55] The other references are not worth listing or examining, as they afford no additional evidence and are clearly against any metaphysical interpretation.

It is not denied that the temporal mission of which the passages speak may require us to postulate a corresponding eternal procession. But the reasons which could make this necessary are strictly theological and not exegetical. We shall have to consider the implications for the doctrine of God of the fact that he has revealed his triune nature in a *sending* of one Person by another. Here we are only concerned with the direct evidence of Scripture. And this, contrary to the beliefs with which St Thomas and others have worked, cannot be said to bear out any doctrine of eternal relations of the origin within the Godhead.

But though sound exegesis affords no direct evidence for such relations, it may be said that they are implied in the subordination of Son to Father, of which the Fourth Gospel in particular speaks. This brings us to the second set of Johannine passages.

These are those which speak of the sending of the Son by the Father and of his dependence on him for everything that he is and says and does (Jn 5:19, 26, 30; 6:57; 8:28–9 etc.). These passages culminate in the famous text, of which the Arians made such capital: 'the Father is greater than I' (14:28). On this Bernard (*St John* II, 1928, 555) makes a comment which will serve as a judgment on them all.

> It suffices to note that the *filial* relationship, upon which so much stress is laid in Jn., implies of itself that the Son is from the Father, not the Father from the Son. There is no question here of theological subtleties about what a later age called the 'subordination' of the Son, or of any distinction between His οὐσία [essence] and that of the Father. But, for Jn., the Father *sent* the Son . . . and *gave* Him all things . . . Cf. Mk. 1332, Phil. 26 1 Cor. 1527, for other phrases which suggest that ὁ πατὴρ μείζων μού ἐστιν [The

Father is greater than I] is a necessary condition of the Incarnation. It is the same Person that says 'I and my Father are one thing' (1030), who speaks of Himself as 'a man who hath told you the truth which I have heard from God' (840).

A sound interpretation of Jn 14:28 and suchlike phrases must steer between two errors. On the one hand, it is impossible, though many have taken such a view (see, Westcott's review of the Patristic interpretations of Jn 14:26 in his commentary ad loc.), to hold that the words implying his inferiority to the Father are spoken by the man in Christ alone. Such an interpretation would involve a fatal splitting of his person, such as vitiated so much of the Alexandrine Christology. Nor again can the words be read in any sense which would entail an eternal subordination of any kind. The relative subordination, which, as all recognize, does not imply a difference of substance, is a necessary condition of the Incarnation; or, rather, it is another way of stating the fact of the Incarnation. The Second Person of the Trinity therein came to live as a son (i.e., in an 'I–Thou' relationship of filial obedience to God). The phrase 'the Father is greater than I' implies no more than that it was *Christ*, the *Son* that is, the one who was living a life of *obedience*, who was speaking about God. This personal situation of the speaker is expressed by saying that the one to whom obedience is due *sent* him and *gave* him all things and must in fact be reverenced and respected as greater, since he is the author of the commands he has set himself to fulfil. But he is called 'Son', and is spoken of as inferior to the Father in virtue of this filial obedience and self-subordination, because he lived in the (human) 'I–Thou' relationship. There are no grounds for saying that this filial relationship, and therefore the subordination, are descriptive of an eternal condition within the Godhead.[56]

It is important to see that this is not the same as saying that it was the man in Christ who said 'My Father is greater than I', whereas it was in his divine nature that he said 'I and the Father are one'. The 'I' in both cases is the same, the 'I' of God living as man, in the human relation to God. It is true that in the former case the words are only applicable to the Incarnation and would not have been spoken apart from it. But it is just as much the God in Christ who speaks them as the man.[57] For the sonship, in itself a human relation, in virtue of which they were spoken, was the sonship of God. Moreover, the latter words, 'I and the Father are one', signify a different kind of unity, being uttered as they were from within the context of the Incarnation, than they would have apart from it. If it had been the God in Christ alone who spoke the words, this would not have been so. But being spoken by him who was both God and man they describe the situation of one who, without ceasing to be God, was united to God in the specifically human mode of union, that is to say, in a personal communion. The words 'without ceasing to be God' are essential. Otherwise the statement 'I and the Father are one' is watered down to an assertion of that complete communion with God which could be predicated as well of one who was just perfect man. The significance of the words lies in the double fact that what appeared as just a perfect human communion was also an essential union, and that what was an essential union could be, and was being, expressed in and through a personal communion.

This brief review of the catena of Johannine passages has disclosed that sound exegesis and interpretation are against any reference to eternal relations of origin or subordination within the Trinity. Hitherto, therefore, we have found no passages which we can or must assign to our third class – those which definitely extend subordinationism to the eternal relations of the Persons in heaven. And yet, as we saw, unless such be found, the doctrine of relations or origin, and its use to establish the real differences within the Godhead, can lay claim to no biblical foundation. There remain, however, a few Pauline texts, which certainly at first sight appear to offer more hope. There are four in particular which must be considered.

The first is Phil. 2:6–11: 'Christ Jesus: who, being in the form of God, counted it not a prize to be on an equality with God, but . . .' This seems clear evidence against any ultimate subordination. But it is mentioned here for two reasons. First, because it completely accords with the interpretation given to the Johannine passages just under consideration – namely, that there is an eternal equality but a temporary self-subordination involved in the Incarnation. And secondly, because of the contrast between the logic of this passage and that of the next we quote.

This, like the other two remaining passages, is from 1 Corinthians. There are obscurities in it, but the setting is plainly eschatological.

> Then cometh the end, when he [Christ] shall deliver up the kingdom to God, even the Father; when he [Christ] shall have abolished all rule and all authority and power. For he must reign till he hath put all his enemies under his feet. The last enemy that shall be abolished is death. For, he put all things in subjection under his feet. But when he saith, All things are put in subjection, it is evident that he is excepted who did subject all things unto him. And when all things have been subjected unto him, then shall the Son also himself be subjected to him that did subject all things unto him, that God may be all in all. (1 Cor. 15:24–8)

The other two texts must be taken together with this, as they can only be interpreted in the light of it. They are 'Ye are Christ's; and Christ is God's' (1 Cor. 3:23) and 'The head of the woman is the man; and the head of Christ is God' (1 Cor. 11:3).

The passage from 1 Cor. 15 has given rise to numerous interpretations. These are set out by Godet in his commentary on the epistle. He rejects, and rightly, all the feats of exegesis which have yielded the view that here there is not necessarily asserted any ultimate subordination of the divine Person of Christ. The only plausible way of escaping this conclusion is to say that the passage speaks of the cessation of Christ's mediatorial function with the handing back of the delegated sovereignty which he held from God. But this, though possible as an interpretation of 5:24, is not sufficient to account for 5:28, which distinctly refers not to the work but to the Person of Christ. There are, then, only two alternatives left. The first is frankly to admit that this passage 'is in contradiction not only to the ecclesiastical dogma of the Trinity, but also to all the expressions of St Paul which imply Christ's divinity and pre-existence' (Godet, ad loc.). This solution Godet rejects on the ground that such a contradiction on such a fundamental point is inconceivable in as logical and careful a thinker as St Paul.

The other alternative, which he adopts, is to regard the subjection of the Son as just as integral to, and compatible with, the Christian conception of the Godhead as his pre-existence and equality in substance with the Father. He interprets the passage as follows:

> The Son, though of the same substance with the Father, yet is subordinate to Him. However, for the purpose of putting all things in subjection to Himself, and of destroying the powers of evil in the world, God gives Christ power to reign and to exercise the Divine sovereignty within the universe. When this object has been achieved, when the Son has established the Kingdom of God, then He hands it over, and His rule and authority, like that of every other power, is at an end. And, in consequence, He returns to His previous and normal position of subordination to the Father.
>
> He effaces Himself to let God take His place. Formerly it was He, Christ, in whom God manifested Himself to the world; it was He who was 'all in all' (Col. 3:11). But He took advantage of His relation to the faithful only to bring them to that state in which God could directly, without mediation on His part, live, dwell in them, reveal Himself, and act by them. This time having come, they are, as to position, His equals; God is all in them in the same way as He was and is all in His glorified Son. They have reached the perfect stature of Christ (Eph. 4:13).

As an exegesis of the passage under review this interpretation has much to commend it. It gives a clear sense and does not labour under the strain which is manifest in those accounts which seek to eliminate the subordinationist element. It is, however, legitimate to ask whether it does not involve a departure from other Pauline thought so great as to incur nearly the same condemnation as the interpretation which would make this passage a denial of Christ's divinity.

It is to be noted that the assertion of equality of essence with the Father is not stated in the passage under discussion. It is assumed by Godet as the Pauline background of the elaboration of the idea of subordination. It would seem, however, that some indication of it might have been given to correct an otherwise unbalanced and misleading statement. The impression inevitably made upon the reader is that the relation of Christ to God is similar to that of John the Baptist to Christ. His function is to lead men to another, to God. When that task is fulfilled, the day of his rule is over. God must increase; for then his sovereignty will be directly exercised. But Christ must decrease; for, instead of being he in whom 'dwelleth all the fullness of the Godhead bodily' (Col. 2:9), he will be subordinated to the Father 'as an elder brother in the midst of many brethren' (cf. Rom. 8:29). The contrast, or rather the contradiction, between this and Pauline thought generally can be easily brought out by a comparison with the passage from Philippians previously under discussion.

	Phil. 2:6–11	*Godet on* 1 Cor. 15:24–8
Status of Christ before Incarnation	In the form of God, on an equality with God.	Of the same substance with God, but subordinate to him.
Effects of Incarnation on this status	Emptied himself, taking the form of a servant. Humbled himself.	Called to reign, to a direct exercise of the divine sovereignty, to be 'all in all'.
Final status (a) *Vis à vis God*	God highly exalted him, giving him a name which is above every name.	He effaces himself and returns to a position of submission and subordination.
(b) *Vis à vis the world and men*	In the name of Jesus every knee shall bow, of things in heaven and things under the earth, and every tongue shall confess that Jesus Christ is *κύριος* [LORD], to the glory of God the Father.[58]	A brother who in relation to his brethren keeps only the advantage of his eternal priority. They are, as to position, his equals.

We have to say that Godet's exegesis goes wrong at exactly the points at which he attempts to assimilate this passage to the rest of Pauline thought, namely:

(a) the assertion of original equality of substance with the Father, which his interpretation assumes, is not found in 1 Cor. 15.

(b) His quotation from Col. 3:11 would lead one to suppose that there Paul regarded, or could have regarded, the complete sovereignty of Christ as something temporary. This is completely belied by the context, which is ethical. The finality of the ethic clearly depends on the finality of the Kingdom of which it is the law. The idea of a temporary Messianic kingdom seems to be a relic of Jewish apocalyptic thought. Johannes Weiss compares with 1 Cor. 15:24 (*Kommentar*, ad loc.) 2 Esdras 7:28f., where the Christ dies after reigning 400 years, and Rev. 20:4ff. – where, however, it is not stated that Christ shall only rule for 1,000 years, but that the saints shall reign with him (on earth) for that period. He has a reference to *Pirke Elieser*, 11: 'The ninth king is the Messiah, who will reign from one end of the world to the other; the tenth is God: therewith will the kingdom return to its original holder.' This conception of a temporary rule, though inevitable as long as the Messiah is regarded as human, is impossible if he is divine. At any rate the Church has expressed itself to be firmly against it. The credal statement, 'whose kingdom shall have no end', is based on much more than Lk. 1:13 (cf. Is. 9:7): it is presupposed in the whole New Testament view of Christ's Person.

(c) His interpretation of Rom. 8:29 ('the first-born among many brethren') is open to two objections. There is no suggestion, either here or in Col. 1:18 ('the first-born from the dead'), that this title of Christ either implies any position of inferiority to the Father or a status of equality with regard to the body of believers. The phrase in Col. 1:18 is immediately followed by the words, 'that in all things he might have the pre-eminence. For it was the good pleasure of the Father that in him should all the fullness dwell (*πᾶν τὸ πλήρωμα κατοικῆσαι*)'. (Incidentally, Lightfoot points out that the force of *κατοικῆσαι* is to emphasize the permanence of the dwelling, as opposed to *παροικῆσαι*, which would indicate temporary residence. This is another indication that the passage from 1 Cor. 15 is unsupported in other Pauline writings.) Moreover, the very close parallelism of Col. 1:15–17 and 18–20 demands that, whatever sense we give to *πρωτότοκος πάσης κτίσεως* (the first-born of all creation) in 5:15, we must give the same to *πρωτότοκος ἐκ τῶν νεκρῶν* (the first-born from the dead) in 5:18. Now Lightfoot has convincingly shown that there is not the slightest ground for interpreting the former to mean that Christ is merely the first of created things, a *primus inter pares* (first among equals) of the old creation. It is then equally impos-

> sible to regard the latter as indicating that with respect to the new creation Christ is merely 'a brother who in relation to his brethren keeps only the advantage of his eternal priority'. The significance of the idea of Christ as 'the first-born among many brethren' is not that we are thereby equal to him, but that he, by becoming man amongst ourselves, has opened up a way which we as men can tread. This is clearly brought out in the Epistle to the Hebrews, of which, indeed, it is the central theme.[59]

The conclusion which seems to force itself upon us is that the idea of the ultimate subordination of the Son, quite apart from its incompatibility with other New Testament writings, is in contradiction with the rest of St Paul's thought. Nowhere else is there any suggestion that the exaltation of Christ is, or could be, anything but the final word on the truth about his Person. What is significant about Godet's interpretation of 1 Cor. 15:24–8 is that as an exegesis of the passage itself it is remarkably convincing. Indeed, no interpretation which denies subordinationism has any plausibility. The choice must lie between the complete subordination of the Son to the Father as *a creature* or as *God*. We may agree with Godet that the former interpretation would involve a denial of too much both within and without the corpus of the Pauline writings to make it at all likely. But the latter appears almost equally unpauline and unbiblical. For although Godet's view, as has been said, is sound enough as an exegesis of the verses in question, yet whenever he seeks to find support for it in other passages of St Paul he is most unconvincing.

Of course, this conclusion with regard to 1 Corinthians is entirely negative and, from the point of view of New Testament criticism and exegesis, leaves a host of questions unasked and unanswered. We should want to know the sources which affects St Paul's eschatology at this point, his reasons for adopting it, and the implications for the development of his thought. But these questions can be left to the commentators – though it must be remarked that they are decidedly inadequate at this point. This is largely due to the limitations of the historico-critical point of view, which alone seems to be of interest to most modern exegetes. It is significant that one has to go back to Godet for the last serious attempt to struggle with the *doctrinal* perplexities of the passage. If its implications for dogmatics are ignored, then it presents nothing very remarkable, and the comparative silence of the commentaries is explicable. (Though even so, the fact that, for instance, a certain idea can be traced back to *Pirke Elieser* is of very minor importance compared with the question of *how* a piece of pure Jewish messianism found its way into a Christian Theology completely incompatible with it.) But from the doctrinal point of view, which is our present concern, the passage is of great significance. The deliberate and studied effect of the verses in question, in which it is obvious that every word is carefully weighed, makes it impossible to treat it as anything but a serious essay in Christian eschatological doctrine. That it was so meant its context leaves us in no doubt. And yet had it had a dominant influence on the development of theology, it would have made Nicaea impossible. Certainly, if we are to reject the passage as a basis of doctrine, it must not be because it is a ἅπαξ λεγόμενον (a word found only once). That is what Forsyth stigmatized as 'concordance criticism'. Like the 'kenotic' passage from Philippians with which comparison has been made, its content is to be estimated, not by the number of times it can be paralleled by in the rest of the New Testament, but by the deliberateness with which it is intended and the intrinsic importance of its theme. It is its incompatibility with the New Testament as a whole and not its uniqueness which must be demonstrated, if the doctrine of God which it implies is to be disregarded. And this incompatibility a study of the evidence must be regarded as having shown.

The conclusion to which the evidence inevitably appears to point is that the idea of the eternal subordination of the Son (and the Spirit) to the Father is in fact unbiblical. With regard to the language about procession which St Thomas found in the words of the Fourth Gospel, it seems perfectly clear that the author is alluding simply to the temporal mission involved in the Incarnation and the gift at Pentecost. The same reference to the Incarnation dominates the passages which speak of Christ's inferiority to the Father, and this determines their meaning for Dogmatics. Lastly, the idea of the final complete subordination of the Son to the one God, to the intent that he may be all in all, is unbiblical, not in the sense that it is not found in the Bible, but that it contradicts the whole tenor of its teaching about the Person of Christ. It may be added that even if this contradiction could be shown to be non-existent – and it would obviously be more satisfactory if it could – the passage in 1 Cor. 15 would still provide the type of subordinationism that is required for the doctrine of the relations of origin. For if the eternal differences between the Persons are to be grounded upon them, the relations of subordination must be shown to be permanent and unchanging. The subordination envisaged by St Paul is something which is connected with the temporal economy of salvation and which only takes effect in the last day. It may be a reversion to an original state, but the relation is certainly not eternal and unvarying.

But, though the doctrine of the relations of origin can claim no direct biblical support, yet it may be said that it is involved in the general rule by which the actions and character of God in revelation are to be taken as determinative for us of the eternal and essential nature of the divine being. May we not – in fact, must we not – argue that the fact of temporal mission implies as its ground the fact of eternal procession? And can this not be called a genuine biblical defence? For it is only taking the historical revelation seriously, as the index of the true nature of God. It is treating the Bible as the Bible itself demands that it shall be treated. The Incarnation is presented by the New Testament as grounded in the eternal purpose of God: nothing in it may be regarded as accidental. What, therefore, it discloses of the historical relation of the Persons bears directly upon their eternal relation. Herein, it may be said, lies the true biblical basis of the doctrine which places the ground of the triune division in the relations of origin of the Persons.

Though it is doubtful whether this doctrine would have established itself had its exponents not believed that the New Testament, and in particular the Fourth Gospel, did speak directly of such eternal relations, those who would confine their defence of it to the lines just set out are certainly on much surer ground. For the general principle they are setting forth is unimpeachable. The thelematological approach which we have been following in our whole doctrine of God requires that revelation be taken absolutely seriously. The will of God as revealed *is* his being or essence. There is nothing behind the God of revelation to which we have to go in order to discover the real God, God as he is in himself. The *τρόπος ἀποκαλύψεως* (the manner in which he is revealed) *is* the *τρόπος ὑπάρξεως* (the manner in which he is). For God is a 'Thou', a being in relation, a being in revelation. God outside this relation or revelation is not more real or more truly himself: he is an abstraction. We must not even say that the economic Trinity is an index of the essential: it *is* the essential. For there is no 'essence' or 'being' of God except 'being in relation', 'being *ἐν οἰκονομίᾳ* (in an economy)'. Not only, therefore, should we be forced to argue from the fact of the historical revelation to God's eternal nature, we should have to go further and say that the temporal mission would not merely point to an eternal procession: it would *be* the eternal procession.

But we can only say '*would* be' – because there is another condition, a condition which rescues the statement from its obvious absurdity. It is the only condition which governs the general rule that everything spoken about God as revealed is spoken about God as he is; but it is one of great importance. The formula which we touched on before must now be set out explicitly. It is that everything in Christ is a revelation of the eternal God except that which is bound up with the fact of his humanity. Of course, the fact that Christ could and did become man at all is indeed a revelation of something about God. It discloses that man is so truly made in the image of God that, within manhood's limits, the divine nature can be itself as truly in the human 'Thou' existence as in its own 'I' existence, of which the human is the analogue. Again, the fact that when God came to earth he appeared as a particular kind of man, as a suffering servant tell us as much about God as it does about men. But the actual facts, physical and otherwise, which are involved in the state of being human cannot themselves constitute a revelation of the divine, beyond the fact that their predication of Christ shows that he assumed everything that is included in manhood. Thus, to take an example, that Christ had flesh and bones is certain; for that is implied in being fully human. But the flesh and the bones do not of themselves furnish any additional revelation of the divine nature: they do not correspond to anything in God.

Our principle of interpretation, then, must be that everything which is not incidental to the fact of existence as man must be predicated eternally of the essential Godhead. Let us now apply it to the defence given above of the doctrine or relations of origin between the Persons of the Trinity.

This defence, as far as it goes, is sound in its insistence on the positive part of the formula: it takes the facts of the historical revelation seriously as indications of their eternal ground. It does, of course, stop short, in that it only regards the *τρόπος ἀποκαλύψεως* (manner of revelation) as an *index* of the *τρόπος ὑπάρξεως* (manner of reality), thereby introducing a fatal distinction between nature and will in God, between the essential and the economic. It is in fact bound to stop short here, because anything further would commit it to the absurd statement, which we saw to be involved if the negative condition was not observed, that the temporal mission *was* the eternal procession.

But what of this negative condition? Does not this theory adequately distinguish and eliminate the human element in the revelation of the Incarnate? We are bound to say that it does not. For Christ's position of inferiority vis-à-vis the Father (the relation of 'being sent'), which is treated as an index of an eternal subordination of origin, is in fact merely incidental to his state of manhood. For to be in an 'I–Thou' relation of obedience, of having to make a response to a higher word, is just a description of what manhood means, in the same way as having flesh and bones is one of its necessary external expressions. If Christ was truly man he could not have appeared in an other relation to God. That he did so is indeed a revelation of his complete humanity; but it is no indication of an essential and permanent relation of subordination. Any fact about the Incarnate which is just another way of saying that he was man is not relevant as a revelation of the eternal nature of God. And to be in a relation of obedience is even more truly another way of stating the fact of humanity than to have flesh and bones. When Christ declared 'I live because of the Father' (Jn 6:57), he is revealing no eternal divine procession: he is simply affirming the basic fact of humanity to which all men must ever bear witness, that 'through Thee I am' (Gogarten). When he said, 'the Son can do nothing of himself' (Jn 5:19), he is just reiterating the truth enunciated by Jeremiah that 'the way of man is not in himself: it is not in man that walketh to direct his steps' (10:23). And when he confessed 'as I hear, I judge' (Jn 5:30), he is but stating again what he quoted to Satan, that man lives 'by every word that proceedeth out of the mouth of God' (Mt. 4:4). All the assertions on the part of Christ of inferiority and dependence attest but the genuineness of his humanity: they provide no evidence of an eternal subordination of him as God to the Father. Of course, his words about being 'sent' and having 'come' from God apply to him in a unique sense and reveal the truth of his Person. To know 'whence he is' is to know who he is. They indicate, indeed, that he is eternally divine, but they neither assert nor imply that he is eternally subordinate.[60]

It is in consequence of this that we are finally bound to reject the doctrine of relations of origin as insufficiently grounded in Scripture. And with it goes, too, the traditional basis for the differentiation of the Persons. This is indeed a serious matter, and we could have wished to retain it if it were at all possible. For it had the merit of really providing the kind of differentiation that is required and facing the problems involved, in a way that its more fashionable alternative does not and cannot do. With the rejection also of this alternative we have reduced ourselves to a position in which it appears that all chance of finding a *locus proprietatis* of the Persons, and with it all chance of formulating any positive doctrine of the Trinity, has disappeared. It would indeed be unsatisfactory if we had to leave the matter here – though hardly as unsatisfactory as resting in a positive solution which is in fact insupportable. The point of agnosticism concerning the nature of the Persons would have been reached even earlier than St Augustine placed it in his most diffident moments. The '*tres nescio quid*' of St Anselm would be the last, and only, word.

But is there no way out, which at least partially, could relieve the purely negative conclusion which the rejection of both the historic solutions has involved? We believe that there is, and that it lies in pursuing further the application of the principle of interpretation which administered the final blow to the doctrine of the relations of origin. Let us return to this, and apply it radically to the revelation of the Incarnation, where, on any count, the basis for Trinitarian doctrine is to be sought.

The situation at the Incarnation – and in the revelation of the Incarnation is here included the whole stretch of the *Heilsgeschichte* from Christmas to Pentecost – may be stated thus. God discloses himself simultaneously in threefold form: first, as loving Father, to whom all men owe the love-in-obedience of the 'I–Thou' relationship; secondly, as Jesus Christ, standing as man in this human relationship to God and yet himself 'very God'; thirdly, as Holy Spirit, who takes the things of Christ, making his work ever-living in us and enabling our response to it – the 'Applicator' and 'Advocatus'. In a real sense the Spirit too is revealed to stand in a 'Thou' relation to the Godhead. For the 'I' who makes the 'Thou' response of faith is in fact the Holy Ghost informing, without superseding, the personality of the believer. Here also God is truly on both sides of the 'I–Thou' relation, as he was in the response of the incarnate Christ. Thus, though the Spirit does not, like the Son, *become* man, he is capable of existing towards God through man, in the polarity of the 'Thou' relationship.

At the Incarnation, therefore, the Godhead is revealed for the first time as existing in three distinct *relations*. It is these differences of relation that make necessary a doctrine of the Trinity, not differences of 'character' or modes of working. The Old Testament, too, knew God in different 'characters', but it was not forced to a Trinitarian Theology. It is only from this point, from the difference of relations, that a satisfactory doctrine of the Trinity can start. We cannot begin with God creating, God redeeming, God sanctifying, or any other such collocation of attributes, and then proceed to identify these with Father, Son and Holy Spirit. On that method there is no compelling reason for stopping at three Persons and no ground for any *real* differentiation. Rather, one must start with the three Persons, no more and no less, which are required by the three relations at the Incarnation. From there it is possible and necessary to go on to a doctrine of appropriations, within the bounds permitted by the Bible. But it is the relations which are the basis for the differentiation.

This is important. For though the 'Thou' relationships of the Incarnation, being human relations, indicate nothing concerning the *nature* of the eternal divine relations within the Trinity, they do give ground for the assertion that there are such relations of the same kind. For the fact that the Persons of the Trinity could exist in the relative opposition of the polar 'Thou' relationship means that there are real distinctions between them. The element of incommunicability must be there if, when it appears in human form, it has to express itself in the real opposition of 'I' over against 'Thou', whose mutual isolation and integrity are the presupposition of their communion. The incommunicability of the Persons is presupposed in, and not constituted by, their revelation as Persons. For if they had first become really distinct at the Incarnation, the fact of a threefold revelation would be purely accidental to the essential nature of God. All we could say is that it has so happened that God revealed himself in three Persons, between whom there existed a real relative opposition. But this would tell us nothing of the real God, who is essentially uni-Personal. Such a position would represent the extremest form of modalism and mark the end of the doctrine of the Trinity altogether.

It is impossible to hold that the fact God revealed himself in three modes differentiated by a real incommunicability is something incidental to the fact that he became man – simply another way of stating what humanity means. And if it is not this, then it must constitute a genuine revelation of his eternal nature. God exists in three Persons, between whom there is a real relative opposition. So much we may assert with confidence. We cannot say that they stand towards each other in 'I–Thou' relationships, that the Persons are persons. For the *nature* of the revealed relationship, the form in which the element of incommunicability is expressed, *is* determined by the fact that God became man. The 'Thou' relationship is the human relationship, and it cannot therefore be predicated of the eternal Persons. Moreover, there is no evidence for saying that the three Persons are not in every sense equal. For any degree of subordination found at the Incarnation is directly due to the fact that one was standing over against the other in the human relation to God.

That there are *real* and essential distinctions within the Godhead and that there are three Persons so distinguished is something that we can assert from the revelation of the Incarnation. The basic presuppositions of the doctrine of the Trinity are thus assured. *How* the Persons are distinguished, and what constitutes the *proprietas incommunicabilis* of each, we cannot say. We may say that it is by their mutual relations and not by their intrinsic qualities and attributes that they are differentiated. For when their real distinctness is expressed in revelation in human terms, it appears as a distinctness in *relationship* (of 'I' over against 'Thou'), not a distinctness of *character* (e.g., the Father as power and the Son as wisdom). If there were any such 'exclusive' appropriation of attribute or function made to the Persons in the historical revelation, then we should be bound to say that it represented an element by which they were eternally distinguished from each other. But in fact the New Testament provides evidence for no such exclusive appropriations: if it did, it would be providing evidence of tritheism.

But for non-exclusive appropriations it does provide ground. Despite the fact that it is possible to produce passages in which the roles are differently apportioned (cf. the list of Dr Kirk's quoted in Note 46), it is generally true to say that the Bible 'appropriates' creation to the Father, redemption to the Son and sanctification to the Spirit. To the extent to which they are appropriated (and this is certainly not anything like exclusively) we must conclude that there is something in each of the Persons which gives a fittingness to their appearing in revelation in these particular roles. In the same way, the fact that of the three Persons the Father has been manifested most especially as Transcendent, the Son as Incarnate and the Spirit as Immanent must point to some eternal fittingness; for nothing is accidental in God. But neither must we argue as the classical writers tend to do that the mission of the *Son* in the world is fitting on account of an eternal subordination to the Father; nor, with others, may we take the three aspects of the relation to God corresponding to this differentiation as the distinguishing approach of the three Persons: we cannot say, with Kirk, that a relation of obedience as to one above us, and of communion as with one among us, and of possession as by one within us constitute the *grounds* of the Personal distinctions.

In the matter of the doctrine of 'appropriations' we may agree with the classical writers that they are both legitimate and necessary. And we may assent to the criteria which they propound for their formulation: they must be neither exclusive nor arbitrary. But the definition of arbitrariness will have to be recast. For these writers an appropriation was arbitrary if it did not show some evident connection with the particular relation of origin of the Person in reference to whom it was made. In many instances, indeed, they were content with associations which appear far-fetched and slight;[61] but this, at any rate, was the theory. For us, however, 'fittingness' is correspondence with biblical ascriptions of some function or 'character' in the historical revelation. It is not compatibility with some eternal relation of origin, for which in fact we have no evidence.

This change enables the doctrine of appropriations properly to fulfil the function for which it exists. Its use, after all, is to relate the real differentia of the Persons, which must lie outside experience and the *opera ad extra*, to the threefoldness manifested in the historical revelation. The very names given to the Persons – Father, Son and Holy Spirit – themselves perform this function. They are indispensable appropriations. They do not describe the actual *proprietas* of each Person – their reference is clearly to the situation of the Incarnation – but they do serve to relate this to the threefold mode of the divine working in the historical revelation. When, however, appropriations are made according to the traditional criterion of 'fittingness', they do in fact fail to fulfil the purpose for which they exist. For being framed solely on the grounds of their connection with the relations of origin they do not effect the link with experience which is required of them. On the one hand, if we start from revelation – say, from the threefoldness in the *opera ad extra* of creation, redemption and sanctification – no observable connection is to be traced between them and those qualities which are predicated of the Persons on the ground of their association with the states of 'being unbegotten', 'having been begotten' and 'having proceeded'. And, if we start from the other end, the same applies. To appropriate, for instance, *unitas* to the Father, *aequalitas* to the Son and *connexio* to the Spirit does nothing to relate the doctrine of the Trinity any closer to our experience of the threefold address of the divine 'Thou'; nor does such a division correspond with anything in the historical manifestations of the Persons recorded in Scripture. Again, a triad of attributes such as 'power', 'wisdom' and 'goodness' has no sort of inevitability about it such as makes us immediately recognize it as an interpretation of present experience or of the historical revelation. It is perhaps significant that St Thomas and Hooker both use the same triad but appropriate them differently (cf. above p. 287): so little difference does it appear to make.

Chapter Twenty

THE PERSONS OF THE GODHEAD AND THE PERSONALITY OF GOD

It will be recalled that the starting point of our discussion of the doctrine of the Trinity was the doctrine of God as eternal 'Thou' confronting the soul as the Lord of its life, giving all as it demands all. The 'essence' of God was his personality, his 'being-in-relation', his 'I'-existence in relation to which ours is 'Thou' existence or 'being-in-responsibility'. If this was the *essentia divina*, the *οὐσία* (essence) or *substantia* of God, what then, we asked, of the fact that Christian theology declares this essence to be known only under three forms, in three modes of being, in three 'Persons'? How were the Persons to be conceived, and what was their relation to the one Essence? In other words, we approached the doctrine of the Trinity by considering the relation of *Persona* and personality. How was the doctrine of the personality of God affected by the fact that he must be regarded as tri-Personal? Did this mean in fact that he was tri-personal; that the Godhead was made up of three divine persons each standing in a 'Thou' relationship to the others and confronting man in distinguishable relations of the same kind? Against such a conception we found many weighty considerations, and we decisively rejected it as a tenable theory of the divine triunity. What then of the other alternative, that God was not merely uni-personal but uni-Personal? According to this, the Persons would possess the same status as attributes. They would not be *really* distinguished from each other by any incommunicable element or mutual opposition. The differences would be differences only relatively to us and to our way of looking at the matter. But the real distinction of 'I' over against 'Thou' at the Incarnation shows that then at any rate there was an element of incommunicability. And unless we are to remain content with an unbiblical modalism, which would rob the Incarnation of its value as a revelation of the eternal nature of God, we have to assume that such real distinctions represent permanent realities in the essential Godhead.

We then spent some time in examining the two alternative theories which claim to locate this element of incommunicability. The first, that it was to be found in the *opera Trinitatis ad extra* (external works of the Trinity), seemed to have little to commend it. The second, which placed it beyond our experience, in the eternal relations of origin of the Persons, went much deeper. Indeed, the Trinitarian doctrine of St Thomas, recently adopted in substance by K. Barth, provides a most convincing account of the relations of the three Persons to the one Essence. The fact that in the end we were obliged to reject the doctrine of relations in which they ground the Personal distinctions need not prevent us from embracing much of their theory. For as long as we are satisfied to preserve an agnosticism on the subject of the precise nature of the internal relations of the Trinity, we may express full agreement with a theory which both safeguards a *real* distinction or mutual opposition between the three Hypostases, and yet does not make them persons by conceiving their relation to each other and to man as one of 'I' to 'Thou'.

As a result of this discussion we are still left with the question from which we started: what is the relation of the divine personality to the divine Persons? If the latter are not constituted by the fact that they stand in 'I–Thou' relations, why are they called Persons at all? What is the justification of the use of the word *persona*? Clearly the use of the use of the terms 'person' and 'Person' as we have defined them is not univocal. But is it even analogical, or must we say that it is just equivocal? And, if the latter, is its retention not merely confusing?

This precise question was asked long ago by St Thomas. He too was concerned with the legitimacy of the word *persona* in Trinitarian theology. Had it the same meaning as when it was applied to human persons? Or if not exactly the same, at least a meaning sufficiently near to justify the employment of the same word? To understand the problem with which he was faced, and with which we are faced, it is necessary to go back in history yet a little further.

Though Boethius was working with a term which had long been in use in Trinitarian debate and had in fact already been fixed in meaning by credal and conciliar statement, it is nevertheless true that it is his definition of *persona* to which time and time again later writers return as their starting point. *Reperta personae est definitio: "naturae rationabilis individua substantia"* [A definition of person has been found: an individual substance of rational nature].' What is of immediate interest here is not so much the content as the context of these famous words. For they come from a discourse *Contra Eutychen et Nestorium*, III, and their immediate reference is not Theological but *Christological*. The *persona* that Boethius has particularly in mind is neither an eternal Hypostasis of the Trinity nor again an ordinary human being, but the divine-human Person of Christ. The significance of the context of the definition for the theory of human personality is not our present concern (cf. pp. 21–2 above). But for Theology it is as great as it is frequently ignored.

It seems to be generally assumed that the usage of the word 'Person' in the phrases 'the Person of Christ' and 'the Persons of the Trinity' is identical. But this is not at all evidently the case. For in the former instance the reference is to the Incarnate Christ, that is to say, to one who was living as a human personality in an 'I–Thou' relationship to God and men. In the latter case it designates an eternal Hypostasis of the divine nature, in which the idea of incarnation and the human 'I–Thou' relationship plays no essential part at all.

Before the word acquired any fixed definition *persona* could of course be used, and was used, to a considerable degree as the particular author desired or contemporary theological fashion dictated. It would clearly be a mistake to read Boethius' Christological definition into the Trinitarian statements of the earlier writers and then accuse them of tritheism. The precise terminology in which the new doctrine was to find safe expression was always a matter of embarrassment to the Church's theologians. And of all the words in the air, none was less fixed in its connotation than *persona*. In consequence, any attempt to say what the fourth- and fifth-century writers must have meant by it is extremely precarious.

Dr J. F. Bethune-Baker appends to his study of 'The Meaning of ὁποούσιος in the "Constantinopolian" Creed' some notes on the meaning of the principal Trinitarian terms. Of *persona* he writes that, in the matter of its history,

> it is first an actor's mask; and then by an easy transition the part the actor plays, which is represented by his mask, and so any part or rôle assumed by anyone without regard to its duration. It is secondly the '*condicio*' [situation], '*status*' [position], '*munus*' [function] which anyone has among men in general, and in particular in civil life. And so it is the man himself so far as he has this or that '*persona*'. Thus slaves, as not possessing any rights of citizenship, were regarded by Roman law as not having 'persona': they were ἀπρόσωποι [without a role/existence] or '*persona carentes*' [not recognized].

He summarizes the connotation of the term by saying,

> Even when it seems to be used very nearly in the sense of 'person' . . . it is always – even in such cases – a person looked at from some distinctive point of view, a person in particular circumstances; and the word conveys the notion much more of the environment than of the subject. (*Texts and Studies*, VII, 70)

Now this may be a true description of the meaning of *persona* in Trinitarian doctrine – indeed, it is surely what the orthodox must have wanted it to mean. But the fact that this same word could be used very soon afterwards in the Christological controversies in the sense which cannot be very different from the modern use of the word 'person', and certainly contains far more reference to the subject than his environment, indicates at least a broader meaning than Bethune-Baker allows for. It is only on a basis of a study of both the Trinitarian and the Christological uses that it is possible to come to any conclusion concerning the connotation of the word in ordinary speech and the extent to which its meaning required to be stretched in order to serve as a technical theological term.

To compare and contrast the two usages is both interesting and instructive. For in the different controversies theologians were attempting to use the one word *persona* for what in fact were two distinct concepts. In the former case the idea for which an expression was needed was the general nature of the three particular modes in which the one divine Essence existed. The subject in each of these was the one God himself: the Persons represented the different manners of partaking of this Essence, different ways in which the subject existed. What was indicated by the nominative was the Essence, God existing: *Persona* stood for a distinction which could only be expressed in the ablative or adverbially. '*Una substantia et tres personae*' must be interpreted as '*una substantia in tribus personis*'. It is not that the three Persons are three subjects who partake of a common nature (like three men): it is the *substantia* which is one subject existing in three modes of being. Dr Prestige has convincingly shown that the orthodox position was never that the divine *οὐσία* was an abstract generic nature in which the three Persons shared: it was a single and concrete substance identically expressed in each Person. *ὁμοούσιος* must be interpreted as implying, not merely similarity of nature, but identity of substance. The doctrine of the Trinity teaches 'one God in three Persons and not three Persons in one Godhead' (*God in Patristic Thought*, 281).

But in the Christological debates the situation was quite different. The entity for which the term *persona* was appropriated was something which could only be expressed in the nominative. It was the subject, the centre of personality, the unity of the self. It was opposed to the term *natura*, whose proper case was the genitive. Christ was one Person consisting of, or constituting the unity of, two Natures. Here it was the actual substantiality which was the essential element contained in the notion *persona*. In the case of the Trinity, substantiality, the fact of being a subject of a verb, was contained in the idea of Essence or Substance. *Persona* did not add another subject. In fact, its definition contained no reference to substance, but only to the way or mode in which the subject subsisted. Each *persona* was substantial or essential, in the sense that each Person *was* the one Essence, each was the whole God. But that in virtue of which *persona* was defined as *persona* as opposed to *substantia* was the peculiar *way* in which the one Essence existed.

Endless confusion arises out of the use of the term *persona* to cover both these concepts. In practice, of course, the definition of the word is silently changed as it is applied first to the one and then to the other. But those who made definitions thought they were making one which was constant throughout. Their definitions differ according to which concept they have primarily in mind when they are making it. Thus, that given by Dr Bethune-Baker is governed by the fact that it is formulated in a Trinitarian context. That of Boethius, in contrast, in which the ideal of 'individual substance' is dominant, arises from the fact that it is called forth by a Christological argument. He goes on indeed to apply it to Trinitarian theology, not imagining any discrepancy to be involved. But it is the other context which has decided the formulation. And through the universal adoption of Boethius' definition this situation was extended to subsequent theology. It meant that Trinitarian doctrine was to be discussed with its most crucial term defined in a foreign context.

It is probable that we should not be too quick to ask which of the two senses noted above – the Trinitarian or the Christological – was most faithful to the current use of the word in common speech. For the vulgar usage was to a large degree governed by the development of the ecclesiastical. Between the time when Tertullian first used the word *persona* in a Theological sense (*Adv. Prax.*, 7 etc.) and the mature reflections of a Boethius at the beginning of the sixth century, a new term had virtually been born. It was the period of the emergence for the ancient world of the concept of personality. At its opening the word *persona* conveyed little or nothing of what we mean by the idea. At its end there was produced a definition which was truly definitive. To it all subsequent definitions up to recent times have been but footnotes and comments, and Professor C. C. J. Webb goes so far as to describe it as 'still, perhaps, take it all in all, the best that we have' (*God and Personality*, 47). Between these two historical poles there was a very considerable development – a development conditioned almost entirely by the fact that the word had been taken out of the histrionic and legal contexts of its birth and brought up in the world of theological debate.

We may surmise a development something like this. *Persona* is chosen in the first place because it most fittingly indicates that each Hypostasis is God in a different character or capacity: each is the whole Essence in a different way of existence. The word draws attention, not to the subjecthood of each

Hypostasis, but to the modes in which the one God is subject. Its use as the translation of ὑπόστασις introduced new associations. The metaphor here was rather of the individual as giving concrete expression to the universal. The universal could only exist in the particular, and each particular was the complete embodiment of the universal. God had no existence outside and apart from the three Hypostases, and each Hypostasis was the whole God. The result was the same as in the *persona* metaphor. For the subject there had reality only as he was a subject in some particular character, in some particular relation; and yet each *persona* was the whole subject. But there was a subtle difference of emphasis and approach between the two ways of expression. The ὑπόστασις metaphor started from the individual instance and emphasized that this was the only form in which substance or subjecthood had any reality. The *persona* metaphor began with the one subject who was the constant factor in all the particular instances and stressed the adverbial nature of its various individual determinations. That there was such a difference of emphasis is shown by the long-standing mutual suspicion of the Eastern and Western theologians on this point of terminology. That the result of both could be shown to be the same is presupposed by their eventual acceptance as official equivalents.

It is this association with ὑπόστασις which Professor Webb regards as the crucial stage in the development of the word *persona*. Coloured by its contact with the Greek term, it acquired a 'substantial' connotation of which its origin gave no suggestion. Just as *persona* gave to ὑπόστασις the connection with 'rational nature' which it did not of itself possess, so ὑπόστασις contributed to *persona* the element of 'individual subsistence', which was necessary before Boethius' definition and the modern concept of personality could be born.

From thenceforward the path of advance was clear. It only required an emphasis on this new element of individual subjecthood to fit *persona* for its Christological use. But this was not the end of the story: the process of development was not yet complete. For it is possible to assume too easily that the idea of the 'Person' of Christ for the first writers on the subject was the same as that with which we are familiar. To us it stands for that psychological unity of the self which gave to the two natures concrete individuality and subjecthood. But the term *persona* was not adopted in the first place to supply a felt need for any such concept. It was not a question of finding a subject or centre of individuality for two general and abstract 'natures' and deciding that *persona* was the most fitting term to describe it. That was there, and the name was there – the ὑπόστασις or *Persona* of the Second Person of the Trinity. The problem was to combine this Hypostasis of the divine nature with manhood. The necessity for the difficult doctrine of anhypostatic humanity shows that the *Persona* or ὑπόστασις was not something that came into being as the result of the union and whose locus theology had to seek. It was there already – the ὑπόστασις of the Son, as the doctrine of the Trinity had defined it. For us the problem of the Person of Christ tends to present itself as the problem of how to find a single personal centre: for them the problem was how to avoid two. The opposite heresies of Apollinarius and Nestorius show how the form of the problem affected the solutions which failed to solve it. The personal centre was a datum from the beginning – the Hypostasis or Person of the Logos. The question was, how could the fact of manhood be united with this. If the humanity did not have its own hypostasis, it must, it seemed, be less than true humanity. If it did, how was a unity of personality to be preserved? The doctrine of ὑποστασία as finally formulated by Leontius of Byzantium, by which the hypostasis of the manhood – what made Christ *a* man – was fully contained in, and not merely replaced by, the Hypostasis of the Logos, given the form of the question, must be the only possible answer, however unsatisfying. It was the point from which the ancient writers started in their understanding of the personality of Christ which determined their whole treatment and their ultimate solution. We must make sure that we know what this was, or we shall misunderstand what they meant by *persona* in its Christological context.

The modern starting point for the doctrine of the Person of Christ tends inevitably to be the psychological unity of self-consciousness of the man Jesus. But the early Church did not thus begin with the human ego as 'an individual substance of a rational nature'. It was rather with the Hypostasis of the Second Person as Trinitarian dogma had defined it. The problem was how this mode of existence of the divine being could live in finite manhood. The new element which the Incarnation appeared to them to introduce was not, as it seems to us with our modern ideas of personality as a centre of self-conscious individuality, that of independent subjecthood in an 'I–Thou' relationship. It was rather what they described as περιγραφή (limitation) – the limitation by the finitude of the human body and its organs (cf. Dorner, *The Doctrine of the Person of Christ*, I, ii, 444). It is for this reason that they could use the word *persona* both for the Second Person of the Trinity and the Person of Christ without being conscious of any shift of meaning. It was not a case for them of a change from something which could properly be expressed only in the ablative to something essentially nominative. *Finitude, not subjecthood, seemed to them the most noteworthy fact about personality*. The change was therefore a change from the Logos infinite to the Logos bounded by human limitations. The divine Hypostasis remained the same: as impassible it could not be essentially changed or affected by the new form of its manifestation. To use *persona* without alteration of both its heavenly and its earthly state was, then, only natural and logical.

The mere fact of the transference of *persona* from its Trinitarian to its Christological context, therefore, does not constitute such a decisive transition as from our point of view we might assume it to be. This in itself does not bring us into the sphere of discussion in which Boethius' definition and the modern concept of personality are immediately relevant. Nevertheless, the final step in the development has in principle been taken. *Persona* is applied to a being, who, whether it was recognized as such from the beginning or not, *was* 'an individual substance of a rational nature', an 'I' in a 'Thou' relationship. Previously it did not have reference to what we mean by a personality: now it did. The realization of the implications of this for the definition of *persona* was only a matter of time. By the age of Boethius they had in principle all been drawn. We need not go into the process by which this end was reached. It is sufficient to point to the Nestorian approach to Christology to see a temper very different from that which was only interested in human personality as a limitation of the divine. And now that a word had been found for it, the fact that the concept of personality had for so long lacked a means of expression in both the Greek and Latin languages naturally had the effect of hastening the process of its final evolution.

But the question with which we began is still with us. The transition in the meaning of *persona* from its early Trinitarian to its later Christological sense may have shown itself historically explicable. And we may also be able to understand how an immature notion of the concept of personality obscured the extent of this change of connotation in such a way that the two senses were regarded as requiring but a single definition. But the fact remains that we can see they were far from univocal. In the course of time, one of them was bound to represent a usage further removed from that of common speech than the other. And of the two there can be no doubt which became the more specialized and technical term.

It is clear that St Thomas, in discussing the difference between *persona* in its *signification communis* (general usage) and its meaning in theology, identifies the former with the definition of Boethius. He at any rate, then, considered the sense which contained stress on the idea of 'individual substance' to be normative. It is also evident that Boethius too regarded his definition as in no way reflecting a specialized Christological usage. He had already defined *natura* in such a way as to indicate that he was using it in the general philosophical sense of the term.[62] He proceeds in the same way with the word *persona* and in Chapter IV of his treatise combines the two definitions: '*Natura est cujus libet substantiae specificata proprietas, persona vero rationabilis naturae individua substantia*' ('Nature is the specific property of any substance, but person is an individual substance of rational nature'). It is evident that he does not regard the two determining words of the Christological formula as being used in any peculiar or technical sense. *Persona* was for him the concrete individual subject or personal centre which gave to the generic term 'rational nature' its actual existence. The fact that in Christ's case this personal centre was the ὑπόστασις of *two* 'natures', humanity and divinity, in no way affected the meaning of *persona*.

If this was, at any rate from the time of Boethius onwards, the common and ordinary meaning of *persona*; if, in fact, it connoted very much more what we mean by 'person' than is usually credited; then the Trinitarian authors must for long have used the term in a very technical sense. For they could not have avoided tritheistic doctrine otherwise; and this they certainly did avoid.[63]

It is true that, at the time when the Trinitarian formula was being hammered out and its terms fixed, there was no such great discrepancy between the ordinary signification of the word *persona* and its Theological use. For it was indeed the latter which largely determined the former. But at least from the sixth century onwards the situation has been very different. The retention of the word in Trinitarian discussion has now to be prefaced by a careful statement that it does *not* mean what the definition of Boethius says it does. Moreover for us, on account of the preoccupation with the problems of the self which has characterized Western philosophy since Descartes, the implications of Boethius' definition have been drawn out in a direction which emphasizes still further the element of self-conscious subjecthood so inimical to the Trinitarian use. The gulf which separates this last from the common connotation of personality has been growing from the moment when *persona* was first applied to the Christological problem. Today it has reached such proportions as to lead us seriously to consider whether the retention of the term in the formulation of the Church's Trinitarian Theology is not considerably more misleading than illuminating. It is not because the doctrine itself has undergone any change that an alteration needs to be contemplated. It is rather to safeguard its abiding truth the more effectively that an archaic terminology may have to be revised.

It is significant that Dr Karl Barth, whose approach in many ways is very different from that pursued here, has come to ask himself exactly the same question. After a long discussion on the history and legitimacy of the use of *persona* in Trinitarian theology (*The Doctrine of the Word of God*, 408–11), he concludes that the word has now to be employed in such a specialized sense that it is better to drop it altogether. He is prepared, however, to regard the terminology as both valid and valuable up to a much later date than our previous conclusions would seem to justify. He sees the decisive change in the meaning of *persona* which rendered its use unsuitable as occurring with the introduction of the attribute of self-consciousness in the seventeenth century. We would say that it had in fact possessed the real element that disqualified it long before this date. In some form the idea of 'an individual centre of consciousness' had in principle attached to it ever since it had been used to designate the Person of Christ. What this fact of personality involves has indeed been made far more explicit in the modern period, beginning from Descartes and continuing through Kant and the nineteenth century. But the emphasis on self-consciousness only explicates what was long ago contained in the *individua substantia* and *rationabilis naturae* of Boethius' definition. This element which made its use in Trinitarian doctrine so dangerous, was present well before the modern period. We see Anselm having to deny what would naturally seem the logical implication of the choice of the term *persona*, namely, that '*omnes plures personae sic subsistunt separatim ab invicem, ut tot necesse sit esse substantias, quot sint personae*' 'thus all the separate persons subsist separately, so that it is necessary that there should be as many substances as persons' (*Monol.* 79). And that the term necessarily conveyed the idea of a separate centre of consciousness before Descartes may be seen from a definition of Melanchthon's, quoted by Barth himself: '*Persona est subsistens vivum, individuum, intellegens, incommunicabile, non sustentatum ab alio*' (Person is a substance that is living, individual, intelligent, which cannot be communicated, not supported by another) (*Exam. ordinand, C.R.* 23, 2). Barth admits that this 'has a somewhat suspicious ring' in connection with the doctrine of the Trinity, 'especially if we put beside it the fact that he was able to say likewise in the plural, *tres vere subsistentes . . . distinctes seu singulares intelligentes* [three intelligences truly existing distinctly or in a singular way] (*Loci, C.R.* 21, 613)' (*The Doctrine of the Word of God*, 411). Similarly Calvin stressed what J. Gerhard later called the '*magnum imo infinitum discrimen*' [great, indeed, infinite difference] (*Loci*, III, 62) between the divine Persons and the human:

> *Les anciens docteurs ont usé de ce mot de personne et ont dit, qu'en Dieu il y a trois personnes: Non point comme nous parlons en notre langage commun appelant trois*

> *hommes, trois personnes ou comme mesmes en la papauté ils prendront ce geste audace de peindre trois marmousets (mannikins) et voilà la trinité.* 'The ancient doctors used this word person and said that there were three persons in God; not as when in our common language when we speak denoting three men, three persons, where as in the papacy they can take this bold gesture to depict three mannikins, and that is the Trinity.' (*C.R.* 47, 473; quoted Barth, ibid., 410)

In the light of this clearly recognized discrepancy between Trinitarian and vulgar usage, we may now return to St Thomas's discussion of the relation between them. He states plainly that 'it is one thing to ask the meaning of this word "person" in general; and another to ask the meaning of "Person" as applied to God' (*S.T.* I, 29, iv). He admits that *persona* must be applied to God *eminenter*, 'not as it is applied to creatures but in a more excellent way' (29, iii), 'since nothing can be said univocally of God and creatures' (29, iv, 4). However, he is not prepared to concede that the two usages are completely equivocal. He will not agree with those 'who say that the definition of Boethius is not a definition of *persona* in the sense we use when speaking of Persons in God' (29, iii). His difficulty is that he has interpreted the differences between the Hypostases of the Trinity entirely in terms of relations. In God the Persons are the relations of origin and vice versa: '*Persona significat in divinis relationem* . . .' (When speaking of God, Persons means relationship . . .) (30, i). Yet in ordinary usage the word *persona* does not 'in itself refer to another (*ad aliquid dicitur*), as do the words which express relation' (29, iv). He admits that the idea of relation is not contained in the idea of a human or angelic person; but he still denies that the word Person is used of God in an equivocal sense (29, iv, 4). He seeks to demonstrate this by use of an illustration, but all that it succeeds in establishing is that there *are* points of similarity between the two usages, not that, on *this* point of relation, the senses are anything but equivocal.

St Thomas proceeds to try and show that the two usages, like all statements about God and men, are neither univocal nor equivocal, but analogical. He takes Boethius' definition of *persona* and corrects it where it is inapplicable to God. The point in it on which he definitely fastens for modification, as we have seen (p. 292), is the notion of individuality. This is applicable to the divine Persons only in the sense in which it indicates incommunicability. For normally it is matter which is the principle of individuation; and this is impossible in one who, as *actus purus*, is essentially *immaterialis*. In consequence he adopts (29, iii) Richard of St Victor's emendation of Boethius' definition. '*Rationabilis naturae individua substantia*' becomes when applied to God: '*Divinae naturae incommunicabilis existentia*' ('individual substance of divine nature' becomes 'the incommunicable existence of the divine nature') (Richard of St Victor, *De Trin.* iv, 18 and 23).

This revised definition, however, conceals a far greater alteration than that of individuality to incommunicability. A human person is a self-subsistent individual partaking of a common rational nature shared alike by all men. He is an individual substance (*substantia prima*) belonging to the species 'humanity' (*substantia secunda*), which constitutes the essence or nature of each individual. But the divine Persons are not related to the Godhead as a whole as men are related to humanity: this would be undisguised tritheism. The difference is that, whereas in men the *essentia* belongs to the *substantia secunda* (humanity) and the *existentia* to the *substantia prima* (the individual), in God *essentia* and *existentia* are one. *Persona* no longer describes a *substance* of *a* rational nature but a *subsistence* of *the* divine nature. In God the *substantia secunda* (*essentia*, *ὀυσία*) actually exists: it is not an abstract or generic term but concrete and specific. And *substantia prima* is not an independent subject or existent, but a way of existence of this one Essence. *Persona* is no longer an individual example of a general, but as such non-existent, concept 'humanity': it is a mode of subsistence of a single existing divine essence or personality. The Persons of the Trinity are not three 'I's' of the same nature, but three different modes of existence of the one 'I'. With the shifting of the property of independent personal existence from the *substantia prima* in man to the *substantia secunda* or *natura* in God, the whole meaning of personhood has changed.

Such is the difference between, on the one hand, not merely the modern usage of 'person' but also the classical philosophical use of *persona* and, on the other hand, the orthodox meaning of *persona* or Person in Trinitarian discussion, that it would seem better to give up using the term in the latter connection altogether. Many writers have admitted that they have employed it merely for lack of anything better. For Augustine such usage was a matter of *necessitas* or *consuetudo loquendi* (habit of speaking) (*De Trin.*, V, 9; VII, 4): its object was '*non ut illud diceretur, ed ne taceretur omnino*' (not that this should be said, but so that there should not be complete silence) (V, 10). Boethius himself envies the Greeks their word *ὑπόστασις* and confesses he would prefer to say *tres substantiae*, were it not for ecclesiastical usage (*Contra Eut. et Nest.* III). Anselm, following Augustine, speaks of the *ineffabilis pluralitas* (the plurality which cannot be spoken about) (*Monol.* 38) of the '*tres nescio quid*', and uses the term *persona* '*indigentia nominis proprie convenientis*' [for want of a truly appropriate name] (ibid., 79). Moreover, we have seen the difficulty of which St Thomas was conscious in his application of *persona* to what was really a distinction of relations. He admits that ὑπόστασις expresses the kind of subsistence he has in mind and says that it is only the fatal ambiguity of *substantia* which rules it out as a synonym for *persona*. He works with *persona*, but anything positive he has to say is drawn, not from the concept of 'person' but from that of internal subsistent relations.

From the point of view, then, of the 'classical' definition of *persona* and personality, the application of the term to the doctrine of the Trinity has little to commend it. What has to be described are forms of being which are distinguished, and solely distinguished, by the relation they bear to each other. Whether these, as St Thomas thought, are relations of origin or not, the term *persona* is clearly inappropriate. For it is defined in exactly the opposite way – not by reference to another, but rather in terms of self-existent independent subjecthood.

But what, if, as we have seen fit to do, we reject the 'classical' theory of personality as expressed in Boethius' definition? Have we not deliberately discarded it in favour of a concept which is explicitly defined in terms of relation? Could we not therefore find in the idea of 'person' just the concept required to characterize the three Hypostases of the Trinity? But this, as we have many times had occasion to see, is in fact impossible. It is true that we have defined personality in terms of relation; but it is in terms of one particular relation, the 'I–Thou' relationship. And though we are in a position to say nothing positive about the relations which differentiate the divine Persons, except that they are 'real', there is one thing we may definitely say by way of negation. They are not, and could not be, 'I–Thou' relationships. For that is the specifically human relation, that which makes man man. This relationship may indeed in some sense be the human equivalent of the divine relations, in that the incommunicability of the Persons has elected to express itself through it. But to describe their eternal divine nature, the idea of the 'I–Thou' relation is wholly inapplicable; and so, in consequence, is the word 'person', which is defined solely in terms of this relationship.

Barth, who appears throughout as the champion of orthodoxy, frankly rejects the term 'Person' as an answer to the question *quid tres*? (what sort of three?). He would reserve it to describe the one 'Thou' or 'I' who exists as personal Lord in this threefold form. 'The man who wishes to keep to it throughout will scarcely find another valid argument to put alongside the undoubtedly honourable position it holds by hoary ecclesiastical and scientific usage, save that he has not another better one to put in its place' (*The Doctrine of the Word of God*, 412). With this conclusion we are forced to agree. *Persona* may have its value as 'a practical abbreviation and as a reminder of the historical continuity of the problem' (ibid., 412). But its special usage in Trinitarian theology bears so little relevant similarity to the modern meaning of 'person', or even to any meaning the Latin *persona* bore outside it, that even as a form of technical shorthand it has little but practical indispensability to commend it.

If, then, we are to reject the word 'Person', or, rather, reserve it for the one Essence or personality of God, what are we to put in its place? There is still the question *quid tres*? There seems no reason to be dissatisfied with Barth's *Seinsweise* or 'mode of being', (τρόπος ὑπάρξεως). He produces a convincing defence of this concept, both historically and doctrinally (*The Doctrine of the Word of God*, 412–15),[64] and there is no need to restate his arguments. The main suspicion, of course, of which such a term must be able to clear itself, is that it involves a form of Sabellian doctrine. Evidence must be forthcoming that what is envisaged by the three 'modes of being' is not just three temporary or temporal manifestations of a God who is 'really' and eternally in himself an undifferentiated unity. It is not simply that the three must not be *successive* modes, as Sabellius asserted, but that they must not be *merely* modes at all. There must be no suggestion that the threefoldness attaches to an 'economic' Trinity alone, and that 'essentially' God is something quite different. To end with a few words on this subject will serve at the same time to relate the whole of this discussion on the Trinity to our general doctrine of God.

We have argued elsewhere that the distinction between the economic and the essential in reference to God is both unfortunate and misleading. It is true that the discrimination which it implies between the divine will and the divine nature has approved itself as useful in theological debate. We ourselves have in fact employed it in dissection whether the locus of Personhood in the Godhead was to be found in the 'opera Trinitatis ad extra' or elsewhere. We can and do differentiate between what God has done historically 'for us men and for our salvation' and what he eternally is in himself. What is so unfortunate and disastrous is that this distinction should be transferred from the realm of methodology to that of metaphysics. The suggestion then at once creeps in that the 'real' God is God-as-he-is-in-and-for-himself, abstracted from all reference to the world and his relation to it. It is in this eternal solitariness, we are told, that God's real nature is to be sought. His will, the reflection, of course, of his nature, is not grounded in it by any necessity of his being. That he created the world and lived and died in it reveals the quality of the love that he essentially is. But he might have done quite otherwise – he might never have created at all – and his essential nature would have been the same and remained unaffected. For the world, and the whole of the divine economy, is in no sense necessary to God. The essential deity can be defined without reference to it.

It is not necessary here to repeat the considerations which we adduced to show the insufficiency of this position. Enough to say in opposition that, from the thelematological point of view we have been adopting, there is no such distinction between being and will in God. His will is his nature. For God's being is being-in-relation, being in decisive action, being in love. God as considered 'in and for himself' out of this relation to other 'Thou's' and apart from his activity in his world is nothing but an abstraction. God as he reveals himself is God as he is essentially. His will is grounded in a necessity of his being: he could not do otherwise, just because he is the love which he is.[65] The *τρόπος ἀποκαλύψεως* (mode of revelation) *is* the *τρόπος ὑπάρξεως* (mode of being), and vice versa. There is no revelation which is not revelation of the Essence, and no Essence which is not existence-in-relation, -in-revelation.

It is thus alone that the status of the Persons can be properly understood. They are not modes in the sense that they are merely 'modes of revelation', behind which stands the real God as he is in himself, who is essentially not three but one. Nor are they 'modes of being' distinguished by mutual relations whose sole connection with this world is to be traced by means of somewhat improbable and far-fetched 'appropriations'. They are modes of being-in-relation, modes of the sort of existence which God has, modes of 'Thou' existence. Perhaps 'modes of loving' comes nearest to what is required. They are ways in which God is eternally personal. They differ from the attributes in that they are really mutually distinct. They are distinct not in character but in relation; and in such relation as when it appears in human guise cannot but take the form of the utterly personal meeting of 'I' and 'Thou'.

It is the 'Thou' relation of the Incarnation which must be the starting point of Trinitarian doctrine. We must take this revelation of the divine will *ἐν οἰκονομίᾳ* [in the economy] absolutely seriously. It is a revelation of God as he essentially is. If the Persons *could* be revealed as thus really mutually distinct, it was because, being what they were, they had to be. The revelation was grounded in a necessity of the divine being. It is this principle which forces us to our beliefs about the Trinity. Because of it we cannot say that the distinction of Persons in God is anything but real, essential and ineffaceable. Moreover, this revelation shows us that the distinction consists in one of mutual relation. It would force us too to go on to say that the relation was one of 'I' to 'Thou', if this was not clearly perceived to be in itself part of the conditions of revelation in manhood at all.

The one and only essential God is God in relation, God in revelation. This does not mean that God is only that which he has revealed himself to us as being, or only that which we have been able to grasp of him. That would be to make our own capacity for receiving it the measure of God's love. But it does mean that God has no other kind of being or reality than being-in-relation. His existence is essentially and only 'Thou' existence. That is what is meant by calling him personal. It is, then, in his self-revelation, and in particular through the revelation of the historical events recorded in the Bible, that we must seek to know his eternal nature. In that sense, the ground for the doctrine of the Trinity, if it is a real doctrine about God's essential being, must be sought in revelation, in the *opera ad extra*. But when we look at these we find for the most part no basis for any exclusive differentiation of Personal working. We find, it is true, a natural threefold division. God is seen to be working in three 'characters' – in creation, redemption and sanctification. But neither these nor any other divisions afford a ground for more than non-exclusive 'appropriations'. In this matter the classical writers were entirely right in refusing the hopeless, and dangerous, attempt to seek the Person-constituting element in the sphere of immediate experience.

But the alternative course was not to flee right away from the God as historically revealed and to take refuge in texts of Scripture which supposedly referred to the eternal 'private' life of the deity. The ground for a 'real' distinction of Persons is, and must be, that they have been *revealed* as really distinct. But they have been so revealed, not in their 'characters', which is always, for some reason, what is meant by the *opera Trinitatis ad extra*, but in their mutual relations at the Incarnation. There they are presented in the incommunicability of personal existence in the 'I–Thou' relationship. This is the basis for any real differentiation.

And yet this love-relationship cannot be transferred *simpliciter* into eternity. That is an illegitimate anthropomorphism and leads to tritheism. Herein consists the paradoxical relation of the Personal distinctions to the revelation of God. We know, and can only know, the Trinity as a trinity in revelation; for it is only 'in relation' that God exists. Whenever we meet God we meet the Trinity; for that is his 'name'. But it is only at the Incarnation that we know him as indisputably three. Only there is it that the 'real' difference, which is not a difference of 'character' but of relation, is revealed. Yet the relationship which reveals it is in itself the human relationship, and cannot be predicated as such of God. It is the translation into human language of the eternal mutual relations of the Persons. Yet these mutual relations, though not the object of direct human experience, are such as only exist in and for revelation. For the Persons which they constitute have only existence as modes of loving. To call them 'essential' as opposed to 'economic' relations is to obscure this. And it is a point which in consequence the classical writers miss. As a result they have great difficulty in linking the real Personal distinctions they find with any living experience of revelation. Their system of 'appropriations' contains little of religious value for the believer. It is for this reason that the opposition of 'essential' to 'economic' is so unfortunate. For there is nothing essential in God which does not *ipso facto* possess existence only *ἐν οἰκονομίᾳ*.

This last sentence may provide the note on which to close. The Christian doctrine of God is the doctrine of One who is eternally 'Thou'. The being of God is not something that can be treated as an 'It'. It is not 'pure', neutral being which can be discussed or proved without its making any demands on him who would investigate it. It is being in whose presence there is a judgment to be faced, a response to be made. The unity of God, as we saw (Ch. 14), is not a proposition to be demonstrated, but a commandment which impinges on every moment and aspect of a man's life. It is something which he has to acknowledge with the response of his whole being or not at all. To make this acknowledgment of the total sovereignty of God is the chief and only end of man. To fail to make it is quite literally his disintegration: for he cannot attain an internal reconciliation or preserve an integrity of personal existence in the face of an ultimate denial of the total claim which is the unity of God. No man can serve God and Mammon. To stand in the presence of the divine 'Thou' is to be presented with the choice of life and death. There can be no escape from this ultimate, exclusive and finally disjunctive Either-Or. Such is the seriousness of the issue with which we have to treat.

The doctrine of the Trinity is nothing other than the inner meaning of the divine unity, the name of the eternal 'Thou'. If the doctrine of the Trinity does not lead to a personal acknowledgment of this name, of this total claim, if it is just so much speculation about a deeply fascinating theological problem, then it is nothing less than sin to touch it. For to regard it thus is a breach of the Third Commandment: it is to take the name of God in vain, to treat the eternal 'Thou' as an 'It'. This may seem a hard saying. But it is only to take seriously the fact that what we have been discussing from beginning to end has been a 'Thou'. And one cannot merely discuss a 'Thou'. Either one judges it and thereby transforms it into an 'It'; or one must allow oneself to be judged by it. The Hebraic witness was that 'our God is a consuming fire' (Heb. 12:29). He remains even in our speculation 'him with whom we have to do' (Heb. 4:13).

The revelation of the Trinity is but another way of stating the fact of the gospel. It is that which enables man to make the total response of faith and obedience to the One Lord of his life which is reconciliation and redemption. In the words of the Collect for Trinity Sunday, it is only by 'acknowledging the glory of the eternal Trinity' that we may 'worship the Unity'. If speculation on the nature of the Persons does not run out into such acknowledgment and worship of a Person, then it is clear that the Essence whose modes of being they are has been regarded as something other than the centre of consuming love which is the Christian God.

NOTES

Chapter 1

1 Bevan also makes the interesting observation that Epicureanism and Stoicism represented two rival rationalists. The one argued that the ascription of personal qualities to the directing powers of the universe must imply the existence of personal deities. The other, while agreeing with the necessity for the ascriptions, denied the implication in the interests of science, which seemed to provide no evidence for such personal forms.

2 It is proposed throughout to make a distinction between two senses in which the word 'theology' is commonly used. It may refer, generally, to that discipline or science whose data are the facts of revelation, and in that sense it is comparable with the other sciences and stands in a similar relation to philosophy. But it may also refer, more particularly, to the doctrine of God, in the strict sense of the term. When employed with this connotation it will be written with an initial capital. This may also serve to bring it into line with its parallel department of Christian doctrine, Christology.

3 For a positive discussion of the meaning of the Augustinian and similar formulae, see below Ch. 16. Here we are only concerned to state that they are not inspired by a consciousness of our immediate problem, even though they may have been employed in this connection by recent writers. One of these writers has himself made this perfectly clear: cf. C. Gore, *Belief in God*, 1921, 70.

4 It may be of interest to record some of the later stages in this process. What follows is not intended to be anything like an exhaustive list, but simply a selection of passages from some fairly representative English authors who have touched on the subject.

B. F. Westcott, *The Epistles of St John*, 1883, additional note 2 on 1 Jn 5:20. 'The words "God is love . . ." must hold good of God in His innermost Being, if we may so speak, apart from creation. Now love involves a subject and an object and that which unites both. We are taught then to conceive of God as having in Himself the perfect object of love and the perfect response of love, completely self-sufficing and self-complete. We thus gain, however imperfect language may be, the idea of a tri-personality in an Infinite Being as correlative to a sole-personality in a finite being.' But there is no attempt here to use this as a philosophical argument, and the passage cannot therefore be quoted as evidence for a consciousness of the problem at issue.

A. J. Mason, *The Faith of the Gospel*, 1888, 43–6; (1892 3rd edn), 56–9, remarks that, to avoid the conclusion of pantheism that God gradually comes to know himself by means of the world, 'it would appear reasonable to postulate that God contains in His own being both subject and object'. God is set off by something in his own nature, by an eternal reproduction of himself. This reflection of himself must be adequate to his being – not a lifeless image, but a 'Thou'; 'and God in turn must be a "Thou" to that which reproduces Him'. And it must be equal to him: nothing but God can represent God. But there must also be a bond between the 'I' and the 'Thou' – itself a Person; since that which mediates and interprets one to the other cannot be less than either. This is an essential part of the Divine nature: 'it is a vital process in the very being of God, without which he cannot be conceived as existing'.

J. R. Illingworth, *Personality, Human and Divine* (1894). To the argument that personality implies a contrast between the ego and the non-ego, and, therefore, a limitation of God by something outside himself, he quotes Lotze with complete agreement, summarizing in the words: 'The function of the non-ego, in short, on human personality, is not to define its circumference, but to stimulate its activity' (244). The contention is that, since God requires no such stimulus, he has need of no such 'other'. But he adds, 'At the same time it is obvious that the Christian doctrine of the Trinity, with the possibilities of Divine self-determination which it involves, is a further assistance towards the conception of a Personality which is at once Infinite and yet definite' (244). He goes on to cite Victorinus Afer, Irenaeus and Origen. But the passages quoted have reference entirely to the delimitation of the Father by the Son (*mensura Patris Filius*), not to the necessity for the existence of a reciprocal relationship. Illingworth makes no reference to the idea of the Trinity as a divine society; nor indeed does he appear to be any more concerned than Lotze with the problems raised by the fact that personality only appears to exist, not merely in relation to some object (the not-self), but in relation to other *persons*.

R. C. Moberly, *Atonement and Personality*, 1901, 164–5. Love must have an 'other' and this, in the case of the divine, implies the existence of mutual relationships within the Godhead. 'I am not sure that this is not the one thing in respect of Divine Personality of which we can with the most unfailing certainty be said to have a real intellectual grasp.' As a matter of fact it is a position which Moberly assumes rather than argues. There is a leap in the conclusion of his syllogism: love only exists in relation: God is love: therefore there are relations *within the Godhead*. (And why necessarily more than one relation?)

W. Temple, *The Nature of Personality*, 1911: 'I must dismiss altogether the argument which urges that in the Godhead, conceived apart from the Creation, there must be Personal distinctions, because otherwise God could not be Love.

This argument maintains that God is Love, and Love requires an object; therefore there must be at least a second Person to be the object of the Love and to return it' (113). This position he accuses of 'sheer Tritheism'. To the argument that knowledge of the self is only reached by distinction from the not-self, he maintains that it is not necessary to regard this condition as valid for God: direct self-knowledge is not an absolute impossibility (86). He agrees that persons only exist in relation to other persons; but he finds no insuperable difficulty in this, since he is not prepared to uphold a doctrine of creation 'in time', nor obliged therefore to assume a situation in which God was ever alone (87, 98).

C. Gore, *Belief in God* (70). He states the problem of the solitary existence of a personal God of love, saying that the Church found the doctrine of the Trinity 'the solution of the intellectual difficulty', although it had originally been formulated in quite another connection. Gore concurs in this solution without question. On the basis of the evidence we have been able to gather 'the Church' is certainly an imposing name for a far from unbroken tradition of less than half a century.

Chapter 2

5 It is worth noting how traditional Catholic doctrine, working with the 'classical' presuppositions, distinguishes in man between the *imago Dei* and the *similitudo Dei*. The former, which represents the 'essence' of man, which he cannot lose without ceasing to be man, is constituted by his freedom and rationality. The latter, which is defined in terms of the relationship in which he exists towards God, may be lost through sin *without in any way affecting his essential humanity*. For a more acceptable statement of the doctrine of the *imago Dei*, cf. Ch. 5 below.

Chapter 3

6 There is an interesting confession by one whose 'classical' definition we have had occasion to quote above, that the egocentric predicament which it creates is in fact inescapable. 'The other', he writes, 'towards whom I feel and act, is thus completely outside me, a non-ego: how then can I come to him or he to me? A person is, by definition, essentially a totality whose actions are directed towards the ends of its own being: how then can my activities pass beyond myself and have reference to the ends of a person whose being and activity lies totally outside my own boundaries?' (W. Stern, *Die menschliche Persönlichkeit*, 48). Stern's own solution is in effect to abandon the individual in favour of supra-individual social units and to substitute a kind of organic union for personal communion.

7 E.g.: J. Baillie, *Our Knowledge of God*, 1939, 201–18; D. L. Scudder, *Tennant's Philosophical Theology*, 1940, Ch. II. Cf. also J. Cook Wilson, *Statement and Inference*, II, 853, 1926; C. C. J. Webb's British Academy Lecture, *Our Knowledge of One Another*, 1930, and his *Divine Personality and Human Life*, 1920, 182; W. E. Hocking, *The Meaning of God in Human Experience*, 1912, Chs XVII–XXI; *God Transcendent*, 84–90, 171–2, 1935.

8 That is to say, it has always historically been associated with it. The absence from the history of philosophy of attention to the problem of our knowledge of others testifies to its dominance. For, according to this theory, there is no peculiar problem here at all, simply because there is not held to be involved a third kind of knowledge over and above our consciousness of ourselves and our knowledge of the external world. Knowledge of other selves is simply a question of combining these other two forms of awareness. In Fichte's words '*der Begriff des Du entsteht durch Vereinigung des Es und des Ich*' ['the concept of the Thou comes into being through the union of the I and the It'].

But there is no *necessary* connection between the 'classical' theory of personality and the view that we only have indirect knowledge of others. It would be quite possible for it to assert that as well as immediate consciousness of ourselves we possess a direct form of intuition of the existence of other such centres, which does not make the process of analogy unnecessary, but which renders it possible. Thus, to take a parallel example, unless we possessed a three-dimensional form of intuition, the familiar optical illusion produced by cubes drawn on a flat surface would simply be pointless. It would never occur to us to imagine that there was a third dimension, and no amount of inference from squares would produce cubes. In the same way, no amount of inference from objects within my own presentational continuum, from the world of my own peculiar possession, could lead to the supposition of another centre of awareness, the very existence of whose world is a challenge to my own, which I must suppose to be unique. What we are asked to credit is that what has hitherto been as it were just a point on the circumference of the subject's presentational field, '*ein Stück Welt*' – a piece of his world – is transformed, *merely* as a result of a closer analysis of this world, into an active centre of a world of its own, in which *he* himself is but one peripheral object. But, given this dimension of awareness, analogical inference is both possible and necessary in order to fill its content. This would be a perfectly reasonable account of how we come to know other selves. But the assumption would still remain that knowledge of ourselves is prior to, or at least independent of, that of others. The 'classical' theory asserts that the self can be defined in terms of itself and that relationship to others forms no part of its essence. An ideal solipsism is always presupposed. For if a person is so defined, then there must always be the possibility that he could be a person even if he knew no other. The fact of self-consciousness, which is the peculiar characteristic of personality, cannot therefore under any circumstances be made to depend on a relation to some 'other'.

9 There arises here the recurrent problem as to how much in Plato is really Socrates. On this point, however, it appears possible to be more than usually confident. That the dialectical method was invented and employed by Socrates himself seems to admit of no reasonable doubt. Besides the *Phaedo* we have the evidence of Xenophon of the effect of this method on his contemporaries (*Memorabilia*, iv, 6). Above all, there is the charge – made in jibe by Aristophanes in the *Clouds*, and brought up with more bitter intent at the trial – that his constant aim was 'to make the worse appear the better case'. This contains clear reference to his conviction that there are two sides to every argument and that truth can only be reached as the conclusion of a debate. Professor A. E. Taylor is confident in tracing the dialectical method to Socrates himself (see his book *Socrates*, 1939, 156–62).

If this connection is established, it may not be fantastic to draw a further inference. It was noted in the previous chapter that on the whole it has been those with a truly personal knowledge of God who have contributed most to the understanding of human personal relationships. Is it a coincidence that he in the ancient world who alone appeared to have any appreciation of the significance of the latter also comes before us as a man who stands out from his age in being aware of an experience of the divine which was in its degree genuinely and intensely personal? Socrates' experience of what he called his 'daimonion' (on this, cf. N. Söderblom, *The Living God*, 1933, 237–45) was something which, because of its personal nature, could not be fitted into the current theological schemes. It seems as far removed from the newer mystery religions as it was an offence to the traditional Olympian cultus.

It should be noted also that it is equally an offence to the Socratic-Platonic theology itself. The system of 'Ideas' is quite incapable of including or explaining such experience of personal communication and revelation. In the light of what was said in the last chapter we may note the gap that had to be filled in the elaboration of a theory of human personality before such an awareness of the divine could be matched by a correspondingly personalistic Theology.

10 There are of course passages in Plato in which God seems to occupy the same position as that enjoyed by the Idea of the Good, say, in the well-known passage in the *Republic* (vi, 505ff.), where the Good is said to be to the intelligible world what the sun is to the physical, in whose light everything else exists and is viewed. But it would appear that this represents little more than a difference of terminology. It is doubtful whether Plato attached much significance to the change. For the emphasis in the word θεός (God) remained on the idea of perfection rather than on the idea of personality. 'To the Greek philosopher the perfection and unity of God was a far higher conception than His personality, which he hardly found a word to express, and which to him would have seemed to be borrowed from mythology' (B. Jowett, *The Dialogues of Plato*, 1875, ii, 149). What is under discussion is what Jowett paraphrases as the 'intelligent principle of law and order in the universe, embracing equally man and nature'. It is

generally safe to say that when this is conceived as energizing primarily teleologically as a final cause (as in the *Republic*), it goes under the name of the Good; when the reference is primarily cosmological, that is, to a first cause (as in the *Timaeus* and the *Laws*, Book X), then we read of God or the Gods. Certainly there is no suggestion that moral values can only exist in the mind of a person, and that therefore the Idea of the Good requires a foundation in a personal God. Perhaps we may see a parallel here with Kant's conception of the Moral Law. To look upon this 'as if' it were the voice of God is a harmless and even, for the religious man, a necessary step. But this is not to say that the Moral Law requires a basis in a personal will for its existence or authority. God may be regarded as the 'Lawgiver', but never as the 'Author' of the Moral Law (Kant, *Lectures on Ethics*, 1930, 51). As a 'rational being' it is binding on him also, though not, of course, in the form of an obligation. 'In the case of God the subjective laws of His divine will are one with the objective laws of the good will in general, but God's subjective law is no ground of morality. God is Himself good and holy because His will conforms to this objective law' (ibid., 24). In this line of thought we are not far removed from those passages in Plato where God is spoken of as a *ψυχή* (soul), and this as being on a lower level of reality than the Idea of the Good.

11 This unlikely source for a philosophy of personality (Feuerbach's most famous saying is the somewhat unpromising formula, '*der Mensch ist nur was er isst*' – a man is only what he eats) has now been widely recognized for its importance in the history of the 'Thou'. Professor Hans Ehrenberg who re-edited his *Grundsätze der Philosophie der Zukunft* in 1922 acclaims him in his introduction as the 'discoverer' of the 'I–Thou' relation. His chief references to it are to be found in the last section of this work, but already in 1839, in his *Critique of the Hegelian Philosophy*, he had used the same terms and suggested the same line of thought. For other references to Feuerbach in this connection, cf. H. Ehrenberg, *Disputation*, 1923, I (Fichte), 165–8; J. Cullberg, *Das Du und die Wirklichkeit*, 1933, 31–4; M. Buber, *Zwiesprache*, 72; N. Berdyaev, *Spirit and Reality*, 1939, 170.

12 For further details of this circle, and especially of the activities of Buber and Rosenzweig, Lev Giluet's *Communion in the Messiah* (1942) may be consulted. Some light is also thrown there on the important influence of the form of Jewish pietistic mysticism known as Chassidism (Hasidism) on Buber's thought (see, especially pp. 141–7). Cf. also: H. Kohn, *M. Buber, Sein Werk und seine Zeit* and W. Michel, *M. Buber, Sein Gang in die Wirklichkeit.*

Chapter 4

13 It is interesting to note how the division among the school of 'Thou-philosophers' runs. The difference of usage, however, is not recognized by the writers themselves, and is therefore not always very precise. On the side of

Buber in regarding the 'I–It' relation as in some sense an 'objectification' of a more primal 'I–Thou' attitude to the whole of reality are E. Grisebach (*Gegenwart: ein kritisches Ethik*, 1928) and N. Berdyaev (especially *Solitude and Society*, ET 1938; cf. *Spirit and Reality*, ET 1939). But even here there is a difference from Buber. The 'It' is indeed a deposit of the 'Thou' relation, but this latter is conceived almost exclusively in terms of the meeting of two persons. Cf., for example, the passage from Grisebach's *Gegenwart*, 148–9, quoted on pp. 63–4 and also Berdyaev's *Solitude and Society*, 90–7, where the terms 'other Ego' and 'the Thou' are used interchangeably. But elsewhere (ibid., 112–13, 187–8) Berdyaev does speak of real 'communion' with nature and animals.

K. Heim (*Glaube und Denken*, 1931/1934 3rd edn, ET *God Transcendent*, 1935) is inconsistent. On the one hand his fundamental distinction between the 'dimension' of the 'Thou' and that of the 'It' definitely refers to the difference between our dealings with other selves and with things. Thus, to be a 'Thou' by definition involves the power of being conscious of oneself as over against the not-self; 'Because . . . you also live in a world which is contrasted with yourself, I can employ this word "Thou" in addressing you. If it were otherwise I could as easily speak about you as an "It" ' (*God Transcendent*, 81). Yet he seeks to combine with this usage a conception of the 'It' world as something past, objectified and static. He definitely identifies the realm of things with the past world of what 'has become' (see Ch. IV, Sec. 17, esp. p. 125). (This identification inevitably involves him in epistemological difficulties. See Note 16 below). But whereas in Buber the creative 'present' is bound up with, and gains its metaphysical significance from, the fact that the 'I' is in the 'presence' of a 'Thou', in Heim there is no direct connection between the world of 'becoming' and the dimension of the 'Thou'. *Temporal* presence is alone of importance – that is, the fact that the course of events is not yet fixed and decided. But the spiritual ancestor of this idea is not Buber but Bergson. Heim's two points of view afforded by 'knowing' and 'willing' correspond exactly with Bergson's distinction between the functions of the 'intellect' and the 'intuition'. The significance of the 'present' lies not in the fact that it is associated with the meeting of 'I' and 'Thou' (i.e., with the fact that it is being created by *persons* in relationship with each other or the world), but just in the circumstance that it is not static but continually in the melting-pot of decision. 'However this decision may come about, whether through conscious Will, or unconscious impulse, or by some completely different way unimaginable by us, at any rate something is really decided' (*God Transcedent*, 183). This reads like mere activism for its own sake: as long as something is happening, it does not matter much whether personal values are being realized or not.

Those writers who definitely identify the 'Thou' and the 'It' with persons and things, though not, of course, denying the possibility of treating 'Thous' and 'Its', are more numerous. F. Ebner (*Das Wort und die Geistigen Realitäten*, 1921) must be placed in this category, since he has no conception of a 'Thou' relation to things. He does, however, have much to say which is very similar to Buber on the objectification which follows the abstraction of the knowing 'I' from its context of relation to the 'Thou'; Ehrenberg (*Disputation*, 1923): 'Only between "I" and "It" is there no speech; a person and a thing cannot speak with each other' (I, 183): F. Gogarten (*Ich glaube an den dreieinigen Gott*, 1926, and *Glaube und Wirklichkeit*, 1928); E. Brunner (especially *Der Mensch im Widerspruch*, 1937: ET, *Man in Revolt*, 1939; and *Wahrheit als Begegung*, 1938: ET, *The Divine-Human Encounter*, 1944); K. Löwith (*Das Individuum in der Role des Mitmenschen*, 1928); Max Scheler, also from within the Phenomenological school, had given a 'non-analogical' analysis of our knowledge of other selves in the 1923 edn of his *Wesen und Formen der Sympathie*. But this was all in terms of the 'Fremd–Ich', which Löwith saw to be very different from the 'Thou', who is the 'other I' *when he is being addressed*; Cullberg (*Das Du und die Wirklichkeit*, 1933); J. Baillie (*Our Knowledge of God*, 1939); H. H. Farmer (*The World and God*, 1942. In Ch. X of *The World and God*, he adopts a 'Bergsonian' distinction between present fluidity and past fixity to account for the compatibility of miracle with natural law, but he makes no attempt to connect this with the difference between 'Thou' and 'It', thereby avoiding the pitfalls into which Heim falls. The use which he permits himself of the phrase 'an "It–It" relationship' in *World and God* (1942) (p. 35) is an indication of how far he has moved from Buber, for whom an 'It' is only constituted by the fact that it stands in a certain relation to an 'I').

In recent years reference to the 'Thou' has become too widespread to chronicle. The editor (Alec Vidler) of *Theology* has gone so far as to say: 'Almost every theological book or periodical that is published nowadays contains . . . some reference to the "I–Thou" relationship' (May 1945). Suffice it to say that it is the second of the two usages we have noted which has gained almost exclusive possession of the field. This seems a pity.

14 The context of this line reveals, however, that, like Lotze, he is thinking entirely in terms of the not-self rather than the 'Thou':

> The Baby new to earth and sky,
> What time his tender palm is prest
> Against the circle of the breast,
> Has never thought that this is I:
>
> But as he grows he gathers much,
> And learns the use of 'I' and 'me',
> And finds I am not what I see,
> And other than the things I touch.
>
> So rounds he to a separate mind,
> From whence clear memory may begin,
> As through the frame that bounds him in,
> His isolation grows defined.
>
> (Tennyson, *In Memoriam*, xliv)

This is quoted in F. D. Maurice's lectures on *The Conscience*, 1868 (Lect. I, 'On the Word "I" '). I find it hard to see with Mr A. R. Vidler, to whom I owe the reference (*Theology*, May 1945), that Maurice is of very great significance for the history of the 'Thou'. The terminology occurs in his *Social Morality*, 1869, 2, 115, 124, but there is little more. Much more impressive from an English author a few years later is the passage from A. J. Mason already quoted (Note 4) on the subject of the internal relations of the Trinity: 'That which truly reproduces God must be to Him, not "It", but "Thou"; and God in turn must be "Thou" to that which reproduces Him' (*The Faith of the Gospel*, 44).

Chapter 5

15 Even the utilitarian value of such an idea of God may be seriously questioned. Beside Laplace's famous retort to Napoleon we may set this confession from Miguel de Unamuno: 'When as a boy I began to be disquieted by the eternal problems, I read in a book, the author of which I have no wish to recall, this sentence: "God is the great X placed over the barrier of human knowledge – as science advances the barrier recedes". And I wrote in the margin: "On this side of the barrier, everything is explained, either with or without Him; on the further side, nothing is explained, either with or without Him. God, therefore, is superfluous". And so far as concerns the God-Idea, the God whose existence is supposed to be logically proved, I continue to be of the same opinion' ('Creative Faith', tr. J. E. Crawford Flitch in *Essays and Soliloquies*, 1925, 217).

16 Berdyaev fails to grasp the significance of symbols for personality, and regards their use as a sign of a defective form of communication. Symbols are condemned as part of the 'objective' world of 'It' and superfluous in true (mystical) communion. There seems to be a confusion here between objects in the sense of 'things' and objects in the sense of the results of the process of 'objectification' (cf. p. 132 above). The symbol (e.g., the word) is essentially something that can be both an 'It' and a revealer of a 'Thou'. If it were always an 'It', then Berdyaev's criticism would be valid and it could never be the medium of real knowledge. If it were always a 'Thou', then it could not perform the concealing function which is necessary for a *personal* revelation. Heim (*God Transcendent*, 167–70) has a clear grasp of the significance of this dual character of the word as symbol. Yet this insistence on the necessity for some meeting point for the 'I' and 'Thou' within the objective world is inconsistent with his view that 'objects' can only exist as the result of such a meeting having taken place.

17 This idea (perhaps most concisely formulated in the words 'We are what we hear from God') is fundamental to Brunner's thought and finds a place in many of his works. A number of quotations from them have been collected by John Baillie and are to be found on pp. 28–9 and 42 of *Our Knowledge of God*. Ebner had already described man's essence as his addressability, *Ansprechbarkeit* (*Das*

Wort und die geistigen Realitäten, 18), and said that only he who has the word from God is a real man: 'God made man in that He spoke to him' (26). Berdyaev in *The End of Our Time*, 1933, and *The Fate of Man in the Modern World*, 1935, has worked out the same idea with reference to the practical consequences of its denial. He elaborates the thesis that 'man without God is no longer man' of modern humanistic civilization of the high ideals for emancipated humanity preached at the Renaissance and the French Revolution.

Chapter 6

18 There is clearly a distinction to be drawn between the theoretical and practical application of the 'instrumental' relation to persons. Scientific psychoanalysis with a view to the establishment of more satisfactory personal relationships is obviously on a different ethical plane from the relation to a person which *consists* in psychological manipulation. The former is a conscious temporary abstraction from the personal relationship for the sake of that relationship. The latter is a deliberate substitution of the 'instrumental' for the 'personal' way of working in the relationship itself. There is always the danger that the psychoanalyst may come to regard his subject as if he or she were purely the sum of the laws he is studying and nothing more. In which case he is forgetting the abstraction upon which his science rests, and is liable to let his impersonal dealings take the place of the relationship which alone gives them justification.

Exactly the same applies in the case of the infinite Person. It is quite legitimate that we should make the abstraction from the relationship to the eternal 'Thou' in which all knowledge of God is given, and stand back from him and talk *about* him (though remembering that, unlike other people, he is always present when we are discussing him in the third person). Such theological reflection, examination and analysis is quite essential if we are to establish a relation to God which is as true and complete as we can make it, and if we are also to be in a position to articulate and communicate our religion to others. It is, indeed, inevitable that thus to treat as 'It' what is essentially 'Thou' will to some extent be to falsify. Brunner has described the sort of distortions which attach to the attempt to comprehend the God-relation under the 'subject–object' antithesis of 'It' knowledge (*The Divine-Human Encounter*, Ch. IV). These will be particularly evident in discussions which revolve around the fact of freedom (doctrines of grace, election, universalism, etc.), which is necessarily foreign to the world of 'It'. Logical completeness here falsifies: theology must be content to leave the antinomy without attempting to resolve it. It has to accept that in these matters paradox is not a concession but a category. But though abstract theology is bound to be inadequate to what it describes, and for correction must continually be being referred to the point of meeting and decision, it remains legitimate and necessary. It only partakes of the nature of sin when it becomes the substitute for religion, when the God of doctrine becomes the object of the relationship itself and faith is understood as assent to a confession or creed.

19 This is bound up with Macmurray's whole conception of religion, which is regarded purely as an activity of the human spirit. It is that activity in which man is most fully rational, when his personality goes out to meet and be met by a rationality equal to his own. It is essentially continuous with the process of acting in terms of the nature of the object as it expresses itself also in science and art. Science represents the 'proper' objective relation to the world when the object is the material order; or rather, it is the relation to the whole in so far as it can be treated as a mechanical system (it includes biology and psychology as well as chemistry or physics). Its rationality consists in the fact that it is a serious attempt by man to relate himself to the object in terms of *its* nature and laws, and not, as in magic, in accordance with the wishes or designs of the subject. Art is the 'proper' relation to reality as conceived organically. The connection here is not immediately evident, but it would divert us too much to examine the grounds of this identification. Lastly, religion is the rational relation to the world of persons, in which the full mutuality of reciprocal communion is achieved.

The question which it naturally occurs to ask here is what has become of God, who, one would think, should appear in any definition of religion. Macmurray answers: 'God is the infinite ground of all finite phenomena in the personal field – and, therefore, ultimately of all phenomena whatever – but the knowledge of God is possible only through the empirical phenomena of personal relationship. In any particular relationship of persons, if it is truly personal, God is known, as that which is partially, but never completely, realised in it' (*Reason and Emotion*, 209–10). Now Buber would fully agree that God can be known only in and through the finite 'Thou' relations of a man's historical existence, of which the mutual personal relation is the chief channel of revelation. But he would also strongly assert that God was himself a 'Thou' over and above, and 'other' than, any finite 'Thou'. Macmurray's conception of the divine could not unfairly be summed up in some old words of the elder Pliny: '*Deus est mortali adjuvare mortalem*' – this *is* God when one mortal helps another (*Nat. Hist.* ii, 18; quoted by C. C. J. Webb, *God and Personality*, 1920, 71). It is really an impersonal view of God. For he is not a Being who can enter into personal relations with men, albeit only through the media of finite relations. He is a mere universal with which we become acquainted through individual personal relations, exactly parallel in reality-status (to use his own illustration) to the general concept of 'matter', which science is bound to postulate, though it can know nothing of it except as it finds concrete expression in individual instrumental relations. And such reality-status, in Macmurray's philosophy, is nil; for 'reality is always something in particular' (*Reason and Emotion*, 165).

In a later work, MacMurray's *The Structure of Religious Experience*, 1936 (79–81 – the only paragraph in which God finds a mention!), he denies that

God is similar to the universals of science, in that, in the mutuality of personal relationships, the self is the object as well as the subject of observation of his world. In the religious universal he meets someone who stands over against him. But this 'universal Other' who stands in a 'universal relation' to the self remains nothing over and above the particular 'others' met in individual relationships, though, *qua* universal, it may be encountered in all of them. A 'universal relationship' is nothing in itself. The 'Other' is not an individualized Being with a purpose and will of his own. There can be no place for particularized divine initiative, no providence, no revelation. There is, in consequence, no one to whom I can owe a responsibility which is not just that required of me by the strictly equal nature of the human being whom I encounter.

Chapter 7

20 The 'Thou' relation, like Christian *ἀγάπη* (love) which is its norm, does not depend upon a response in order to be itself. 'Even if the man to whom I say "Thou" is not aware of it in the midst of his experience (*Erfahrung*), yet relation (*Beziehung*) may exist' (Buber, *I and Thou*, 9). It is ever seeking response and is fulfilled in that response, yet it is not destroyed if it is not forthcoming. It is because a man is what *God* 'says' to him, rather than what *he* 'says' to God, that his humanity is ever preserved.

21 Purely mental relationships may be excluded from consideration here. It is hard to see that a brick is any different from the fact that I am thinking about it or that *to me* it is to the left or right of some other brick. At the same time, the fact that it has another brick beside it does make it, however slightly, different from what it would have been without it, by virtue of the force of pressure exercised upon it. This, as opposed to the mental relationship can be included among the mechanical determinations which make it what it is.

Chapter 8

22 Cf. Kierkegaard, *Training in Christianity*, 127: 'Unrecognisableness, the absolute unrecognisableness, is this: being God, to be also an individual man. To be the individual man, or an individual man (whether it be a distinguished or a lowly man is here irrelevant), is the greatest possible, the infinitely qualitative, remove from being God, and therefore the profoundest incognito.' He has a nice reference to those who 'by force of lecturing . . . have transformed the God-Man into that speculative unity of God and man *sub specie aeterni*, manifested, that is to say, in the nullipresent medium of pure being, whereas in truth the God-Man is the unity of God and an individual man in an actual historical situation' (ibid., 123).

23 There is no equivocation here. For 'the individual' (in Kierkegaard's sense of the term), although it means more than a particular historical existent, always includes this connotation. An 'impersonal' Man could not exist in an 'I–Thou' relation.

Chapter 9

24 All references to the *Summa Theologica* will be shortened as follows: *S. T.* Pt. I, Qu. XXXVIII, Art. 2 will read 'I, 38, ii'. When the passage quoted occurs, not in the corpus of the Article, but in the reply to one of the 'objections', instead of 'Pt. I, Qu. XXXVIII, Art. 2, adversus 3' will be written 'I, 38, ii, 3'. The English translation when given is that of the Dominican Fathers.

Chapter 10

25 *Potentia* (potentiality) here stands, as normally in St Thomas, for *potentia passiva. Potentia activa* (power or potency) is something very different and exists pre-eminently in God.

26 St Thomas never actually discusses the possibility of self-limitation in God. But there is no doubt what his answer would have been. He starts from the assumption that omnipotence means that God can do all things. He goes on to say that things intrinsically impossible are excluded. The impossible is essentially that which involves non-existence or the absence of being. This is made clear in the following passage, which also shows how power, like everything else in God, is made a function of his Being. 'The Divine Existence . . . upon which the nature of power in God is founded, is infinite, and is not limited to any genus of being; but possesses within itself the perfection of all being, whence, whatsoever has or can have the nature of an entity, is numbered among the absolutely possible things; and it is in respect of these that God is called omnipotent. Nothing is opposed to the idea of entity except nonentity; that, therefore, is repugnant to the idea of an absolutely possible thing, coming within the scope of the Divine Omnipotence, which implies existence and non-existence at the same time . . . Everything that does not imply a contradiction in terms, is numbered among those possible things, in respect of which God is called omnipotent' (*S. T.*, I, 25, ii).

27 It should be noted that this very preference for the data of 'reason' over those of revelation as the starting point of a theological system in itself commits that theology to a view of God which is less than personal. For the conclusions of 'reason' are empirically derived, whether with divine assistance or not, from the existence and general nature of the universe (*ex creaturis*). Actually it seems

certain that the facts by themselves make it possible to assert by logical inference neither the existence, infinity, goodness, nor any of the other statements about God listed above. But let us suppose for the sake of argument that the Thomistic claims are justified. Reason can tell us all that, and can provide the categories and framework for the interpretation of the rest. But then, what is being asserted is that the entirely general revelation (if it is even so called) vouchsafed through the general structure of the universe as a whole is more indicative of the divine nature than the special revelation given in the history of religion, and pre-eminently in the face of Jesus Christ. Thus, in the example under discussion, omnipotence is defined by inference from the cosmic functions of the deity, rather than in the terms of the Incarnation and the Cross. It is this preference for the general over the particular that depersonalizes God. For it employs a principle of interpretation which is valid only for the study of things. It is when we have reduced things and their functions to instances of certain known general and invariable laws that we can claim to have understood them. Though only in so far, it is true, as it is grounded in the general and normal, it is yet the particular, the occasional, the exceptional, which is most 'revealing' for the understanding of personality. To repeat some words of Temple's quoted before: 'It tells us something about a man's character if we know that he rises from his bed every day at the same hour: it tells us much more about him if we know that he even once rose a great deal earlier to do some act of kindness' (*Nature, Man and God*, 305). And this illustration brings out the further point that only in its dealings with other persons does personality come to its fullest and most characteristic expression.

The most deeply revealing and characteristic manifestation of the divine essence, if he is really personal, should therefore be sought in the *particularities* of his dealings *with persons* in history. It is this double implication of the ascription of personality to God which the biblical writers recognize in claiming the life and death of Jesus Christ to be the key to the interpretation of the cosmos. It may indeed be 'the glorious God that maketh the thunder' (Ps. 29:3); but thunder might be attributed to numerous other causes, all quite impersonal. But of the Cross there could be no other category of interpretation than that of personal love. Here, we know we are dealing with a will with a purpose, and we can discern much of its quality. It is therefore by the evidence of such personal, particular facts that our theological categories must be determined. It is only then that we can set about the interpretation of the cosmos as a whole. The exact reversal of this procedure by the view under discussion reveals that it is thinking fundamentally in terms of a deity who is not fully personal: the absolute of Greek philosophy is still on the throne.

28 The aspect of faith which is here referred to is that which the New Testament has in view when it sees it as the opposite of 'offence' (σκανδαλί]εσθαι). The offence which our Lord's kindred and acquaintance found in him derived from the fact that an ordinary finite individual, whose measure they thought they had

('Is not this the carpenter, the son of Mary, and brother of James, and Joses, and Judas, and Simon? and are not his sisters here with us?' Mk 6:3), should claim to be the embodiment of the eternal, the infinite and the divine. The spirit of 'offence' is that which in the finite sees only the finite and finds the further claim wholly perverse. The spirit of faith is that which in the *finite* sees the whole infinitude of God and 'beholds his glory'.

For the same reason the spirit of faith is always antithetical to that which asks for a 'sign'. For such a request is fundamentally a desire to gratify the rationalistic presupposition of the natural man that the infinite authenticates itself by overriding the boundaries of the finite and stands towards them as their negation. If, say the Jews, Christ will perform some supernatural act revealing a power which oversteps the limits of the human, *then* they will belive that he is infinite and divine. And so ingrained in all of us is the prejudice of the natural wisdom of this world, which makes us immediately turn to the spectacular for the revelation of omnipotence, that we cannot but confess to an initial sympathy with Dives' rejoinder. 'Nay, father Abraham: but if one go to them from the dead, they will repent' (Lk. 16:30). But, as we know, history only too exactly bore out the truth of the reply, that 'if they hear not Moses and the prophets, neither will they be persuaded, if one rise from the dead'. When it was acted in front of their eyes, the Jews did not believe. The raising of Lazarus is no more and no less a manifestation of the divine omnipotence than the lifting up of the Son of Man on the Cross. Both are foolishness to them that are perishing: both the power of God to them that believe. The Jews did not believe though one rose from the dead: the Centurion knew the living God in the dying Christ.

It should be noted that those miraculous acts of Jesus which appear to reveal a heightening of normal human powers no more *prove* omnipotence than do the moments of his severest weakness. At no point did his infinity come to expression except through *some* limitations, even though at some points the constructions upon his activity were less pressing than at others. Five thousand loaves are no nearer to infinity than five. The most that miracles could prove would be a power of more than ordinary greatness: the judgment of omnipotence is just as far distant. By the unbeliever they could be explained away as the action of a somewhat abnormal being. The reaction of Christ's contemporaries, even when favourable, was by no means necessarily an ascription of divinity. All that Nicodemus was prepared to venture was: 'We know that thou art a teacher come from God: for no man can do these signs that thou doest, except God be with him' (Jn 3:2). Even the raising of the widow's son at Nain provoked no stronger comment than: 'a great prophet is arisen among us' (Lk. 7:16). Again, the power of his teaching 'with authority', while of a kind which made man confess that 'never man spake like this man' (Jn 7:46), yet could be regarded as something perfectly human (cf. Mt. 21:46, 'they took him for a prophet').

29 The deliberate revaluation of the Synoptic conception of the 'glory' of Christ by the author of the Fourth Gospel may underlie his omission of the story of the

Transfiguration. In Mark this incident is doubtless intended as a symbolic turning back of the corner of the veil, to reveal what was indeed throughout the truth about the Person of Christ but which had only recently been disclosed to Peter's faith. But there is clearly a danger in representing what, because of unbelief, the disciples are able to *see* in Christ only from time to time, as something which was *manifested* only from time to time. The impression might be left that Christ could only be seen as the embodiment of the divine glory and infinity when the terrestrial limitations which constricted it were lifted by some supernatural act. For St John every moment of the life of Christ was instinct with 'glory' for those who could behold it: the idea of a localized transfiguration was misleading. Moreover, if there was one place and time of glorification above all others, according to him it should be fixed elsewhere. It is of another 'lifting up' that it must be said par excellence: 'now is the Son of Man glorified'. By thus focusing attention on the Passion he is concerned to correct the association, liable to be encouraged by the Synoptists, of power and glory with the spectacular and miraculous. The one act to which he specifically ascribes omnipotence is, significantly, the complete passivity of the Crucifixion (Jn 12:32).

Chapter 11

30 For the history of the doctrine, from Origen onwards, see J. Hastings, *Encyclopaedia of Religion and Ethics*, Art. 'Universalism'. Among contemporary universalists may be mentioned Nicolas Berdyaev, Abp Temple, Profs John Baillie, Raven, Dodd and Farmer. But the question is as open as ever. The latest compendium of Anglican doctrine contains the summary sentence: 'Universalism – the belief that all men will necessarily be saved – is contrary both to Scripture and reason and has been condemned as a heresy by the Church at the Fifth Oecumenical Council' (C. B. Moss, *The Christian Faith*, 1943, 452).

31 The unsatisfactory antithetical view of the relation of love and justice in God, which clung to so much of the work of the Reformers, continues to appear in Brunner. See, the sentence quoted in p. 171 above, and cf., 'This is the place (*sc.* the Cross) where the love of God breaks through the wrath of God' (*The Mediator*, 520) and 'Even as the God of love He cannot deny His wrath' (ibid., 520). There is also the rather extraordinary statement: 'God is not simply Love. He *defines* Himself as Love. Love is His Will, not His Nature, although it is His eternal Will. As His Nature, however, even in Christ, we must worship His sovereign Majesty and His Holiness' (ibid., 282). Cf. *The Divine-Human Encounter*, 43–4: 'This is not to be understood as if in the final analysis Lordship or the holiness of God could be reduced to His love, so that it would suffice to speak about God's love. Not without reason the Bible time and time again speaks of both as of two very different things.' We would admit that the

identification of the two only took place gradually, but surely the Old Testament leaves no doubt as to the direction of the movement (cf. especially Hosea). In the New Testament 'God's Sovereign majesty and holiness' reveals itself as none other than the love of him who 'took a towel and girded himself'. 'Ye call me, Master, and, Lord, and ye say well; for so I am. If I then, your Lord and Master, have washed your feet . . .' (Jn 13:13–14). The divine will to power and lordship is none other than the omnipotence of dying love (Jn 12:32–3).

32 Cf. some other lines of Wesley's:

His love is mighty to compel;
His conquering love consent to feel,
Yield to His love's resistless power,
And fight against your God no more.
(*A Collection of Hymns for the Use of the People called Methodists*, No. 2)

33 The similarity and differences between the Calvinistic and universalistic forms of predestination are interesting. Calvinism represent the supreme assertion of the sovereignty of God, God's nature being regarded as *justice*. Universalism is the same, with the divine essence defined in terms of *love*. For reasons which will be clear from the earlier part of this chapter, the Calvinistic conception of the divine decree is necessarily a double one: justice appoints one end for the wicked, and another for the good. But love cannot be content to rest at the damnation of the wicked. It must go further: if it shuts up all in disobedience, it is only that in the end it may have mercy on all.

34 The practical difference to belief made by the fact of the Cross of Christ could not be more clearly illustrated than by a comparison of two contemporary writers of the first century AD, the one a Jew and the other a Christian. The first is the author of 2 Esdras (4 Ezra), the second the Epistle to the Romans.

The early chapters of 2 Esdras contain the most remarkable discussion of the problem of universal salvation to be found in the biblical writings. The treatise takes the form of a dialogue between God and man, which opens as follows: 'In the thirtieth year after the ruin of the city, I Salathiel (the same is Esdras) was in Babylon, and lay troubled upon my bed, and my thoughts came up over my heart: for I saw the desolation of Sion, and the wealth of them that dwelt at Babylon' (3:12). After recalling the process of creation and its culmination in the making of Adam and the election of Israel as the chosen nation, he presents his problem to God with penetrating clarity. 'All this have I spoken before thee, O Lord, because thou hast said that for our sakes thou madest this world. As for the other nations, which also come of Adam, thou hast said that they are nothing, and are like unto spittle: and thou hast likened the abundance of them unto a drop that falleth from a vessel. And now, O Lord, behold, these nations, which are reputed as nothing, be lords over us, and devour us. But we thy people, whom thou hast called thy firstborn, thy only begotten, and thy fervent lover, are given into their hands. If the world now be made for our sakes, why do we not possess for an inheritance our world? how long shall this endure?' (6:55–9). The answer to this, couched in terms of the apocalyptic of the time, is given in a vision of the day of judgment, when God's righteousness shall be vindicated and the wicked condemned. But here comes the critical transition. The seer, unlike most of his contemporaries, is not willing to stop here. 'And I answered, I said even then, O Lord, and I say now: Blessed are they that be now alive and keep the statutes ordained of thee. But as touching them for whom my prayer was made, what shall I say? for who is there of them that be alive that hath not sinned, and who of the sons of men that hath not transgressed thy covenant? And now I see, that the world to come shall bring delight to few, but torments unto many. For an evil heart hath grown up in us, which hath led us astray from these statutes, and hath brought us into corruption and into the ways of death, hath showed us the paths of perdition and removed us far from life; and that, not a few only, but well nigh all that have been created' (7:45–8). To this God replies that in all matters the rarer a thing is the more precious it is; a few choice stones are worth any amount of lead or clay. 'So also is the judgment which I have promised: for I will rejoice over the few that shall be saved, inasmuch as these are they that have made my glory now to prevail, and of whom my name is now named. And I will not grieve over the multitude of them that perish; for these are they that are now like unto vapour, and are become as flame and smoke; they are set on fire and burn hotly, and are quenched' (7:59–61). To this cynical answer Ezra expresses a sentiment reminiscent of Schopenhauer or the Preacher of Ecclesiastes. If this is the case he says, why was the mind of man ever evolved? Why not be as the beasts that perish? 'For it is far better with them then with us; for they look not for judgment, neither do they know of torments or of salvation promised unto them after death' (66). Here God rightly reminds his accuser that the gift of moral freedom and responsibility which man enjoys entails acceptance of the consequences of its misuse. Hell is something that man brings upon himself and in its most terrible form it is nothing external but the recognition by the sinner of the righteous holiness of God (87). But this does not satisfy Ezra, who is still oppressed by the great preponderance of the damned over the saved and the stultification of God's purpose which it implies. For 'if thou shalt lightly and suddenly destroy him which with so great labour was fashioned by thy commandment, to what purpose was he made?' (8:14). God in reply directs his attention to the order of nature, where the same wastage is seen, with no apparent frustration of the end. 'For as the husbandman soweth much seed upon the ground, and planteth many trees, and yet not all that is sown shall come up in due season, neither shall all that is planted take root: even so they that are sown in the world shall not all be saved' (41). Ezra here appeals on behalf of man against the callous valuation which would make the loss of a soul of as little account as the failure of a seed to germinate. 'Man, which is formed with thy hands, and is called thy own image, because he is made like unto thee, for whose sake thou hast formed all things, even him hast thou made like unto the husbandman's seed' (44). Let it not be thought, replies God, that I am not aware of this or do not care about the fate of my creation; 'for thou comest far short that thou shouldest be able to love my creature more than I' (47). These things must be; the wicked have brought it upon their own heads; 'for when they had received liberty, they despised the Most High, thought scorn of His law, and forsook His ways' (56). 'And therefore be thou no longer curious how the ungodly shall be punished, but enquire how the righteous shall be saved, they whose the world is, and for whom the world was created' (9:13). This is clearly an evasion, and Ezra recognizes it as such. 'And I answered and said, I have said before, and now do speak, and will speak it also hereafter, that there be more of them which perish, than of them which shall be saved: like as a wave is greater than a drop' (14–16). But God has no satisfactory reply, and the problem is shelved.

Here is a man who is desperately anxious to believe in universal salvation, and yet who can fasten on no religious certainty upon which he might rest such a belief. In Rom. 9–11 St Paul is tormented by exactly the same problems, namely, the relation of Israel to the Gentiles and the destiny of those who reject God. For him, no less than for Ezra, the difficulties are immense. But whereas suspense of judgment is the most that the latter can achieve, St Paul, confident in the omnipotent love of God revealed in Christ, wins through to a triumphant universalistic conclusion (Rom. 11:32). In consequence, the appeal which is made in the two works to the inscrutability of the divine wisdom is very differently inspired. For Ezra it is a counsel to resignation, for St Paul an expression of wondering faith and hope (Rom. 11:33–6).

Chapter 12

35 It should be stated that the simile of the row of houses, though given by Professor Broad, does not represent his own view, which is that the present precedes literally nothing at all (*Scientific Thought*, 66; quoted, Bevan, *Symbolism and Belief*, 88).

36 It is, of course, obvious that different observers may see the same thing at different times. If I could take up a position on one of the moons of Saturn, I should see events on the planet considerably before an observer on earth. But that does not mean to say that I am seeing them before they happened (i.e., on Saturn). It may be that it is impossible to obtain a single unchanging standard which can give us an absolute measure of time. But that does not affect the fact that there is a public time. Indeed this fact is presupposed in the statement of Einstein, which is an axiom of his theory of relativity. 'I call two events *simultaneous* for a given observer when they are perceived or seen at the same time by that observer while he is equidistant from both' (*The Theory of Relativity*, quoted Bevan, *Symbolism and Belief*, 106). 'Simultaneity' can only involve 'equidistance'

if there is a 'real' time which light takes to travel from two events, which 'really' happened together. In the same way, by travelling faster than light I might catch up the rays which had left the earth and see things happening backwards. But this is only possible (a) if the events really *have* happened, (b) if they 'really' happened in the 'right' order, and (c) if there is a 'real' speed at which light travels, and which I am exceeding.

37 One of the earliest arguments which follow this line occurs in Origen, *Contra Celsum* II, 20. He does not make a point of the difference between knowledge and foreknowledge, but it is assumed in the reasoning. 'Celsus imagines that an event, predicted through foreknowledge, comes to pass because it was predicted; but we do not grant this, maintaining that he who foretold it was not the cause of its happening, because he foretold it would happen; but the future event itself, which would have taken place though not predicted, afforded the occasion to him, who was endowed with foreknowledge, of foretelling its occurrence.' This statement is equally vulnerable to the objection urged below against the positions of Boethius and Aquinas.

38 For the Bible, the expression of what is most real is not timeless being but historical event. This corresponds to the difference between the Hellenic ontological and the Hebraic thelematological conceptions of metaphysics. For the latter it is action-in-relationship and not being-in-itself that constitutes reality. It is for this reason that, for the Jew, insight expressed itself as foresight, and that the prophet took the place of the seer. Much of what the prophets had to say cannot on any reckoning be explained as judgments extracted from an analysis of the contemporary political situation and its prospects. Thus, the 'hopeful' passages in Hosea or the promises of Jeremiah 31 bear no relation to the immediate state of affairs, which only justified the blackest prognostications. They stem, rather, from an insight into the eternal realities of God's nature, a God whose last word, they knew, could not be one of wrath and destruction. That is the ground of their assurance. But – and this is what is significant – this assurance expressed itself in the form of *hope*, that peculiarly Hebraic virtue. They were not content, as the Greeks would have been, to comfort themselves with the knowledge that, in the midst of temporal disaster, the eternal, timeless realities of God stood unshaken and that they could fix their minds on these. Though the message of the prophets did not derive from history, it inevitably formulated itself in the terms of history. For their way of saying that these truths about God were realities was to say that they must be realized, and realized in historical events. For that was for them the key of reality. The real was an attribute of the 'Thou' world, of the 'I' in a relation of decisive action. If truths or insights did not validate themselves in events, then they could not be real. It was neither the false philosopher nor the false mystic who was the type of deception in Israel, but the false prophet.

For the Hebrew mind, God is essentially and always the God of history. The ultimate and final truth about God is necessarily presented as the ultimate and final event in history. If the last word about God is that he is mercy and loving-kindness, then this must express itself for a Jeremiah or a Second Isaiah in the assurance of a new covenant and a recreated universe as the last word about history. This prophecy is not a more-or-less confident guess about the future turn of events: it is a solemn assertion of what God is like, now and ever. It is that which for the Greeks would be expressed in a proposition about a timeless truth. But with history as the key of the real, ultimate actualization becomes the meaning of truth. May we say that even for God, in Kierkegaard's phrase, 'truth is subjectivity', that the real is only real in so far as he makes it real for himself? Reality is not something timelessly existent in heaven: it awaits its establishment on earth. It is this which gives the time-process its eternal significance. Time 'makes a difference' to eternity. It is not just the moving image of something which is completely and eternally real in itself. On any such theory as this, no adequate reason can be given for the necessity of time at all. Why should a record of the perfection of self-complete simultaneity need to be played off in the labouring key of temporal succession? Even if a purpose can be seen for it in the economy of God's plan for men, for himself it remains entirely superfluous: he is not really, only and essentially a God of history. Only if history is itself metaphysical, only if it is a sphere where reality is not mirrored but made, is the biblical doctrine of God preserved.

39 Cf. Lovell Cocks, *By Faith Alone*, 201: 'The contemporaneity of faith with the Word is not the relation of consciousness to a content but an act to an act, for faith is not a world-view but a decision.' The Epistle to the Hebrews is certainly not propounding a 'world-view', which absolves the individual from decisive commitment, but of all the New Testament books it is the one which chiefly lends colour to the Hegelian interpretation of Christianity, against which Kierkegaard waged continual battle.

Chapter 13

40 The following note on the LXX usage is derived from Kittel's *Theologisches Wörterbuch zum Neuen Testament* (*Theological Dictionary*) (καιρός), q.v. for further references. It will be seen that this usage generally supports the conclusions to be drawn from the New Testament. The fundamental meaning of the term is that of a moment, determined by God and decisive for man: the double reference is never far away. The word is applied to any definite time, whether in the normal course of human and natural existence or outside it, set by God for a particular purpose. It is extended, indeed, to measures of time in general, but the original connotation of the term is seldom entirely lost sight of. Thus, when it is applied to the length of a man's life, there is the suggestion in the background that the number of his days is not merely fortuitous but corresponds exactly to the span decreed for him by God. As the obverse of this divine appointment of

all things, there is the claim which the *καιρός* makes for human response. It is the moment for decision, the critical situation from which there is no escape, the crucial opportunity which must not be allowed to slip.

The divine determination of all time is a familiar theme. God takes up the *καιροί* in his hand (*ὅταν λάβω καιρόν* (when I choose the time) Ps. 74:3) and disposes of them (*αὐτὸς ἀλλοιοῖ καιρούς* Dan. 2:21). Time is God's time, *καιρός αὐτοῦ* (Eccles. 3:11; 51:30; Ps. 20:10), and this applies in particular to the religiously decisive times, the times of consummation, whether of blessedness (Dan. 7:22) or of death (Eccles. 7:17). *καιρός* can stand alone as a technical theological term, without requiring further definition, as indicating the day of judgment or of the end (particularly the former, where it is equivalent to *κρίσις*) which God appoints (Lam. 1:21; 4:19; Ezek. 7:12; 22:3; Gen. 6:13; Dan. 8:17). So close, indeed, is the connection of the idea with that of the divine appointment that God himself is boldly compared to *καιρός* (*καθὼς καιρός* (Judg. 13:23; cf. Num. 14:9: *ἀφέστηκεν γὰρ ὁ καιρὸς ἀπ' αὐτῶν, ὁ δὲ κύριος ἐν ἡμῖν μή φοβηθῆτε αὐτούς*) (Opportunity has withdrawn from them. The Lord is with us. Do not fear them.)). There is nothing in life which falls outside this divine decree, 'no purpose under heaven' for which there is not a *καιρός* given by God (Eccles. 3:1–8, 17, the *locus classicus* for the use of the term), and, in the ordered sequence of *καιροί* of which his life is composed, the pious man will see the hand of God, in gift and demand.

41 Exactly when and how this will come about cannot be known by God; for that would imply that he had a detailed map of the future spread before Him. Mark 13:32 might seem to contradict this: 'Of that hour or that day knoweth no one, not even the angels in heaven, neither the Son, but the Father.' The contradiction only arises, however, if the 'hour' is thought of in terms of *χρόνος*. The chronological moment of the end of the world is itself a matter of no importance for God's purpose. It is only of interest to the curious, to the 'spectators' of history. When the New Testament speaks of 'knowing the hour' it is not referring to a time which can be calculated in terms of years and months (as certain of the apocalyptists thought, and certain of their modern disciples still think, only to be confounded time and time again by the evidence of history's continuance). It is referring to a time, rather, which can be calculated only in terms of the purposes yet to be achieved in it. The Father knows the *καιρός*, not the *χρόνος*. And he alone knows it, because he alone can determine the hour when his purpose has reached its maturity. In his omniscience he declares the final *καιρός*. Creatures, as beings 'in time', cannot know this until the word has been spoken. And the Incarnate, as man, is equally subject to this limitation. But the Father is the one in whose power the times and the seasons are. He knows the end as Lord of the *καιροί*, not as the Spectator of the *χρόνοι*.

All this does not mean to say that the *καιρός* does not occur at any particular date. There is, of course, the peculiar difficulty which adheres to the final *καιρός* in that it seems impossible to attach a date *in* time to an event which marks the end of time. But the idea of καιρός in itself is not unrelated to time as measured in months and years: the 'seasons' of the natural order can be marked on the calendar. καιρός is, rather, the truth about such times. The difference between καιρός and χρόνος is not that one plays fast and loose with time-intervals, whereas the other is measured by the regularities of days and months. Night and day, summer and winter, which form the basis of calendar time, are themselves, for the Bible, God's καιροί. The καιροί of the natural order, like everything else in this realm, occur with that predictable regularity and existence. χρόνος represents simply the abstraction of these ordered sequences from the personal purpose which appoints them. They are regarded as self-determined mechanical regularities. 'Clock time', which is only these regular time-intervals ironed out to exclude any slight variations, is made the ultimate measure of everything, personal purpose included. Thus, the true relation is reversed, and an 'objective' temporal order is set up as the canon by which God's purpose is to be judged and calculated. The only difference which the theory of relativity makes to this is to say that in fact we have no single fixed point from which to measure this time. It does nothing to correct the false order by which time is made the lord of purpose instead of its subject.

The Bible asserts that all time is subordinate to God's purpose. Some καιροί God has decreed should follow a regular course, in order that human life can have that settled foundation without which personal existence would be impossible. These afford us dependable measurements of temporal duration. But they must not be used to judge God's purpose itself. The biblical writers would see no insuperable obstacle to those measurements themselves being altered, if sufficient reason justified it (cf. 2 Kings 20:8–11). The regularities are part of a larger purpose and do not exist for their own sake. Even if they remain constant they cannot form the clue to the whole. To ask, when is the last day? is to interpret the ultimate self-justifying καιρός in terms of the καιροί which are subordinate to it. It is not these that determine the end. Although this will occur at a certain date, it cannot be calculated in terms of years and months. For it depends on the fulfilment of a purpose; and for this a thousand years are as one day. Personal response, whenever it may come, is the decisive factor. Beside that, the καιροί of the years are as χρόνοι – they determine nothing.

Chapter 14

42 It should be perfectly evident, of course, that St Thomas's position is here under consideration *solely* as exemplifying the assumption the the doctrine of the Trinity is properly to be treated at the end of Christian Theology, as a differentiation within an already fully cognized unity. In no other sense has our approach been that of Aquinas, which is fundamentally opposed to the 'Hebraic' position we have adopted throughout this work.

43 It is no accident that there should be a parallel here between the doctrine of the nature of God and the commandment of love. For, as we saw, the commandment is but the shadow or obverse of the belief. The commandment of God is essentially to 'love as I have loved you'. As the Incarnation and the revelation of the divine Trinity gave new content to the old idea of the love of God, so the old idea of human love, the one commandment, is transformed while it remains the same.

Chapter 15

44 The following distinction will be observed throughout. Whenever 'person' is used of the Godhead in the sense which that word bears in popular modern usage – namely, when it means a self-conscious centre of personality, capable of entering into distinct 'Thou' relationships with some 'other' – it will be spelt with a small 'p'. When it signifies the Latin *persona* and is used as a technical Trinitarian term, without any implications concerning the possibility of such relationships, it will be written 'Person'. Thus a tri-Personal God (i.e., a being existing in three Persons) might be uni-personal, in the sense of being related to another person (i.e., man) as a single 'Thou'.

45 There is a certain amount of ambiguity in this word 'possession'. The definition of Kirk's here quoted could cover two distinct sets of phenomena: (a) Conscious awareness of coming under the control of a power other than one's own will, a control which issues in actions for which one has no direct responsibility. Examples of such experiences would be those attributed to the priestess of Delphi, or to Cassandra in the *Agamemnon* (of Aeschylus) (cf. ll. 1072ff.; 1214–16), the 'speaking with tongues' referred to in the New Testament, the trance of a medium etc. (b) The action of a power working through the normal processes of circumstance and volition, guiding, inspiring or sanctifying the subject in such a way that he is not conscious at the time of any will not his own, but which, on reflection, he can see to have been at work in the situation. It is in the latter sense in which the great majority of Christians would claim experience of the operations of grace or providence.

Hodgson appears to have this meaning alone in mind when he speaks of 'possession' as the distinguishing mark of the presence of the Spirit. 'Our primary notion of the Spirit is that of God working in and through us without our being aware of the fact at the moment' (*The Doctrine of the Trinity*, 51). His continual use of the past tense (e.g., 39) implies that the Holy Spirit is an object not of direct present experience but of indirect inference after the event.

In contrast, Kirk does not confine himself to the second sense. It is not clear whether he regards the sanctifying work of the Spirit, which he calls, somewhat unfortunately, 'compulsory moralisation', as a matter of immediate present experience or not. Probably not; but he treats it as essentially continuous with, and almost as a sublimation of, the more abnormal and pathological ecstatic manifestations of possession.

Perhaps the difference between the normal and the abnormal is only a matter of degree, and for most of what follows the distinction is not important. It is, however, relevant when we come to consider the scriptural basis for the confinement of the work of the Holy Spirit to experiences of possession. For, according to Hodgson, there could be no present experience of the Spirit, while for Kirk this would appear to be confined to abnormal psychic phenomena; and each of these positions it is difficult to support by the New Testament.

46 Cf. Jn 14:16, 18; 16:16, 19, 22; 1 Jn 3:24; 4:13; Rom. 8:9–10; 2 Cor. 3:17, 18; Gal. 4:6; Phil. 1:19. Cf. 1 Pet. 1:10, 11; Acts 16:7. Cf. also the apparently identical use of the phrases 'in the Spirit', 'in the Lord', 'in Christ'. Kirk points out (*Essays on the Trinity and the Incarnation*, 205) that the same results are predicated of relations with both the Son and the Spirit. We are justified in Christ (Gal. 2:17) and in the Spirit (1 Cor. 6:11); sanctified (1 Cor. 1:2; Rom. 15:16), sealed (Eph. 1:13; 4:30) and circumcised (Col. 2:11; Rom. 2:29) in both; we have joy (Phil. 3:1; Rom. 14:17), faith (Gal. 3:26; 1 Cor. 12:9), love (Rom. 8:39; Col. 1:8), communion (1 Cor. 1:9; 2 Cor. 13:14) in both.

Chapter 16

47 Dr R. C. Moberly appends a careful note 'on the question how far the title "Son" is directly used of the Logos as pre-Incarnate; with special reference to Hippolytus against Noetus, and to Marcellus of Ancyra' (*Atonement and Personality*, 208–15). He examines the biblical evidence and concludes that, whereas there is inevitably a measure of uncertainty in exegesis, scriptural usage is against any unequivocal predication of the title 'Son' of the Pre-incarnate. 'The fact remains that the only passage in the New Testament which goes wholly and obviously behind the fact of the Incarnation, drops altogether the words "Father" and "Son" ' (namely, Jn 1:1–14) (ibid., 214). His own position is not essentially dissimilar to ours, though he would be prepared to assert that the filial relationship provides a more positive analogy of the eternal relationships within the Trinity than we feel justified in allowing. The difference is due to divergent views on the nature of man. Our position is substantially that adopted by Hippolytus, though for different reasons. An exactly contrary position is argued by Mr J. Burnaby, 'The Divine Sonship', in *The Journal of Theological Studies*, July–October 1944.

48 Without committing ourselves in any way to Hastings Rashdall's own doctrine of the Trinity, we may point to his works as containing the most effective castigation of recent tritheism (see *Principles and Precepts*, 1927, 44–6; *Doctrine and Development*, 1898, 21–32; *Philosophy and Religion*, 1909 181–5. Cf. W.

Temple, *The Nature of Personality*, 113–15). It is, of course, arguable that tritheism in itself is not necessarily a bad thing. If one has no concern in aligning oneself with the formulae of the Church's Councils, it is possible to make out a case for regarding the communion between three (though why three?) persons, even on the basis of the complete individuation which it presupposes, as the most ultimate and complete unity, more complete than that of a single personality. Moreover, if it could be shown that experience of God as three 'Thous' were necessary to effect our total reconciliation and, therefore, a monotheistic faith, then the existence of three divine personalities could hardly be regarded as destructive of the unity of the Godhead.

Against such a position two things may be said. First, a doctrine of a divine society, though philosophically tempting, can scarcely claim a place in a *Christian* theology. For, in order to commend itself as the presupposition of monotheism rather than its destruction, it has to assume an analysis of experience which is not that of the Bible. And for this reason, it is also irreconcilable with the definitive statements of the Church on the nature of the Trinity. Secondly, whereas the 'I–Thou' philosophy willingly concedes that the ultimate unity is not that of the 'I' in isolation, it never goes as far as saying that the real unit of existence is two (or three) persons in relationship. It is impossible to go beyond the individual as the irreducible reality and the final seat of value, even though he possesses this reality and value only in relation to an 'other'.

49 By this is not meant that, according to St John, Christ thought that Christians would experience the Spirit as 'the terminus of a distinct and recognisable relationship'. John 14 points to a considerable 'confusion' of the Persons in the believer's awareness: 'I will pray the Father and he shall give you another Comforter, that He may abide with you for ever' (v. 16); 'I will not leave you comfortless: I will come to you' (v. 18); 'If a man love me he will keep my words: and my Father will love him, and we will come unto him, and make our abode with him' (v. 23). Our Lord here recognizes that the ordinary Christian's experience of God will be one of a single personal love manifested in three distinguishable though not separable forms.

50 This reluctance extends to the Early Fathers. Adolf Harnack examines the evidence (*History of Dogma*, I, 187–8) and concludes that 'there cannot have been many passages in the earliest literature where Christ was roundly designated θεός'; 'θεός, even without the article, was in no case a usual designation for Jesus. On the contrary, it was always quite definite occasions which led them to speak of Christ as of a God, or as God'. And all that can be said of this indirect *theologia Christi* applied a fortiori to the divinity of the Spirit.

51 The use of this word is in no way intended to imply at this stage any particular theory as to the nature of the Persons of the Godhead.

Chapter 17

52 The situation contemplated actually presupposes a position that could not be held with any logical consistency. If the 'Thou' relationship is not peculiarly human, then the fact that Christ is eternally man cannot of itself introduce one into the Trinity. Only if it is peculiarly human does this doctrine imply it; and if it is peculiarly human, then it is not there already between the Persons in general.

53 The thought, given as the content of faith, that 'he that cometh to God must believe that he is, and that he is a rewarder of them that seek after him' (Heb. 11:6) is one which, in the less personal terms of the Idea of the Good and the supreme worthwhileness of its pursuit, might well have come from Plato himself. The ὅτι ἐστιν (that he is) has been described as the most Greek phrase in the Bible.

Chapter 18

54 The New Testament grounds for such a statement, which is unlikely to be challenged, will be discussed on pp. 314–15 below, when we come to set out more carefully what exactly can and cannot be deduced from the Incarnation concerning the differentiation of the Persons.

Chapter 19

55 See, J. H. Bernard, ICC, St John, ad loc., for the linguistic evidence. It is to be noted that ἐκ, which is especially meant to represent the unique divine origin of Christ, is used in 8:47 of any believer: 'he that is of God heareth God's words'. The parallelism of 16:28 is decisively against anything but temporal procession: 'I came out from the Father (ἐξῆλθον ἐκ τοῦ πατρός), and am come into the world: again, I leave the world, and go unto the Father.' Just as the last two clauses speak of the double aspect of the ascension, so the first must both have reference to what is involved in Christ's coming into the world.

56 See, pp. 470–1 above. Cf. F. Weston, who gives a similar interpretation of Mk 13:32 ('But of that day and that hour knoweth no one, not even the angels in heaven, neither the Son, but the Father'): 'The Incarnate Son in manhood, conditioned by manhood, self-conscious through manhood, is the Son who did not know the day of the last judgment. And in the Gospel the word Son has no other connotation' (*The One Christ*, 199–200). In view of the last words, it is curiously illogical for him to argue (314–15) to the fittingness of the Second Person becoming incarnate on the ground that it is he who 'possesses the Godhead . . . by an eternal act of reception and dependence' (309–10). For his

statement about the simple identification in 'the gospel' of the Son with the Incarnate is not merely a judgment about Mark. It is part of his whole Christology, which would deny that any other interpretation was possible from the point of view which the Gospels record. Jesus 'knew Himself only as God in manhood, within the sphere of the Incarnation' (199). Thus, even if Christ had been eternally subordinate to the Father, he could not have known it or revealed it while he was in the flesh. If, then, the statements of dependence on the part of the Son refer entirely to the Incarnate (cf. 157), it is impossible to argue that this subordination is somehow grounded in, and made fitting on account of, 'an eternal act of reception and dependence'. Moreover, if, without any evidence, the relation of subordination ('the Father is greater than I') is transferred to eternity, then so must ignorance of the judgment day. For both are equally conditions of 'sonship' or manhood.

57 F. Godet points out that it was only a divine being who could make such a statement; for one who was merely human it would be just as blasphemous as to claim equality with God. 'God alone can compare Himself with God' (*Commentary on the Gospel of St John*, III, 1890, 156).

58 Even in this passage we have that degree of subordinationism which reserves ὁ θεός for the Father alone and halts at the transition from 'the Son of God' to 'God the Son'. But this, which we have already discussed, is very different from that which seems to be implied in 1 Cor. 15:28. From the former the crucial transition could be, and was, made; from the latter it is quite impossible.

59 Cf. especially Heb. 2:8–12, where the words 'both he that sanctifieth and they that are sanctified are all of one: for which cause he is not ashamed to call them brethren' are set in close proximity to 'in that he (God) subjected all things unto him (Christ), he left nothing that is not subject to him'. There is no suggestion here that a further subjection, of Christ to the Father, is ultimately necessary.

60 The foregoing discussion provides an interesting illustration of the essential interdependence of the doctrine of God and man, and the importance for each of a true theory of the personality of the other. It is because of a false doctrine of the nature of man that the relation of the Incarnate to the Father is held to point to an eternal relation of subordination as its ground. For it is not seen that such a relation is part of the essence of humanity. And it is because of a desire to postulate such an eternal relation as the basis of the temporal that the doctrine of revelation which identifies the 'economic' and the 'essential' cannot be accepted; for that would make this eternal procession the same as the temporal mission, which would be absurd. But this doctrine of revelation is implied in a Theology which conceives the divine Essence as being-in-relation, as eternal 'Thou' existence. And, in its turn, it is this doctrine of God which alone provides the basis for the true estimate of man's nature – being-in-responsibility to the divine 'Thou'. If one starts from one doctrine of man, one necessarily reaches its corresponding Theology. The repudiation of the 'classical' view

of the nature of personality, the doctrine of God as 'Thou', and the denial of relations of origin within the Trinity are all bound up together.

61 Thus, the only ground which could apparently justify the appropriation of 'wisdom' to the Son and 'love' to the Spirit is that given by St Thomas, when he asserts the procession of the Son to be 'by way of the intellect', whereas that of the Spirit is 'by way of the will'. But this distinction has no authority, and is in fact little more than a metaphor whereby the mind is enabled more easily to picture two kinds of procession, the difference between which it is impossible to define. It is not a distinction which is known to Augustine, who nevertheless makes the same appropriation. But, when pressed, the classical writers seem prepared to embrace any argument which will attest some fittingness somewhere. The appropriateness of attributing the name 'Love' especially (*proprie*) to the Holy Spirit is elaborately demonstrated by Augustine by means of a dexterous juggling of texts from 1 Jn 4:7–19 (*De Trin.* XV, 31). And St Thomas even thinks it worthwhile to quote the following: 'Power is appropriated to the Father, as Augustine says, because fathers by reason of old age are sometimes feeble; lest anything of the kind should be imagined of God' (*S.T.*, I, 39, vii).

Chapter 20

62 '*Natura est vel quod facere vel quod pati posit.*' (Nature is what can do or suffer something)

'*Natura est motus principium per se non per accidens*' (Nature is a movement which happens in principle and not by accident) (i.e., a wooden bed falls to the ground because it is made of wood and not because it is a bed).

'*Natura est unamquemque rem informans specifica differentia*' (Nature is a specific difference informing a particular thing) (*Contra Eut. et Nest.*, I).

63 As we have seen, St Thomas certainly did not regard the Persons as anything like personal centres of consciousness existing in 'I–Thou' relations to each other. And the same is true of the earlier writers. Bethune-Baker summarizes the Catholic use as it was at the time of the 'Constantinopolitan' Creed: '*οὐσία* the existence or essence or substantial entity of the Trinity as God; *ὑπόστασις* the existence in a particular mode, the manner of being of each of the "Persons".' 'Thus there is *μία οὐσία* and *τρεῖς ὑποστάσεις* [three modes of being] or *μία οὐσία ἐν τρισιν ὑποστάσεσιν* [one being in three modes of being] – one substance or essence in three subsistencies, or forms or modes or spheres of existence: one God permanently existing in three eternal modes' (*Texts and Studies*, VII, 80, 81). Such a statement is strongly supported by the conclusions of Dr Prestige (see, *God in Patristic Thought*, Chs XII and XIII).

64 For the Patristic evidence, cf. also G. L. Prestige, *God in Patristic Thought*, 245–9.

He points out that the regular association of the phrase *τρόπος ὑπαρξέως* with 'mode of derivation' (*ἀγγενησία*, unbegottenness, *γέννησις*, begottenness, *ἐκπόρευσις* procession) is not necessary to it. In itself it simply means 'mode of existence', and the association arises solely from the fact that from the beginning relations of *origin* alone were regarded as distinguishing the modes. It is then quite legitimate to retain the phrase while rejecting the traditional doctrine of relations.

65 Cf. *The English Hymnal*, No. 380, v. 2:

Ere He raised the lofty mountains,
Formed the sea, or built the sky,
Love eternal, free, and boundless,
Forced the Lord of life to die,
Lifted up the Prince of princes,
On the throne of Calvary. (J. M. Neale)

The juxtaposition of 'free' and 'forced' is well calculated to bring out the paradox of the inescapable necessity laid upon God by his own unfettered nature. The alternation of 'forced' to 'moved' in *Hymns Ancient and Modern* is an interesting reflection on the pressure of traditional 'orthodoxy' in the direction of safety.

INDEX OF SUBJECTS AND AUTHORS

INDEX OF REFERENCES

ANCIENT AND CLASSICAL AUTHORS